Therapeutica Sacra
Showing briefly the method of healing the diseases of the Conscience, concerning Regeneration
David Dickson

Therapeutica Sacra: Showing briefly the method of healing the diseases of the Conscience, concerning Regeneration

by David Dickson

This text has been initially updated from EEBO-TCP by Project Puritas, Further revision and editing done by Monergism.

Copyright Monergism via universal text usage permission from the above.

Copyright © 2024

Published by by Monergism Books

P.O. Box 491West Linn Oregon 97068

www.monergism.com

ISBN: 978-1-961807-91-4

Editor's Note – During the EEBO-TCP Transcription Process, all the text was hand transcribed according to visual representation; and as such, sometimes the letters s, l, f & t are misconstrued with each other, these letters regularly being almost illegibly similar in the original facsimile script. Though it is rare for these errors to remain post-edit, unfortunately they may remain if uncaught. My apologies in advance where such errors occur. Also, the symbol <H&G>, when included, signifies omitted Hebrew & Greek. Lastly, some archaic words may be updated to more contemporary terminology; but changes have been kept to a bare minimum.

Contents

TO THE RIGHT HONORABLE AND VERY NOBLE:

THE COUNTESS DOWAGER OF Glencairn.

Madam,

After the Author had written and published this Treatise in Latin, for the use of young Students in Theology; by the earnest and frequent entreaty of friends, he was induced and persuaded to translate it into our vulgar Tongue, for the benefit of these who understood not the Latin; and for preventing the labor of others, who, more forward then skillful, were about the doing of it, and had once so far proceeded, as to offer it to the Press, without acquainting him therewith.

When he had finished the Translation, his purpose was to have dedicated it to your Ladyship, and to have sent it abroad into the world under your protection: but weakness and sickness, the ordinary companions of age, and after them, death (whereby God Almighty and Gracious, called him from his labors to enter into his Master's joy) seizing upon him, before he could write an Epistle Dedicatory, it was his will, that your honorable Name should be prefixed unto it. In pursuance whereof, it comes now, as an Orphan, to kiss your noble Hands, fraughted with hopes of favor and shelter for the Parent's sake, and of acceptance, as a testimony of the sincerity of the respects he carried to your Ladyships virtues.

It hath the stronger plea for a tender reception, that it is the child of his age, being his last labor, and being brought forth in his seventy and second year; and that it comes arrayed in a suit of Country-clothe, which himself put upon it, being published according to the Copy written with his own hand.

That it may be, as it was designed by him, useful for the good of souls, and that God may comfort you under your present sad affliction, and make up the loss of your noble Husband, the late Lord high Chancellor of Scotland, is the prayer of,

Madam,

Your Ladyships most humbly devoted Servant, Alexander Dickson.

Edinburgh, 13. June, 1664.

CHAP. I. - Of Conscience in general.

SEEING OUR PURPOSE IS to speak of the curing of sundry ordinary cases, or diseases concerning Regeneration, by a prudent application and use-making of divine Covenants, made about and with man, for his coming to eternal life; it is needful to speak in the entry a little, first, of the nature of the Conscience, and use thereof in general; next, of the cases of the conscience in general; thirdly, what Regeneration is, and who is the man regenerate; fourthly, of divine Covenants, relating to everlasting happiness; and, fifthly, of the orderly and prudent application of these Covenants in general, that thereafter we may descend to speak of application thereof in particular Cases the more clearly.

2. As to the first, what conscience is, It hath pleased God, the sovereign Lord and Judge of all men, in the Creation, to put in man's soul a natural power or faculty, whereby he might not only understand the revealed will of God, (the only Lord of, and Law-giver to, the Conscience) not only concerning what he should believe and perform, but also might judge of his own faith and obedience, whether performed or not performed; yea, and might judge also of the faith and obedience of others, in so far as evidences may be had of their conformity unto, or dis-agreement from, the revealed rule of faith and manners. This power of the soul of man, whether it be considered

only in its natural aptitude and fitness to judge, (though not as yet, or for the time, actually judging) or whether it be looked upon as it is putting forth itself in exercise, we call it by the name of Conscience.

3. The word Conscience is divers ways taken; for sometime by it is meaned the natural power of the mind, to judge both of our own and others conformity to the rule: and in this larger acception we say, Every man hath a Conscience, that is, every man, whether male or female, whether old or young, whether sleeping or waking, hath a faculty, which may, and sometime shall, judge of their own and others behavior towards God. Sometime it is taken for that natural power of the mind, putting forth itself actually in exercise, by judging of others; So doth the Apostle take it, 2 Cor. 5:11. I trust, saith he, we are made manifest in your consciences. But here, in this Treatise, we take Conscience more strictly, as it examineth and judgeth of ourselves; for, in this sense, it is most properly called Conscience, or joint knowledge; partly, because it supposeth, that God and we know our obedience, or disobedience, to the rule prescribed to us by Him; partly, because Conscience imports, first, our knowledge of the rule; and, next, our knowledge of our behavior in relation to the rule, and our comparing of these two together, and passing of sentence of ourselves answerably.

4. Conscience, as it doth respect ourselves, is no other thing, in effect, then the understanding power of our souls examining how matters do stand betwixt God and us, comparing His will revealed, with our state, condition and carriage in thoughts, words or deeds, done or omitted, and passing judgment thereupon as the case requires: So that in the court of Conscience, (which is God's Depute in us, as it were) these five things are to be considered; 1. the duty of self-examination; 2. the thing we are to examine; 3. the rule whereby

we are to examine; 4. the process of the Conscience unto sentence giving; and, 5. the execution of the sentence, so far as the Conscience may.

5. As to the first, the duty of examination of ourselves and judging ourselves, it is required of us, lest we be judged of God and chastised with sharp rods, 1 Cor. 11:31,32, and hereunto we are exhorted, Psal. 4:4, Commune with your own hearts upon your beds, and be still.

6. As for the second, the thing which we are to examine concerning ourselves, it is one of three, or all the three, in their order; to wit, either our estate, whether we be in the state of nature, under wrath, or not; or whether we be regenerate and in the state of grace through faith in Jesus Christ, or not. Of this speaketh the Apostle, 2 Cor. 13:5. Examine yourselves whether ye be in the faith. Or it is our condition, whether being in the state of grace our present disposition or inclination of heart and affections be such, as becometh a man reconciled or not. To this point of examination, Christ doth call the Angel of the Church of Ephesus, Rev. 2:5. Remember therefore from whence thou art fallen. Or, the thing we are to examine is our deeds, words and thoughts actually done or omitted; the neglect of which examination is reproved, Jer. 8:6, and Rev. 2:19,20.

7. The third thing to be looked unto in the court of Conscience, is the rule whereby we are to examine ourselves in all, or any, of the former respects, which is the revealed will of God in holy Scripture; wherein is set down to us what we should believe, and what we should do, and what is the reward of the obedience of faith, and what is the punishment of disobedience. And here if the Conscience be not well informed, and the rule closely cleaved unto, the erring Conscience may swallow down the grossest idolatry, and cry up Diana

for a great goddess, Act. 19:28, and make the murderers of the Saints conceive, that in killing them they do God good service, John 16:2.

8. The fourth thing is, the judicial process of the Conscience, for giving such a sentence of direction for what is to be done, or of absolution or condemnation, in the point examined and found done or not done: which process, if the Conscience be well informed, is after the manner of clear reasoning, by way of Syllogism, wherein we lay down the rule given by the supreme Law-giver, in the major or first proposition. Then we do lay ourselves to the rule in the minor or second assumed proposition; and from the comparison of ourselves, with the rule, we give out sentence in the third room, which is called the Conclusion. As for example, If the Conscience be about to give direction for what is to be done, it reasoneth thus,

What God hath appointed to be the only rule of faith and manners, I must take heed to follow it as the rule.

But, the holy Scripture, God hath appointed to be the only rule of faith and manners.

Therefore, I must take heed to follow the Scripture as the only rule.

Or more shortly, the Lord hath commanded to repent and turn unto him, (offering reconciliation in Christ) therefore it is my duty so to do.

But in the process of the Conscience unto conviction or absolution, sometime more, sometime fewer reasonings are used.

As for example, for conviction, the process goeth thus, That which God hath commanded me, I should have done: But, to repent and turn to Him, He hath commanded me; Therefore, I should have repented and turned to God.

Again, He that hath not obeyed the Lord, in repenting of his evil ways and turning unto God, is under great guiltiness, and worthy of death, by the sentence of the Law;

But, such a one am I, may every impenitent person say of himself:

And, therefore may conclude of himself, I am under great guiltiness, and worthy of death, by the sentence of the Law.

Like-ways, in the process of the Conscience, a humbled person well informed, may reason thus,

That way of reconciliation which God hath appointed a self-condemned sinner to follow, I am bound to follow;

But, this way (and no other) hath God appointed, that the sinner, convinced of sin and of deserved wrath should flee to Christ Jesus the Mediator, that by Him he may be justified, sanctified and saved:

Therefore, this way of reconciliation, and no other, I am bound to follow.

Again, Whosoever, by the grace of God, in the sense of sin and deserved wrath, is fled unto Christ for righteousness and eternal life and in Christ's strength, is endeavoring to give new obedience to the will of God, is undoubtedly a true believer and child of God;

But, such a one am I, may the humbled sinner, fled to Christ, say of himself:

Therefore, I am, by the grace of God, undoubtedly a true believer and a child of God.

And yet again he may go on, to strengthen his faith, and to comfort himself in the Lord, thus,

Whosoever in the sense of sin, poverty and weakness, hath fled to Christ the Redeemer, resolved never to part with Him, and hath consecrated himself, in the strength of Christ, to endeavor to give new obedience to the will of God, he is an heir with Isaac of the promised blessings, and may hope to have them perfectly in possession at last;

But such a one am I, may the humbled sinner, fled to Christ, say of himself:

Therefore, I am an heir of the promised blessings with Isaac, and may hope to have them perfectly in possession at last.

Such a process as this doth the Conscience of the regenerate man follow, when he reneweth the acts of his repentance, and sentenceth himself worthy of what the Law pronounceth against his sin; and when he reneweth the acts of his faith in Christ, through whom alone he is freed from the deserved curse of the Law.

9. As to the fifth thing to be observed in the court of Conscience, which is, the execution of the sentence it hath pronounced; because the Conscience is set over the man by God, as Judge-depute: therefore it goeth about, in the name of God, by and by to execute, as it may, the sentence justly pronounced by it; and according to the nature of the sentence, of condemnation or absolution, pronounced by it, it stirreth up divers motions and affections in the heart; some of them sad and sorrowful, some of them joyful and comfortable. The sad and bitter passions that follow upon the sentence of conviction and condemnation, justly pronounced, are shame, grief, fear, anxiety, vexation and such-like; whereby the guilty sinner is either fretted, as with a worm, or fired and tormented. Of this we have an example in our first parent Adam, who, being convicted in his conscience of sin and deserved wrath, did flee from the face of God, all amazed and a frighted, Gen. 3:9,10. The Lord called unto Adam, and said unto him where art thou? And he said, I heard thy voice in the garden, and I was afraid, because I was naked, and I hid myself.

But the Conscience, after it is furnished by the Gospel to absolve the penitent believer fled to Christ, doth stir up more sweet and comfortable motions in the heart, such as are, peace, comfort, joy, gladness, exultation, confidence, and such like. An example whereof we see in Paul, 2 Cor. 1:2. Our rejoicing, saith he, is this, the testimony of our conscience, that in simplicity and godly sincerity, not with fleshly wisdom, but by the grace of God, we have had our conversation in the world.

So the Conscience, after it is wounded by the man's transgression, doth the part of a Judge, citing the man before its Tribunal; and the part of an Officer, presenting the man at the Bar; and the part of an Accuser, challenging the man for his transgression; and the part of the Recorder, producing the book of Statutes; and the part of sufficient witnesses, proving and convincing him of the deed done.

Again it doth the part of a Judge, pronouncing sentence and condemning the convicted transgressor; and the part of a Sergeant and Marshal, binding the condemned wretch; and the part of the Prison and Stocks, pinching and pressing the bound sinner; and the part of the Burrio, scourging and tormenting him.

But the Conscience, after examination, finding the man either innocent and free of the crime, or forgiven and reconciled to God by Christ, after repentance and faith, embracing the Redeemer, it doth the part of an honest Friend, carefully comforting the innocent or penitent; and the part of an Advocate, excusing and defending the man against all challenges; and the part of Witnesses compurgators; and the part of the Judge absolving; and the part of the Rewarder. And so much concerning the nature and use of Conscience, as may suffice our purpose.

CHAP. II. - Of Cases of Conscience in general.

A CASE OF CONSCIENCE, taken in a large sense, comprehends every accident which any way affects or qualifieth the Conscience, And in this sense, the persuasion and certainty, which the Conscience may have, the soundness, health and strength of the Conscience, may be called Cases and good Cases of the Conscience.

So also, any effect which the Conscience doth work on the soul, such as are peace of conscience, comfort and joy in the heart, may be called Cases of the Conscience also.

But the Cases whereof we are to treat, are the ill Cases of the Conscience, whereby it is fallen from the soundness and straightness it should have, which we call by the name of wounds, diseases, and sickness of the Conscience: whereunto, that we may descend to speak more orderly, a twofold difference is to be observed.

2. First, we must put difference between a healthy and a sick Conscience. A healthy Conscience is that, which after examination of our ways, according to the rule of God's Word, doth justly absolve us, and speaketh peace to us toward God. Of such a conscience it is said by Solomon, A sound heart is the life of the flesh, Prov. 14:30, by the heart he meaneth the conscience, which ordinarily in Scripture is called the heart. And he saith, the sound conscience is the life of the flesh;

because the body is so much in better case, that the conscience be at peace toward God. And this blessing is allowed upon every believer in Christ, in his orderly walking, 2 Tim. 1:7. God hath not given us the spirit of fear, but of power, of love, and of a sound mind. A Conscience in this disposition needeth not medicine, but spiritual nourishment and exercise in all Christian-duties.

A sick Conscience we call, that which either is senseless of its own evils and dangers it is in, and sitteth down securely, and resteth without a warrant; Or, which is justly wounded, and labors under the sense of its pain; or, which is unquiet upon mistakes and ignorance of making use of the true remedy: of such a sick Conscience we are to speak, if possible, by God's blessing, a word in season may be spoken, to waken a secure conscience, or to refresh the weary soul, that being recovered from its malady, it may be able to feed upon the bread and water of life, and work the works of God in the strength of Christ.

3. Secondly, we must put difference between a troubled Soul and a troubled Conscience; for, the Soul is more largely taken then the Conscience. The Soul comprehendeth all the powers and faculties of the man; but the Conscience, as we speak of it, is only one faculty of the mind, judging of the man's moral ill or well-being; and so all cases of the Conscience are cases of the Soul: but, all the cases of the Soul are not cases of the Conscience. For, the Soul may be troubled while the Conscience is not troubled at all; yea, a man may have a commendable trouble in his soul, when he seeth God dishonored or His Church in hazard, whereby his conscience is so far from being troubled, that such a holy trouble strengthens his conscience in his address to God, as is in many places of the Psalms to be seen.

Again, a man's mind may be troubled by sundry natural or civil motives; while the conscience is allowably quiet, as in losses of things

temporal, fears, pains or unexpected inconveniencies occurring; yea,
there may be passions and perturbations of the mind in persons that
are not capable for the time of the exercise of Conscience, as may be
seen in young infants, and in the elder sort, in fits of fever, melancholy
and frenzy: and yet further, it is possible that passions, perturbations
and troubles of soul, may be found without any disease of the Conscience; because our Lord Jesus, in the days of his humiliation, was a
man acquainted with sorrows, but was not obnoxious to sin or any
self-challenging; for, he knew no sin in himself. He had trouble in his
soul, but could not have trouble of conscience, Job: 12:27. Now is my
soul troubled, and what shall I say? Father, save me from this hour;
but for this cause came I unto this hour. Of the cases of the Soul we
speak not here, but of the sinful diseases of the Conscience.

4. There is also a third difference to be observed between common
cases of Conscience, and these that specially concern Regeneration.
Common cases comprehend all these questions and doubts, wherein the Conscience is seeking light and resolution about the rule of
faith and manners, that it may better inform itself about the sense of
Scripture, and about the application thereof in the point of direction
in faith and practice. These common cases are of as large extent, as
the bulk of Divinity, as large as the Doctrine held forth in Scripture
concerning faith and manners: for, there is not any one article of faith
or duty prescribed, as a point of piety or righteousness, about which
questions may not be moved and cases propounded, wherein the
Conscience may seek satisfaction.

Of this huge great tree, we take but only one branch to speak of, so
far as maketh for our purpose concerning Regeneration.

CHAP. III. - Of Regeneration, what it is; and the regenerate man, who he is.

WE SPEAK NOT HERE of the regeneration of elect infants, dying in their infancy, God hath His own way of dealing with them; but of the regeneration of those who are capable of being outwardly called by the ministry of the Word which we may thus describe,

Regeneration (being one in effect with effectual calling) is the work of God's invincible power and mere grace, wherein, by His Spirit, accompanying His Word, He quickeneth a redeemed person lying dead in his sins, and reneweth him in his mind, will and all the powers of his soul; convincing him savingly of sin, righteousness and judgment, and making him heartily to embrace Christ and Salvation, and to consecrate himself to the service of God in Christ, all the days of his life.

2. The main thing we must take heed to in this work, is to give to God entirely the glory of His Grace and Power and Wisdom, so that the glory of man's regeneration be neither given to man, nor man-made sharer of the glory with God, but God may have the whole glory of His free grace, because out of His own goodwill, not for anything at all foreseen in man, He lets forth his special love on the redeemed in a time acceptable; And the glory of His Almighty power,

because by His omnipotent and invincible working He makes the man dead in sins to live, opens his eyes to take up savingly the things of God, takes away the heart of stone, and makes him a new creature, to will and to do His holy will; And the glory of His Wisdom, who dealeth so with His creature as He doth not destroy, but perfect the natural power of the man's will, making the man regenerate, most freely, deliberately and heartily to embrace Christ, and to consecrate himself to God's service. The reason why we urge this, is, because Satan, by corrupting the doctrine of regeneration, and persuading men that they are able of themselves by the common and the natural strength of their own freewill, without the special and effectual grace of God, both to convert themselves and others also, doth foster the native pride of men, hindereth them from emptying and humbling themselves before God, keepeth them from self-denial, doth mar the regeneration of them that are deluded with this error, and obscureth what he can, the shining of the glory of God's grace, power and wisdom in the conversion of men: for, whatsoever praise, proud men let go toward God for making men's conversion possible, yet they give the whole glory of actual conversion to the man himself, which Christ ascribeth to God only, and leaveth no more for man to glory in his spiritual regeneration, then he hath to glory in his own natural generation, John 3:5-8. And the same doth the Apostle teach, Ephes. 2:8-10, and, Philip. 2:13. It is God (saith he) which worketh in you both to will and to do of His own good pleasure. And therefore it is the duty of all Christ's disciples, but chiefly their duty who are con-secrate to God, to preach up the glory of God's free grace, omnipotent power and unsearchable wisdom, to live in the sense of their own emptiness, and to depend upon the furniture of grace for grace, out of Christ's fullness; and zealously to oppose the proud error of man's natural ability for converting himself, as they love to see, and find the effectual blessing of the Ministry of the Gospel, and themselves accepted for true disciples at the day of their meeting with Christ the Judge at His second coming.

3. For opening up of regeneration, these five propositions must be holden. The first is this, the natural man receiveth not the things of the Spirit of God; for, they are foolishness unto him; neither can he know them, because they are spiritually discerned, 1 Cor. 2:14.

The second is this, it is the Spirit of God which convinceth man of sin, of true righteousness and of judgment, John 16:9-11.

The third is this, in regeneration, conversion and quickening of a sinner, God, by his invincible power, createth and infuseth a new life and principles thereof, Psal. 110:3. Thy people shall be willing in the day of thy power, and, John 5:21, and 6:63.

The fourth is this, the invincible grace of God, working regeneration and a man's conversion, doth not destroy the freedom of man's will, but makes it truly free, and perfects it. Jer. 31:31. I will make a Covenant with the house of Israel and with the house of Judah, and will put My law in their inward parts, and write it in their hearts, &c.

The fifth is this, albeit a man, in the act of God's quickening and converting of him be passive, and in a spiritual sense dead in sins and trespasses, yet, for exercising external means, whereof God maketh use unto his conversion, for fitting him and preparing of him for a gracious change (such as are, hearing of the Word, reading of it meditating on it, inquiring after the meaning of it, &c.) the natural man hath a natural power thereunto as to other external actions, which sufficeth to take away excuse from them who have occasion of using the means and will not use them, Matth. 23:37.

For clearing of the first proposition, we must remember, that the object of actual regeneration, conversion and effectual calling, is the man elected or redeemed by Christ, lying in the state of defection from God destitute of original righteousness, at enmity with God, bently inclined to all evil, altogether unfit and impotent, yea even spiritually dead to every spiritual good, and specially to convert, regenerate or quicken himself: for albeit after the fall of Adam there are some sparks of common reason remaining, whereby he may confusedly know that which is called spiritual good, acceptable and pleasant unto God and fit to save his soul; yet the understanding of the unrenewed man judgeth of that good, and of the truth of the Evangel wherein that good is proposed, to be mere foolishness, and doth represent the spiritual object, and sets it before the will, as a thing uncertain or vain; and the will of the unrenewed man, after deliberation and comparison made of objects, some honest, some pleasant and some profitable in appearance, naturally is inclined to prefer and choose any seeming pleasant or profitable thing, whether the object be natural or civil, rather than that which is truly honest and morally good. But if it fall out that a spiritual good be well and in fair colors, described unto the unrenewed man, yet he seeth it not, but under the notion of a natural good, and as it is clothed with the image of some natural good, and profitable for preserving its standing in a natural being and welfare therein. So did the false prophet Balaam look upon the felicity of the righteous in their death, when he did separate eternal life from faith and sanctification, and did rent asunder the means from the end appointed of God, saying, Let me die the death of the righteous, and let my last end be like his, Numb. 23:10.

After this manner the woman of Samaria apprehended the gift and grace of the holy Ghost, and saving grace offered to her by Christ, Lord (saith she) Give me of that water, that I may not thirst again, and may not come again to draw water, Joh. 4:15. So also did the misbelieving Jews judge of the application of Christ's incarnation and suffering for their spiritual feeding, Joh. 6:33-35, for, The natural man cannot know the things of the Spirit of God, because they are spiritually discerned, and the natural man is destitute of the spirit of illumination. 1 Cor. 2:14. And the wisdom of the flesh is enmity to God: for it is not subject to the law of God, yea, it cannot be subject unto it, Rom. 8:7. The power therefore of the natural or unrenewed man is not fitted for the discerning, and loving of a spiritual good, because he is altogether natural and not spiritual: For, a supernatural object, requireth a supernatural power of the understanding and will, to take it up, and rightly conceive of it: But of this supernatural faculty, the unrenewed man is destitute, and in respect of spiritual discerning, he is dead, that he cannot discern spiritual things spiritually.

4. As for the second proposition anent a man's regeneration, the Lord, that He may break the carnal confidence of the person whom He is to convert, first, showeth him his duty by the doctrine of the law and covenant of works, making him to see the same by the powerful illumination of the holy Spirit, and so taketh away all pretext of ignorance. Secondly, He showeth him his guiltiness and deserved damnation wherein he is involved, and so taken away all conceit and imagination of his innocence. Thirdly, He doth convince him of his utter inability to satisfy the law, or to deliver himself from the curse thereof, either by way of action and obedience, or by way of suffering and paying of the penalty of the violate law of God: And so overtur-

neth all confidence in himself, or in his own works. Whence followeth
the elect man's desperation to be delivered by himself, because he
seeth himself a sinner, and that all hope of justification by his own
deeds or sufferings, is cut off. Now, that this is the work of the holy
Spirit, is plain, John 16:8. When the comforter, the spirit of truth, shall
come, He shall convince the world of sin, &c. And in this condition
sundry of God's dear children, for a time are keeped under the bonds
of the law, under the spirit of bondage and sad conviction.

5. As for the third proposition, the Lord after He hath laid the sin of
His elect child, who is to be converted, to his charge by the doctrine
of the law, first, openeth up a light unto him in the doctrine of the
Gospel, and lets him see, that his absolution from sin and his salvation is possible, and may be had, by flying unto Christ the Redeemer.
Secondly, the Lord drawing near hand the humbled self-condemned
soul, deals with him by way of moral suasion, sweetly inviting him
in the preaching of the Gospel, to receive the Redeemer Christ Jesus,
the eternal Son of God manifested in the flesh, that by receiving of
Him as He is offered in the Evangel, for remission of sin, renovation
of life, and eternal salvation, he may close the Covenant of grace and
reconciliation with God. Thirdly, because the fall of Adam hath bereft
man of all spiritual and supernatural power, till he be supernatu-
rally quickened and converted by the omnipotent power of God's
grace: Therefore the Lord superaddeth unto moral suasion, effectual operation, and formeth in the soul a spiritual faculty and ability
for doing what is pleasant unto God, and tendeth to save himself
according to the will of God. This infusion of a new life, sometime
is called the forming of the new creature, sometime regeneration,
sometime rising from the dead and vivification, or quickening of the
man, sometime saving grace and the life of God, and the seed of God,

having in it the principle of all saving graces and habits, which are brought forth afterward to acts and exercise.

Meantime, true it is, that all men, because of their inborn corruption, have an inclination and bent disposition to resist the holy Ghost; But when the Lord will actually convert the man, He overcometh and taketh away actual resistance, and doth so break the power of natural rebellion that it doth not forever after reign in him: for, if God did not take away actual resistance of the man in his conversion, no conversion should certainly follow, and God should be disappointed of His purpose to convert the man, even when He hath put forth His almighty power to work conversion; But God doth so wisely and powerfully stir up this new infused life of grace, and setteth it so on work, that the understanding and judgment like a counselor, and the Will like a commanding Emperor, and the active power of the new infused faculty as an officer, do all bestir themselves to bring forth supernatural operations. Whence it cometh to pass, that the new creature beginneth to look kindly on Christ the Redeemer, and to desire to be united unto Him, and doth stretch forth itself to embrace Him heartily, for obtaining in Him righteousness and salvation, as He is offered in the Gospel: And so he casts himself over on Christ with full purpose never to shed from Him but by faith to draw out of Him grace for grace, till he be perfected. And here the man that was merely passive, in his quickening and regeneration, beginneth presently to be active in his conversion, and following conversation: for, God giveth to him to will and to do of His good pleasure; And he having obtained by God's effectual operation to will and to do, doth formally will and do the good which is done.

6. As to the fourth proposition, when the power of God is put forth, invincibly for the converting of a soul, that invincible working is so

far from destroying the natural liberty of the will, that it doth indeed preserve it, and sets it right on the right object, and doth perfect it: For, as when God openeth the eyes of a man's understanding, that he doth behold the wonders of His law, when he removeth the natural blindness of the mind, and maketh a man see that the Gospel is the wisdom and power of God unto salvation; which sometime he counted to be mere foolishness, he doth no ways destroy the man's judgment, or understanding, but doth correct, help, heal, and perfect it; So when the holy Spirit doth powerfully and effectually move and turn the Will of the man to embrace the sweet and saving offers of Christ's grace in the Gospel, and maketh him deliberately choose this blessed way of salvation, and to renounce all confidence in his own, or any others worth or works, He doth not destroy, but perfect the liberty of the Will, and raiseth it up from death and its damnable inclination, and maketh it most joyfully and most freely to make choice of this pearl of price, and bless itself in its choice forever. Therefore, let no man complain of wrong done to man's free-will, when God stops its way to hell, wisely, powerfully, graciously and sweetly moveth it to choose the way of life; But rather let men beware to take the glory of actual conversion of men, from God, and either give it wholly to their idol of free-will, or make it sharer of the glory of regeneration with God, which glory God will not give to another, but reserve wholly to Himself: for, all men, in the point and moment of regeneration, are like unto Lazarus in the grave, to whom God, by commanding him to arise, gave life and power to arise out of the grave where he lay dead and rotting.

7. As to the fifth proposition, We must distinguish the work of regeneration from the preparation and disposition of the man to be regenerate, whereby he is made more capable of regeneration to be

wrought in him: for, the material disposition of him, fitting him for regeneration, is neither a part nor a degree of regeneration; for, albeit the Lord be not bound to these preparatory dispositions, yet He will have man bound to make use of these external means which may prepare him; because, by the use of external means (such as are, hearing of the word, Catechizing and conference, &c.) a man may be brought more near unto regeneration, as Christ doth teach us by His speech to that Pharisee, who was instructed in the law and answered discreetly unto Christ; Thou art not far (saith He) from the kingdom of God, Mark. 12:24. This preparatory disposition, in order unto regeneration, is like unto the drying of timber to make it sooner take fire, when it is casten into it. For, dryness in the timber, is neither a part nor a degree of kindling or inflammation of it; But only a preparation of the timber to receive inflammation when the fire shall be set to it, or it put in the fire, possibly, a long time after. In these preparatory exercises then, no man will deny, that the natural man unrenewed, hath a natural power to go and hear a Sermon preached, to read the Scripture, to be informed by Catechizing, and conference of Religion and regeneration, whereof God when He pleaseth may make use in regeneration of the man. Wherefore, whosoever in the preaching of the Gospel, are charged and commanded to repent, to believe in Christ, or turn unto God, they are commanded also to use all these external means whereby they may be informed of the duty required, and of the means leading thereunto; in the exercise of which external means, they may meet with sundry common operations and effects of God's Spirit, before they be regenerate or converted, whereof the use may be sound not only in, but also after, conversion; And if any man shall refuse, slight or neglect to follow these preparatory exercises, which may prepare him for conversion, he is inexcusable before

God and man, and guilty of rejecting of the offer of reconciliation, yea guilty of resisting of the holy Ghost, of which sin and guiltiness the holy martyr Stephen chargeth the misbelieving Jews, Acts 7:51.

8. As for the regenerate man, he it is who in the acknowledgement of his sinfulness and deserved misery, and of his utter inability to help himself, doth cast away all confidence in his own parts, and possible righteousness of his own works, and fleeth to Christ offered in the Gospel, that in Christ alone he may have true wisdom, righteousness, sanctification, and redemption; and doth with full purpose of heart consecrate himself, and endeavor, in the strength of Christ, to serve God acceptably all the days of his life.

For the ground of this description, we have the words of the Apostle, Philip. 3:3. Where putting a difference between the true people of God, and the counterfeit, he saith. We are the circumcision who worship God in the spirit, and rejoice in Jesus Christ, and have no confidence in the flesh. In which description of the regenerate man, the Apostle first points forth unto us three special operations of the Spirit of regeneration, then three duties of the man regenerate.

The first operation of the Spirit of God, the only circumciser of the heart, is the humbling of the man in the sense of his sin by the doctrine of the law, and cutting off all his confidence in his own worth, wit, freewill and strength to help himself. So that the man hath no confidence in the flesh.

The second operation, is the infusion of saving faith, making the man humbled to close with Christ in the Covenant of reconciliation, and to rest upon Him as the only and sufficient remedy of sin and misery, so that Christ becometh to him the ground of rejoicing and gloriation.

The third operation, is the upstirring and enabling of the believer in Christ, to endeavor new obedience, and to worship God in the spirit.

As for the three duties of the man regenerate. The first is, to follow the leading of the Spirit in the point of more and more humbling of himself before God in the sense of his own insufficiency, and eschewing of all leaning on his own parts, gifts, works, or sufferings, or anything else beside Christ; He must have no confidence in the flesh.

The second duty, is to grow in the estimation of Christ's righteousness and fullness of all graces to be letten forth to the believer employing Him by faith, and comforting himself in Christ against all difficulties, troubles and temptations; He must rejoice in Jesus Christ.

The third duty, is to endeavor communion-keeping with God in the course of new obedience in all cases, worshiping and serving God in sincerity of heart; he must be a worshiper of God.

As to the last thing holden forth in the Apostles words, which is the undoubted mark and evidence of the man regenerate and circumcised in heart, it standeth in the constant endeavor to grow in these three duties jointly, so as each of them may advance another: for, many failings and short-comings will be found in our new obedience and worshiping of God in the spirit; but, let these failings be made use of to extinguish and abolish all confidence in our own parts and righteousness, that our daily failings may humble us and cut us off from all confidence in the flesh.

But let not these failings so discourage us, as to hinder us to put confidence in Christ; but by the contrary, the less ground of confidence we find in ourselves, let us raise so much higher the estimation of remission of sin and imputation of Christ's righteousness, and stir up ourselves by faith to draw more strength and ability out of Christ for enabling us to walk more holily and righteously before God; and having fled to Christ and comforted ourselves in him, let us not turn his grace into wantonness; but the more we believe the grace of Jesus Christ, let us strive, in his strength, so much the more to glorify God in new obedience: And in the circle of these three duties, let us wind ourselves up stairs toward heaven: for, God hath promised, that such as wait on the Lord, shall renew their strength, they shall mount up with wings as Eagles, they shall run and not be weary, they shall walk and not faint, Isaiah 40:31.

In the conjunction of these three duties, the evidence of regeneration is found. If there be not a sincere endeavor after all these three duties, the evidence of regeneration is by so much darkened, and short for probation: for, it is not sufficient to prove a man regenerate, that he is driven from all confidence in his own righteousness, and filled with the sense of sin and deserved wrath, because a man that hath no more than that, may perish in this miserable condition, as we see in Judas the traitor, whose conscience was burdened with the sense of sin, but did not seek mercy and pardon. Neither is it sufficient to boast of acquaintance with Christ, and profess great respect to him, because many do cry, Lord, Lord, who neither renounce their confidence in their own righteousness, nor worship God in spirit; for, of such Christ saith, Matth. 7:21. Not everyone that saith to Him, Lord, Lord, shall enter into the kingdom of God. Neither is it sufficient to pretend the worshiping of God in spirit: for, all they who think to be justified by their own works, do esteem their manner of serving of God, true and spiritual service and worship, as may be seen in the proud Pharisee glorying before God in his own righteousness, and acknowledging that God was the giver unto him of the holiness and righteousness which he had, Luke 18:11. I thank Thee, O God, saith he, that I am not like other men, extortioners, unjust, adulterers, or even as this publican: for, of this man Christ saith, he returned to his house unjustified, that is, a man lying still in sin unreconciled.

Neither is it sufficient to prove a man regenerate, to confess sin and by-gone unrighteousness, and to promise and begin to amend his ways and future conversation; for, so much may a Pharisee attain. And there are many that profess themselves Christians, who think to be justified by the merits of their own and other saint's doings and sufferings, and do disdainfully scoff and mock at the doctrine of the imputed righteousness of Christ; how many are they also, who think their bygone sins may be washen away, and be recompensed by their purpose to amend their life in time to come? How many are they, who, being willingly ignorant of the righteousness of God, which is of faith in Jesus Christ, go about to establish their own righteousness as the Jews did? Rom. 10:3.

And how few are they who follow the example of the Apostle, who carefully served God in spirit and truth, but did not lean to his own righteousness, but sought more and more to be found in Christ, not having his own righteousness, which behooved to be made up of his imperfect obedience of the law, but that righteousness which is by faith in Jesus Christ? Philip. 3:9.

But that man, who daily in the sense of his sinfulness and poverty fleeth unto Jesus Christ, that he may be justified by His righteousness, and endeavoreth by faith in Him to bring forth the fruits of new obedience, and doth not put confidence in these his works when he hath done them, but rejoiceth in Jesus Christ the fountain of holiness and blessedness; That man (I say) undoubtedly is regenerate, and a new creature, for so doth the Apostle describe him, Philip. 3:3.

CHAP. IV. - Of divine Covenants about the eternal salvation of men; and in special, of the Covenant of redemption, showing that there is such a Covenant, and what are the articles thereof.

BECAUSE THE HEALING OF the sickness of the conscience cometh by a right application of divine Covenants about our salvation: therefore it is necessary, that some measure, of the knowledge thereof be opened up.

1. A divine covenant we call, a contract or paction, wherein God is at least the one party contractor. Of this sort of covenants about the eternal salvation of men (which sort chiefly belong to our purpose) there are three. The first is, the covenant of redemption, past between

God, and Christ God appointed Mediator, before the world was, in the council of the Trinity. The second is, the covenant of works, made between God and men, in Adam in his integrity, endued with all natural perfections, enabling him to keep it, so long as it pleased him to stand to the condition. The third is, the covenant of grace and reconciliation through Christ, made between God and believers (with their children) in Christ.

2. As to the covenant of redemption; for clearing the matter, we must distinguish the sundry acceptions of the word redemption: for, 1. Sometime it is taken for the contract and agreement of selling and buying-back to eternal salvation, of lost man, looked upon as in the state of sin and misery. In which sense, we are said to be bought by Christ, both souls and bodies, 1 Cor. 6:19,20. Ye are not your own; for ye are bought with a price: therefore glorify God in your body, and in your spirit, which are God's. And this may be called redemption by paction and agreed bargain. 2. Sometime redemption is taken for the paying of the price agreed upon. In which sense, Christ is said to have redeemed us, by suffering of the punishment due to us, and ransoming of us. Gal. 3:13. Christ hath redeemed us from the curse of the law, being made a curse for us. 3. Sometime redemption is taken for the begun application of the benefits purchased in the covenant by the price paid, Ephes. 1:7. In whom we have redemption through His blood, even the remission of sins, according to the riches of His grace. 4. Sometime redemption is taken for the perfect and full possession of all the benefits agreed upon between the Father and Christ His Son the Mediator. In which sense, we are said to be sealed with the holy Spirit of promise, which is the earnest of our inheritance, until the redemption of the purchased possession, Ephes. 1:14, and Ephes. 4:30, it is said, Grieve not the holy Spirit of God, whereby ye are sealed

unto the day of redemption; which is the day of Judgment, when Christ shall put us in full possession of all the blessedness which He purchased by bargain and payment for us.

In this place we take redemption in the first sense, for the covenant past between the Father and Christ His Son, designed Mediator, about our redemption.

3. When we name the Father as the one party and His Son Christ as the other party in this covenant, we do not seclude the Son and holy Spirit from being the party offended; but do look upon the Father, Son and Spirit, one God in three Persons, as offended by man's sin; and yet all three contented to take satisfaction to divine justice for man's sin in the Person of the Son, as designed Mediator, to be incarnate. Whereby the Son is both the party offended as God, one essentially with the Father and holy Spirit; and the party contractor also, as God designed Mediator personally for redeeming man, who with consent of the Father and holy Spirit, from all eternity willed and purposed in the fullness of time, to assume the human nature in personal union with Himself, and for the elects sake to become man, and to take the cause of the elect in hand, to bring them back to the friendship of God, and full enjoyment of felicity for evermore.

When therefore we make the Father the one party, and the Son designed mediator the other party, speaking with the Scripture, for the more easy up-taking of the Covenant, let us look to one God in three Persons, having absolute right and sovereign power according to His own pleasure to dispose of men, looked upon as lying before God (to Whom all things are present) in sin and death, drawn on by man's own deserving, and yet for the glory of His grace resolving to save the elect, so as His justice shall be satisfied for them, in and by the second Person of the Trinity, the co-eternal and co-essential Son of the Father.

4. This covenant of redemption then may be thus described. It is a bargain, agreed upon between the Father and the Son designed Mediator, concerning the elect (lying with the rest of mankind in the state of sin and death, procured by their own merit) wisely and powerfully to be converted, sanctified and saved, for the Son of God's satisfaction and obedience (in our nature to be assumed by Him) to be given in due time to the Father, even unto the death of the cross.

In this bargain or agreement, the Scripture importeth clearly, a selling and a buying of the elect, Acts 20:28. Feed the Church of God, which He hath purchased by His own blood, 1 Cor. 6:20, ye are bought with a price, and 1 Pet. 1:18. The seller of the elect, is God; the buyer, is God incarnate; the persons bought, are the Church of the elect; the price, is the blood of God, to wit, the blood of Christ, who is God and man in one person.

This covenant of redemption, is in effect one with the eternal decree of redemption, wherein the salvation of the elect, and the way how it shall be brought about is fixed, in the purpose of God, who worketh all things according to the counsel of His own Will, as the Apostle sets it down, Ephes. 1 unto the 15th verse.

And the decree of redemption is in effect a covenant, one God in three persons agreeing in the decree, that the second Person, God the Son, should be incarnate, and give obedience and satisfaction to divine justice for the elect: unto which piece of service the Son willingly submitting Himself, the decree becometh a real covenant indeed.

But for further satisfaction, that there is such a covenant between the Father and the Son, as we have said, for redeeming of the elect, Scripture giveth us evidence six ways.

The first way is by expressions, which import and presuppose a formal covenant between the parties, buying and selling; the second way is, by styles and titles given to Christ the Redeemer; the third is, by expressions relating to an eternal decree for execution and performance of the covenant of redemption; the fourth is, by representation of this covenant in the Levitical types; the fifth is, by Christ the Redeemer now incarnate, His ratification of the covenant; and the sixth way is, by holding forth to us the heads and articles agreed upon, wherein the covenant consists.

The first poof.

As to the expressions, importing a formal covenant, first, Ephes. 1:7, it is called a redemption, or a buying of the elect out of sin and misery by blood, showing that no remission of sin could be granted by Justice, without shedding of blood, and Christ undertook to pay the price, and hath paid it.

Again, the inheritance which the elect have promised unto them, is called a purchase, importing, that the disponer of the inheritance to the elect, must have a sufficient price for it, and that the Redeemer hath accepted the condition and laid down the price craved for it, Ephes. 1:14, and so bought back lost heaven and forfeited blessedness to so many sinners, who other ways for sin, might justly have been excluded and debarred therefrom forever.

A third expression is holden forth, Acts 20:28, wherein God disponer and God Redeemer, are agreed, that the elect shall go free for God the Redeemer's obedience unto the death, who hath now bought them with His blood.

A fourth expression is in plain terms set down by Paul, 1 Cor. 6:20. Ye are bought with a price: God the disponer selleth, and God the Redeemer buyeth the elect to be His conquest, both body and spirit. And Peter more particularly expresseth the price of redemption agreed upon, to be not gold or silver, but the blood of the Mediator Christ, the innocent Lamb of God, slain in typical prefiguration's from the beginning of the World, and slain in real performance in the fullness of time, 1 Pet. 1:18-21.

A fifth expression is, that of our Lord Jesus in the institution of the Sacrament of His Supper, Matth. 26:28. This is my blood of the New Testament, which is shed for many, for remission of sins. Here an agreement between the Redeemer and God disponer, that these many which are the elect, shall have remission of sins for the Redeemers ransom of blood paid for them. The purchase of this ransom of blood, He maketh over in the Covenant of grace and reconciliation to believers in Him, and sealeth the bargain with them by the Sacrament of His Supper.

The second proof.

The second evidence of this Covenant of Redemption past between God and God the Son Mediator designed, is from such titles and styles as are given to Christ in relation to the procuring of a Covenant of grace and reconciliation between God and us. First, He is called a Mediator of the Covenant of reconciliation, interceding for procuring of it, and that not by a simple entreaty, but by giving Himself over to the Father (calling for satisfaction to Justice, that reconciliation might go on) for paying a compensatory price, sufficient to satisfy Justice for the elect, 1 Tim. 2:5,6. There is one God and one Mediator between God and man (to wit, God incarnate) the man Christ Jesus who gave

Himself a ransom for all (to wit, elect children) to be testified in due time.

Another title is given to Him by Job, Chap. 19:24. Where He is called a Redeemer, a near kinsman, who before His incarnation had obliged Himself to take on human nature, and to pay the price of Redemption (represented by slain sacrifices) for the elect His kinsmen.

A third title is held out, in that He is called a Surety of a better Covenant, Heb. 7:22. Whereby is imported, that God would not pass a Covenant of grace and reconciliation to men, except He had a good Surety who would answer for the debt of the party reconciled, and would undertake to make the reconciled stand to his Covenant. And Christ undertook the Suretyship, and so hath procured and established this Covenant of grace, much better than the Covenant of works, and better than the old Covenant of grace with Israel, as they made use of it. This necessarily imports a Covenant between Him and the Fathers Justice, to whom He becometh surety for us: for, what is suretyship, but a voluntary transferring of another's debt upon the Surety, obliging to pay the debt for which he engageth as Surety?

A fourth title given to Christ, is, that He is a reconciliation by way of permutation; the atonement, Rom. 5:11. We have by Christ received the atonement, that is, that which hath pacified the Fathers Justice and reconciled Him to us, is made over in a gift unto us; for, by Christ, procurement we have God made ours, and Christ pacifying God, put, as it were, in our bosom: for, God having sold us to Christ, by taking Christ's satisfaction for ours, He hath come over to us as reconciled, and given us Christ the Reconciler and the atonement, to be ours. Here is an agreement made between God and Christ, and the condition of the agreement between the parties for our behoof, clearly imported and presupposed.

The fifth title given to Christ, is this, He is called the propitiation, 1 John 2:2. Whereby God is pacified, not only for the believing Jews, but also for the whole elect World, which should believe in Him. And if He be the pacifying propitiation, then God hath satisfaction in all that His Justice craved from Christ for the elect; and, Rom. 3:25. He is called a propitiatory sacrifice, wherewith God is so well pleased, that He makes offer of Him to us, and sets Him forth to us for pacifying our Conscience through faith in His blood, to declare His righteousness for remission of sins, without breach of Justice; wherein, what price God required and was paid by Christ, is insinuate and presupposed; for, satisfaction could not be, except the price agreed upon, had been promised and accepted before in Covenanting.

The third proof.

The third evidence, proving that there was a Covenant of Redemption past before the beginning of the World, is, because the eternal decree of God was fixed about the way of Redemption to be fulfilled in time: for, Known unto God were all His works from the beginning, Acts 15:18. And whatsoever God doth in time, He doth it according to the eternal counsel of His own Will, Ephes. 1:9. Now, Christ the eternal Son of God, being made man, laid down His life for His sheep. The Son of man goeth, as it was determined, but woe unto that man by whom He is betrayed, Luke, 22:22. And whatsoever Christ suffered, was by the determined counsel of God, Acts 2:23. And God the Son, before He was incarnate, declares the decree of the Kingdom promised unto Him by the Father, and of the victories which He should have over all His enemies, and of the felicity and multitude of the subjects of His Kingdom, that should believe in Him, Psal. 2:7. I will declare the decree, saith He; presupposing therefore the decree of God, of sending His eternal Son into the World, to become a man and to suffer, and thereafter to reign forever, we must also necessarily presuppose the consent of the Son, making paction with the Father and the Spirit, fixing the decree and agreement about the whole way of Redemption, to be brought about in time: for, the same Person, Christ Jesus, who dwelt among men in the days of His humiliation, John 1:14. Was with the Father from eternity: and as by Him all things were made, which were made, John 1:2,3. So without Him nothing was decreed which was decreed, Prov. 8:22 to 32, which also is manifest in the Apostles words, 2 Tim. 1:9. He saved us, and called us with a holy calling, not according to our works, but according to His own purpose and grace, which was given us in Christ Jesus before the World began.

For, as before the beginning of the World, the elect were given to the Son designed Mediator to be incarnate, and the price agreed upon; so also grace to be given in time to the redeemed by compact, was given from eternity unto Christ, their designed Advocate. Also, Ephes. 1:3-5, we were elected in Christ, unto holiness and salvation and unto all spiritual blessings, and were predestinate to the adoption of sons by Jesus Christ. And 1 Pet. 1:18-20, we are redeemed, not with gold or silver, but by the precious blood of Christ, who was predestinate before the beginning of the world. Whereby it is manifest, that the Covenant between the Father and the Son, was transacted concerning the incarnation of the Son, and His sufferings, death and resurrection, and all other things belonging to the salvation of the elect.

The fourth proof.

The fourth evidence of the passing a Covenant between the Father and the Son, is holden forth in the typical priesthood of Levi, by the altar and sacrifices, and the rest of the Levitical ceremonies which were prescribed by God: for, as these things were testimonies, preachings, declarations and evidences of a Covenant, past of old between God the disponer, and the Son the Redeemer, about the way of justifying and saving such as believed in the Messiah by an expiatory sacrifice, to be offered in the fullness of time, for the redeemed; So also they were prefiguration's, predictions, prophesies and pledges of the Redeemers paying of the promised price of Redemption. And this agreed-upon-price (because of the perfections of the parties contractors, the Father and the Son) was holden and esteemed as good as paid from the beginning of the World; and the agreed-upon-benefits purchased thereby to wit, grace and glory, were effectually bestowed on the faithful before Christ's incarnation, as the Psalmist testifies, Psal. 84:11. The Lord, saith he, is a sun and a shield, the Lord will give grace and glory, and no good thing will He withhold from them that walk uprightly; and, Psal. 73:24. Thou shalt guide me with Thy counsel, and afterward receive me into glory; and that because the promised price of Redemption was of no less worth, to give righteousness and life eternal to believers in the Messiah to come, then the price now paid is now of worth to give for it, righteousness and life eternal to these that believe in the Messiah now come, Jesus Christ incarnate. And this donation of saving graces, as remission of sin, and carrying on to life eternal, was sealed unto believers in the Covenant of reconciliation, by the appointed Sacraments of circumcision and the paschal lamb.

The fifth proof.

The fifth evidence of a Covenant past between the Father and the Son Mediator to be incarnate, is this, Christ now incarnate, doth ratify all these things which the Father and Himself not yet incarnate, and the holy Spirit had spoken in the Old Testament about the salvation of the elect, and the price of their redemption, and of the conditions to be performed on either hand; And, as it were of new, doth repeat and renew the covenant which before was past between the Father and Himself before He was incarnate: for, Luke 2:49, speaking to Joseph and His mother when He was about twelve years old, He saith, Wist ye not, that I must be about My Fathers business? And, Matth. 3:13. He presents Himself pledge and surety for sinners before the Father, to be baptized for them with the baptism of affliction, and to fulfill all righteousness, as was agreed upon before, verse. 15, whereupon the Father doth receive and admit the surety and His undertaking for payment, verse. 17, and, Lo, a voice from heaven, saying, this is My beloved Son, in whom I am well pleased; and John 5:39. He standeth to all things which were testified of Him in the Scriptures; Search the Scriptures: for in them ye think to have eternal life, and they are they that testify of Me. And verse. 36. He professeth, that all that He doth, is with the Fathers consent and concurrence, and that He came into the World, that He might finish what the Father had sent Him to do and suffer, which He calls His work that He was about. And more specially He shows the agreement past between the Father and Him before He came into the world concerning his incarnation, and the discharge of his Mediatory office, and his power to give eternal life to those that believe in him: for, the Father sent him to be incarnate, verse. 37, and that he with the Father, might give eternal life to whomsoever he will, and might quicken the dead, verse. 21, and that he might exercise judgment, authority was given to him as the Son of man, verse. 27. Yea, he showeth, that it was agreed upon between the Father and him about all the doctrine which he should reach, John 8:26. I speak to the World these things which I have heard of him; and he showeth that they were agreed about the price of redemption of the elect, and about his resurrection from the dead, and that his death did fully satisfy the Father, John 10:15. As the Father knoweth Me, even so know I the Father; and I lay down My life for the sheep; and verse. 17, therefore doth the Father love Me, because I lay down My life that I might take it again; and, verse. 18, this commandment have I received of the Father. And, Luke 24:25, he propones in short the sum of the covenant past between the Father and himself, speaking to the two disciples going to Emmaus; O fools and slow of heart, to believe all that the prophets have spoken, ought not Christ to have suffered these things, and to enter in his own glory? But most briefly he showeth the whole matter so oft as he calleth the Father his God, and that in respect of the covenant past between God and him to be incarnate, and now incarnate indeed.

The sixth proof.

The sixth evidence of the Covenant of Redemption, past between the Father and the Son, standeth in the heads and articles of the Covenant wherein they were agreed.

Now there are as many articles of the Covenant, as there are injunctions, commands and conditions required on the one hand, and promises to fulfill all on the other hand; as many predictions as there are of Christ's sufferings, and promises made to the Church through and for Him. Of these many, we shall touch only at four, whereby the faith of believers in Him may be confirmed about their Redemption by Him, and whereby the erroneous doctrine of them who evacuate the Covenant of redemption of the elect, may be refuted: wherein they teach, that Christ, by His obedience yielded unto the Father, even to the death of the cross, did purchase no more but a possibility of salvation, and no more grace for the elect then for the reprobate, as if He had not purchased a certainty of salvation to be given to any, but had suspended all the fruit of His suffering upon the frail, mutable, inconstant and corrupt free-will of men; so that no man can by their doctrine have more certainty of their own salvation, then they have of the certainty and stability of their own sickle mind and will: and so no more certainty of their own salvation, then of their own perdition. The order we shall keep in speaking of the articles of the Covenant of Redemption, shall be this.

The first article, shall be of the persons redeemed.

The second article, shall be of the price of Redemption to be paid by Christ in the fullness of time.

The third article, shall be about the gifts and benefits purchased for, and to be given unto, the persons Redeemed.

The fourth article of this Covenant of redemption, past between the Father and the Son, shall be of the means and ways whereby the gifts and benefits purchased, may be wisely, orderly and effectually applied to the Redeemed.

In ranking of these articles, we do not presuppose a priority of one of them before another in order of nature or time; But we choose to speak of them in order of doctrine, for our more easy understanding of the matter.

For, the Covenant of Redemption past between the Father and the Son, is by way of an eternal decree of the Trinity, comprehending all and whatsoever belongeth to Redemption. In the decerning of which decree, there is not a first nor a last, but a joint purpose of God to bring about and accomplish all the heads and articles of the Covenant, each in their own due time, order and way appointed.

The first article of the Covenant of Redemption concerneth the persons redeemed.

The redeemed in Scripture, are pointed forth under sundry expressions; sometime they are called the predestinate; sometime the elect; sometime these whom God foreknew; sometime they who are called according to His purpose; sometime they that were given to Christ of the Father; sometime Christ's sheep; sometime the children of God, &c. But whatsoever name they have, the persons are the same, according to that of the Apostle, Rom. 8:29,30, whom He did foreknow, them He did predestinate to be conform to the image of His Son—Moreover whom He did predestinate, them He also called; and whom he called, them he also justified; and whom he justified, them he also glorified. The number and the names of the persons here spoken of, are the same; and they are called the predestinate, in regard that God hath appointed them to a certain end, to wit, eternal life, to be brought thereunto effectually by certain means for the glory of God's grace. They are called elect, verse. 33, in regard God in the purpose of his good pleasure, hath severed them from among the rest of men, lying with them in the state of perdition by their own procurement, and hath designed them to be partakers of eternal salvation. They are called foreknown, and written in the book of life, in regard God hath comprehended them in his special love, no less distinctly and unchangeably, then if he had their names written in a catalogue, or book. And they are called given unto Christ, in regard the redeeming of them, and bringing them to life is committed to Christ. But by whatsoever name they are designed, the persons redeemed are still the same.

2. But whereas the elect, given to Christ, are called the redeemed, it presupposeth, that they were considered and looked upon as now fallen by their own fault, and lying by their own merit in sin and misery, enemies to God, and altogether unable to help themselves.

For, this much doth the notion of Redemption, or buying back again import: and that it is so, is clear, because the mercy of God, the grace of God, the good-will of God, is put in Scripture for the only motive and impulsive cause of Redemption, Ephes. 1:7-9. In whom we have Redemption through his blood, even the forgiveness of sins according to the riches of his grace, wherein he hath abounded toward us in all wisdom and prudence, having made known unto us the mystery of his will according to his good pleasure, which he had purposed in himself.

3. The Scripture showeth us that there is an innumerable multitude of redeemed persons, and a sort of universality of them, extended unto all nations and ages and states of men; so that this huge multitude for whose redemption Christ's blood was shed, Matth. 26:29, is justly called by the name of a world, an elect world, John 3:16, to be called out of that reprobate world, for which Christ refuseth to intercede, John 17:9, the truth of this matter, the redeemed do acknowledge in their worshiping Christ their Mediator, Rev. 5:9, and they sang a new song, saying, Thou art worthy to take the book and to open the seals thereof; for, thou wast slain, and hast redeemed us to God by thy blood, out of every kindred and tongue and people and nation These are the all men whom God will have saved and doth save, 1 Tim. 2:4, these are the all men of whom the Apostle speaks, 2 Pet. 3:9. God is patient toward us (to wit his elect) not willing that any of us should perish, but that we all should come to repentance: And this the Apostle giveth for a reason of the Lord's deferring his coming, till all the elect should be brought in, of whom many were not yet converted in the Apostles time and many were not yet born, and if Christ should not delay his coming, till they were born and brought

in to reconciliation with God, the number of the elect should be cut short.

4. In no place of Scripture is it said, that all and every man are elect, or every man is given to Christ, or every man is predestinate unto life; in no place of Scripture is it said, that Christ hath made paction with the Father for all and every man without exception; But by the contrary, it is sure from Scripture, that Christ hath merited and procured salvation for all them for whom he entered himself Surety. Their sins only were laid on Christ, and in him condemned, satisfied for, and expiate, Isa. 53, for these, and in their place he offered himself to satisfy Justice, for them he prayed, them only he justifieth and glorifieth: for, the sentence of the Apostle, 2 Cor. 5:15, standeth firm; in Christ all are dead (to the law) for whom and in whose room Christ did die. And therefore for these his people the law is satisfied: from these the curse is taken away, to them heaven and all things necessary to salvation are purchased, and shall infallibly in due time, yea invincibly be applied.

Christ hath not sanctified, consecrate, and perfected all and every-one, Heb. 10:14, only for his sheep predestinate, he laid down his life, John 10:15,16,26, he did not buy with his blood all and everyone, but his Church called out, and severed from the world, Acts 20:28, he saveth not all and every man from their sins, but his own people only, to wit, whom he hath bought with his blood to be his own, Matth. 1:21, whom he hath purchased to be his own peculiar, whom he doth purify, and kindle with a servant desire to bring forth good works, Tit. 2:14.

Such as Christ hath redeemed, he loveth them infinitely, and counted them dearer to him then his life. But many shall be found to whom Christ shall say I never knew you, to wit, with approbation and affection, Matth. 7:23.

They for whom Christ hath died shall sometime glory against all condemnation; but so shall not every man be able to glory, Rom. 8:34,35.

Christ never purposed to lay down his life for those, whom going to die he refuseth to pray for; only for those who are given to him out of the world will he pray and die, and rise, and will raise them to eternal life, John 17:9.

So far is it from God's purpose and Christ's to redeem all and every man, that he hath not decreed to give every nation so much as the external necessary means for conversion and salvation, Psal. 147:19,20. He showeth his word unto Jacob, his statutes and his judgments unto Israel; He hath not dealt so with any nation; and as for his judgments they have not known them.

And for this wise and holy course of hiding the mystery of salvation from many, even wise men in the world, Christ Jesus glorifieth and thanketh the Father, Matth. 11:25. I thank thee, O Father, Lord of heaven and earth, because thou hast hid these things from the wise and prudent, and hast revealed them to babes, even so, Father, for so it seemed good in thy sight.

The second article.

As to the second article of the Covenant of Redemption concerning the price of Redemption, and the sitting of the Redeemer for accomplishing the work of Redemption, God would not have silver, or gold, or any corruptible thing, 1 Pet. 1:18. He refuseth all ransom that can come from a mere man, Psal. 49:8. But He would have His own co-eternal and only begotten Son to become a man, to take on the yoke of the law, and to do all His will, that He alone might redeem the elect, who by nature are under the curse of the law. He would have Him the second Adam to be obedient even to the death of the cross, that by His obedience many might be justified, Rom. 5:19.

This is clearly confirmed by the Apostle, Heb. 10:5-10, commenting upon the 7th and 8th verses of Psal. 40. In burnt offerings and sacrifices for sin thou hast had no pleasure, then said Christ coming into the world, Lo, I come (in the volume of the book it is written of Me) to do thy will O God—by the which will we are sanctified, by the offering up of the blood of Jesus once for all.

2. By Christ's obedience we understand not only that which some call his active obedience, nor that only which some call his passive obedience: for, his active and passive obedience, are but two notions of one thing; for, his incarnation, subjection to the law, and the whole course of his life was a continued course of suffering, and in all his suffering he was a free and voluntary agent, fulfilling all which he had undertaken unto the Father, for making out the promised price of Redemption, and accomplishing what the Father had given him command to do. His obedience, even to the death of the cross, did begin in his emptying himself to take on our nature, and the shape of a servant, and did run on till his resurrection and ascension. As for these his sufferings in the end of his life, which he suffered both in soul and body, they were the completing of his formerly begun and running obedience, but were not his only obedience for us, or his only suffering for us, for he had done and suffered much from his incarnation before his last passion and death, but the highest degree of his obedience, whereby he bought deliverance unto us from sin and misery, and whereby he bought unto us, immortality and eternal blessedness in heaven, was his death on the cross completing our ransom.

3. Whereas some have said, that one drop of His blood was sufficient to redeem more worlds then one, if there were any more, it is but an inconsiderate speech, and destitute of Scriptural authority; for when Christ had suffered all things before the time of His death, it behooved Him to be crucified also, Luke 24:26, but it behooved Him not to suffer more than justice required for a ransom, but only as much as was agreed upon, and no less could satisfy. Now this commandment He received of the Father, that He should lay down His life for His sheep, John 10:18. For, the wisdom of God thought good, to testify His own holiness and hatred of sin, and to testify His love to the elect world, and riches of His grace toward them to whom He would be merciful, by inflicting no less punishment of sin on the Mediator His own dear Son (taking upon Himself full satisfaction to justice for all the sins of all the Elect given unto Him to redeem) then the death both of His body and soul for a season.

And indeed it was suitable to His holy and sovereign Majesty, that for the ransom of so many thousands and millions of damnable sinners, and saving of them from everlasting torment of body and soul, no less price should be paid by the Son of God, made man and surety for them, then His sufferings both in His body and soul for a season, as much as should be equivalent to the due deserved punishment of them whom he should redeem; and it became the justice of the infinite Majesty offended, to be reconciled with so many rebels, and to bestow upon them heaven and eternal blessedness, for no less price then the sufferings of the eternal Son made man, whose humiliation and voluntary obedience, even to the death of the cross, was of infinite worth and value; and therefore he yieldeth himself to the sufferings agreed upon in the covenant of Redemption, both in body and soul.

Of the sufferings of Christ in His soul.

Our Lord's sufferings in His body did not fully satisfy divine justice; 1. because as God put a sanction on the law and covenant of Works, made with us all in Adam, that he and his should be liable to death, both of body and soul, (which Covenant being broken by sin, all sinners became obnoxious to the death both of body and soul) So the redeemed behooved to be delivered from the death of both, by the Redeemers tasting of death in both kinds, as much as should be sufficient for their redemption. 2. As sin infected the whole man, soul and body, and the curse following on sin, left no part nor power of the man's soul free; So justice required, that the Redeemer, coming in the room of the persons redeemed, should feel the force of the curse, both in body and soul.

Obj. But how can the soul die, seeing it is, by the Ordinance of God in creation, made immortal?

Ans. The death of the soul is not, in all things, like to the death of the body; for, albeit the spiritual substance of the soul be made immortal and not to be extinguished, yet it is subject to its own sort of death, which consists in the separation of it from communion with God, in such and such degrees, as justly may be called the death of the soul, from which sort of death, the immortality of the soul, not only doth not deliver, but also it doth augment it and perpetuate it, till this death be removed.

Obj. But, seeing the human sold of our Lord could never be separated from the permanent holiness wherewith it was endued in the first infusion of it in the body, and could never be separated from the indissolvable personal union with the second person of the God-head assuming it, how could His soul be subject to any degrees of death?

Ans. Albeit the con-natural holiness of the soul of Christ could not be removed, nor the personal union of it be dissolved no not when the soul was separated from the body, yet it was subject, by Christ's own consent, to be emptied of strength-natural, to be deprived for a time of the clearness of vision of its own blessedness, and of the quiet possession of the formerly felt peace, and of the fruition of joy for a time, and so suffer an eclipse of light and consolation, otherwise shining from His God-head; and so in this sort of spiritual death might undergo some degrees of spiritual death.

The degrees of the suffering of Christ's holy soul.

Among the degrees of the death suffered by Christ in His soul, we may number, first, that habitual heaviness of spirit which haunted him all the days of His life, as was foretold by Isa. 53:3. He was a man of sorrows, and acquainted with grief. We hear He weeped, but never that he laughed, and but very seldom that he rejoiced.

2. He suffered in special, sorrow and grief in the observation of the ingratitude of them, for whom he came to lay down his life, we hid as it were our faces from him; he was despised, and we esteemed him not, Isa. 53:3.

3. The hardness of men's hearts, and the malice of his own covenanted people, and the daily contumelies and despiteful usage he found from day today, increased his daily grief, as by rivulets the flood is raised in the river; he was despised and rejected of men, Isa. 53:3.

4. He was tempted in all things like unto us, and albeit in them all never tainted with sin, Heb. 4:15, yet with what a vexation of his most holy soul, we may easily gather by comparing the holiness of our Lord with the holiness of his servants, to whom nothing is more bitter then the fiery darts of the devil, and his suggestions and solicita-

tions to sin: especially, if we consider the variety of temptations, the heinousness of the sins, whereunto that impudent and unclean spirit boldly solicited his holiness, Matth. 4, and withal, the importunity and pertinency of the devil, who never ceased, partly by himself, partly by those that were his slaves, and partly by the corruption which he found in Christ's disciples, to pursue, press, and vex the God of glory all the time he lived on earth.

5. The guilt of all the sins, crimes, and vile deeds of the elect, committed from the beginning of the world, was imputed unto him, by accepting of which imputation, albeit he polluted not his Conscience, yet he burdened his soul, binding himself to bear their deserved punishment.

Now when we see that the vilest sinners, as liars, thieves, adulterers, cannot patiently hear themselves called liars, or thieves, nor bear the shame of the vileness, whereof they are really guilty, with what suffering of soul? With what clouding of the glory of his holiness, think we that our Lord took upon his shoulders such a dunghill of all vileness, then which, nothing could more be unbeseeming his holy Majesty?

6. Unto all the former degrees of suffering of his soul, the perplexity of his thoughts fell on him, with the admiration and astonishment of soul, when the full cup of wrath was presented unto him, in such a terrible way, as made all the powers of his sense and reason for a time to be at a stand. Which suffering of his soul, while the Evangelist is about to express, he saith he began to be sore amazed, and also to be very heavy; and to express himself in these words, My Soul is exceeding sorrowful unto death, Mark 14:33,34.

Obj. But did not this astonishing amazement of Christ's soul speak some imperfection of the human nature?

Ans. It did no ways argue any imperfection or deficiency of sanctity in him, but only a sinless, and kindly infirmity in regard of natural strength, in the days of his flesh; for, the mind of a man, by any sudden and vehement commotion arising from a terrible object, may without sinning be so taken up, that the swift progress of his mind in discourse may for a while be stopped, and the act of reasoning suspended a while: all the cogitations of the mind fleeing together to consult, and not being able to extricate themselves in an instant, may stand amazed, and sit down a while, like Jobs friends astonished. Now our Lord, taking on our nature and our common sinless infirmities, became like unto us in all things except sin. Daniel's infirmity at the sight of an Angel, was not sin, Dan. 10.

Obj. But doth not this astonishing admiration, suddenly lighting upon Christ's soul, prove that something unforeseen of him did befall him?

Ans. Not at all; for, he knew all things that should befall him, and told his disciples thereof, and was at a point and resolved in everything, which was to come before it came. But this astonishing amazement did only show forth the natural difference between things preconceived in the mind, and these same things presented to sense: for, there is in the mind a different impression of the preconceived heat of a burning iron, before it do touch the skin, from that powerful impression which a hot iron thrust into the flesh doth put upon the sense. In regard of which natural difference between foresight and feeling, between resolution and experience, this astonishment befell our Lord, and in this regard, Christ is said to learn experimental obedience by these things which he suffered, Heb. 5:8.

7. Another degree of the suffering of our Lord's soul, is the interruption, for a time, of the sensible uptaking and feeling of that

quiet and peaceable enjoyment of the felicity of the human nature, given (for the point of right) unto it in its personal union with his God-head, in so far, that in the midst of many disciples, Greeks and Jews looking on him, the vehemency of his trouble did not suffer him to hide his perturbation; for, (John. 12:27) our Lord cried out, Now is My Soul troubled, and what shall I say? And, Mark 14:34, made him declare his exceeding heaviness; My Soul is exceeding sorrowful unto death. In which words he insinuates, that to his sense, death was at hand; yea, that in no small measure, it had ceased on him, and wrapped him up in the sorrows of death, for the time, as in a net of which he knew he could not be holden still.

Obj. But did not this huge heap of miseries take away from the human nature, the felicity of its union personally with his God-head?

Ans. It did indeed hide it for a time, and hinder the sensible feeling of it for a time, as it was necessary, in his deep suffering; but it did not take it away, nor yet eclipse it altogether: for, as a corporal inheritance hath a threefold connection with the person owner thereof; so a spiritual inheritance hath a threefold connection with the believers soul. The first is, of lawful title and right; the next is, of possession of the inheritance according to the lawful right; the third is, an actual fruition and present feeling of the use of the inheritance. The fruition and felt benefit and use, may be marred or suspended, and the possession stand: and the possession may be interrupted and suspended, and the lawful right remain firm. Christ had not only an undoubted right to this felicity standing unto him, by the personal union, but also a fast possession of it, in as far as the personal union was indissolvable. But the actual felt fruition in his human sense and uptaking, was so long interrupted as the human nature was diverted from this contemplation for its present exercise, and turned to look toward the sad spectacle of imminent and incumbent wrath: especially when, and how long it was, as it were, bound to the feeling of the present stroke which did fill the soul with sadness and grief, anxiety and vexation, without sin.

8. Neither did the vindictive justice of God, pursuing our sins in our Surety, stay here, but in the garden went on to show unto Christ the cup of wrath, and also to hold it to his head, and to press him to drink it; yea, the very dregs of the agreed-upon curse of the law, was poured into his patient and submissive mouth, as it were, and bosom, and the most inward part of soul and body, which as a vehement flame, above all human apprehension, so filled both soul and body, that out of all his veins it drew and drove forth a bloody sweat (the like whereof was never heard) as when a pot of oil, boiling up and running over by a fire set under it, hath yet further the flame increased by the thrusting of a fiery mass of hot iron into it.

Hence came such a wasting and eating up of all his human strength, and emptying of his natural abilities, such a down-throwing of his mind, such a fainting and swounding of his joy, and so heavy a weight of sorrow on him, that not only he desired that small comfort of his weak disciples watching with him a little, and missed of it, but also stood in need of an Angel to comfort him, Luke 22:43.

It is without ground, that some of the learned have denied the cause of this agony to be the drinking of the cup of wrath holden forth to him by the Father, saying, that the sight of it only and of the peril he saw we were into, was the cause of this heavy exercise: for, the cup was not only shown unto him, and the huge wrath due to our sin set before him that he should see it, and tremble at the apprehension of the danger we were in, but it was poured into him, and not only on him, that he for the sins of his redeemed should suffer it sensibly, and as it were drink it, that the bitterness thereof might affect all the powers of soul and body: for, the Scripture testifies, that not only upon the sight and apprehension of this wrath and curse coming on him, the holy human nature did holily abhor it, but also that he submitted to receive it, upon the consideration of the divine decree and agreement made, upon the price to be paid by him, and that upon the feeling of this wrath this agony in his soul, and bloody sweat of his body, was brought on.

Obj. But, how could the pouring forth of the Fathers wrath upon his innocent and dear Son consist with his Fatherly love to him?

Ans. Even as the innocence and holiness of Christ could well consist with his taking upon him the punishment of our sins; for, even the wrath of a just man, inflicting capital punishment on a condemned person, put case his own child, can well consist with fatherly affection toward the child suffering punishment; therefore it is not to be doubted, but these two can well consist in God, in whom affections do not war one with another, nor sight with reason, as it falleth forth among men; for, the affections ascribed unto God, are effects rather of his holy will toward us, then properly called affections in him; and these effects of God's will about us, do always tend to our good and blessedness at last, however diverse one from another in themselves.

9. Among the degrees of the sufferings of Christ's soul, we may number not only the perturbation of his mind and thoughts, but also the perturbation of his affections, and especially his fear; for, his human nature was like unto ours in all things except sin, and was indeed feared when it saw and felt the wrath of God, least it should have been swallowed up by it, and of this fear the Apostle (Heb. 5:7) beareth witness, saying, who in the days of his flesh, when he had

offered up prayers and supplications, and strong cries and tears, unto
him that was able to save him from death, and was heard in that he
feared.

Now, albeit this seemeth the saddest passage of all his sufferings,
that he was feared for being swallowed up, yet this his fear is not
to be wondered at, nor is it inconsistent with his holiness; for when
Christ assumed our nature (as hath been said) he assumed also all
the common and sinless infirmities, passions, and perturbations of
our nature: Now it is kindly that the creature, at the sight of an angry
God should tremble; for, we read, that the rocks and mountains have
trembled before God, when he did let forth his terror; and it is natural
to man, at the sight of a terrible object, at the sight of a peril and evil
coming upon him, but much more already come upon him (especially
if the evil and peril be above all his natural strength) to tremble and
fear the worst; and this becometh holy nature very well to fear present death, off-cutting, perdition and swallowing up in the danger,
when God appeared angry and was hasting to be avenged on sinners
in the person of their Surety, what could the human soul of Christ
gather from this terrible sight, but that which sense and reason did
teach? In the meantime there was no place here for his doubting of
the issue and his escaping from being swallowed up; for, natural fear
of the manly nature, arising from the infirmity of the creature, differs
very far from the fear arising from the infirmity of faith in God's
faithfulness and power; and natural fear of the worst, can very well
stand with the strength of faith to overcome the natural fear: for, as
the sensitive appetite may abhor a bitter cup of medicine, and cause
all the body tremble for fear to take it, while in the meantime, the man
by reason is resolved to drink that bitter cup of medicine, because
he confidently hopeth to help his health thereby; so natural fear in

Christ to taste of the cup of wrath, could very well consist with strong faith and assurance to be delivered therefrom: for, it is very suitable that faith should as far overcome the natural apprehension of sense and reason natural, as reason doth overcome sense in drinking a loathsome and bitter cup of medicine.

And to clear this yet further, that extreme fear to be swallowed up of wrath, could well consist in Christ with strong faith to overcome and bear out that terrible wrath, Let it be considered, that as it was needful Christ should be subject to the infirmity of natural strength, that he might suffer death; so it was needful, that he should have strong faith to enable him to bear out, in a holy way, that which he behooved to suffer: for, if on the one hand, Christ had not been weakened, and emptied of all human strength in his flesh, he could not have been humbled enough for us, he could not have suffered so much, as Justice did exact for satisfaction for us; and on the other hand, if he had not stood firm in faith and love toward God's glory and our salvation, he could not have satisfied Justice, nor been still the innocent and spotless lamb of God, nor have perfected the expiatory sacrifice for us.

Obj. But was he not tempted to doubt by Satan?

Ans. We grant that he was indeed tempted by Satan to doubt, yea we shall not stand to grant that he was tempted to desperation; But we altogether deny, that he was tainted with sin by temptation in the least degree: for, the Scripture saith, he was tempted in all things like unto us, but yet without sin in him or yielding in any sort to any temptation. And seeing by the Evangelist, Matth. 4, we understand, that he was tempted in the wilderness by the devil unto the most horrible sins that Satan could devise, and yet was not stained or polluted in the least degree, with the least measure of yielding to the sinful temptations; we need not stand to grant, that he might be tempted, or that he was tempted unto doubting and desperation; for, this was among the most notable and prime temptations, whereby Satan, in his impudent boldness, solicited the Son of God, very God and man in one person, even to doubt of that what Satan knew he was; If thou be the Son of God, saith he. It is true indeed, that we who are sinners by nature and corrupted in all the powers of our soul, cannot be tempted, tossed, and troubled, but therein our sinful nature in some measure may appear, and be polluted: But the matter was not so with our holy Lord, the God of glory, who was separate from sinners; for our impure nature is like to water in a puddle, which being stirred, doth presently become muddy and foul; but the holy human nature of Christ, was altogether pure, like unto clear and pure fountain water in a glass, which howsoever it be troubled and tossed, remaineth most pure and free of all muddiness.

Obj. But at least, was there not a conflict in our Lord between his faith, and the temptation to doubting?

Ans. We grant not only a conflict of Christ's human natural strength, with the burden of affliction, but also a conflict and wrestling of his faith against the temptation to doubting; for, wrestling doth not always argue the infirmity of the wrestler, for the Angel who is called God, Hos. 12, wrestles with Jacob, and in God was no infirmity. Again, wrestling doth not argue always infirmity, but doth only evidence the wrestler's power and the importunate obstinacy of an adversary, who being repulsed and cast down, doth not at first leave the field, but riseth up again, insists and presseth on so long as it pleaseth the most powerful party to suffer the adversary to make opposition.

Obj. But you must grant, that in the conflict of Christ's human natural strength, with the affliction and burden of the punishment laid upon him by the Father, he was overcome, and succumbed and died.

Ans. Yes indeed: but we must put a difference between the conflict of natural strength with the burden of affliction, and the conflict between faith and a temptation unto sin; in the conflict of holy human nature in Christ with the punishment of our sins laid on Him, it was not a sin to have his natural strength overpowered, and to lie down under the burden and to lay down his life and die; but it was a main part of His obedience, it was the performance of His promise and undertaking, to yield himself to Justice and to die for us, that we might be delivered from death eternal. But in the wrestling of His faith with the temptation unto doubting, it had been a sin to have yielded in the least degree, and that which could not consist with the perfect holiness of the Mediator, Surety for sinners.

Obj. But, did not the perplexity of His thoughts and the anxiety of His mind, diminish something of the vigor and constancy of his faith?

Ans. It did diminish nothing of the vigor and constancy of His faith; for there is a great difference between the troubling of the thoughts, and the hesitation or weakening of faith, as there is also a great difference between the perturbations of the mind and the perturbation of the conscience. For, as the mind may be troubled, when in the consideration of some difficulty it cannot at first perceive an out-gate, meantime the conscience remaining sound and quiet; so may the work of the mind's discoursing, be interrupted and at a stay for a time, faith (mean time) remaining untouched, wholly sound and quiet. For example, upon the sudden receiving of a wound, or upon an unexpected report of some great loss, such as befell Job, the wheels of the reasoning faculty may be at a stand for a time, and the conscience in the meantime be quiet; yea, and faith in the meantime, remain strong, as we see in Jobs first exercise.

Now if this may be found in a holy imperfect man in any measure, why shall we not consider rightly of the exercise of the holy one of Israel suffering in His human nature the punishment of our sin?

Let us consider but one of the passages of our Lord's exercise, John 12:27,28. Now (saith He) My Soul is troubled: wherein behold the perplexity of His mind, smitten with the horror of the curse due to us, coming upon Him; then cometh forth, what shall I say? Wherein, behold! Reason standing mute and altogether silent, only He lets forth the confession of His perplexity: presently after this, He subjoineth Father, save Me from this hour; wherein behold! Holy nature, trembling and shrinking to fall into the wrath of the Father, and according to the principles of holy nature, testifying the simple abhorrency of His soul from such an evil as is the wrath of God His Father, which had it not been for love to save our souls. He could not have yielded his human nature to endure, or bear it: therefore He, considering that we were but lost forever, if He should not suffer wrath for us, He repeats the sum of the Covenant of Redemption agreed upon, But for this cause came I unto this hour. And last of all, shuts up His speech and exercise in the triumphing voice of victorious and untainted faith, Father, glorify thy Name; and here He resteth: wherewith the Father is so well pleased, as that from heaven He speaketh to the hearing of the multitude standing by, I have both glorified it, and will glorify it again.

10. Among the deepest degrees of the suffering of Christ in His soul, we reckon that desertion whereof Christ on the cross giveth an account, crying out, My God, My God, why hast Thou forsaken Me?

By which speech He doth not mean, that then the personal union of the natures was in him dissolved, nor yet that God had withdrawn His sustaining strength and help from the human nature, nor that the love of the Father was taken off him, nor that any point of the perfection of holiness was taken from him; but his true intent is, to show, that God for a time had taken away sensible consolation, and felt joy from His human Soul, that so justice might in His sufferings be the more fully satisfied: And this is the forsaking of Him here given to us to understand. In which desertion Christ is not to be looked upon simply as He is in His own person, the Son of the Father, in whom He is always well pleased, but as He standeth in the room of sinners, Surety and Cautioner, paying their debt: In which respect He behooved to be dealt with as standing in our name; guilty and paying the debt of being forsaken of God, which we were bound to suffer fully and forever, if He had not interposed for us.

11. The last degree of Christ's sufferings (wherein He may be said to have descended into hell so far as Scripture in the Old Testament or the history of Christ's passion in the new, will suffer us to expound that expression) is that curse wherein the full wrath of God, and the dregs of that horrible cup was poured forth upon His holy human nature, while heaven and earth and hell, seemed to conspire to take vengeance on Him, and fully to punish our sins in the person of Him our Surety by that cursed death of the cross, which was the evidence foretold of the malediction of God lying on Him, in so far as was necessary to complete the punishment of loss and feeling both in soul and body. And therefore not without ground have Orthodox divines taken in Christ's suffering in His soul, and the detaining of His body in the grave (put in as the close and last part of Christ's sufferings) as the true meaning of that expression He descended into hell: not

only because these pains which Christ suffered both in body and soul, were due to us in full measure; but also because that which Christ suffered in the point of torment and vexation, was, in some respect, of the same kind with the torment of the damned: for, in the punishment of the damned, we must necessarily distinguish these three things, 1. the perverse disposition of the mind of the damned in their sufferings; 2. the duration and perpetuity of their punishment; and, 3. the punishment itself, tormenting soul and body. The first two are not of the essence of punishment, albeit by accident they are turned into a punishment, for the wickedness, vileness and unworthiness of the damned, who neither will nor can submit themselves to the punishment (and put the case they should submit, are utterly unable to make satisfaction forever) do make them in a desperate, doleful condition forever, though obstinate sinners do not apprehend nor believe this, but go on in treasuring up wrath against themselves, pleasing themselves in their own dreams, to their own endless perdition. Of these three, the first two could have no place in Christ: Not the first, because He willingly offered Himself a sacrifice for our sins; and upon agreement, paid the ransom fully: Not the second, because He could no longer be holden in the sorrows of death then He had satisfied Justice, and finished what was imposed on Him; and His infinite excellency made His short suffering to be of infinite worth, and equivalent to our everlasting suffering.

The third then remaineth, which is the real and sensible tormenting of soul and body in being made a curse for us, and to feel it so in His real experience. And what need we question hellish pain, where pain and torment, and the curse with felt wrath from God falleth on, and lieth still, till Justice be satisfied? Concerning which, it is as certain, that Christ was ceased upon by the dolor's of death, as it is certain in Scripture, that He could not be holden of the sorrows of death, Acts. 2:24.

Quest. But what interest had Christ God-head in His human sufferings, to make them both so short and so precious and satisfactory to Justice for so many sins of so many sinners, especially when we consider that God cannot suffer?

Ans. Albeit this passion of the human nature, could not so far reach the God-head of Christ, that it should in a physical sense suffer (which indeed is impossible) yet these sufferings did so affect the person, that it may truly be said, that God suffered, and by His blood bought His people to Himself, Acts 20:28, for, albeit the proper and formal subject of physical suffering be only the human nature; yet, the principal subject of sufferings, both in a physical and moral sense, is Christ's person, God and man, from the dignity whereof, the worth and excellency of all sort of sufferings, the merit and the satisfactory sufficiency of the price, did flow.

And let it be considered also, that albeit Christ, as God, in His God-head could not suffer in a physical sense; yet, in a moral sense He might suffer, and did suffer: for, in as much as He, being in the form of God, and without robbery equal to God, did demit His person to assume human nature, and empty Himself so far as to hide His glory and take on the shape of a servant, and expose Himself willingly to all the contradiction of sinners which He was to meet with, and to all railings, reviling's, contempt, despising's and calumnies, shall it seem nothing, and not enter in the count of our Lord's payment for our debt?

Obj. But, how could so low a down-throwing of the Son of man, or of the human nature assumed by Christ, consist with the Majesty of the person of the Son of God?

Ans. We must distinguish in Christ these things, which are proper to either of the two natures, from these things which are ascribed to His person, in respect of either of the natures or both the natures; for, infirmity, physical suffering, or mortality, are proper to the human nature. The glory of power and grace and mercy, and superexcellent Majesty and such like, are proper to the Deity; but the sufferings of the human nature, are so far from diminishing the glory of the divine nature, that they do manifest the same and make it appear more clearly: for, by how much the human nature was weakened, depressed, and despised, for our sake, by so much the love of Christ, God and man in one person, toward man, and His mercy and power and grace to man, do shine in the eyes of those that judiciously look upon Him.

Obj. But seeing Christ's satisfaction for sinners, doth not stand in any one part of His doings and sufferings, but in the whole and entire precious pearl, and complete price of His whole obedience from His incarnation even to the death of His cross, how cometh it to pass, that in Scripture the whole expiation of our sins, is ascribed so oft to His passion, and particularly to His blood?

Ans. This cometh to pass, 1. Because the certainty and verity of His assumed human nature, and the certainty of His real suffering, and the fulfilling of all the Levitical sacrifices, did most evidently appear unto sense in the effusion of His blood. 2. Because the expression of His sufferings, both in soul and body, appeared in the effusion of His blood: for, in the garden, while His body was not as yet touched, or hurt by man, from the mere pains of His soul, drops of blood fell down out of all His body to the earth. 3. Because His blood-shedding and death, was the last act of completing the payment of the ransom to the Father for us, which payment began in His humble incarnation and went on through all His life, and was completed in His bloodshed and death, whereof our Lord gave intimation on the cross, when He cried as triumphantly victorious, it is finished.

The use of this article of the covenant of Redemption.

We have at some length spoken of the price of Redemption, and of Christ's defraying the debt by His passion. 1. That hereby the merit of our sins, may the more clearly be seen. 2. That the sublimity and excellency of divine Majesty, offended by sin, may appear. 3. That we may behold the severity of God's justice, till He have satisfaction and reparation in some sort of the injuries done to Him. 4. That the admirable largeness of God's mercy may be acknowledged and wondered at.

For in the price of Redemption paid, as in a mirror we may see, how greatly the Lord hateth sin,; how great His love is to the world in sending his Son Christ amongst us; how heavy the wrath of God shall lie upon them that flee not to Christ's satisfaction for their delivery; how great the dignity and excellency of the Lord our Redeemer is, for whose cause reconciliation is granted to all that take hold of the offer of grace through him; how great the obligation of believers is to love God, and serve him; and how greatly the glory of all the attributes of God, doth shine in the work of Redemption.

2. By this doctrine, it appeareth how vain and wicked the devices of superstitious men are, who, for pacifying of God's wrath, have appointed penances, and pilgrimages, and self-scourging's, and soul-masses, and purgatory, and such like other abominations, whereof the word of God hath not spoken, but forbidden all the inventions of men, as unworthy conceits, to bring about men's salvation: which inventions tend only to derogate from the dignity of the price of Christ's ransom, and to cry down the fullness and perfection

of the price paid by our blessed Redeemer Jesus Christ, and to set up other Savior's in his room.

3. Hence also it is manifest, how fit a high Priest is appointed over us, who is touched with our infirmities and temptations; by whom we may have so solid consolation in all the pangs of our tormented consciences, and in whom we have a solid foundation laid down to all that flee to him, for settling our faith and hope in the Son of God, who hath of set purpose, with the Fathers consent, suffered so many and great evils that he might redeem us.

4. And hereby we may perceive also how well divine Justice is satisfied, and with what warrant the consciences of the weak believers may be quieted, who so use to exaggerate the grievousness and the multitude of their sins, that they forget to put a right estimation upon the satisfaction made by Christ for all that come unto God through him.

The third article.

The third article of the covenant of Redemption, past between the Father and the Son, concerneth the benefits, gifts and graces to be given unto the redeemed: all which gifts and graces, are summarily comprehended in that one gift of God, spoken of, John 4:10, which gift is Christ, who is freely offered unto, and given to, the elect believer for righteousness and eternal life, according to what was said, Isa. 9:6, for, unto us a child is born, a Son is given, on whose shoulders the government is laid, whose Name is called Jehovah, the wonderful counselor, the strong God, the eternal Father and Prince of peace. And, 2 Pet. 1:3, who according to his divine power, hath given unto us all things which pertain to life and godliness, through the knowledge of Him who hath called us to virtue and glory.

2. The benefits which are appointed for the redeemed, are so conveyed and brought unto them, that first, they are Christ's riches which he hath purchased unto the elect, and being resolved to die, that the purchase might be made fast to his people, he hath made his latter Will and Testament once and again, and left in legacy to all that believe in him, all things which belong to righteousness and salvation; and these benefits, in an acceptable time, he effectually applieth and puts them in possession thereof. Of which gifts, we shall name chiefly three: the first is regeneration, or turning of the man toward himself; the second is the gift of saving faith; the third is perseverance. In which three gifts, the patrons and magnifiers of the power of man's freewill, do what in them lieth to obscure the glory of God's free grace, by glorying that without the special grace of God they can convert themselves or not, as they please, so that when God intends their conversion, and useth all means for their conversion, they are able to resist all his gracious operation, and make void his purpose and endeavor. But this covenant of Redemption, past between the Father and the Son, Mediator and Redeemer, doth decide the question and give them the lie: for, only they whom God did foreknow, did he predestinate to be conform to the image of His Son—and whom he did predestinate, them he also called; and whom he called, them he also justified; and whom he justified, them he also glorified, Rom. 8:28.

Concerning these three gifts.

It is agreed between God and Christ, that the elect shall be converted invincibly and infallibly, and that saving faith shall be bestowed on them, and that they shall persevere in the obedience of faith so, as they shall not totally and finally fall away from God's grace.

It is promised to Christ, Psal. 110:3, that in the day of His power, His people shall be willing; for, albeit the native corruption of their will, opposeth itself and resisteth the holy Spirit, when he is using the means to convert them. Yet in an acceptable time, the invincible power of God's free grace toward them, so taketh away all actual resistance, that the man, unwilling of himself, is made most freely and heartily willing to be reconciled to God: for, God can both preserve the natural liberty of the will, and take from it that crookedness and frowardness that is in it; he can infuse and create in the man a right spirit, and new habits of grace, and can bring forth these habits unto exercise, making the redeemed man not only able to will, but also actually to will and to do what is pleasant to him, Philip. 2:13, and, Ephes. 2:8, we are taught, that faith is not of ourselves, it is the gift of God; not of works, least any man should boast. And this gift of saving faith, is bestowed only on the elect; and therefore it is called the faith of the elect, Tit. 1:1, and only they believe in Jesus Christ, that are ordained unto eternal life, Acts 13:48, yea, every one cometh to Christ, who is given to him of the Father, John 6:37, and no man cometh to Christ, save he whom the Father draweth, John 6:44, but they that are not redeemed, do not come to Christ for righteousness and life, John 10:26, ye believe not, saith Christ to some Jews, because ye are not of my sheep, My sheep hear My voice and I know them, and they follow Me.

As for perseverance, the Father promiseth to the Son, that the work of grace shall be firm in all the redeemed ones, or in his elect seed, Isa. 59:21, as for Me (saith the Lord to Christ) this is my covenant with them, my spirit that is upon thee, and my words which I have put in thy mouth, shall not depart out of thy mouth, nor out of the mouth of thy seed, nor out of the mouth of thy seeds seed, saith the Lord, from henceforth and forever. And, Jer. 32:40. I will make an everlasting covenant with them, that I will not turn away from them to do them good, but I will put my fear in their hearts, that they shall not depart from me.

And a special command is given unto Christ, for preserving all unto eternal life who come unto him, John 6:39, this is the Fathers will, which hath sent me, that of all which he hath given me, I should lose nothing, but should raise it up at the last day: which Christ undertakes, that he will faithfully perform, John 10:28, while he saith, I give unto them eternal life, and they shall never perish, neither shall any man pluck them out of my hand, &c. But, that we insist not too long in this argument (whereof the Orthodox divines have written abundantly in their disputations against the foresaid error) because the adversaries take their pretended arguments from the instability of men's will, in the matter of perseverance, and from the freedom and power of man's changeable will in the matter of conversion and saving faith, and from the manner of God's speaking to the mixed multitude of both called and not chosen, and to them that are both called and chosen, we shall content ourselves for clearing this covenant betwixt the Father and the Son, Mediator and Redeemer, to make the matter fast concerning the elect, founding their conversion, faith, repentance, perseverance, and salvation, upon the unchangeable covenant of Redemption, fixed upon the settled agreement between God, and God the Son Mediator and Redeemer, as shall be proven from five places of Scripture.

The first proof, is from verse. 13, of Isa. 52, to the end of Chap. 53.

The first place is Isa. 52:13, and forward to the end of chapter 53, where we have, first, the two parties contractors, God the Father, and Christ; for, the Father brings forth his confederate Son to be incarnate by covenant, his servant, whom he employs in the whole work of Redemption, as the meritorious cause and accomplisher of it; behold My servant, saith God the Father by his Spirit, speaking by the Prophet, Chap. 52:13. Next, both parties are sure of the event of the paction, and of the accomplishing of the whole work gloriously, behold, (saith he) My servant shall deal prudently and prosperously, He shall be exalted and extolled and be very high, verse. 13. Thirdly, he tells the proper price, which Christ the Son shall pay for the Redemption of his people, agreed upon by paction, to wit, the Exinanition and Humbling of the Son incarnate unto the ignominious death of the cross, that His visage shall be marred more than any man, and His form more than the sons of men, verse. 14, and more particularly, Chap. 53:2. He hath no form nor comeliness, and when we shall see Him, there is no beauty that we should desire Him, He is despised, and rejected of men, a man of sorrows and acquainted with grief, &c. verse. 2:3. He was wounded for our transgressions, verse. 5. He shall make his Soul an offering for sin, verse. 10.

Fourthly, Christ the Son of God incarnate, is assured and confirmed of the sweet fruit of his passion in the conversion of many nations, whom he should sprinkle with the blood of the covenant and sanctify by the water of His holy Spirit, Chap. 52:15. He shall sprinkle many nations, &c.

Fifthly, God and Christ are agreed and well pleased in the conversion of so many as are elected, and given to Christ, to have in Him the right of adoption, Chap. 53:10. He shall see his seed, that is, He shall regenerate the elect, and make them His children, and see them so, to His satisfaction.

Sixthly, no meritorious nor impulsive cause is found in the persons redeemed, for which the punishment due to them should be transferred upon the Mediator Christ our Redeemer; for, they should be found in themselves but despisers of Christ, because of His sufferings, Chap. 53:4. Surely he hath born our griefs, and carried our sorrows; yet we did esteem him stricken, smitten of God and afflicted.

Seventhly, no sin nor meritorious cause of punishment is found in Christ the Redeemer, for which He should be smitten, Chap. 53:5,9. He was wounded for our transgressions—he had done no violence, neither was any deceit in his mouth.

Eighthly, peace and reconciliation and healing of our sinful and miserable sicknesses, and deliverance from wrath, are purchased by the price of His blood, Chap. 53:5, the chastisement of our peace, was upon him, and with his stripes we are healed.

Ninthly, these sufferings Christ did not endure unwittingly, or unwillingly, but by consent, by covenant deliberately, Chap. 53:7. He was oppressed, and he was afflicted, yet he opened not his mouth; he is brought as a lamb to the slaughter, and as a sheep before his shearers is dumb, so he opened not his mouth.

Tenthly, the cause of this covenant, whereby the price is called for a yielded unto, and paid, is the only free grace of God and His good pleasure, Chap. 53:10. It pleased the Lord to bruise him, He hath put him to grief.

Eleventhly, It is agreed between the Father and the Son, that our sins should be imputed unto Him, and His righteousness imputed unto us, and that the redeemed should believe in him and so be justified, Chap. 53:11, he shall see of the travel of his Soul, and shall be satisfied, by his knowledge, or faith in Him, shall My righteous servant justify many: for he shall bear their iniquities.

Twelfthly, It is agreed between the parties, that for whom Christ should lay down His life, He should stand intercessor also, for bringing unto them all the purchased graces and blessings, Chap. 53:11, he bare the sins of many, and made intercession for the transgressors: the rest of the world beside the elect, He interceded not for, John 17:9,10.

Hence it followeth, that God and Christ did not bargain for the Redemption of all and every man; no not for the Redemption, conversion and salvation of all and every man to whom the Gospel was to be preached: for, many were to be called, who were not chosen, to whom the gift of saving faith was not to be given, nor the power of God to salvation was never to be revealed; and this is the observation which the Evangelist makes upon the 1st of Isa. 53, John 12:37, &c. But though he had done so many miracles before them, yet they believed not on him, that the saying of the prophet Isaiah might be fulfilled which he spake, Lord, who hath believed our report? And to whom is the arm of the Lord revealed? Therefore they could not believe, because Isaiah said again, (Isa. 6:9,10) he hath blinded their eyes, and hardened their hearts, &c.

Secondly, it followeth hence, that election and Redemption were not for the foreseen faith or works of the elect redeemed, but of the mere grace and goodwill of God, and all done for them and in them, contrary to their deserving's: for, it is said, Isa. 53:6, all we, like sheep have gone astray, and the Lord hath laid on him the iniquity of us all.

Thirdly, it followeth hence, that it was agreed upon, that saving grace and conversion and sanctification should infallibly and invincibly come to pass and be given to the redeemed, Isa. 52:13. Behold, My servant shall deal prudently and prosperously; and, verse. 15, he shall sprinkle many nations; and, Isa. 53:11, by his knowledge shall my righteous servant justify many.

Fourthly, hence it followeth, that the agreement is past for their final perseverance and full salvation: for, Isa. 53:5, with his stripes we are healed: now our healing, is our full salvation from our sin and misery, or our deadly sicknesses. And, Isa. 53:10, the pleasure of the Lord shall prosper in his hand: the pleasure of the Lord is partly our sanctification, 1 Thes. 4:3, partly, our salvation and glorification, Joh. 6:39, this is the Fathers will which hath sent me, that of all which he hath given me, I should lose nothing; but should raise it up again at the last day. And to this purpose powerfully doth his intercession serve, from which the Apostle concludes, that believers shall be perfectly saved, Heb. 7:25, wherefore he is able also to save to the uttermost, them that come to God by him, seeing he ever liveth to make intercession for them.

The second proof is from Isa. 59:20,21.

The second place is from Isa. 59:20,21, where, first, we have the parties agreeing pointed at: the Lord Jehovah saith and of the Redeemer He saith, that He shall come to Zion as Redeemer. Next, we have the kind of agreement between the parties, God on the one hand, and the Redeemer with the redeemed, for whom and in whose name he makes the agreement; this is my Covenant with them, but first with Christ, as the words following do show. Thirdly, we have the party redeemed, Zion and Jacob that turn from transgression, which is the mark of true believers in Christ and of the elect, for whom this grace is appointed, as Rom. 11:7. Israel hath not obtained that which he seeketh for, but the election have obtained it, and the rest were blinded. And, Rom. 11:26, all this Israel shall be saved, as it is written. Fourthly, we have the sort of their delivery, which shall be not only by price paying, but also by powerful and effectual working, as the original imports, Rom. 11:26, and, Isa. 59:20. Fifthly, the benefits bestowed upon the elect, are comprehended under the designation of the redeemed; they are to be turned from their iniquity by effectual conversion, by granting them faith in Christ, repentance and reconciliation. Sixthly, it is showed how these graces shall be brought to pass, to wit, by application thereof by the word and Spirit of Christ; from which, sanctification, salvation, and the perpetuation of all graces unto salvation, do flow and follow on them; My Spirit that is in thee, saith the Lord to the Redeemer incarnate, and My word which I have put in thy mouth, shall not depart out of thy mouth, nor out of the mouth of thy seed, &c.

These articles of the covenant of Redemption make expressly, first, against universal Redemption of all and every man: because Christ, as is showed before, makes his bargain for the elect, and leaves the rest in blindness, and is a Redeemer of none but of these to whom He is a deliverer actually, from whom He turneth away iniquity and ungodliness; which benefits befall none, but the elect and the re-deemed.

Next, they make against election for faith and foreseen works, because when Christ cometh to call-in the Jews. He finds nothing commendable in them but impiety and transgression and defection, and whatsoever might provoke Him to reject them; they are turned from transgression.

Thirdly, they make against a mere possible and contingent con-version: for, invincible grace is promised here; for, the word and the Spirit of Christ shall take up a dwelling in them, and not depart from them.

Fourthly, they make against the doctrine of the Apostasy of the saints, and uncertainty of their perseverance, because here it is promised to Christ, that from the heart and mouth of His seed, the word and Spirit of Christ shall never depart.

The third proof is from, Joh. 6:37, &c.

The third place is, John 6:37-45, where, first, is set down the party contractors in the Covenant of redemption; for, the Elect are given over into the hand of Christ by the Father; All that the Father giveth to me, cometh to me. v. 37.

Secondly, upon the Fathers giving of the Elect unto Christ followeth, in due time, the conversion and saving faith of the redeemed; All that the Father giveth me, cometh to me, saith Christ.

Thirdly the redeemed are committed unto Christ, as to their leading on, preservation and perfecting of their salvation; This is the Fathers will which hath sent me, that of all which he hath given me, I should lose nothing, but should raise it up again at the last day.

Fourthly, it is agreed by what means the faith of the redeemed shall be formed in them, which are, the revealed sight of Christ the Son of God in the Word; the powerful drawing of the illuminate soul unto Christ, which powerful draught overcometh all opposition and resistance, because it is omnipotent and invincible: for, no man cometh to Christ, but he whom the Father draweth, v. 44, and that by making them savingly, and in a lively manner see the Son and believe on him. v. 40.

Hence followeth, 1. that it is false Doctrine to teach, that there is a universal redemption unto life of all and every man; because not all, but only some are given, and made to come to Christ; the rest that are not given, come not.

Secondly, it followeth, that Election is of mere free grace; because men come not unto Christ that they may be given, but they are given unto Christ, that they may be brought and come unto him.

Thirdly, by this agreement, the powerful conversion of the redeemed and their powerful preservation unto eternal life, is as certain as the power, and constancy, and obedience of Christ unto the
Father, is firm and certain; This is the will of him that sent me, that
of what he hath given me, I should lose nothing, but raise it up at the
last day, ver. 39.

The fourth proof is, Joh. 10:14.

The fourth place is, John 10:14-30, where we see, that the Lord
Jesus, the true Pastor of Israel, before he was incarnate, Psal. 23,
continueth in that same office now, being incarnate, and gives his
people to understand this, when he saith, I am the good shepherd.

Secondly, the care and custody of all the redeemed, both converted
and unconverted, was put upon Christ, v. 14,16. I know my sheep, and
am known of mine; and other sheep I have, which are not of this fold,
them also I must bring in, and they shall hear my voice.

Thirdly, the price of their redemption is clearly agreed upon, v. 15.
As the Father knows me, even so know I the Father; and I lay down
my life for my sheep.

Fourthly, the Father accepts the price, and is satisfied and well
pleased with it, v. 17,18. Therefore doth my Father love me, because
I lay down my life, that I may take it up again. &c.

Fifthly, all the redeemed are infallibly converted, but they that are
not redeemed are not converted, v. 27, My sheep hear my voice, and I
know them and they follow me; and, v. 26, but ye believe not, because
ye are not of my sheep.

Sixthly, albeit the redeemed and converted shall not want enemies, who shall go about to mar their perseverance and salvation, yet
shall they not prevail, v. 28. I give them eternal life, and they shall
never perish, neither shall any man pluck them out of my hand.

Hence followeth, first, that the doctrine of universal redemption of all and every man unto life is false; because only the redemption of the elect sheep is agreed upon, for whom he layeth down his life, v. 15, and the rest are not redeemed nor ordained to life, for these he speaks to, v. 26, they were not of his sheep, but remained unbelievers.

Secondly, it followeth, that the election of men is not for faith or works foreseen, but on the contrary, faith is ordained to be given unto the redeemed, because they are elected and given over unto Christ to convert and save them, v. 16, other sheep I have, and them I must bring in, and they shall hear my voice.

Thirdly, it followeth, that the conversion of the Elect doth not depend on their will, but upon Christ's undertaking to make them believe and upon His omnipotency, verse. 16, other sheep I have, and them I must bring in and they shall hear my voice.

Fourthly, it followeth, that albeit the redeemed believers be in themselves witless as sheep, and weak, and ready to be destroyed, and compassed about with many enemies as sheep among wolves, yet because of the omnipotency of the Father and of the Son, that have taken the care and custody of them, they shall persevere, and it is impossible they should perish or not persevere, John 10:28,29. I give them eternal life; and they shall never perish, and none can take them out of My Fathers band.

The fifth proof.

The fifth place is, Psal. 40, explicate by the Apostle, Heb. 10:5-7, where, first, the Spirit of God expounds the covenant whereof we are, speaking, and brings in the parties, God and Christ as speaking one to another, and as it were, in our sight and audience, repeating the terms thereof. The price of Redemption is first spoken of, for expiation of sin, not to be forgiven without blood, without better blood then the blood of beasts, Heb. 10:4.

Secondly, all satisfactions by men, and whatsoever price can be paid by mere man, are rejected; sacrifice and oblation thou wouldest not, verse 5.

Thirdly, nothing except only the incarnation of the Son the Mediator, His obedience and suffering to the death, could satisfy divine Justice; But a body hast thou prepared Me, verse 5.

Fourthly, the Mediator Christ, offers Himself pledge and Surety of His own accord, and takes the condition; then said I, lo, I come, to wit, as Surety to pay the ransom and to do thy will, Heb. 10:7.

Fifthly, Christ the Surety; not only condescends upon the price, but also upon the persons to be redeemed, and their sanctification; by which will we are sanctified, by the offering of the body of Christ once for all: and this price is now actually paid, Heb. 10:10.

Sixthly, the price being paid, the Mediator goeth about the application of the purchased benefits, by His intercession, Heb. 10:12,13, this man after he had offered one sacrifice for sin forever, sat down on the right hand of God from henceforth expecting till his enemies be made his footstool.

Hence followeth, first, that there is no universal Redemption of all and every man unto life, because by one offering he hath perfected forever, them that are sanctified, Heb. 10:14, therefore they were never redeemed, who are never sanctified; and only they are perfected, who are redeemed.

Secondly, it followeth, that not for anything in man, neither foreseen faith or works, are men elected and redeemed, because all is rejected that mere man can do, that the mere grace of God may appear in Christ's undertaking for men of His own accord; Sacrifice and oblation thou wouldest not, then said I, behold! I come, Heb. 10:5,7.

Thirdly, by Christ's death, purchase is made of the infallible conversion and sanctification of the redeemed, and of their perseverance unto perfection. By one offering of Christ He hath perfected forever them that are sanctified, Heb. 10:14, and therefore the redeemed cannot but be converted, cannot but be sanctified, cannot but persevere unto perfection, and that forever, Heb. 10:12-14.

The use of this article is, first, that all these who hear the Gospel, and have in any sort embraced it, should in the acknowledgement of their natural corruption and perverse wickedness, humble themselves before God, and pray for, and expect grace according to the promises offered in the Gospel.

Secondly, that they who are already sensible of their sins and ill deserving's, may not run away or be discouraged, but so much the rather, flee to Christ in whom relief from sin and misery is promised to such.

Thirdly, that they who have fixed their eye on the Son, resolving to cleave unto him, should acknowledge the powerful draught of God's almighty hand, who hath caused them to come to Christ, and should upon the begun work of grace, conceive lively hope of salvation, and study to purify their souls in this hope.

Fourthly, that they who find the instability and inconstancy of their own free-will, and have experience of their own heart, deceiving them frequently, after they have engaged themselves by promises and vows to take better heed to their ways, should not cast away their confidence in Christ because of their own infirmity, but that they should lean less to their own strength, and lay hold on Christ's power, fidelity and constancy so much the more, for to help the weak at such a dead lift. The Apostle, looking to Christ's engagement in the covenant, for those who in any measure of sincerity adhere unto him, hath said, 1 Cor. 1:8,9. Christ shall confirm you unto the end, that ye may be blameless in the day of our Lord Jesus Christ. God is faithful, by whom ye are called unto the fellowship of his Son Jesus Christ our Lord.

Fifthly, let us not take the guiding of our own freewill, but let so many as are fled to Christ, give him the glory of the inclining of our heart to his testimonies, and to his obedience in any measure, and know that every spiritual motion floweth from his purchase, and application of what is bestowed on us. And when we find his hand withdrawing, and our heart inclining to what is not right, let us run to him to right it, in hope to be helped by his grace to fight against whatsoever adversary of our salvation.

The fourth article.

As to the fourth article of the covenant of Redemption, it concerneth the means and manner how the elect shall be called forth from the perishing world, and be effectually called and turned unto God, so as the world among whom the elect do live, shall not have cause of stumbling justly: for, he hath taken a most wise course so to execute the decree of election and Redemption, as he shall be sure to bring in his own to himself, and not open up his counsel in particular to the discouraging of any, as is told by the father, Isa. 52:13. My servant shall deal prudently and prosper. The chief mean appointed, is the preaching of the Gospel to all nations, commanding all men, where the Gospel is by God's providence preached, to repent and believe in the Name of Jesus Christ, and to love one another as he hath commanded them, Acts 17:30, and, 1 John 3:23, and they who refuse to obey are without excuse.

Another mean is, the bringing of so many as profess their accep-tation of the offer of grace by Christ Jesus, them and their children into the bond of an express solemn covenant, that they shall submit themselves to the doctrine and government of Christ, and teach their children so to do, as Abraham the father of believers did, Gen. 18:19, Matth. 28:19,20, make disciples of all nations, or, make all nations disciples to Me.

A third mean is, the sealing of the covenant by the Sacrament of baptism, Matth. 28:19,20, make all nations disciples to Me, baptizing them in the Name of the Father, of the Son, and of the Holy Ghost.

A fourth mean is, the gathering them into all lawful and possible communion with others his disciples, that by their Church-fellow-ship one with another, they may be edified under their officers, ap-pointed in Christ's Testament to feed, govern and lead them on in the obedience of all the commands which Christ hath commanded his people in his Testament: by which means he goeth about his work, and doth call effectually, sanctify and save, his own redeemed ones, leaving all others without excuse.

Concerning all these and other means and manner also of exe-cuting his decree, it is agreed upon between the Father and His Son Christ, as His holy Spirit hath revealed it to us in Scripture. All which may be taken up in two heads; the one is the agreement about the doctrine, and directions given to His Church; the other is about ac-tions, operations, and all effects to be brought about for making his word good.

Concerning his doctrine, Christ saith, John 12:49,50. I have not spoken of myself, but the Father who hath sent me, he gave me a commandment what I should say, and what I should speak, and I know, that his commandment is life everlasting, whatsoever I speak therefore, even as the Father said unto me, so I speak.

Concerning actions and operations, and the execution of the decrees, it is agreed also between the Father and the Son, John 8:16. If I judge, my judgment is true; for, I am not alone, but I and the Father that sent me; and, verse. 29. He that sent me, is with me, the Father hath not left me alone: for, I do always these things that please him; and Joh. 6:38. I came down from heaven, not to do my own will (without the consent of the Father) but the will of him that sent me.

In a word, the consent and agreement of the Father and the Son Jesus Christ our Lord, is such, that the Son doth nothing by his Spirit, but that which the Father doth work by the same Spirit from the beginning of the world, John 5:17. My Father worketh hitherto and I work; and, Col. 1:16, for by Christ were all things created that are in heaven and that are in earth, visible and invisible, whither they be thrones or dominions, or principalities, or powers, all things were created by him and for him. He is alpha and Omega, the beginning and the ending, the first efficient, and the last end of all things. Rev. 1:8, because for the glory of Christ, the creation, the covenant of works and the covenant of grace, were made, and had, and shall have their full execution, all for the glory of God in Christ, by whom all things were made and do subsist.

CHAP. V. - Of the Covenant of works.

WE HAVE SPOKEN OF the first divine covenant, wherein God, and God incarnate are the parties; it followeth to speak of the next divine covenant, to wit, the covenant of works between God and man, Adam and his posterity, made in man's integrity. In which covenant, God is only the one party of the covenant, and man created with all natural perfections, is the other party. In this covenant, man's continuing in a happy life, is promised, upon condition of perfect personal obedience, to be done by him out of his own natural strength bestowed upon him, as the Apostle teacheth us, Gal. 3:12, the Law is not of faith, but the man who shall do these things shall live by them. And unto this law or covenant of works, is added a threatening of death in case man should transgress: the sense whereof is told by the Apostle, Gal. 3:10, cursed is everyone who doth not abide in all things, that are written in the book of the Law to do them.

The difference between the law, and the Covenant of works.

The word Law, is sometime taken for the matter or substance of the law of nature, written in the hearts of our first Parents by creation; the work of which law, is to be found in the hearts of their posterity unto this day. And in this sense the word Law, is taken by the Apostle, Rom. 2:15, the Gentiles (saith he) show the work of the Law written in their hearts, their conscience also bearing witness, &c. Sometime the word, is taken for the formal covenant of works, as Gal. 3:10, as many as are of the works of the Law, that is, under the covenant of works, are under the curse; for, it is written, cursed is everyone that continueth not in all things that are written, in the book of the law, to do them.

2. The law as it is taken for the covenant of works, differeth from the law of nature, written by creation in the hearts of our first Parents; first, because the law of nature, written in the heart of man, in order both of nature, and time, went before the covenant made for keeping that law; because the covenant for keeping that law, was not made till after man's creation, and after his bringing into the garden to dress it and to keep it, Gen. 2:16,17.

Secondly, God by virtue of the law written in man's heart, did not oblige Himself to perpetuate man's happy life: for, albeit man had kept that law most accurately, God was free to dispose of Him as he saw fit before he made the covenant with him; But so soon as he made the covenant, he obliged himself to preserve him in a happy life, so long as he should go on in obedience to his law and commands, according to the tenor of the covenant, do this and live.

Thirdly, death was the natural wages and merit of sin, albeit there had no covenant been made at all: for, sin against God, deserveth, of its own nature, death of soul and body, by the rule of simple justice, whether the sinner had consented to the punishment or not. But man by entering in the covenant actually gave a formal voluntary consent, that death should cease upon him, if he should sin, as Eve beareth witness in her conference with the serpent, while she doth repeat the condition put upon the breaking of the particular command given by God, and accepted by man, Gen. 3:3.

Fourthly, when the covenant of works is abolished so far, as it can neither justify, nor condemn the man that is fled to Christ, and entered in another posterior covenant of grace, the natural obligation of the man standeth still, for taking direction from, and giving obedience to, the law; for, it remaineth still the rule of a man's walking, and it is impossible that a mere man should be exempted from the authority of God over him, and from subjection due by nature to his Creator: for upon this account, that man is a reasonable creature, understanding God's will about his behavior toward God, he is always bound forever to love God with all his mind, heart and strength, and his neighbor as himself. Neither can the natural merit of sin be taken away, nor death deserved be eschewed but by forgiveness of it for Christ's merits.

The covenant then was superadded unto the law in the deep wisdom of God: for, this way of dealing with man by a Covenant, was, of its own nature, a most fit mean unto man's felicity, and unto the glory of God.

How the Covenant of God with man was a mean to man's felicity.

The Covenanting of God with man, tended of its own nature to man's good and happiness.

First, because a singular respect and honor was put upon man, when he was made a confederate friend of God: for, if it be an honor to a mean and poor man to be joined with a King or Prince in a formal bond of mutual friendship, how much greater honor is it unto man, to be joined in a bond of mutual love and friendship with God?

Secondly, before the making of the Covenant man had no promise made to him by God, but so soon as the Covenant was made, the Lord did freely oblige himself to give, and made to man a right to ask, and to expect of God, with a ground of certainty, to obtain of him such things, as without promise past, he could not ask, or at least, he could not certainly expect to have granted unto him.

Thirdly, before the making of the Covenant, nothing hindered the Lord, if he had pleased, to command man to return to dust whereof he was; but after the Covenant, it pleased God, by his own free promise, to oblige himself to perpetuate man's happiness wherein he was made, so long as he should go on in obedience.

Fourthly, by the making of the Covenant, a door was opened, and a fair entry to a higher degree of felicity then he possessed by his creation: for, when a natural life and earthly felicity was given to Adam to enjoy upon the earth, God, by the Covenant, made paction with him upon condition of perfect obedience, to give him a life and felicity super-natural, opposite unto death bodily and spiritual, which was threatened unto him if he should transgress the command.

Fifthly, Adam, by the Covenant, had a sort of help to make him keep the Law written in his heart more carefully and cautiously, and a prop to make him stand more fixed: for, on the one hand, he was advertised and forewarned of the danger of sinning, that he might beware to offend God; and on the other hand, he was encouraged and allowed to serve God more cheerfully, and to perform due obedience to God the more diligently: for, in the Covenant, the greatest reward that could be thought upon was set before him, and promised unto him; to wit, eternal life upon his obedience and the greatest punishment threatened if he should dis-obey; both which served greatly to move him to be constant in his obedience.

How God's covenanting with man served for God's glory.

In God's covenanting with man, his glory did notably shine and show forth itself to man. First, the goodness and bounty of God, did manifest itself therein: for, in making a Covenant with man, the Lord demitted himself, and in a manner humbled himself to deal with man for the standing of mutual friendship between himself and man forever: and when we consider this, as the Psalmist saith, Psal. 8:4. What is man that thou are mindful of him? And the Son of man that thou visitest him? So may we say, what is man? Or the Son of man that thou shouldest enter in covenant with him?

Secondly, by covenanting with man, God did show his wonderful moderation: for, God is sovereign Monarch and absolute Emperor over his own creature, to make of it what he pleaseth; yet, in covenanting with man, he did sweetly temper his supremacy, seeking, as it were, to reign with man's consent. And when because of his sovereign Authority and absolute Right and Interest, he might have put upon man harder commands and conditions of the Covenant, and these also altogether righteous and just, he chose to use such moderation, that he would require nothing of man, except that which man should, and behooved in reason judge both a just and an easy yoke, and in accepting the condition of the Covenant, acknowledge it to be such.

Thirdly, the Lord declared his wisdom in covenanting with man, because when he had made man a reasonable creature, he chose to draw forth a free and voluntary service, most suitable to his reasonable nature, and that in a most sweet way; to wit, not only by giving unto man a most equitable Law, but also by setting before the man, by way of paction, the highest reward that he could be capable of, even life everlasting.

Fourthly, in covenanting with man, God did most wisely and holily have a respect to the glory of his own, both sovereignty and holiness; because after he had made man by nature good and holy (albeit mutable and subject to change, if the man pleased to essay another way) he took course to help the mutability of his free will, not only by setting a reward of obedience before him, but also by a threatening of punishment, if he should transgress, and so on the one hand and the other to hedge him in, and guard him against all temptation unto sin, that neither he should be forced by any external power to sin, nor by any counsel or suggestion or moral suasion (whereunto only man was exposed in the trial of his obedience) should have so strong motives to draw him to disobedience, as the promise of God and the threatening should have force in all reason, to keep him fast to his due and loyal obedience. Thus was Adam fore-warned and fore-armed against whatsoever, without himself, might assault him: for, what reward for disobedience could be offered unto him, so great as the favor of God and everlasting life in the fellowship of God promised to him, if he continued fast in obedience? And what terror could be so great to affright and scare him from sin, as the threatening of death bodily and spiritual, if he transgressed?

Quest. But the profane curiosity of man dareth to ask a reason, why God did not make man both good by nature and immutably good also?

Ans. It is indeed proud curiosity to inquire for reasons of God's holy will, which hath its own most sufficient reason in its self, and may satisfy all his subjects, who will not devilishly prefer their own wisdom and counsel to his: But we shall content ourselves soberly to answer the question thus; To be both originally, or by nature good, and unchangeably good also, beseemeth God himself only, as his property and prerogative, which it became his Majesty to reserve to himself as the fountain of all goodness, and not to communicate this glory either to Man or Angel in their creation, that the due distance between God and the natural perfections of the creature, should not only be provided for, but made manifest to the creature also. It's true, Christ's human nature, was so sanctified in his conception, that there was no possibility that sin should be in it; but let us consider, that Christ's person which did assume the human nature into personal union with his God-head, is not a creature; and to assume the human nature into a personal union with his divine nature, is the proper privilege of God over all, blessed forever. And what the human nature of Christ hath of holiness, it hath it not of itself, but of grace from the second person of the God-head, who did assume it. And the Angels that stood when the mutability of angelical nature was manifested in the fall of many of them, did stand by the grace of free confirmation of them in their station.

Fifthly, God in covenanting with man, made way for the demonstration of his most holy Justice in the execution of punishment, which was not only the natural wages and deserved reward of sin, but also by paction and covenant appointed by mutual consent of parties, if man, so much obliged to God, should break so equitable and easy a command, as was given to try him by, being fore-warned of his danger.

Sixthly, this way of covenanting with man, was a most holy and fit mean to manifest the vanity and instability of the most perfect creature, except in the exercise of all its abilities and habits, it do acknowledge God, and in everything less and more, constantly employ him, and depend upon him.

Last of all, this was a most holy mean to bring forth to light the grace and mercy of God in Christ, providing a remedy for fallen man before he fell, and to open up the decree and covenant of Redemption in due time to be brought about by Christ, to the glory of God in Christ, by whom, and for whom all things were made, Col. 1:16.

Quest. Had this Covenant of works no Mediator, no Surety engaged for Adam and all his posterity?

Ans. No Mediator was in this Covenant; for, the party on the one hand, was God, and on the other hand was Adam and Eve our common parents, standing upon the ground of their natural abilities, representing and comprehending all their natural offspring; and according to the condition of the Covenant in their own name and name of their posterity, promising obedience, and receiving the condition of life if they continued, and of death in case they failed, Gen. 2:17. In whose sin we all have sinned, Rom. 5:12.

Now, the necessity of a Mediator, did not appear in this Covenant so long as it stood, that afterward in the making of another Covenant it might more timeously appear. First, because man, being created holy according to the image of God, was the friend of God while he had not sinned; and again his service, while he stood in obedience, was very pleasant and acceptable to God, because so long freely and sincerely he served God according to the command and rule written in his heart.

Quest. After that his Covenant was broken, was it not abolished altogether, seeing it could not now be any longer perfectly obeyed, nor save us who are sinners?

Ans. Albeit this Covenant, being broken on man's part, did become weak and utterly unable to produce Justification by works, or eternal life to us, by our inherent righteousness; yet, on God's part, the bond of this Covenant, doth stand firm and strong against all men by nature for their condemnation, who are not reconciled to God: Wherefore all that are not renewed and made friends with God by another Covenant of faith in God incarnate (the seed of the woman, who destroyeth the work of the devil) do lie bound under the bond of this Covenant of works, as Christ testifies, John 3:18. He that believeth on me, is not condemned; but he that believeth not, is condemned already; to wit, by the force of the Covenant of works violated by them, and are nor delivered from the curse by Christ the Son of God, till they fly to him: And this doth the Apostle confess, speaking of himself and other elect Jews before their regeneration, Ephes. 2:3. We also were children of wrath, even as others: for, whosoever is not reconciled to God by Christ, against him doth the sentence of the Law, and curse for violation of the Covenant, stand in force; for, sinning against the Covenant, doth not loose the man from the Covenant, neither from the obligation to obey it, nor from the punishment of breaking it.

Obj. But seeing a man is utterly unable to obey the Law, or to keep that Covenant, doth not his utter inability excuse him and dissolve the bond?

Ans. No ways: Because that inability is the fruit of our sin, and is drawn on by ourselves; nor doth God lose his right to crave the debt due to him, because the Bankrupt is not able to pay what he oweth: For, even among men, such as have mis-spent their patrimony, are not absolved of their debt because they are not able to pay the debt; yea, even the children of the mis-spender of his goods, do stand debtors so long as the debt is neither paid nor forgiven.

The Covenant of works therefore being broken, the obligation standeth, to make us give obedience so much the more in time to come, and because of the curse pronounced for the breaking of the Covenant in time past, the obligation to under-lie the punishment for by-gone sins doth stand; and so both the obligation to underlie the punishment, and the obligation to give obedience, do stand together, while a man is not absolved from the Covenant of works, by entering in a new Covenant, whereby the debt is paid and the sinner absolved.

Whosoever then conceive, that they may be justified from by-gone sins by their own obedience in time to come, either by way of doing or of suffering, they but deceive themselves, dreaming they can do impossibilities; for, the punishment to be suffered for sin by the sinner, is the curse-everlasting of soul and body, seeing a mere creature cannot forever satisfy for his rebellion, how long soever we presuppose his duration under suffering. And for obedience by way of doing perfectly what the Law doth crave, it is utterly impossible, because we are carnal, sold under sin, and cannot satisfy the Law; and because we cannot satisfy the Law, the Law becometh weak and unable to justify and save us, Rom. 8:3.

How the Covenant of works may be called the Covenant of nature.

Albeit the Law written by nature in men's heart, differeth from the Covenant for performance of the Law, as hath been shown before; yet, the Covenant of works made with Adam before he fell, tying him to keep that Law, may be called the Covenant of nature.

First, because the Covenant of works is grounded upon the Law of nature, and doth exact nothing of man, save that which God might require of him according to the Law of nature.

Secondly, because when the Covenant of works was made with Adam, it was made with all his natural posterity, which was to spring of him by natural generation; and so the obligation thereof did pass upon all his natural posterity, by the Law of nature, which maketh the child begotten to bear the image of the begetters.

Thirdly, that the Covenant of works may justly be called the Covenant of nature, appeareth by the force of the conscience being wakened from its sleepy security; for, it challengeth for sin according to that Covenant, and pronounceth the sentence of God's wrath against the sinner: For, the conscience doth acknowledge the Judgment of God, that they which commit such things, are worthy of death, Rom. 1:32.

Fourthly, because the conscience naturally inclineth a man to seek justification by his own works, if it can any way find pretense for it, as we may see in the Pharisee, who in his speech to God, doth judge himself a holy man, because he is not amongst the worst of men, and hath many good works above others to reckon forth and lay before God, Luk. 18:11.

Fifthly, the inclination of man's heart, to expect a reward of every good work he doth, whether it be in some part real, or only apparently such, testifieth so much, Judge. 17:13. Micah so reasoneth, Now know I the Lord will do me good, seeing I have a Levite to my Priest. And how miserably the conscience may be deluded in this case, when men do dote upon their own well-deserving, appeareth in Leah: for, Gen. 30:18. Leah saith, God hath given me my hire, because I have given my maiden to my husband.

Sixthly, this point is also made manifest by the natural ignorance of righteousness by faith, and affectation to be justified by works, which the Apostle finds fault-with in the Israelites, Rom. 9:31. They sought righteousness not by faith, but as it were by works: And, Rom. 10:3, being ignorant of the righteousness of God, and going about to establish their own righteousness (to wit, righteousness by works, according to the tenor of the Covenant of works) they did not submit themselves to the righteousness of God.

Seventhly, the same course followed by Papists and other erroneous teachers, testifieth the natural inclination of men to seek righteousness by works according to the tenor of the Covenant of works, and not by faith in Christ Jesus, that righteousness may come by grace only: And so are some men's hearts glued to this error, that they do transform justification by faith in justification by one work instead of all, as if the work of faith were the man's righteousness, and not Christ him-himself laid hold on by faith: Not considering, that to the man that renounceth all confidence in any work of his own, and flieth to Christ by faith, Christ is made of God unto that man wisdom and righteousness, 1 Cor. 1:30.

Last of all, this natural inclination, even of the regenerate, to seek righteousness by works, doth prove the Covenant of works to be naturally ingraft in all men's hearts, as appeareth in the Galatians, who being instructed in the doctrine of justification by faith in Christ without the works of the Law, did easily upon a temptation offered, look back, with liking, to the way of Justification by works, for which the Apostle reproveth them, Gal. 4:21. Tell me (saith he) ye that desire to be under the Law, or Covenant of works; and ver. 9. But now after ye have known God, or rather are known of God, how turn ye again to weak and beggarly elements, whereunto you desire again to be in bondage?

Obj. But, the Galatians as it seemeth, did not reject Justification by faith, but, did join with it Justification by the works of the Law, thinking that the safest way was to join both together.

Ans. The inconsistency of these two ways of Justification, the Apostle showeth, Rom. 11:6. For, Justification by grace, is no more by works, otherwise grace is no more of grace, and what Justification is by works, is no more of grace, otherwise work is no more works. And therefore, the Apostle makes the joining of these two ways of Justification to be nothing else but a plain seeking of Justification by the Covenant of works, which cutteth a man off from any benefit by Christ, Gal. 5:2, and whosoever seeketh to be justified by the Law or Covenant of works, is fallen from grace, ver. 4.

For further clearing this matter, we may distinguish two sorts of the Covenant of works: The one is true, genuine, and of God's institution, which God made with all men in Adam, for perfect obedience unto God's Law, out of man's own natural abilities. There is another counterfeit, bastard covenant of works, of man's own devising, which a sinner, lying in his sins (unable to do what the Law commands, or to suffer what the Law being broken binds upon him) of his own head devileth, upon other conditions then God hath set, and will have God to take his devised covenant instead of perfect obedience to the Law, that so he may be justified. Such was the covenant, which the carnal Israelites made with God in the wilderness, and which their posterity did follow, turning the Covenant of grace, whereunto God was calling them, into a covenant of works of their own framing: For, the grace which was offered to them in Christ under the veil of Levitical types, figures and ceremonies, they turned into an external service of performance only of bare and dead ceremonies, and into a ministry of the letter and death; for they did not take up Christ to be the end of the Law for righteousness to everyone that believes in him, but did think, that both the moral and ceremonial Law was given unto them of God, to the intent that they should do the external works of the moral Law, so far as they could; and when they transgressed the moral Law, they should fly to the ceremonial Law, and make amends for their faults by satisfying for their sin by the external sacrifice of some clean beast offered to God, or by the washing of their body, and their clothes. Such also is the covenant, which now adays many make with God, cutting short, with the old Pharisees, the sense of the precepts of the Law, by extending it no further then they may keep the same, that so they may make their own inherent righteousness the longer, and conform unto their own clipped rule of righteousness: and this they do by denying themselves to be guilty of original sin after baptism, and by extenuating and diminishing many faults, as but light and venial as they call them, and by devising satisfactions for expiating the sins of the living, by penances and pilgrimages, and of the dead by their sufferings in their imaginary purgatory, that so they may be justified by their works and sufferings. Such also is their covenant, who seek justification by deceased Saints merits, hoping they may so have absolution from sin, and obtain life eternal. And all these sorts of covenants of men's framing, we call bastard-covenants of works, because God will not admit any other Covenant of works then that which requireth perfect personal obedience. And therefore so many as seek to be justified by works, do stand under the obligation of perfect personal obedience under pain of death, and will be found not only utterly unable to do any good work, but also to be without Christ, and to be fallen from grace, as the Apostle (Gal. 5:3,4) doth teach us.

Obj. Seeing God doth abhor these bastard-covenants of works, and doth well know, that men are so far from performance of the due obedience of the Law, that they are utterly unable before they be reconciled through faith in Christ, to do so much as one acceptable work, as the Psalmist teacheth, Psal. 14:1-3. Why doth the Lord exact perfect obedience unto the Law from sinners? Why doth he press so instantly the slaves of sin to perform the duties required in the true Covenant of works?

Ans. The Lord justly doth abhor and reject these bastard-covenants, because they evacuate and make void both the Covenant of works and the Covenant of grace which is by faith in Christ; and he doth press all men to perform perfect obedience to all the commands whereunto they are naturally obliged, to the end that proud men, conceity of their own natural abilities, may find by experience, that they are unable to perform the condition of the

Covenant of works, and may acknowledge the same, and so despair of righteousness by their works, and be forced to fly to Christ, and to the Covenant of grace through him, that they may be freed from that covenant; and being justified by faith in Christ, may be enabled to begin new obedience to the Law in the strength of Christ's furniture: For, Christ is the end of the Law for righteousness to everyone that believeth, Rom. 10:4. And the Law entered, that men might by the Law see and acknowledge that the offense did abound, and then might perceive, that the riches of grace by Christ, did super-abound, Rom. 5:20,21 and, 1 Tim. 1:5. The end of the command, is love out of a pure heart, and a good conscience and faith unfamed.

This was the end of the promulgation of the Law in mount Sinai, that a stiff-necked people trusting in their own abilities, might be made sensible of their imperfection, by the repetition of the Law. And to this also God super-added the external yoke of the ceremonial Law, which neither they nor their posterity were able to bear, Acts, 15:10, that the people perceiving their manifold pollutions and guiltiness, wherein they were daily involved by breaking of God's Law: might in the sense of the burden lying on them, and of their damnable estate under it, fly to Christ the lamb of God that takes away the sins of the world, as he was, represented and offered to their sight in the sacrifices and burnt offerings.

Of this end of pressing the Law upon proud men, we have an example, Math. 19:16-22. In the conference of Christ with the young conceity rich man, who in the opinion of his own inherent righteousness, and of his abilities, was hugely swelled, as if he had already for time by-gone satisfied the whole Law, and that he was able and ready to do any good work which could be prescribed unto him, for obtaining of eternal life; whose proud conceit that Christ might humble and bring down, he craveth nothing but that he would keep the commands: And when the young man denied that he had broken the Law, he proveth him guilty of gross and vile Idolatry, from this, that he put a higher estimation on his riches than on remission of sin, and did love them more then heaven and fellowship with God in eternal life.

In all this let it be considered, that albeit men's confidence in their works, doth displease God; yet good works do not displease him, but they are so far pleasant unto him, that there is no moral motive which may serve to stir up in his people, an endeavor to follow after good works, which the Lord doth not make use of; partly, by setting before them the reward if they obey; partly, by setting punishments before their eyes if they obey not: yea, and the very observation of external moral duties and obedience, such as may be discharged by the unregenerate man (albeit God in relation to Justification do esteem it polluted and vile) yet he doth sometimes reward their external works by giving them external and temporal benefits for their encouragement: for, even Ahab's temporary humiliation the Lord so far accepted, that there-upon He took occasion to delay to take vengeance upon him, 1 Kings, 21:27-29. Likewise the Lord useth to recompense the civil justice of Pagans with a temporal reward, yea and to reward the outward diligence of every man in every lawful occupation, with some answerable outward reward.

The very Pharisees, who for the raising to themselves a fame and higher estimation for holiness, did take a great deal of pains, in prayers in the streets, and Market-places, and other exercises of Religion, wanted not an answerable reward; verily (saith Christ) they have their reward, Matth. 6:2.

And this course the Lord doth keep, that he may entertain and foster the civil society of men among themselves, and that His people looking on this bounty of God, may be stirred up the more to bring forth the fruits of faith, in hope of a merciful promised better reward of grace in the life to come, beside what they may have in this life.

CHAP. VI. - Of the Covenant of Grace.

THE THIRD AND LAST covenant concerning man's eternal salvation, is the covenant of Grace made between God and man, through Christ the Mediator.

Grace, sometimes simply and absolutely taken, is opposed to merit; and in this sense, every good thing, which of God's good pleasure is ordained, or promised, or actually bestowed on the creature, presuppose innocent, is called Grace: because it is impossible that a mere creature, can properly merit any good thing of God: because the creature neither hath nor can have, that which it hath not received, Rom. 11:35, who hath first given to Him, and it shall be recompensed to him again?

Sometime Grace is taken for every gift or good, bestowed by God upon the ill deserver: in which sense, gifts, common to elect and reprobate, are called by the name of Grace, Rom. 1:5. Ephes. 4:7.

Sometime Grace is taken in opposition to the pactional merit of works, or to the reward due by debt covenanted, as Rom. 4:4. To him that worketh, the reward is not reckoned of grace, but of debt. In which sense, that which is given for works, is not given of grace, Rom. 11:16, and in this sense, we take Grace as it is opposed to the covenant of works: for, the condition of the covenant of works, is the giving perfect obedience to the law; But the condition of the covenant of grace, is the receiving of Christ by faith unto righteousness and life, offered in the Gospel, without the works of the law; which covenant, may thus be described. The covenant of grace is a contract between God and men, procured by Christ upon these terms, that whosoever in the sense of their own sinfulness shall receive Christ Jesus offered in the Gospel, for righteousness and life, shall have Him and all the benefits purchased by Him, according to the covenant of Redemption; and that God will be his God, and the God of his children. This covenant of grace is founded upon the covenant of Redemption, past between God and Christ, wherein it was agreed, that all the elect given unto Christ, shall be reconciled in due time to God, and that to this end, this grace should be preached to bring about the reconciliation; and therefore Christ is called the Mediator of the new covenant, Heb. 12:22.

Of Infants interest in this Covenant.

Quest. What interest have infants in this covenant?

Ans. The same which they had since the first express and formal making thereof with Abraham, to whom God promised to be his God, and the God of his children, whose children all are, who are in Christ, Gal. 3:27-29.

For, of the redeemed some come to age, whom God, having called by the preaching of the Gospel, doth induce and effectually move to embrace solemnly the offered fellowship with God and his saints in Christ, and to consecrate themselves and their children unto the service of God. There are other redeemed ones, who die in their infancy, before they come to the use of reason, to whose salvation God hath express respect in making his covenant with their parents, that he will not have them excluded from the blessing, when he calls their parents to him, but in the common offer of grace and reconciliation by Christ, he makes the promise jointly to the parents and the children; for, in one sentence, and, as it were, with one breath, He saith, I will be thy God and thy seeds after thee, Gen. 15:17, whereof the Apostle maketh good use, Acts 2:39, declaring the promise to be made to the Jews and their children, and to the called Gentiles and their children. And upon this ground Paul and Silas, timeously did offer consolation to the Jailor, trembling and anxious what way he should be saved, Acts 16:31, saying, Believe in Christ Jesus, and thou shall be saved, thou and thy house.

As for the manner how the Lord dealeth with the souls of infants in converting them, the Scripture doth not speak, for this lieth among the secrets of God, which doth not concern us to search after, Deut. 29:29. It should be sufficient to us, that God in covenanting with the parents, promiseth to be the God of their children. And according to this covenant the Lord complains of their staying and offering their children unto idols, calling them His own sons and daughters, Ezek. 16:20, and upon this ground, in the second command, the Lord promiseth to show mercy to the thousand generation of believing parents; and, 1 Cor. 7:14, the Apostle doth call the children of one of the parents believing, holy children, because of their consecration unto God by the believing confederate parent, and in regard of God's right and interest in them as the children of His own family by covenant.

And Christ our Lord upon this ground, doth call the children of confederate parents, burgesses of heaven; of such is the kingdom of heaven, Matth. 19:13,14, and because infants are dedicate to Christ, to be taught and governed by Him in His own way and order, they are called disciples, Acts 15:10, as the disputers for the circumcision of Christians children, as well as of their parents, after the law of Moses, do make it manifest: and in the institution of baptism, our Lord gives the privilege of the covenant unto every nation, no less then to the Jews, that by covenant whole nations might be drawn in and given up as disciples to His doctrine, Matth. 28:29, make all nations disciples by your doctrine, baptizing them, &c. that the children with the parents, might be partakers by baptism, of the seal of the covenant for the righteousness of faith, no less than the children of Israelites were by circumcision.

Of the means to draw on the making of this covenant.

Of these means we have spoken in the fourth article of the covenant of Redemption, and need not to insist more about them then to name them.

The first mean to draw men into this blessed covenant, and to keep them in it, is the external revelation of the will of God, for teaching men how great their sin and misery is, and how they may be reconciled and delivered by the grace of our Lord Jesus Christ, and how they may testify their thankfulness (being reconciled) for such a mercy; which grounds of saving knowledge, are fully and faithfully set down in holy Scripture, and committed to His servants in the ministry, who should in preaching of the Gospel, inform and persuade men to repent and embrace the grace of Christ, and put on His sweet yoke of obedience upon them.

The second mean is, after application of the Lord's word to the hearers for convincing them of sin in them, and righteousness in Christ, and judgment to follow, to wit, of absolution of the believer, and of condemnation of such as believe not, To receive into the bond of this covenant of grace, all that appear seriously to consecrate themselves and their children to the faith and obedience of the doctrine of our Lord Jesus Christ, without determining whether they be regenerate for the present or not.

The third mean, is the solemn sealing of this covenant, for right-eousness of faith and salvation through Christ, by baptizing both the parents that accept the covenant, and their children also; and by exhortations, promises and commination's, and all other arguments, which may more and more convince them of their need of Christ, and duty of following Him, to fix and strengthen their hearty purpose to cleave unto the Lord. Such as are, the Lord's command to believe in Christ and love one another, 1 John 3:23, and His threatening, if they believe not, John 3:18, and, 1 John 5:10,11.

The fourth mean, is the gathering of these that have embraced this covenant, into all lawful and possible Church-communion with other His disciples, and fixing them in their several congregations, that they may be edified under their Officers, appointed by Christ in His Testament in their most holy faith, and obedience of all His ordinances. And for further clearing the way of God's bringing the visible Church of Christ into this covenant with Himself, let it be considered.

1. Albeit of those that are come to the use of reason, with whom God doth formally and solemnly make this covenant of grace and reconciliation, many are externally only called, and few in compar-ison chosen, Matth. 20:21, yet, it is not the will of God, other ways then by doctrine to separate the elect from the rest of them that are externally called, or to make the elects name known to the world: for, the kirk knoweth not, but God only knoweth who are His, 2 Tim. 2:19. And therefore He hath ordained means common to the elect and reprobate, to bring both unto the external embracing of His covenant, and continuing externally therein, and He doth bestow gifts both to the one sort and to the other, and He worketh in both the one sort and the other according to His own will; But as for inward and effectual

calling, or special saving graces which do accompany salvation, and the special operations of the holy Spirit, He reserveth to the elect and redeemed only, to whom in a time acceptable, He revealeth Himself, and sealeth them for His own service.

2. By this wise and holy dealing with the hearers of the Gospel, whereby the Lord so makes good the covenant of Redemption, and bringeth His decrees to pass, as none shall have just reason to stumble; no wonder, that many be compassed within the draught-net of the Gospel, and be moved to enter into this holy and blessed covenant, of whom there may be elect, not as yet converted, whereupon by God's appointment, followeth a solemn covenanting of all that consent to the condition of the covenant, and profess their faith in Christ: all whom (with their children) Christ translates from the Pagan world, into His visible kingdom and fellowship of His Church militant and grants unto them right to the common privileges of Citizens, in the order appointed in His word, that keeping all lawful and possible communion with the Catholic visible Church of Christ, they may be edified in their particular congregations, and governed with others by Ecclesiastical discipline.

3. Together with these external means, serving for drawing on the covenant and going on in it, the common operations of God do concur; common to all the called, both elect and reprobate, and gifts common to both, are bestowed, such as illumination, moral persuasion, historical, dogmatical and temporary faith, moral change of affections, and some sort of external amendment of their outward conversation, saving grace being the special gift of God to His own.

4. Of this manner of covenanting and taking into Church-fellowship, all the called that consent in a moral way to the condition of the covenant, regenerate and unregenerate, we have a pattern in the

Lord's covenanting with all Israel, Exod. 19, the covenant is offered
to all the Israelites, without exception; all are invited to enter in
covenant without exception, arguments, motives and moral inducements are made use of, from their experience of the Lord's goodness
and gifts given to them before; most ample promises of spiritual benefits, are made unto them, conditionally to be bestowed on them both
in this life, and in the life to come, verse. 4,5,6, the people embrace
the condition of the covenant, V. 7,8, the people are sanctified, and
prepared to receive the holy commands and will of God, in the rest
of the chapter; then, in the 20th chapter and in the rest of the book,
the duties of the covenanters are propounded, which concern the
acknowledgement of sin and deserved death; and these also which
concern obtaining of justification and sanctification by Christ, and
which concern their showing forth their thankfulness, all the days of
their life.

The same covenant, after forty years, is repeated and renewed by
Moses, a little before his death in the land of Moab, Deut. 29, the
Lord commands Moses to renew the covenant with all the people,
verse. 1, all the people of Israel, are gathered together, regenerate and
unregenerate, verse. 2, the sum of arguments and motives to enter in
covenant of new, is shortly set down, verse. 3, the greatest part of the
people to be joined to God in covenant, are openly declared by Moses
to be unregenerate, verse. 4.

After that, arguments are used to move them, in all time coming,
to trust in the Lord and to obey him, to verse. 9, the covenant is made
with the heads of the tribes, and elders of the people, and their governors, and with all the men of Israel, with their little ones, with the
women, and with the strangers that were in the midst of their camp,
verse. 10,11, the covenant is solemnized with adjuration of all to keep

the conditions thereof, verse. 12,13, the covenant is extended with adjuration to the posterity, verse. 14,15, neither is there any exception made, or exclusion of any that consented to the covenant, whether unregenerate Israelites or strangers, but all are admitted within this covenant.

The same way of covenanting did John the Baptist follow, admitting to his baptism the seal of this covenant, all those that came from Jerusalem and out of all Judea, and from the borders of Jordan, without exception; whosoever confessed their sins, or that they were sinners, and professed they did receive the offer of grace, made in the Name of Christ Jesus, the true lamb of God, that takes away the sins of the world, Matth. 3:5,6, and so far was John from waiting for evidences of saving grace and regeneration, before he admitted them that came to his baptism, into the fellowship of the external covenant of grace and reconciliation, that on the contrary, he made public profession, that the fan whereby the chaff is separated from the wheat, and the hypocrite discerned from the sincere Christian, was not in his hand, or in any other man or men's hands, but in the hand of Christ Jesus Himself only. And therefore (which is worthy to be observed) after he had publicly testified his suspicion of the hypocrisy and old poisonable disposition, in the Pharisees and Sadducees that came to his baptism, and offered to receive the covenant of grace and the seal thereof, verse. 7, forthwith, without inquiring into their regeneration and sincerity of heart, he baptized them among the rest, v. 11, and left them to be examined thereafter by Christ Himself, whether they were upright in heart or not.

The same way of gathering members of the visible Christian Churches out of the world, did Christ's own Apostles follow in His own company, Christ himself being present bodily, beholding and approving their baptizing of multitudes, who after hearing of Christ's sermons offered to receive baptism, and went down to the water Arnon, where Christ's Apostles did make and baptize more disciples than John, John 4:1, that is, they admitted multitudes into the holy covenant, and sealed the same with baptism, taking no stricter course of examination of them then John did, but admitting all that craved the benefit of the covenant and the seal of it, though they had no certain evidence of their regeneration, being satisfied, that Christ did not forbid to baptize them, when he saw them go down to the water to be baptized, after hearing His sermon. Now, there is no question He knew their hearts, all of them, and that many of them would afterward shortly make defection from Him, and depart from him, and from his disciples fellowship, as is plain, John 6:66,70.

This way of receiving into external covenant, all these who receive the offer and the condition of the covenant, without inquiring into their election or reprobation, their regeneration or unregeneration for the time, (which may be called a covenanting outwardly and in the letter) in the deep and wise counsel of God, is appointed for the gathering and constitution of the visible kirk: for, by this mean, first, God so executeth and perfecteth the decree of election, that in the meantime he hindereth none, of all the hearers of the Gospel from receiving the grace of Christ offered therein. He excludeth no man from embracing the covenant; but, on the contrary, he opens the door to all that are called, to enter into (as it were) the outer court of his dwelling house, that they may so draw more near to him; and so he doth not particularly manifest any man's reprobation.

Secondly, by this means also he hideth the election of the elect from others, and from themselves till they repent their sins and flee to Christ, and bring forth some evidences of their election, in their obedience of faith and begun sanctification.

Thirdly, the Lord makes use of this outward and common covenanting with all receivers of the offer, as a mean to draw the confederate in the letter, to be confederate in the spirit; for, the faith which he requires as the condition of the covenant, he worketh in the elect, if not before, or with the external covenanting, yet undoubtedly after, in a time acceptable, and that by the ordinary means, the use whereof is granted to all confederate externally: and so as common illumination is a mean to that special, spiritual and saving illumination; and dogmatical or historical faith, is a mean unto saving faith; and external calling, is a mean of effectual calling, So external covenanting in the letter, is a mean most fit, and accommodate to make a man a covenanter in the spirit.

Fourthly, this external covenanting, wherein God promiseth to be the believers God, and the God of their children, is a mean not only to beget and foster faith in the covenanting parents, for their own salvation, but also a mean to comfort them about the salvation of their infants, dying in their infancy, whether before or after their baptism; and a mean to give them good hope of those children's blessed resurrection, by virtue of the promise, because in covenanting, the Lord doth promise to be the believers God, and the God of his children, and doth not exact the condition of actual faith from their dying infants.

From these grounds, it followeth, first, that some are taken externally and conditionally into the covenant, upon their engagement unto the righteousness of faith, and their baptism is a seal of their engagement unto it, who albeit they be not as yet regenerate, yet they are to be esteemed members of the Church, and Christians outwardly, Christians by calling, and in the letter, whose praise is of men, as they were also in the Church before Christ's coming, Jews outwardly and in the letter, whose praise was of men, commended indeed for so much: but if they came not up to lay hold upon, and follow after, righteousness by faith, were not Jews in God's account, and unto them circumcision was but in the letter, and the sealing of the engagement only, and not of the good things covenanted, Rom. 2:28,29.

Secondly, it followeth, that there are some covenanters outwardly and inwardly also, in the flesh and in the spirit also, whose praise is not of men only, but of God also, to wit, such as not only have engaged to fulfill the condition of living in the faith, and following after the righteousness of faith, but are performers really of their engagement, and unto those their baptism, is not only outward and in the flesh, but inward also, in the spirit also, approven of God also. Such as were in the visible Church of old, Jews inwardly, performers of their engagement to live by faith, Jews in the spirit and not in the letter only, whose praise was of God, and not of men only, Rom. 2:28,29.

Thirdly, it followeth, that some are in the covenant absolutely, or without condition required of them for their part, whom God taketh in his own hand absolutely, such as are elect infants, dying in their infancy, for whom, that they might be delivered from original sin and deserved wrath, Christ hath engaged and laid down his life, and promised in the covenant to be their God; whom therefore ere they die, he doth immediately quicken, and sanctify, and translateth to heaven after death; of such (saith Christ) is the Kingdom of heaven, Mark, 10:14.

How the external dispensation of the Covenant of old, differeth from that which now is under the Gospel.

Albeit the covenant of grace in itself, be one and the same, from the first preaching of it in Paradise, unto the end of the world, because Christ the Savior of his people, is one and the same, yesterday and today and forever, and because the faith of the elect is of one kind, and was and shall be to the worlds end; yet, the external outletting and dispensation of the covenant differeth, as it was propounded before Christ's incarnation and after it: for, in Paradise this covenant was set forth by way of promise, (according to the articles of the covenant of Redemption) that Christ should assume the seed of the woman, and should suffer in the flesh, or human nature, and by his power destroy the works of the devil, in favors of his own chosen people, which should militate against the devil under his banner.

2. And least any man should fancy, that the covenant of grace, founded upon this promise, was made with all the posterity of Adam, as the covenant of works was made with Adam and all his posterity the Lord, in the uttering of the promise, did not direct his speech unto Adam and Eve, but to the devil by way of threatening, and cursing him and his seed, even all the reprobate, in the audience of Adam and Eve, that our first parents over-hearing the curse of the serpent and his seed, and the promise of Christ's incarnation, in laying hold upon the promiser by faith, might be justified and saved as private persons, after the same way as other believers after them should be justified and saved. This their faith in Christ, the Lord did foster and augment by his doctrine taught unto them, and by the prescribing typical sacrifices to be offered in faith to God for remission of sins: And the Lord did admit their children into the external fellowship of this covenant, without putting difference between one and another outwardly, as we see in Cain and Abel: of which two, the one, to wit, Cain, was a covenanter in the flesh outwardly and in the letter only;

for he was destitute and void of saving faith; the other, to wit, Abel, was both outwardly and inwardly a covenanter, not in the letter only, but in the spirit also, endued with lively, justifying and saving faith in Christ to be incarnate, and to die for his own people, as the Apostle testifieth, reckoning him up among believers justified by faith, Heb. 11:4.

3. After the flood, God did not make the covenant with every man, nor with any family by way of explicit and formal paction, except Abraham and his family only, of whom the Messiah, God the Mediator, was to come according to the flesh; and with him the Lord confirmed the covenant, by adding unto it the Sacrament of circumcision, as the seal of righteousness and justification by faith.

4. In the wilderness at mount Sinai, that the Lord might make evident the necessary of justification by faith in Christ to come, he did repeat the law to works; and to them that did acknowledge their sin, he did set forth Christ their deliverer, under the vail of sacrifices and Levitical types, and the very same is the covenant now, whereunto Christ and his ministers, laying aside the veil of the ceremonies, did openly invite their hearers, that acknowledging their sins, and renouncing confidence in their own power and worth, they should cast themselves into the arms of Christ the Savior, that through him they might obtain justification and life eternal. We see here indeed a diverse manner of dispensing, and outward managing the making of the covenant with men, but the covenant was still the same, clothed and set forth in a diverse manner, and did no other ways differ then and now, but as one and the self-same man differeth from himself, clothed suitably one way in his minority, and another way in his riper age.

5. If the covenanters therefore be compared among themselves in respect of diverse dispensations, the covenanters in spirit after Christ's incarnation, are in a better condition, then the believers before Christ's coming; for, the believers before Christ incarnate under the pedagogy of the law, did lie under a servitude and bondage as to the outward man, for then the sons and heirs not come to age, did differ nothing from servants, Gal. 4:1, and in regard of the inward man, they saw the mystery of salvation, albeit savingly, yet more obscurely, for, through the veil they saw the mystery of salvation to be had by Christ; but after Christ's coming, the Lord dealt more liberally with believers, because by their freedom from the Levitical ceremonies, taking away the veil, they may behold with open face the glory of the Lord, as in a mirror, and be transformed into the same image, from glory to glory, even as by the Spirit of the Lord, 2 Cor. 3:18.

6. But as for what concerns the covenanters in the letter and outwardly only; they are in worse condition after the coming of Christ, then the literal covenanters before his incarnation: for, the unregenerate under the Gospel, are in danger of more heavy judgment, then the uncircumcised in heart were before Christ came, in regard it is a greater sin to neglect and despise Christ speaking from heaven, in the more clear manifestation of himself in the Gospel, then it was before Christ came to contemn the darker doctrine of Moses, Heb. 2:3, and 10:20.

Concerning the condition of the Covenant.

In receiving or admission of persons, who are come to the use of reason into the covenant, these three things are to be observed, and distinguished one from another; first, the condition of the person, desiring to be in covenant with God, for reconciliation and grace through Christ; 2. The condition upon which he is entered in covenant; 3. The condition required of him, for evidencing of his sincere covenanting.

The first condition required of the man who desireth to enter in the covenant of reconciliation, is the acknowledgement of his sins; for, except a man confess himself a sinner, and unable to help himself, Christ rejecteth him, and will have nothing to do with him, for Christ hath said, I came not to call the righteous, but sinners to repentance, Matth. 9:13.

As for the next, the condition of the covenant upon which the man is received, and whereby the man becometh a confederate, it is his consent to receive the grace offered, even Christ with his benefits, as he is holden forth in the Gospel; or, the condition of the covenant is faith, receiving Christ for righteousness and eternal life.

As for the third, the condition required of the man now entered in the covenant, for evidencing the truth and sincerity of the faith which the covenanter professeth, it is the taking on him the yoke of Christ, which he layeth on his confederate people; or, this condition, is the covenanters up-giving of himself to Christ's government, and obedience of his commands: and all these three, are expressed by Christ, Matth. 11:28,29.

First, they that labor, and are heavy laden, are they whom Christ calleth unto a covenant and fellowship of his grace.

Secondly, he propounds the condition of the covenant, to wit, that they believe in Christ, or come unto Him, that in him they may find full relief from sin and misery, and in him full righteousness and felicity.

Thirdly, he requires of them who do embrace him by faith, and so have accepted the condition of the covenant, that they give evidence of their faith in him, by taking on of his yoke on them; take my yoke upon you, saith he.

All these three, a covenanter in the letter externally, will profess to have, and to purpose to follow; but the true covenanters in spirit, have indeed all the three: for, true faith in Christ, or the receiving of Christ offered in the Evangel for justification and salvation, which is the condition of the covenant, presupposeth the condition of the man who is called to embrace Christ, and draweth after it the condition required of the man covenanting: for, he that receiveth Christ for righteousness and eternal life, of necessity must acknowledge himself a man in himself unrighteous, and a lost man, and that he cometh to Christ to be justified, and sanctified and saved by him, and so to persevere in this course unto life eternal.

Of the terms whereupon this Covenant is offered and pressed in Scripture.

The terms of the covenant, are diversely propounded in Scripture, Exod. 19:5, the Lord propounds it thus, if ye will obey my voice indeed, and keep my covenant, then ye shall be a peculiar people unto me, &c.

In these words, the condition required of those that are already entered in covenant is most eminent; for, this people was in covenant from the time of Abraham's covenanting, and was admitted to the Sacraments before their coming forth of Egypt; and therefore the conditions previous to their entering in covenant, and required for closing the bargain, are not so much insisted on at this time. This condition the people do accept, and give answer to God by Moses, verse. 8, all that the Lord hath spoken we will do.

Another form and expression, is used, Acts 16:31. Paul and Silas say to the Jailor, now anxious how to be saved, believe in the Lord, and thou shalt be saved; thou and all thy house. The Jailor accepts of the condition, and he is baptized and all his house, verse. 33.

The condition of his person taking with guiltiness, and granting his lost condition is spoken of, verse. 37, the condition of the covenant therefore is propounded in the next room, and is accepted, where-upon baptism is administered unto him.

Psal. 27:8. In other words the same condition is propounded: the Lord craveth faith, seeking communion on with God for the condition, seek ye my face; the Psalmist accepteth the condition and answereth, Thy Face, O Lord, will I seek.

Isa. 45:22. Christ requires faith in these he calleth, and upon that condition promiseth salvation, Look unto me, all ye ends of the earth, and be ye saved: the answer of the believer is set down, verse. 24. Surely shall one say, in the Lord have I righteousness and strength.

Likewise the way of making this covenant, is set forth by Christ, offering himself a Savior on the one part, and the believers receiving Christ on the other part, John 1:11,12, as many as received him, to them he gave power to become the sons of God, even to them that believe on his Name.

And, 2 Cor. 5:19,20, upon this only condition of consenting to reconciliation offered, he summeth up most shortly and clearly the covenant-making, We are ambassadors for Christ, as if God did beseech you by us, we pray you in Christ's stead, be reconciled to God. There remaineth no more for making of the covenant, but that the hearer do honestly answer, thus, the offer and condition pleaseth me well, I consent to be reconciled. Now he who consenteth to be reconciled, 1. Granteth his natural enmity; 2. Accepteth Christ the Mediator, Redeemer, Reconciler, offered to him by God, whose fullness is in Christ; And, 3. Obligeth himself to entertain this friendship all his life after.

Last of all, the making of the covenant, is sometime pressed to be received and followed under the form of a precept, 1 John 3:23, this is his command, that ye believe in the Name of His Son Jesus Christ, and love one another as he hath commanded us: In which words the condition, or estate of the person, who is called to believe and enter in covenant, is presupposed: for, it is imported, that he must acknowledge, nor only that he is a miserable sinner, and unable to relieve himself, but also that he is naturally averse from the way of seeking righteousness by faith in Christ, and hath need that the sovereign power of God draw him to Christ. Secondly, the condition of the making of covenant is propounded, which is to believe in Jesu, Christ. In the third room, the condition required of him that is entered in covenant by believing in Christ, is, that we love one another as he hath commanded us.

This offered and commanded condition of the covenant of grace, some by the grace of God do accept, and engage to perform, and do perform sincerely, albeit weakly; other some, trusting in their own strength, engage unto the obedience of faith, and with their mouth profess they are sinners, and do believe in Christ, and that they will submit themselves to his Government, drawing near to him with their lips, when their hearts are far from him; and such men's faith, changeth not their old disposition and way of living, but it suffereth them to serve their belly, or mammon, or vain glory, and such other idols; yet because the Church are not judges of the secrets of the heart, they must receive into Church-fellowship, all who confess themselves to be sinners, and profess they do accept the offer of Christ's grace, and promise subjection to his ordinances.

Obj. But how can the Church receive men in Church-fellowship, who are destitute of lively faith?

Ans. The Church is not judge of the heart, or of the secrets thereof, because it cannot see faith in itself, but must look to the profession of faith, and to the fruits thereof in the own order and time; the Church is witness to their engagement, but not judges of their sincerity.

2. The covenant of grace doth not exclude the most vile sinners, if they acknowledge their sinfulness, and do solemnly consent unto the condition of the covenant: because, according to this covenant nothing is bestowed on the covenanter, of merit, but of grace only, which the Church knoweth God can give, and sometimes doth give unto counterfeit confederates, making them sincere in his own time, and that by the means of the ordinances, made use of in the visible Church.

3. It is one thing to be a confederate Christian in the letter, externally in the sight of men; another thing to be a covenanter in the spirit, inwardly in respect of the heart and inward man, Rom. 2:28, and albeit the external covenant doth not bring on righteousness and life, except a man be also a covenanter inwardly in his heart, in the sense of sin and imperfection, making daily use of Christ: yet it is certain, that outward covenanting, is an ordinary and blessed mean unto many, to beget and foster faith, and help forth the fruits thereof.

4. It may and should suffice us, that God, in the first framing of a national Church, did admit, and commanded Moses to admit all the Israelites in covenant, of whom very few were converted, or reconciled to God in their spirit; and this was not hid from Moses, or from the truly godly in the camp of Israel, as is plainly shown to us, Deut. 28:29, where God bears witness against the people, that their heart was not according to their profession and engagement:

and Moses speaketh out this truth in all the people's audience, while he is renewing the covenant with them, notwithstanding they were unregenerate, Deut. 29.

Obj. But some will insist and tell us, that the visible Church is a society of Saints or regenerate persons, and that they who live in the visible Church, must be visible Saints, whole life at least doth not contradict their profession, and such as by the judgment of charity we must esteem regenerate.

Ans. Christ's visible Church, is the company of them that are called out of the world unto him; the company of them that are consecrate to God, and engaged by solemn covenant to follow the course of holiness: By calling they are Saints, albeit many of them may be found polluted in their manners: thus doth God Himself reach us to judge, Psal. 50:5. Gather unto me my saints, saith He, and who are these? These who have made a covenant with me by sacrifice. Now, of these, many did not worship God in spirit, but placed all their religion in ceremonies, and went about by their outward sacrifices to pacify God, and to expiate their sins, as is plain, verse. 7:8, others of these called saints, consecrate unto God, and joined with him in a visible covenant, were very wicked, who no ways behaved themselves as became covenanters with God; and who therefore were to be excluded from the benefit of the covenant, except they repented: for, they hated true holiness, and did cast the commands behind their back, verse. 16, were thieves and adulterers, slanderers and calumniators of their brethren, verse. 18,19, and yet for all this, the Lord doth not exclude them out of the visible Church, but doth in a fatherly manner reprove them, that they might repent and not perish.

2. There is no question, whether all in the visible Church ought to be both in open conversation, and in heart holy, and that they shall

certainly be damned and perish, that are not such? But the question is here, about the duty of the Governors of the Church, and of the godly in it, whether they should exclude from Church-membership all who are not regenerate, at least so to be esteemed in the judgment of charity? Or, whether all are to be holden for Church-members, and keeped within the Church, who are in covenant with God, and sealed with the seal thereof, to the intent that by doctrine and censures of the Church (so far as may be by means) they may be regenerate, and being regenerate, be helped on in the way of holiness?

3. There is a difference to be put betwixt the precepts, concerning the personal sanctification of every man in himself, and the precepts given for the governing of others, and keeping holy society with the called saints, renewed or unrenewed in the visible Church, so far as God's word giveth light and order: for, it is commanded to me and thee, that we pursue peace and holiness, without which none shall see the face of God; but it is not commanded to me or thee, that we should keep no Church-fellowship in God's ordinances, except with the regenerate. It is not commanded to the Governors of the Church, that they must examine every person concerning their regeneration; neither are they forbidden to admit any into the society of the Church, save these whom they esteem regenerate: But they are commanded to bring in to the Church, all that oblige themselves to be Christ's disciples, with their children, and by the means appointed of God, in doctrine and censures of the Church, to promove their sanctification and salvation; for, so many doth Christ's commission to the Pastors of the Church import, Math. 28:19,20.

4. Regeneration is not the just measure, whereby to square the dimensions and extent of the visible Church; but, confederation and obsignation of the Covenant by baptism: For, the Church is Christ's

visible kingdom, whose visible subjects are all they who solemnly are engaged to subject themselves to his doctrine and government; and therefore the Church visible, is not to be defined, the company of the regenerate, but the company of the confederate with God, and called unto holiness; among whom, Christ tells us, there are few elect, and so fewer regenerate; and therefore the Church of Christ, is compared to a barn-floor, whereinto is gathered both the chaff and the wheat, both they that have faith and they that profess faith, out of whom Christ doth gather his own Elect and redeemed ones.

Obj. But at least in gathering of a Church out of the world, respect must be had, that the consenting of the covenanter be serious; and how can the consent be serious, where the heart is not sincere, where the person is not regenerate? Such a man's consent to the covenant, as is without saving faith, is but feigned, counterfeit, hypocritical, and such a consent as may hinder the man's regeneration, and do nothing but provoke God's wrath against the man and the receivers or admitters of him also.

Ans. Serious is sometime opposed to sport or play, and so a matter may be serious which is in earnest gone about, and is not openly histrionical. And sometime, serious is opposed to the intention of fraud and deceit; and so that may be called serious, which is done without a purpose to deceive or beguile the party. But when the consenter to engage in covenant, speaketh as he thinketh, albeit possibly his own heart deceive him, his consent to the condition of the covenant may justly be called serious, because he intends to deal in earnest, as in a weighty business. And such was the consent of the people of Israel unto the covenant made with God, Exod. 19.

Likewise, counterfeit and hypocritical, is sometime called so, in opposition to that which is real, true and spiritual: And so all consent to the covenant of Grace, which doth not proceed from the spirit of Regeneration is but feigned faith, and indeed is not saving faith; yet, it may be serious and morally honest, like Israel's, Exod. 14:20, and so sufficient to make a covenant, and to tie an obligation on the man to such duties as may lead to salvation.

Again, feigned, counterfeit, hypocritical, is called that which a man purposely doth fain, making show of that which he knows not to be, being conscious to his own wickedness; and such a feigned consent, we grant, doth provoke God against such a person; but the Church is not judge of this, so long as they know not of this gross hypocrisy.

We hold then, that there may be, and usually fall forth, such a moral consent unto the covenant of Grace without saving faith, which may be called a serious, really honest consent, as to the agreement of the mind and mouth of the covenanter, such as is found in ordinary civil contracts, between one man and another, and must be acknowledged to be an external Church-covenanting with God, and with the rest of the members of the Church: and so the consent in respect to the making a covenant, is not feigned, neither is it displeasing unto God in the own kind, albeit it be not sufficient or acceptable to God unto the persons salvation: For, so much doth God himself testify (Deut. 5.) speaking of the Israelites (who were ignorant of the deceitfulness of their own heart, and of their inability to perform what they promised) he saith, (ver. 28,29) They have well said, all that they have spoken. Therefore unto the tying a man in this bond of the covenant, this moral honesty, is sufficient, albeit to salvation it is not sufficient, but in order thereto a mean of God's appointment.

Now, that there is such a thing as we call moral integrity or honesty, which differeth from the true Christians spiritual honesty, or sincerity, it is plain from these places of Scripture, which speak of this integrity of heart in such persons as were not renewed, because they intended no other thing then they pretended. Thus Abimelech excuseth himself to God when he took away Sarah, Abraham's wife from him, thinking Sarah had been his sister and not his wife, Gen. 20:6. In the integrity of my heart and innocence of my hands, have I done this. And this the Lord doth acknowledge to be true, ver. 17. So also the captains that came with their companies to David in Ziklag, are said to have a perfect heart, because they were morally honest, and resolved, as they professed, uprightly to make David King, and to help him in the war, and not betray him, 1 Chron. 12:33,38.

Of the sundry ways of men's framing of the covenant of Grace.

As we told there was a covenant of works, one truly so called of God's institution; and another false sort of covenant of works, of man's framing: So it is also in the matter of the covenant of Grace, there is one truly so called, and another sort false and counterfeit of man's framing. That which is of God's framing is the covenant, that God makes with the Church, for giving righteousness and life by faith in Jesus Christ: that which we call a counterfeit covenant, is the covenant, which men frame unto themselves upon any other condition then faith: Such was the counterfeit covenant of the false apostles, who corrupted the Gospel-covenant among the Galatians, whereof the Apostle Paul complaineth, Gal. 1:6,7, challenging them, that they had forsaken God, who called them to the grace of Christ, and were turned over to another Gospel, that is, to another covenant of grace, then the true one, which is only one, and not various, but by the troublers of the Church was changed into another frame; for, the true covenant, was perverted and corrupted by these who went about to join together Justification by works, and Justification by grace through faith in Christ: which two sorts of covenant, are inconsistent, and do mutually overthrow one another; So also did the Pharisee (Luke, 18:11,12) corrupt and pervert both the covenant of works and the covenant of grace; he corrupted and perverted the covenant of works, because he put up to God some external good works for the perfect obedience of the law; and he perverted the covenant of grace, because albeit he did acknowledge the grace of God, and gave him thanks for giving him ability and power to do good works, and for infusing habits of piety and justice in him; yet, he exalted himself, and took the thanks and praise to himself who had made good use of these virtuous habits, God, I thank thee, (saith he) that I am not like other men, &c.

2. Like unto this fault, is the error of many, of whom some makes the act of faith brought forth by the power of natural free-will, to be the condition of the covenant, contrary to the doctrine of the Gospel, which makes faith infused, to be the gift of God, renouncing its own righteousness and the merit of all works also, and resting on Christ, to be the condition: For, the sentence of the Apostle, standeth firm and unmovable, Rom. 11:16. If it be by grace, it is no more of works, &c.

Other some make this the condition of the covenant, that Christ should pay for mortal sins by his own temporal sufferings, and so take away everlasting punishment, but will have the sinner himself to pay for venial sins by temporal sufferings, partly in this life and partly in purgatory.

Other some dream of framing the covenant of grace thus, if a man do all the good he is able, and hath a will to serve God better than before, they conceive, that God must take the will for the perfect dead, and so for good payment.

Which counterfeit conditions, and other such like inventions of self-pleasing conceits, are all of them nothing else but the adulterating both of the covenant of works, and of the covenant of grace appointed of God, by which inventions men deceive themselves to their own perdition.

Now, that such perverting of the covenant of works and of grace, are rife and frequent among men, experience may prove: For, before Christ's coming, this was the way of carnal Israelites, Rom. 10:3, and Rom. 9:30. For they being ignorant of the righteousness of God, went about to establish their own inherent righteousness, and would not subject themselves to the righteousness of God. And of the Galatians, it is said, chap. 5:4. Christ is become of none effect unto you, whosoever of you are justified by the Law, ye are fallen from grace; that is, ye who seek righteousness or justification by work, have renounced so far as in you lieth grace to be had by Christ; and experience daily showeth the same disposition in many professed Christians.

Quest. Are not then such corrupters of the covenant of grace loosed from their obligation, wherein by their baptism they were tied to seek righteousness by faith only?

Ans. No: for, albeit by so doing they prove themselves to be corrupters and falsifiers of their covenant, to their own perdition, if they repent not; yet they stand obliged still before God to their covenant sealed in baptism: For, the covenant of God with man, cannot be dissolved by men's treachery, and without God's consent, not only because the covenant of God, with men, in regard of the perpetual equity thereof, hath in it a perpetual obligation, but also because the sovereign dominion of God, hath the force of a law to oblige them whom God hath taken in among his people, that being once his confederate subjects, they should remain still his subjects: For,

as circumcision was a seal of covenanted righteousness by faith, So
baptism is a seal of the same covenanted righteousness by faith,
whether the covenanters remain constant unto their covenant or not,
as we see in the Israelites, who albeit they were polluted with idolatry
in Egypt, and albeit they proved rebellious in the wilderness, and in
the land of promise were found often guilty of breach of covenant;
yet, still in the Scripture they are called God's people, and the Lord's
interest and right in them, stood fast, and their right also unto the
external privileges of the citizens of God's kingdom, remained fast
also, until the time that for their open and obstinate rejecting of
Christ, the children of the kingdom were cast out and were broken
off the true olive tree: So also, the obligation of the baptized, who
turn the true covenant of grace in another of their own framing, doth
still stand, tying them to perform the condition of the true covenant:
and their right to the external privileges of the confederate, doth
remain still in some sort, even when they are inter-dieted from the
honorable possession thereof by excommunication: For, the Apostle
teacheth us, that the excommunicate remain, as to their ecclesiastic
state, (albeit not as to their present ecclesiastic condition) citizens
and members of the Church, and subject to Jurisdiction ecclesiastic,
and to Christ's discipline; because when they are judged, and are
under censure, they are said to be within the Kirk, and not without
it, 1 Cor. 5:12. What have I to do to judge also them that are without?
Do not ye judge them that are within? And these that were delivered
unto Satan, as to their present external condition, remained notwithstanding, as to their external state, the domestics of God, under the
discipline of God's house, and were pressed by the censure laid on
them, to learn to cease from their sinful course, and specially from
these faults for which they were censured and corrected by their

excommunication, 1 Tim. 1:20. Hymenaeus and Alexander were given over to Satan, that they might learn not to blaspheme; that is, that being humbled and brought to repentance they might return to the acknowledgement of the truth and to a reverent speaking of holy things, and so the right to be counted brethren and members of the Church (albeit under censure, restraint and disrespect till they repented) was not taken altogether from them, even under excommunication; nor yet were the private duties of charity, due to brethren in that fearful condition, to be altogether denied unto them, even when the possession of the former honor of blameless brethren, was taken from them; for, the Apostle will have them, albeit excommunicate, to be esteemed still censured brethren, and not looked upon as enemies, 2 Thess. 3:14,15. If any man obey not our word by this epistle, note that man (to wit by putting the censure of excommunication on him) and have no company with him, that he may be ashamed, yet count him not as an enemy, but admonish him as a brother; and this is so much the more carefully to be observed, that the constitution of the visible Church of such and such members, and the use of excommunication may be the better understood: least the excommunicate, being over-burdened by the sharpness of the censure, should seem to themselves altogether excluded from Church-society, and so despair of returning to the full possession of their privileges, but might know, that the right of citizens of the city of God, was reserved unto them, and was to be restored by way of possession after their repentance, and that they were not cut off from the Christian charity of the brethren, no not when they were lying under the sentence, that they might so much the sooner return to repentance and to the possession of their Ecclesiastic honor.

Obj. But here there ariseth a greater doubt and objection, how, and upon what reason God doth require the condition of faith, which men cannot perform, except it be given of God, as the Apostle testifieth, Ephes. 2:8, you are saved of grace by faith, and that not of your selves, it is the gift of God?

Ans. The equity of the duty required, doth not depend upon men's present power or strength, of whom the condition is required, but upon this ground, that ability was given to Adam, and to his posterity in him: for, all enjoined service, and so the duty of believing in Christ, is founded upon man's natural obligation to obey the moral law; for, by virtue of the first command, Adam was bound, and we in him, not only to believe the word of God already revealed unto him, but to believe also every word of God to be revealed, and he was bound to give unto God the glory of all his attributes, not only of these which already did show forth themselves in his works, but also of these attributes, which as yet did not put forth themselves in actual exercise: for as it cannot be denied, that man was bound to give God the glory of his avenging justice, upon his threatening to inflict the punishment of death in case man should sin, albeit he could not see the execution of it before he fell; So also it is manifest, he was bound to give God the glory of his goodness and mercy, albeit no object of showing mercy was yet to be found: and that partly, because it was his duty to give the glory of all perfections unto God, whereof mercy is one; and partly, upon the experience he had of God's manifested goodness in his creation, and God's making a covenant with him about eternal life, upon so easy and equitable terms: upon the same ground, even after the fall, Adam was bound not to despair, nor fly, nor hide himself from God, from whom it was impossible he could escape.

It cannot then be reasonably denied, but man by the law of nature, is bound to give credit to God when he speaketh, and bound to trust in God when He offereth himself as a friend and a father to him, and when God bids him seek his face, he is bound to obey him, and seek his face, and to follow after more and more near communion with him.

It is true indeed, that Adam in his integrity, could not formally and actually believe in God as a Redeemer: partly, because this mystery was not yet revealed; partly, because he, not having yet sinned, had not need of a Redeemer or of remission of sin; but yet, the power and ability of believing in God, according as God should let forth his will, and the power to adhere unto God, and rest on his goodness and good-will, was given to man in his creation: for, this perfection was a part of the image of God, wherein man was created, even as the habit of showing mercy on the miserable (though such an object was not to be found, while man continued in the state of innocence) was a part of that original holiness in him; and if this ground hold not, sinners by their sinning once, should make themselves free to sin forever after, and exempt themselves from all the duties of the moral law, upon this pretense, that they were unable to give obedience to it, which is most unreasonable. And, 2. Because the hearers of the Gospel esteem themselves able to perform the condition of the covenant of grace offered, and to believe in Christ, yea and to give credit, or not, to what is preached unto them, as they see reason; is it not equitable then to put all men to it, who judge themselves able to perform what is required; to the end that after experience, and trial taken of themselves, they should either acknowledge their natural inability to believe in Christ, and so go seek of God the gift of faith, or else be destitute of all excuse, if they shall not do what they conceive and profess themselves able to do?

Thirdly, it is equitable to crave faith from them who are able to promise morally the obedience of faith, and are able to use the external means leading unto true faith; for, the Lord Himself followed this way in his covenanting with the Israelites, Exod. 19, where the Lord propounds the condition of the covenant, and promiseth to be their God, if they should hearken to His voice, verse. 5,6, the people did accept the condition, and undertook to perform it, verse. 7,8, and upon these terms the covenant was made with them morally, in an external way, which did bind the obligation fast upon them.

Fourthly, by preaching of the covenant of grace, God doth ordinarily bestow grace, and grace for grace, on the redeemed in a time acceptable; and in craving the condition, the Lord giveth grace to accept the condition, and to perform it; and this course is very suitable to God's sovereignty or supremacy, suitable to His wisdom and his justice, and suitable to the freedom of his grace: for, it becometh the absolute supremacy of God, and the liberty of His most holy will, to send the Gospel only to whom He will; it becometh his wisdom, where ever He doth send the Gospel, to make offer of grace indifferently to all the hearers, whether elect or reprobate, that all may be tried, whether they please to receive the offer or not; It becometh his justice to withhold grace from such as refuse the offer of it; and it becometh his wisdom, mercy, grace, truth and justice, both to exact from the elect, for whom Christ did satisfy, the performance of the condition of the covenant, and in the meantime, by the offer of grace, to make them savingly to believe, using the command of believing in Christ for a fit mean to beget faith: hence it is, that saving faith is given only to the elect; which faith therefore, is called the faith of the elect, Tit. 1:1. Hence it is, that the elect are called heirs of the promises, Gal. 3:29, and children of the promise, Heb. 6:17, partly, because they are the children promised to be brought in to Christ, Isa. 53:10, partly, because by the promises they are regenerate to a new life, and by believing in Christ, they obtain righteousness and eternal life: for, 1 Pet. 1:23, they are called begotten again, not of corruptible seed, but of the incorruptible seed of the word of God.

Quest. If it be asked, since faith is so necessary, what is the object of faith?

Ans. We answer, the truth of God revealed in Scripture, or God speaking in Scripture, and promising eternal life upon conditions holden forth in these promises: among these promises, some pertain to the covenant of works, such as, Gal. 3:12, do this and live: and, Matth. 19:17. If thou wilt enter into life, keep the commandments; and sundry other particular promises of blessings, both spiritual and temporal annexed unto the promulgation of the Law; which promises do serve to encourage them to make good their undertaking if they be able, as they conceive they are, and to humble them when they shall find by experience, that neither threatening nor promises can make them to fulfill that law. Beside the promises annexed to the covenant of works, there are other promises, which pertain to the covenant of reconciliation, and tend to the making men embrace the covenant of grace, and to continue therein, such as these which are propounded in the Gospel, for giving unto the believer all the sure mercies of David, and the benefits purchased by Christ. And of this sort, some are more general, some more special, some of them belong to this life, some of them to the life to come: for, true godliness comprehending faith and the fruits of it, hath the promises both of this life, and of the life to come: of all these promises, the foundation and fountain is the covenant of Redemption (whereof we have spoken, Chap. 4.) wherein Christ promiseth to the Father to do his will, and the Father promiseth to Christ as Mediator and head of the Church, in favors of the redeemed, that he shall see his seed and be satisfied, and the pleasure of the Lord shall prosper in his hand: upon this covenant of Redemption, all the promises, made to the Church, do depend, whether they be absolute promises, whether conditional promises, whether qualified promises, which are like unto conditional. Absolute promises we call (for example) such as do promise absolutely the taking away the heart of stone and the conversion of the Elect, and their perseverance and salvation, Jer. 31:31,32. &c. and 32:40. Such are the promises of gathering, edifying propagating and perpetuating of the Christian Church to the worlds end, as Math. 16:18. Upon this rock I will build my Church, and the gates of hell shall not prevail against it. Which sort of promises, do serve to move men to come and embrace Christ; and after men have fled to Christ, in whom all the promises are Yea and Amen, the believer may make application and comfortable use of all the precious promises of righteousness and eternal life, set forth in the Gospel. Conditional promises are such, as make offer of Christ and reconciliation to the hearers of the Gospel, upon this condition, that in the sense of sin and fear of wrath, they fly to Christ as the only and sufficient remedy of sin and misery. Qualified promises like unto conditional, are these that have in them some qualification of the person who is already a believer, and do seem to make that qualification or designation of the believer to be a condition of the blessing promised therein: which promises, if they be well considered do presuppone the qualified person, to whom the promise is made, to be both a believer and also to be evidently endued with the named quality; as for example, Math. 5. Blessed are the merciful, the peace-maker, the meek, the mourners, the poor, the sufferer of persecution for the Gospel, or for Christ, &c. which virtues, if the person be not a believer in Christ, do as yet signify nothing in him, nor do not entitle the man to this Gospel-blessedness; and being the designations of believers, they give the persons endued therewith, encouragement to go on and increase in that grace and all other graces, that they may thereby more and more give evidence of their being real believers: Such also are the promises which are made to the confident waiters on God, rejoicers in God, lovers and fearers of God, &c. In which promises, grace for grace to be derived out of the fullness of Christ, is promised to the believer. Some promises design fit persons to enter in covenant, and do invite them to come to Christ, Such as are, come unto me all ye that are weary and heavy loaden, Matth. 11:28. And Ho! Everyone that thirsts, come to these waters, &c. Isa. 55.

And besides these promises which contain the condition of the covenant, made to them who embrace the condition, and do already believe, such as is, they that believe in me, shall not perish, but shall inherit eternal life; there are also promises conditional, serving to make men who profess faith in Christ to be real and steadfast in the covenant wherein they are at least outwardly, and solemnly entered, such as, John 15:7,10. If ye abide in me, and my words abide in you, ye shall ask what ye will, and it shall be done unto you, and if ye keep my commands, ye shall abide in my love, &c. And, John 12:26. If any man serve me, him will my father honor; and, John 14:21, he that loveth me, shall be loved of my father; and I will love him and manifest myself unto him.

Obj. Seeing it is certain, that the condition of the covenant of grace, is not the doing of one or more works, but faith receiving Christ offered, without respect to our works, as any part of the condition; and seeing the condition of the covenant, is not the having, or exercising of such and such virtues, but the receiving of Christ through faith unto righteousness and eternal life, by the man who hath renounced all confidence in his own works; how cometh it to pass, that such conditional promises are made to them that are endued with, and do exercise, such virtues?

Ans. Albeit the endeavor to work good works, or the exercise of such and such virtues prescribed by Christ, cannot be the condition of the covenant (for then no man could close covenant with Christ till first he shall find these virtues in himself, and have given proof of his constant exercise thereof) yet such conditional promises are made use of after a man hath closed covenant with Christ by faith, as conditions required in a true believer, to evidence the sincerity of his faith. And that because many make pretense of their faith in Christ, and yet do turn the grace of God into wantonness, and do no ways set themselves to new obedience unto God law, and are no ways careful to bring forth fruits suitable to professed repentance, but are indulgent to their vicious and fleshly lusts, and in effect do renounce all endeavor to exercise good works instead of renouncing a carnal confidence in good works: Therefore God doth put the endeavor to exercise Christian virtues on all professed believers, as a condition distinguishing a sincere believer from an hypocrite, least any man should please himself, because he is externally in the covenant of Grace, while, it may be, as yet his faith is but a dead faith, not working by love: Against which sort of pretended believers James (chap. 2.) disputeth. Such conditional promises are directed toward them that are outwardly already in covenant, and do serve for these several uses.

First, that such as both profess faith in Christ and are endeavoring the duties required in such conditional promises, may acknowledge, that they have obtained of the Lord grace for grace, grace to believe and grace to bring forth the fruits of faith.

Secondly, that the honest hearted may be encouraged to set upon these duties, and may hope to be furnished for them, out of the rich fountain of Christ's grace, John 1:16.

Thirdly, they serve to make such as believe in Christ, when they feel the in-lake of any such commanded duty, or the bitter root of any vice in themselves, to humble themselves in the sense thereof, and to fly more earnestly to Christ the Redeemer, that first they may be covered with his righteousness, and then from him receive the power of the holy Ghost, to bring forth good fruits, as he hath promised, John 15:5. If ye abide in me, ye shall bring forth much fruit.

Fourthly, they serve to make believers in Christ subject themselves to the order of the operation of the holy Ghost who giveth grace for grace, and worketh one grace before another in his own order, as the foresaid promises do import

Fifthly, they serve to stir up believers in Christ, to the love and exercise of such and such virtues, in the hope of the promised reward.

Sixthly, they serve to move believers to join one virtue to another, for certifying themselves of their own calling and election by their growth therein, 2 Pet. 1:3,4,12.

Last of all, they serve to make these who are destitute and void of such qualifications, and are careless to have them, manifest to themselves and others, that they are blind, and cannot see a far off: and that they have forgotten that they were in baptism, ecclesiastically purged form their old sins, 2 Pet. 1:9.

Obj. How can this offer of grace to all the hearers of the Gospel, and the solemn making of a covenant with all that profess they do accept of the offer, stand with the doctrine of election of some, and reprobation of others, or, with the doctrine of Christ's redeeming of the Elect only, and not of all and every man?

Ans. The election of some and reprobation of others, was made clear of old by God's making offer of grace unto, and covenanting with, one nation only, and not with any other. Psa. 147:19,20. He showed his word unto Jacob, his statutes and his judgments unto Israel; he hath not dealt so with any nation, and as for his judgments they have not known them.

2. And the offer of grace to all hearers of the Gospel, and covenanting with all that profess to accept the offer, do consist with the election of some only, as well now as of old when God made a covenant external and conditional with all Israel, of whom the great part were not elected to life, and of whom it is said, albeit they were in number as the sand of the sea, yet a remnant of them only were to be saved Isa. 10:22. For, by this course, God was not frustrate of his purpose and fruit of his covenanting with the mixed multitude of Israelites; for, the Elect by faith obtained righteousness and life, but the rest were blinded, Rom. 11:7.

3. This common offer of grace to all the hearers of the Gospel and the making of a moral covenant with all that do profess that they accept the offer, may stand with the doctrine of Christ's redeeming the Elect only, no less now, then of old, when Christ did make offer of grace to them that were not his sheep, John 10:26, and did receive sundry in among his disciples in external covenant, who did afterward forsake him, John 6:66, but yet he did save, and doth save all his Elect sheep whom the father hath given unto him, Joh. 10:65.

And however this doctrine soundeth harsh in the ears of many, when they hear of any reprobate or not elected, or when they hear that Christ did not lay down his life for all and every man, but for the Elect only, and proud men cannot submit themselves to the truth; yet this doctrine, is found to be most true: for, Christ the Redeemer, teacheth us, Math. 22:14, that many are called and few are chosen. And the Apostle teacheth us the same, for (Rom. 9:15) he citeth Moses to prove the point; I will have mercy on whom I will have mercy, and I will have compassion on whom I will have compassion; and, ver. 18. God hath mercy on whom he will have mercy, and whom he will he hardeneth. And the Evangelist (John 12:37-40) teacheth us, that there is a number, to whom God hath decreed not to give grace to believe in Christ, albeit they shall hear him preached unto them, from Isa. 6:9,10, but to the Elect only, ver. 13. And, chap. 53:1, he teacheth, that few shall believe in Christ, yea, none save the Elect, to whom the arm of the Lord shall be revealed. And our Lord Jesus teacheth the same, John 6:37,44, that all the Elect shall come to him, and that no more then the father shall powerfully draw unto him, can come unto him.

Obj. But there is another forged way of propounding this covenant which sundry learned men hold forth, who have made many disciples and followers of their opinion, because of the seeming plausibleness of their doctrine: wherein they teach, that Christ Jesus hath died not only for all sorts of men, but also for all and every man, as well for them that perish as for them that are saved; and that albeit he hath not purchased righteousness and life eternal determinately to any man, yet he hath purchased by this universal redemption, power to every man's free-will, to believe in Christ and persevere in his obedience, without any special operation of the holy Spirit in one more then another. And this power of man's free-will, wherewith every child of Adam they say is born, they call by the name of universal grace, albeit in effect it is nothing but universal unrenewed nature, common to every man.

Ans. We answer, how learned soever the teachers of such doctrine seem to be, yet in this doctrine they are not taught of God: Over such men's learning and wisdom, Christ doth glory (Math. 11:25) saying, I thank thee, O father, Lord of heaven and earth, because thou hast hid these things from the wise and prudent, and hast revealed them to babes: even so Father, for so it seemed good in thy sight. Therefore of such doctrine we say, that it is false, and contrary unto Scripture, how plausible so ever it seem to proud sinners, yea it is a mocking of Christ, and an hindrance of men's repentance and conversion unto God.

1. Their doctrine is contrary to Scripture, because contrary to the covenant of Redemption wherein the Father and the Son Mediator, are agreed upon the persons to be redeemed, to wit, the elect only, given unto the Son to be redeemed; and agreed upon the price of their Redemption, to wit, the obedience of Christ, even to the death of the cross; and agreed upon the graces and gifts to be given to the elect, to wit, all saving graces, as faith, repentance, perseverance, and whatsoever belongs to righteousness and eternal life; and agreed upon the means and way of gathering in the redeemed, out of all tongues and kindreds and nations, prudently and prosperously, as is proven from Scripture, Chap. 4, and shall be more confirmed in the next following chapter.

2. Their doctrine it mocketh Christ, because it chargeth Christ with folly in His making covenant so, as neither God's justice nor man's common wisdom, would allow, to lay down the price of his blood,

and not be sure who should be saved by his blood, to pay as much for Judas as for Peter, to redeem all and every man, and yet put the disposing of the benefit of Redemption, and fruit of his death out of his own hand, into the hand of men's free-will, to make of it something or nothing as they pleased; to buy a possibility unto men to save themselves actually, without the special grace of the holy Ghost, and to cut himself off from having the glory of the actual conversion of sinners, as far as he is from the blame of men's remaining in sin and infidelity; for, they say he hath purchased alike power to all and every man's free-will, to believe or remain in infidelity as they please; if they use it ill, bear they the blame; if they use it well, they have the praise. They make him to lay down his life for all and every man, and to purchase unto all and everyone, power to believe in him, and yet never to purpose to make offer of the Gospel to the thousand part of men. These and many more blemishes they cast by their doctrine upon the wisdom and power, and grace of our Lord Jesus, who is infinitely wise and holy in all his doings.

3. This doctrine is a great hindrance of men's repentance and conversion unto God, and to the exercise of all holy duties; for, whosoever believeth this their doctrine, he cannot renounce nor deny his own wit, worth, and ability, that he may come humbly unto Christ and follow him, but he must stand to this conceit of himself, which this doctrine teacheth him: yea, such a man cannot say to God in humble and hearty prayer, open mine eyes, that I may behold the wonders of thy Law, and teach me thy statutes; he cannot in earnest say with David, incline my heart to thy testimonies, and not unto covetousness: for, he hath (in his conceit) this power of free-will in himself, by common gift to every man, he cannot heartily thank God (if he seem to himself to do any good) for giving him both to will and to do of

his good pleasure; for, this he hath in his own hand, as this deceitful doctrine persuadeth him.

Obj. But some there are who maintain the decree of Redemption, and covenant between God and Christ (which in substance, is one with the decree) to be absolute, concerning the powerful and invincible conversion, perseverance and salvation of the elect; but concerning the rest of the world, they tell us of a conditional decree of saving everyone who shall believe in Christ Jesus, which doth make some difference from what is said before.

Ans. There is indeed an offer to be made to all the hearers of the Gospel, to whom God in his providence doth send his messengers, who are appointed to make offer of peace and reconciliation through Christ, upon condition of hearty receiving it, even to such as the Lord knoweth will reject the offer altogether; against whom, his sent messengers, are to shake off the dust of their feet, for a witness against them, Matth. 10:13-15, which accordingly was done by Paul and Barnabas, Acts, 13:46,51, and our Lord made offer of himself to his covenanted people the Jews, who did not receive him, John 1:11,12, and this is to be done according to one of the articles of the covenant of Redemption, concerning the prudent way and manner of Christ's singling forth his own elect, from the rest of the world; But this doth no ways import, or infer, an universal conditional Redemption or any conditional decree of God: for, there is a vast difference between a conditional decree of God, and a decree for bringing about God's purpose, by offering peace unto men upon a condition. A conditional decree presupposeth, that God is not resolved what to do about them to whom he shall make offer of peace upon condition, but that he doth suspend the determination of his own will, till the offer be made, and the man hath refused or accepted of the condition propounded unto him; which sort of decree cannot be in God, to whom are known all his own works, and all men's works from the beginning, Acts, 15:18, and who doth all things according to the determinate counsel of his own will, Ephes. 1:11. But a decree to offer peace, upon condition of believing in Christ, is a wise mean both of hiding and executing his own secret decree, and putting the persons to whom he makes the offer unto trial; that after the drawing forth of the natural enmity and backwardness, which is in all men to come unto Christ, till they be drawn by God, He may have mercy on whom He will, and take the refuse at the hands of others for the glory of His justice and grace, according as He hath determined in Himself. The one way determineth man, as God willeth; the other way determineth God, as man willeth. Moreover such a conditional decree concerning all the rest of mankind, beside the elect, is inconsistent with the Scripture, and the way of God's dispensation toward the most part of mankind: for, it was not God's purpose to make the offer of grace, upon condition of believing in Christ, to all and every man, Psal. 147:19,20. He showeth his word unto Jacob, His statutes and His judgments unto Israel, He hath not done so with any nation. And as for His judgments they have not known them. This same doth Moses insinuate, Deut. 4:7,8, and for his dispensation, experience in all ages showeth, that the grace of the Gospel, is not offered to all and everyone, and so they cannot be said to refuse the condition, who never have the offer of grace upon condition; for, our Lord giveth us ground so to reason, speaking of them who should refuse the offer of the Gospel, Joh. 15:22, if I had not come and spoken unto them, they had not had sin, (to wit, the guiltiness of rejecting the offer made in the Gospel) but now they have no cloak for their sin. Wherein also he giveth a reason wherefore the offer is made to them, whom he knew would refuse the offer, to wit, that they may be rendered inexcusable, and be without the cloak or pretense of this allegiance, that if they had gotten the offer, then would they have believed and repented: for, this is the pride of Adams posterity, they conceive they can believe and obey God, if he shall be pleased to reveal His will to them. And this is suitable to the covenant of Redemption; which, because it was not made for the saving of all and every man, therefore it was not God's purpose to reveal his Gospel, and make offer of his grace to all and everyone, but out of all sorts of men to call effectually the elect, sending the Gospel where they live, or bringing them to the place where the Gospel is preached, that the predestinate might be of purpose effectually called, and justified and sanctified and saved, Rom. 8:28,30, and because the elect and predestinate were to live in the civil society of the rest of the world, it was agreed and decreed, that the offer of the Gospel, should be made to all indifferently where God should send his messengers, because God had determined to bring about the salvation of the elect, so wisely and holily, as none of the hearers of the Gospel should be stumbled, or hindered from embracing the offer made to all the hearers indifferently, without letting any man know of his election, till he have received Christ offered to him and other self-condemned sinners, or declaring any man reprobate in particular, to whom he maketh offer of grace.

Obj. But except we grant a universal redemption and the universal grace (as they call it) of the power of free-will to all and every man, how shall we satisfy ourselves about God's dispensation toward them, who live without the Church, strangers and aliens from the commonwealth of Israel?

Ans. As for the elect among them, either they shall be brought to the hearing of the Gospel where it is preached, or the Gospel shall be sent unto them where they do live; and for the rest, the Lord dealeth with them on the terms of the covenant of works, the power of keeping whereof, albeit they have lost in Adam, yet they are not loosed from the obligation and penalty of violating thereof, and even they have not laid aside the proud opinion of their ability to follow virtue, and eschew vice as they please. And the course which God followeth concerning them, the Apostle showeth us, Rom. 2:12-15. As many as have sinned without the written law (saith he) shall perish without the law, &c. for, when the gentiles which have not the law (to wit, the written law given to the Church) do by nature the things of the law; these having not the law, are a law to themselves.

Obj. But if the doctrine of redemption of the elect only unto life, be maintained, and power of free-will to believe and obey the Gospel, be not given to every man, specially of these that have the offer of the Gospel, and that without any special operation of the holy Ghost, how can it be said, that God dealeth justly, in earnest and fairly, with miserable sinners, when he exhorts, requests and obtests all that hear the Gospel, to come to Christ, and persevere in obedience of the faith, when he knoweth that none of them have power to believe or obey, and that to many of them he hath no purpose ever to give grace to repent and believe that they may be saved?

Ans. First, what can the patrons of the power of men's free-will, speak against the justice and goodness of God, when they hear his complaint against Israel, Psal. 81:8-10. &c. Hear O my people, and I will testify unto thee O Israel, if thou wilt hearken unto me, there shall be no strange God in thee, neither shalt thou worship any strange god; I am the Lord thy God, which brought thee out of the land of Egypt; open thy mouth wide, and I will fill it; but my people would not hearken to my voice, and Israel would none of me, So I gave

them up to their own hearts lust, and they walked in their own counsels. What can they say against God's justice and fair dealing, when
he, having drawn forth to light, by his long continued preaching of
his word, the obstinate enmity of the reprobate multitude against
him, opened up his decree against all that sort in the sad message
committed to Isaiah, Chap. 6:9,10. Go and tell this people, hear ye
indeed, and understand not; see ye indeed, but perceive not: make
the heart of this people fat, and make their ears heavy, and shut their
eyes, least they see with their eyes, and hear with their ears, and
understand with their heart, and convert and be healed, verse. 13, yet
there shall be a tenth part, the holy seed, (to wit, the elect) shall be
the substance thereof? And of this prophesy use is made, when the
multitude of misbelievers was like to obscure the glory of Christ, Joh.
12:37-42, they heard the offer of grace preached by Christ himself, and
saw his manifold wonders, yet they believed not, neither could they
believe, because God had rejected them, as John doth prove from the
prophesy of Isaiah.

Secondly, Is it not fair dealing, when the Lord professeth, that his
word shall be preached, and his wonders manifested (for the elects
cause, albeit they were but as a tenth part) to a cursed and reprobate
multitude, who should hear and see without his blessing, and in his
dispensation, doth in effect as he hath professed? As it is a reasonable
answer of a husband man and Gardener to his child, asking him, why
he beats the whole sheaf and watereth all the Garden, seeing the
sheaf is most part straw and chaff, and the garden full of weeds, to
say to his child, that he beats the sheaf, that he may sever the corn
from the straw and chaff, and that he watereth the ground, where
herbs and weeds do grow together, that he may make both to come
up above ground, and after that, may pull out the weeds, and foster

the herbs for the masters use? So it is a reasonable answer to such as cavil against the preaching of the Gospel, to a mixed multitude of elect and reprobate, to say that the Gospel is preached to both, for the conversion of the elect, and bringing to light the hatred of the reprobate against God, and the offer of his grace.

Thirdly, we grant the Lord knoweth men's wickedness and inability to obey his commands, and their natural enmity against him; but he knoweth also, that all men by nature are proud and puffed up with the conceit of their own wisdom and righteousness, and ability, so as they will not acknowledge their sinfulness, nor be sensible of their misery and danger of perdition, but do entertain a high esteem and opinion of themselves, and in special this, that they love God above all things, and that they can do anything commanded, at least in such a measure as may reasonably satisfy God, as is to be seen in the example of the Israelites undertaking, Exod. 19, therefore, God, in His wisdom before he convert any man, doth pull down this false conceit, by putting his ability to proof by the preaching of the law, to the intent, that as the Lord knoweth what is in man, so man may know it also both in his own and other men's experience: and this is brought to light yet more clearly by the preaching of the Gospel, wherein albeit God make the precious offer of life and salvation to every hearer of the Gospel, if he will acknowledge his sin, and betake himself to Christ; yet no man of himself will either believe or receive the offer, but will go on in his own counsel and ways, till God by his grace convert him. This sickness is common both to the elect and the reprobate, but when the natural perverseness of both is manifested, God cometh and maketh the difference of the one from the other, out of his mere grace, by drawing the elect powerfully to Christ and letting the rest go on to their own perdition in his righteous judgment.

And our Lord doth so expound the matter, John 8:47. He that is of God, heareth God's words; ye therefore hear them not, because ye are not of God.

Fourthly, the Lord professeth plainly, that in the dispensation of his word and works of providence, he intendeth the trial of men, and the discovery of their hearts to themselves and to others; and what fairer dealing can there be then this? For, Exod. 16:4. He tells them, that he will rain down Manna upon them, to prove them, whither they will walk in his law or not: and, Exod. 20:20. He tells them, he will give them his law and preaching of his word, to prove them, that his fear might be before them: and, Deut. 8:2, that the dispensation of his providence toward them, all the forty years in the wilderness, was to humble them, and to prove them, to know what was in their heart, whether they would keep his commands or not: and, Deut. 13:1-3, that he would suffer false prophets to arise among them, to prove them, and to try whether they would love the Lord their God with all their heart. And to this same intent, we are advertised, that Christ should be not only a tried stone, but also a stone for trial, set for the ruin of some, and raising up of other some, Isa. 28:16,17, and 8:14, compared with Luke, 2:34,35, for, by this manner of dispensation, the Lord maketh manifest, that both the elect and reprobate are concluded under sin and unbelief of themselves, and that no man can come to Christ, except the Father draw him, that he may have mercy on whom he will have mercy. And this manner of probation of men by a common offer of grace unto all, is a part of that prudence, whereby Christ, by his conditional promises and exhortations, and the preaching of the Gospel to all hearers, maketh all these that are outwardly called, to be without excuse, and fisheth forth the elect out of the sea of sin and misery, and out of the society of those that perish:

of which prudence, Isaiah speaketh, chap. 52:13. Behold, my servant shall deal prudently and prosper, and be extolled, and be very high.

Wherefore this wisdom of God in converting the elect, without giving cause of stumbling unto any of the rest, is rather to be admired and praised, then to be disputed against, as we are taught, Rom. 11:33-36. O the depth of the riches, both of the wisdom and knowledge of God, how unsearchable are his judgments, and his ways past finding out?

Obj. But for all this, the carnal wisdom of proud men is such, as neither is it subject to God, nor indeed can be, but standeth in hostile enmity against him, and will not be quiet, but when it heareth what is said, Rom. 9:18, that God will have mercy on whom he will have mercy, and whom he will he hardeneth, will say, as it is, verse. 19, why doth God yet find fault? For, who hath resisted his will? This doctrine, say they, doth hinder men's repentance altogether.

Ans. We answer with the Apostle, verse. 20. Nay but O man, who art thou that repliest against God? Whether dost thou compear procurator for the reprobate and for Satan the enemy of God, to quarrel and dispute with God anent his righteous decrees? If thou wilt avow this, we leave thee and all such proud and presumptuous misbelievers of plain doctrine to reckon with your Judge. But if thou speak only for thyself, we shall let thee see, that this doctrine shall not hinder thee from repentance. If then thou shalt say, I will not dispute against God, but do desire earnestly to be satisfied about myself, for I believe, that many are reprobate and few are chosen; and my fear is, that I be found of the worst sort, and do not know how to rid myself of my doubts and fears. For answer, we shall deal with thee in a friendly manner; and, first, we put thee in remembrance, that God hath served an inhibition on all men, not to meddle with the secret counsel of God, Deut. 29:29. The secret things belong to the Lord our God, but these things that are revealed belong unto us and our children forever. Therefore do not hearken to this suggestion, but go about thy duty. We ask then, first, art thou convinced of thy sin and ill deserving? If thou say, I am a sinner, and cannot answer for one of a thousand of my by gone sins, for which God may justly, and I fear he shall in effect reject me, we answer unto thee, it is to good purpose that thou are so far convinced of sin, as to judge thyself worthy of death, and utter extermination from his mercy: mean time be comforted thus far, that thou art not of the number of those who confide in their own righteousness, nor of the number of them who trust in their own strength, or power of their free-will.

We ask again, doth thy by gone life displease thee? And wouldst thou have thy sins forgiven, and thyself reconciled with God? Doth Christ, offering himself in the Gospel, please thy soul, when thou hearest from his word, that he craveth nothing of thee, save that thou welcome his offer, and consecrate thyself to him, that so in him thou mayest have righteousness and sanctification and salvation? If thou answer, that the searcher of hearts knoweth thy hearty desire to be reconciled to God in Christ, to live before him hereafter as a reconciled child, there is good hope of salvation for such a one as thou art.

Thirdly, we say, seeing thou hast heard the law convincing thee of sin, and hast believed God's word so far, why dost thou not believe him also, when in the Gospel thou hearest his offer and call unto all self-condemned sinners, to come unto Christ, and rest their weary souls upon him? Who hath excepted thee from the embracing of mercy offered in Jesus Christ? Look therefore what his word saith to all sinners flying for refuge unto Christ, who is the hope set before sinners, and leave him not, whatsoever be thy fears; for, he that hungereth and thirsteth for righteousness through Christ, shall be satisfied.

CHAP. VII. - For a further clearing and confirmation of the doctrine about the three Covenants, from Jer. 31, and Heb. 8.

THE PROPHET JEREMIAH GIVETH us a short compend of the former doctrine anent these three covenants, chap. 31, verse 31, &c. whereof the Apostle giveth a clear commentary, Heb. 8, verse 6,7, &c.

As to the covenant of Redemption, it is here presupposed to be past, as the Apostle, expounding this place of Jeremiah, giveth us to understand, while he showeth us, that the covenant of grace was no other ways purchased, then by the Mediation of our Lord Jesus, transacting about the covenant of Redemption with the Father. And that he may give us to understand this,

1. Christ is called the Mediator of a better covenant, Heb. 8, to wit, of the covenant of Grace.

2. The covenant of Grace is designed by the name of a Testament, which giveth us to understand, that Christ the Mediator, did not ob-

tain the making of this covenant on a less price then the laying down of his life, that all the benefits contained in these better promises, might first be his goods, to dispone upon, as he pleased; and that he being resolved to die, did make his Testament, and leave them all in legacy to the redeemed, his heirs and assignees, designed from eternity.

3. The Mediator making his Testament, is called Jehovah, not a mere man, but God to be incarnate, making an unchangeable Latter-will or Testament, which of necessity required the death of the Testator, that it might be ratified, Heb. 9:15,16, and the death of a Testator not a mere man, but the Son of God to be incarnate and to die, who had life in himself, that he might lay down his life, and take it up again.

4. The goods which he purchased according to the covenant of Redemption, and left in legacy to his heirs, are all and every blessing which do belong to godliness and life eternal, as remission of sin, and writing of the law in their hearts, &c.

5. The redeemed, and designed heirs, are not all and every man, but the elect only, these that were to be saved only, and who were to be effectually called, and endued with the saving knowledge of God, who from the least to the greatest, were all of them to know the Lord: not such as were the reprobate fathers, nor their unbelieving children, but the chosen society of the Israel of God and of Christ's family, the house of Judah, which is the tribe of Christ; for, the Apostle doth extend these promises unto the covenant between God and the elect, to be gathered under the Evangel unto Christ, out of Jews and Gentiles.

As to the covenant of works, it is certain, first, that God made a covenant of grace in substance, and upon the matter with the fathers

that were brought out of Egypt, as we may gather from the consideration of the parties and articles of that covenant: for, albeit God
repeated the covenant of works, and declared the force of the law,
for binding the curse upon all transgressors thereof; yet he did press
the law on them in order unto their reconciliation, by the sacrifice of
the Lamb of God, to be in due time offered up, and did teach them,
that Christ was the end of the law, for righteousness to everyone that
believed.

2. It is certain, that in the framing of this covenant of grace, between God and the visible Church of the fathers, God did make the
promises of righteousness and eternal life and spiritual blessings,
under the veil of temporal types, upon conditions more hard and
difficile in appearance, then the new covenant doth require: for, this
the Apostle showeth to us plainly, Heb. 8:6.

3. It is certain, that the un-believing Fathers did not take up, nor
understand the covenant of Grace, but turned it over in a covenant
of Works, which is manifest by comparing the words of Jeremiah
and the commentary thereupon by the Apostle: For, Jeremiah saith,
that they did transgress the Covenant, albeit God did show himself
a husband unto these un-believing Fathers; that is, they changed the
covenant of Grace in a covenant of Works of their own framing, and
transgressed that Covenant also. And the Apostle saith, they did not
continue in that covenant, because they changed it to themselves
in a covenant of Works, according to which Covenant God did deal
with them: for, instead of being a husband to them, he exacted of
them the penalty of the broken covenant of Works, and Lorded it over
them, and did not regard them. Heb. 8:6. For, they sought after the
righteousness of works, and not to have righteousness by faith; and
therefore did he despise them, and dealt with them after the tenor

of the covenant of Works. And it is observable, that the words of Jeremiah do comprehend the Apostles meaning; for, the words may bear both, that God was a husband unto them, to wit, in making a covenant of Grace with them; and that he dealt with them as a Lord over them, by exacting of them the penalty of the broken covenant of Works, and of the rejected covenant of Grace.

As to the covenant of Grace, the Apostle speaketh of it in express terms, first, by God's promising that he would make a new Covenant with the house of Israel and Judah.

Secondly by his setting better promises before them then these were which were made to the Fathers in the wilderness.

Thirdly, by his giving no other cause of bestowing so great blessings on them, but his own good-will and pleasure.

Fourthly, by his requiring no other condition of them but faith, that they who feel in themselves, the want and need of the promised blessings, and are convinced of their own unworthiness, might give credit unto God that maketh the promise, and so embrace the promises, and apply them to their own use.

As to the external dispensation of the Covenant, it is certain, first, that it was common to all that were externally called, to all the members of the visible Church: for, the covenant made in the wilderness with the elect Fathers and reprobate, with the believers and un-believers, with those that rejected the covenant of Grace and the offer of Righteousness by faith, and with those who looked through the veil afar off to Christ coming, and were saved, was one and the same.

2. It is certain, that the external form of the covenant of Grace, was more obscure and veiled over by the types and figures of the Levitical ceremonies before Christ came; but after his coming, it was propounded in clearer and better promises.

3. A day is set, to wit, the fullness of time, when these shadows and typical figures should be abolished, and the grace of God should be set before his people, to be looked upon with open face.

4. And yet, the grace of God was not so hid and obscurely propounded to the Church before Christ's coming, as it could not be taken up by the children of God; for in the midst of the shadows and dark types the star-light of gracious promises did shine, and the doctrine of the new Covenant, was in substance holden forth by the Prophets; and one instance thereof doth appear in this place of Jeremiah.

As to the internal covenant of Grace, first, these things which are promised in that Covenant, do declare in what state God doth find men whom he doth convert and draw into covenant with himself; for, when the Lord taketh in hand, that he will write his law in their heart, that he will teach them himself to know him, by the teaching of his Word and Spirit; and that he will forgive their sins, he presupposeth, that lawless rebellion did reign in them, with blindness of mind and hardness of heart; and that the Elect, by nature, are without law, without God, without faith, before he reform them according to the Articles, or tenor of the covenant of Redemption.

2. Albeit, by nature, the law be written in men's hearts, as to the knowledge of sundry moral duties, and so far as is sufficient to make them inexcusable for their contravening these sparks of light, Rom. 1:20, and, 2:14,15. Yet, the writing of the law, here promised is spiritual and super-natural, enlightening their minds by the light of God's Spirit, and renewing their heart; and, in effect, the thing promised is actual conversion of them.

3. And seeing conversion is here promised by Christ the Testator absolutely, he hath taken in hand absolutely to effectuate it: for, it is

not said, I will put my law in their heart if they please to suffer me, but determinately, I will put my law, I will write my law in their heart and inward parts, that is, I will make them willing who were averse, and obedient to my law who were rebellious.

4. Christ, the Testator, doth in all this, not satisfy himself by promising the illumination of the mind and the inclining of the heart, for a time; but promiseth also to make a solid and permanent work of it, by making them persevere, which is imported in the words I will put, and I will write it; for, to write it, is as much as to fix and engrave it, that it may remain.

5. The chief head of the Covenant, and which in substance doth contain all blessings, is set down in these words, I will be their God, and they shall be my people: for, by this promise, right is granted unto the true heart-convert and confederate, first, unto God himself, then unto all his benefits, whereof he hath need, in order to righteousness and eternal life: for, they whose God the Lord is, they do live, and shall live forever, as Christ saith, God is not the God of the dead, but of the living, Matth. 22:32. And all particular promises, what are they else but explications of this great and first promise, and applications thereof to his children's cases in particular?

Gifts of the Spirit are promised here, and enduements whereof disciples have need, whereof pilgrims going home to that heavenly city have need: yea, the Spirit himself is promised to them, who is to remain with them to the end of their life, as a director and leader, They shall all know me, saith the Lord, that is, as Christ doth interpret it, They shall be all taught of God, Joh. 6:45.

7. The Lord showeth here, that he will deal with men, in their regeneration and reconciliation, as with reasonable creatures, by preserving and not destroying them in their simple naturals, by main-

taining and not over-turning the liberty of their free-will; I will make a Covenant, saith he, with the house of Judah. Now a Covenant is a free and voluntary Contract.

8. He showeth, that he is Lord and Over-ruler of man's will, who can turn it about as he pleaseth, and that he is not hindered nor impeded to execute and bring to pass, whatsoever he hath purposed to do, by the variable contingency or differency of man's will, but can work upon the will of man, and by the will of man, what pleaseth him; and by second causes, whether working freely and contingently, or by a natural necessity, can wisely, holily and powerfully bring about his own purpose in his set time; the days come, saith he, wherein I will make a covenant with the house of Israel. Wherein he taketh upon him the effectual work of covenanting, promising not only for his own part, but also for the elect of Israel and Judah's part; for, his promise is, that it shall come to pass, that by inclining their will unto reconciliation, they shall willingly consent unto a covenanting with God: for, he saith, I will make a covenant with them; he saith not, if they will, but absolutely, I will make them close a covenant with Me heartily.

9. The party to be converted and to enter in covenant, is not all men, nor every society, but the Church, God's own family; not every nation, but God's people, chosen out of all nations on the whole earth, I will make a covenant with the house of Israel: as it is also cleared, Deut. 7:6-8.

10. The Church of Christ under the Gospel, as the Apostle looketh on this place, is comprehended under the name of Israel and Judah; partly, because Israel hath the priority of all other people in God's covenant; and partly, because all the Christian Church of the Jews and Gentiles, is comprehended under the name of the house of Ju-

dah, which is Christ's tribe, whereof he came, who is the prince and head of all believers and confederate persons, reconciled to God; and partly, because the Israelites or Jews, have this prerogative above all other people and nations on the earth, that of that race of people, the posterity of Abraham, Isaac and Jacob, there shall be in all ages some elected persons till the great bulk of the now scattered people turn Christians, and till the end of the world, Rom. 11:5.

11. No age, old nor young, no sex, man nor woman, nor any external difference of men that can be put between one and another in this life, doth exclude any man from the benefit of this covenant, or commend a man to God that his person should be respected of God, but all and everyone whom God shall externally call, may safely accept the offer of grace, and join themselves to Jesus Christ; for, the grace of God here, is extended unto all degrees and sorts of men, from the least to the greatest.

12. In the meantime God knoweth his own, man be man, both great and small, and with the same love, doth embrace them all; for, the promise is, that all those elect who are known to God, shall know him from the greatest even to the least.

13. The great obstacle which may be supposed to exclude any from coming in to God through Christ, is here removed; to wit, the greatness and multitude of by-gone sins, cast up against the in-coming of some when they are called: The mercy and grace of Christ the Testator, taketh this doubt out of the way, saying, I will forgive their iniquity, and their sins I will no more remember, Jer. 31:34.

14. This promised remission, the Lord will not have limited nor abridged, neither by the number of sins, nor grievousness thereof, nor kinds of sins, but he purposeth and promiseth to take away all iniquity by forgiveness, and to forget their by-gone sins, ver. 34. And

confirmeth this by repeating the promise of not casting them off who shall acknowledge him, ver. 37.

15. From this promise the Apostle (Heb. 10) draweth this consequence, that under the Gospel, or new covenant, there is but one offering for sin; which offering cannot be repeated, in regard that full remission thereby is purchased: For, (ver. 14) he saith, by one offering he hath perfected forever them that are sanctified, and this he proveth from the words of the covenant, ver. 15-17, whence he concludes, ver. 18. Now, where remission of these are, there is no more offering for sin.

16. If any shall ask for the cause of so rich mercy and grace covenanted, he shall find none in man at all. The only cause is set down here, to wit, the will and good pleasure of God, I will forgive their iniquity, saith the Lord, and their sins will I remember no more, that is, I will have mercy on whom I will have mercy.

17. Because the Lord our God and Mediator, is here making his Testament, wherein also he taketh upon him to be executor of his own latter will, and to perform all that is promised, therefore in confirmation, he subscribeth and sets down his name, Jer. 31:35. Thus saith the Lord; and that his subscription may be of weight with all men, he designs himself by his stately stiles or titles, taken from his creation and government of the creatures, Thus saith the Lord, which giveth the sun for a light by day, and the ordinances of the moon and of the stars for a light by night, which divideth the Sea when the waves thereof roar; the Lord of hosts is his name.

This he saith, least the faith of his people should be shaken by their looking to impediments and difficulties, and that they may gather strength and courage to go on in the Lord's way constantly, when they consider the power of God in the workmanship and government of the world.

18. Unto his subscription, he addeth, both witnesses and pledges of his promises, ver. 36. If those ordinances depart from before me, saith the Lord, then the seed of Israel (which comprehendeth the seed of Abraham's faith) shall cease from being a nation before me forever, ver. 36.

19. Last of all, least any man, in the consideration of the grievousness of his sin, or of the apparent impossibility of performing these promises, should doubt, of remission of sins to be granted to the confederate, or of the perseverance of the true believer, or of the perpetuation of the Church, the Lord bids his people that come in to him, be confident and quiet, ver. 37, saying, If heaven above can be measured, and the foundations of the earth searched out beneath, I will also cast off all the seed of Israel for all that they have done, saith the Lord, Now, both these are impossible, that we can measure the heavens, or search the bottom of the earth: Therefore it is impossible, that this covenant and the promises made therein, should fail.

The manner of dispensing the new covenant outwardly and inwardly.

As to the dispensation of this covenant, both outwardly and inwardly, first, this promise of a new covenant, is a challenge against the misbelieving fathers, who slighted the offer of grace and followed after the covenant of works, seeking righteousness by works; which covenant of works, they were not able to perform and it served unto them only for their condemnation: This the Apostle doth collect from this place of Jeremiah, Heb. 8:8. He found fault with the fathers.

Secondly, the Apostle observeth the wonderful mercy of God, that while he is finding fault with the incredulity of the fathers, who lived under this old covenant, he will avenge this their incredulity, ignorance, foolishness and ingratitude, by telling them, that he will make a new covenant and give them that were then living a taste of it, for recovering them, finding fault with them, he saith, the days come, that I will make a new covenant.

Thirdly, this covenant of grace made with the Church, is procured by Christ, to this end, that the covenant of Redemption might be brought unto a real accomplishment by the covenant of Grace. This observation is grounded upon this, that Christ is called the Mediator of this better covenant, Heb. 8:6. For, he will draw up a clear covenant of grace with his people, that the blessings purchased unto them according to the covenant of Redemption, may be applied unto them by this covenant of grace and reconciliation.

Fourthly, the preaching of the promise of this new covenant, is a most fit mean to draw on and close this covenant of grace between God and his people, who are the called according to his purpose: This observation is gathered from Jeremiah's preaching and Paul's preaching of this unto the hearers of the Gospel, to this very intent and purpose.

Fifthly, in the promising and preaching of this covenant of grace, God will have all men's opinions, thoughts and conceptions about this mystery, limited unto, and depending upon, his mouth alone, revealing the same in his Word: This observation is gathered from the Lord's invitation of all men to take heed what he is to say, and what he is to let forth in this matter, Behold the days come, saith the Lord, wherein I will do such and such things, which now I fore-tell I will do.

Sixthly, both the making and way of making a covenant with man, dependeth absolutely on God either to make a covenant or not, to make what covenant he pleaseth to make, upon what conditions he pleaseth, and with what persons he pleaseth to make his covenant. No man ever preveened God, desiring him to make a covenant, but God did preveen all men, he preveened Adam once before his fall, and again by preaching the Gospel in his audience after the fall, he preveened the fathers in the wilderness, he preveened his posterity, that have lived or shall live in the latter days, promising to make a covenant with those who were not come into the world, but were to come long after the promise.

Seventhly, the Lord will have all men to understand, that the end of his covenanting with men, both in that old dark form, and in the new clear form, is his own glory: For, he hath made all things for himself, even the wicked for the day of evil. This observation is gathered, partly, from this, that the Lord bringeth forth his sovereignty for a reason of his rejecting of the misbelieving fathers in the wilderness, I despised them, I regarded them not; I Lorded it over them, as the original may bear. And partly, from this, that he bringeth forth his own will and pleasure, for a reason of his showing grace to their posterity, I will forgive their sins, &c.

8. He showeth also, that in his works he doth not depend upon man, but that all his works are known unto him from the beginning, and that it is determined by himself, what, and how, and by what means, he will do everything. This may appear from this, that he doth fore-tell what he is to do about the saving of his elect, Jews and Gentiles, being no less certain to do what he promised about the posterity to come, then he was certain of what was past already about their incredulous fathers.

9. The Lord will have us to know, that laying aside the considera-tion of his decrees, it is simply in the power of God to punish sin, in

whom he will and to pardon sin through a Mediator, to whom he will, that is, to have mercy on whom he will have mercy, and to pardon whom he will pardon. This is collected from this, that the fathers do sin in the wilderness and justly perish and the posterity do sin and are graciously pardoned.

10. In all this proceeding, no violence is used upon the will of men, whether of them that perish, or of them that are saved. The saved do walk freely and willingly in the way of salvation, as their hearty choice; and these that perish, walk willingly in the way of perdition. God proceeds with both by a voluntary covenant, as this place doth show.

11. In them that perish the meritorious and culpable cause of their perdition is in themselves; but in them that are saved, no cause is found at all, but the cause is found in God's grace allenarly. This is collected from this, that the Lord giveth the reason of the perdition of the misbelieving fathers, from their sins and transgression of covenant, they transgressed my covenant, and I despised them; and of the salvation of their posterity, no other cause but this, their sins I will not remember anymore.

12. The Lord's justice is cleared in the perdition of them that perish, because he gave precepts and promises, and other moral motives, to hinder them from sinning, and to move them to keep his ways, albeit he did not effectually impede their running on to sin according to their inclination, and proneness to follow their own way. This is collected from this, that the Lord saith, he made a covenant with their fathers, and they did break it.

13. It pleaseth God, not only to give his precepts unto men, concerning their duty, but also to condescend so far unto them as to open up in a part his decrees and deep designs about men's salvation,

that they, being admitted somewhat near to the treasures of His wisdom, goodness, justice and mercy, might be so much the more wise, and the more stirred up to discharge their duty, and make use of his dispensation. This we collect from his revealing of the decree of election of the posterity of Israel, and drawing them effectually into a covenant of grace with himself.

14. The Lord doth reveal to the world the doctrine of election unto life, only in the general, and doth not descend to the nomination of them in particular. This is collected from this, that he doth promise to convert and draw into a new covenant of grace, the posterity of Israel and Judah, without naming particularly these that were designed for that salvation.

15. Albeit the Lord keepeth up the names of the elect (except of some few) before their conversion, yet, he giveth forth marks and evidences, whereby after their conversion, they may be known both to themselves and others. This we collect from this, that He sets down infallible marks of the elect, who are to be God's covenanted people or worshipers of God, that they do know God, and have his law written in their hearts and inward parts.

16. As for the reprobation of any man, the Lord hath given no certain mark as long as they live, (except that malicious and willful rejecting and opposing of known Christ Jesus) to the intent that none should dare to exclude, either themselves or others from repentance and hope of mercy, so long as the day of God's longsuffering and patience doth last. This is collected from this, that God doth not make mention of the reprobation of these misbelieving fathers, while they are living, but now long after they are dead; and this mention making of them, is in general only, and not by naming them particularly.

17. Albeit in the dispensation of the covenant of grace, for application of saving mercies, the matter be so wisely carried by God, that both the decree and covenant of Redemption is kept close, as to particular names, and yet it is effectually made out in the applying of grace to individual persons, as the agreement is made between God and Christ Mediator; yet, the covenant of Redemption, is made this far clear, that it did not pass for the conversion and salvation of all and every man, by this evidence, that not so much as the offer of the covenant of grace, and reconciliation shall be made to all and every nation, far less to all and every singular person: but that the people and nation of Israel and Judah is chosen out of all people and nations in the world, comprehending such others as should be called unto their society, and the fellowship of the olive tree among them, as Psal. 147:19,20, holdeth forth. And in this place the whole elect, under the Gospel, are taken up under the name of this one nation.

18. That the decree of election of some, may both be kept up as to particular nomination, and yet have certain execution and be performed, the Lord taketh up all his confederates whether in the letter or spirit also, under the same common name. This is gathered from this, that the misbelieving Israelites that perished in the desert, with whom God made a covenant and they did break it, are designed under the common name of fathers, and are taken up in that covenant under the name of spouse, Jer. 31:32, and the elect posterity are taken up under the common name of the house of Israel and Judah.

19. Such as the covenanters are, in regard of their inward estate, such is the covenant wherein they really are, or such is the covenant in relation to their persons. Unto the reprobate who do change for their part, the covenant of grace into the covenant of works, the

covenant of grace becometh in effect the covenant of works, and is rendered void to them, as the Apostle doth threaten the Galatians, Gal. 5:4, and as did befall the pharisaical fathers, who are here declared as instances; but the covenant of grace unto the elect and true believers, remains still the covenant of grace, from which they do not fall, nor can altogether fall, as the comparison here between the fathers in the wilderness and their elect posterity maketh evident.

20. The Lord hath wisely joined life with the means and way to life and death with the way to death, and will not have that separated which he hath joined. This is collected from this, that the fathers by not continuing in the covenant, are despised and rejected of God, and so perished; but their elect posterity, having the law of God in their hearts, and cleaving constantly unto the Lord, are saved.

21. The Lord will have this doctrine taught where His word is preached, concerning the election of some, and reprobation of other some; of God's covenanting with some people and persons, and not offering a covenant to other some; of covenanting with some in the letter, and with other some in the spirit also, to this end and intent, that men, leaving the searching in particular of that which God hath kept secret in the particular, may follow commanded duties, repent their sins and flee to Christ offered unto them, and take up his yoke upon them, and beware that they neither despair, nor yet presume, or turn the grace of God into wantonness. This we gather from this, that God sendeth forth Jeremiah to preach these things, not only to the visible Church of the Jews going into exile and captivity, but also to all who shall hear this doctrine from him to the end of the world. And the Apostle, repeating this doctrine for the use of the Christian Church of Jews and Gentiles, doth confirm this.

CHAP. VIII. - Of the prudent application of divine covenants in general.

HAVING SPOKEN OF THESE three divine covenants concerning men's salvation, it follows now to speak of the application thereof, first, in general, and then more specially.

In the matter of application, we must, first, look upon God's effectual applying and working in the hearers of these covenants, such effects as he hath intended by these covenants to bring to pass: Next, we must look upon the means whereby he ordinarily doth convey and work his intended works in men. And thirdly, we must look upon the prudent way of use making of these means, both by Pastors and people for people's good.

2. As to the first, the Lord's effectual application, is a real and actual bestowing the good of these covenants upon his own, by way of powerful working on their spirits. Such as are, 1. the giving the grace of understanding of the Scripture; And, 2. the belief of what is understood; And, 3. the application of the doctrine of the law, concerning men's sin and misery, to their own conscience; And, 4. the making them judge themselves according to the law; And, 5. the raising of sorrow in their hearts and fear of wrath; And, 6. the setting of their eye upon Christ for delivery from sin and death; And, 7. the

making them perceive a possibility and probability that they may be saved: And, 8. to have an earnest desire after reconciliation with God in Christ; And, 9. the making of his own to cast themselves over on Christ and to believe on him; And, 10. the making them to consecrate themselves to God in Christ, reconciling the world of mere grace to himself, not imputing transgression to the reconciled through Christ; And, 11. the making them to wonder at the riches of the free grace of God, who in a self-condemned sinner, desirous to be reconciled with him, requireth no personal dignity, no good work, which may commend him to God, but only that he would receive and welcome Christ offered in the Gospel, as the only necessary and sufficient remedy against all sin and misery, requiring no other condition, but that he flee from the curse of the law, and the wrath to come, unto Christ the Redeemer, who offereth himself unto lost sinners in the preaching of the Gospel, that through him the believer may be justified and sanctified, and saved for ever; And, 12. after wondering raised in the hearts of his children, the making them cleave closely to Christ, and to strive against all temptations, which might weaken their faith, and to rejoice in believing, and to be zealous for the Lord's glory, and careful to bring forth more and more fruits of faith and love, and working such other gracious works of his Spirit in his children, as may more and more mortify sin in them, and perfect the image of God in his new creature. This divine, magisterial and effectual application of real blessings, belongeth to God only, and is the end of all ministerial application, which is of the external means appointed of God, to be made use of by men, the blessing whereof must be left to God to bestow, on whom, how, and in what measure, and in what time it pleaseth him, as the Apostle doth show unto us, 1 Cor. 3:6. I have planted, and Apollos hath watered, but God giveth the increase.

3. The external means, which do serve unto the foresaid divine operations, are, 1. The doctrine of life and salvation, set down in the Scripture, to be heard and read by all men, and meditate upon with prayer for a blessing; And, 2. sent ministers, to whom God hath committed the word of reconciliation, by whose ministry disciples may be made unto Christ out of all nations; And, 3. the administration of the Sacrament, whereby they with their children are baptized, and gathered together in several Churches, and put under the government of such Church-officers, as his Testament hath appointed; And, 4. these Churches joined together in the most edifying way of mutual communion, and strengthening one another in true doctrine, pure worship and discipline, which God's providence doth make way for, that the Kingdom of our Lord Jesus may continue and grow in the world, and all his ordinances may be exercised publicly and privately to the best advantage of the Church, for perfecting of the Saints, for the work of the ministry, and for the edifying of the body of Christ, as the Apostle requireth, Ephes. 4:12-14.

4. In the use of these external means, and specially in the application of these three covenants, prudence is required, both in Pastors and people, to which intent and purpose these following considerations may serve.

1. The remedy of every sickness of the conscience, must be grounded on the doctrine of salvation set down in Scripture; which doctrine must first, be known and believed by the party diseased, before he can receive benefit thereby: And therefor that a prudent application of wholesome and saving doctrine may be made, of necessity the party diseased must be acquainted with the doctrine to be applied unto him, before he can make use thereof to his advantage: for, experience teacheth us, how hardly gross ignorants can be convinced

of sin, add how hardly such can be comforted, when their conscience is wakened with the terrors of God, because they neither know from the Word of God, the cause of the terror and anxiety wherein they are, nor can they be capable of the remedy of their evil, except they, first, be catechized in the heads of saving doctrine, held forth in the Law and Gospel, which instruction can hardly be given or received in a short time; and howsoever, a prudent Pastor must make use of time as it is offered, yet when death is near to the party to be instructed, how little is it that can be expected to be done?

2. The order of applying saving doctrine, doth not begin at the application either of the covenant of Redemption, or at the covenant of Grace, but he that will follow a right order, must begin at the law and covenant of works, under the yoke whereof we are all born by nature, children of wrath. And if a man apply that covenant and law to his heart, and subscribe his own ditty and deserved condemnation, then may he turn up his soul to Christ Jesus the Redeemer, and fly to him for refuge, and accept the offer which he makes in his Gospel of a new covenant of grace for pardoning of sin and reconciling unto God in himself the person who is fled unto him, and for sanctifying and saving of him; which covenant, when a chased soul doth consent unto, and layeth hold on Christ offered for relief from sin, wrath, death and hell, then may he ascend by faith unto the covenant of Redemption, and apply to himself with God's allowance all the saving graces purchased by Christ, by that covenant, to all that fly unto him and believe in him.

3. This order of making use of these three covenants, many do not follow, but they begin at the covenant of Redemption, and will either be satisfied about this, whether they be elected or not, given to Christ to be redeemed or not, (which is a secret and not to be inquired into,

save in God's order as we have shown) or else they will not enter upon
the use-making of these means which God hath appointed to bring a
man to repentance and faith in Christ. This is a temptation of Satan,
which if they yield unto, it shall lead them either to resolute profanity
with Cain, or to anxious desperation with Judas.

4. There are some also, who make leap-year of the covenant of
works, and do take no notice of their own natural sinfulness or wrath
due to them, and lying on them by nature; but neglecting this order,
do start a race, and run to a presumptuous avouching of their faith
in Christ, and will thrust in themselves in the number of the elect,
given before the world was, unto Christ to be redeemed and saved,
pretending their believing of the Gospel, when they have not believed
the doctrine of the law, and so do turn the grace of God into lasciviousness and wantonness, and go about the satisfying and fulfilling
of their own lusts. Wherefore it is necessary, that every man who
seeketh to be saved, and hath resolved to follow God's way to attain
unto salvation, do begin first, at the covenant of works, and examine
himself according to the rule of the moral law, how he hath behaved
himself in obedience unto the first and second table, and having
sound a ditty great enough, that he judge himself and pass sentence
on himself as guilty and worthy of everlasting wrath for his sins.
Secondly, when he is convinced of sin and deserved wrath, and of his
own utter impotency to deliver himself, then let him flee to Christ
and lay hold on the grace offered in the Gospel, applying the same
to his burdened conscience, according to the tenor of the covenant
of grace, fully revealed in the Gospel. And, thirdly, when he hath
in earnest consented unto the covenant of grace and reconciliation,
and hath laid hold on Christ, with unfeigned faith, seeking in him
remission of sin, and renovation of life, being resolved by the grace

of Christ, to use the means appointed of him for that end; Now it is time and not till now, to look up unto the covenant of Redemption, and there to read his own name, as it were, written in the book of life, and to acknowledge that the measure of repentance and faith in Christ bestowed on himself now in experience, hath flowed from that fountain of God's love and free grace through Christ.

Except this order be keeped, a man cannot warrantably, and with confidence and comfort, make application of these covenants. Hence it followeth, that it is a preposterous and perilous course which some do follow, and press others to follow, that presently upon the hearing of the Gospel, every man should believe, that Christ hath died for him: for, Christ calleth no man, warranteth no man to come to him, except he, first, do acknowledge his sins, and himself to be worthy of wrath, condemnation and hell for his sins, and to be utterly unable to save himself by any mean, save by Christ: for, (Luke, 5:32) Christ saith, I came not to call the righteous, but sinners unto repentance. Neither doth Christ require of any man, to believe himself to be of the number of Christ's sheep for whom he laid down his life, except he come by faith as a lost sinner to him, and submit himself to his doctrine and discipline, and pastoral care over him: for, (John 17:9) Christ saith, I pray not for the world, but for these thou hast given me out of the world: and no man shall know, that himself is given of the Father to Christ, till first he come in the order foresaid unto Christ, and when he is come to Christ, resolveth to abide with him, then may he say, the Father hath given me to Christ, and drawn me to Christ: for, this is the mark which Christ giveth, John 6:37. All that the Father hath given unto me, shall come to me. And again, verse. 44. No man cometh unto me, except the Father draw him.

3. There is an order also to be observed in the application of the graces offered in the Gospel; for, in the Evangel, first, Christ himself is offered, as the only and sufficient remedy against sin and misery; and next, unto the person that receiveth Christ heartily, all Christ's benefits are promised to come to him by Christ, and are to be found in and through Christ, such as are Justification, Adoption, the indwelling of the holy Ghost, love, joy, peace, gentleness, bounty, fidelity, meekness, temperance and other Christian graces, Gal 5:22, for, no man hath right unto Christ's benefits, before he be a believer in Christ. But so soon as a man, in the foresaid order, is fled unto Christ, and hath laid hold on him by faith, straight way a door and entrance is opened unto him unto the rich treasure of grace, and right is given to him unto all the benefits of Christ; for, all the promises are yea and amen, not before a man come to Christ, not to a man without Christ, but they are all yea and a men in Christ.

4. Therefore they wrong both God and their own selves, who when they come unto the throne of grace, do prescribe unto God another order of working, then he hath set down in his word, craving, in the first place, consolation and sensible peace in their conscience, felt in their hearts; and that God would work some such saving graces in their heart, which the reprobate cannot counterfeit: which directions, if God will take off their hand, and bestow his graces on them sensibly as they prescribe unto him, then they will stand obliged to continue in the faith of Christ; but if they find not their directions obeyed, and their petitions in their order granted, then with grief of heart they begin to complain, and to pretend that they dare not approach unto God or Christ, so long as these petitions are not first granted and felt to be granted.

This temptation doth invert and overturn the order of Gods calling: for, Christ doth not call unto him well-doers, or these that do found their faith upon their own good behavior, and lean to their own works, which they desire to find in themselves, before they fasten faith on Christ; but Christ doth call sinners in their own sense and acknowledgment, who renounce all confidence in their own works, past, present or to come; He calleth such as are lost in their own sense, and do feel themselves utterly unable so much as to think a good thought of themselves, that they may be clothed with the imputed righteousness of Christ, and endued with the spirit of sanctification by him; and Christ's will is, that they who believe in him, abide in him, and suck by faith out of him (as the branches do suck sap out of the tree) grace to bring forth fruits more and more abundantly: for, this is the order which Christ doth prescribe unto his disciples, John 15:5. He that abideth in me, and I in him, the same bringeth forth much fruit: for, without me ye can do nothing. Whosoever therefore will not believe in Christ or do think it is not lawful to approach unto him, till first they find in themselves amendment of life and evident fruits of saving faith, they do in effect change the condition of the covenant of grace, and do suspend their faith in Christ till they find works to build upon, when it were their duty, the more they feel their barrenness, so much the more straitly to lay hold on Christ and hold him fast, and ply him with earnest supplications to make good his promise to them who do abide in him, John 15:5.

5. It is necessary to press every man, who doth believe his justification by faith, that he be careful to observe the moral law, or ten commands, as the perpetual and unchangeable rule of good works prescribed of God: for, Christ came not to destroy the law, but to fulfill it, Matth. 5:17. He hath indeed unto believers in him, dissolved

the covenant of the law, not only by his doctrine, teaching them, that by the works of the law no flesh shall be justified in the sight of God, because by the law, is the knowledge of sin gotten, but no absolution from sin, Rom. 3:20. But also by absolving every believer in him, that walketh not after the flesh, but after the spirit, from all condemnation, Rom. 8:1. Meanwhile he hath not broken the yoke of obedience of the law from off the believer, as he hath broken off the yoke of the covenant of works; but by the contrary, he prescribes to them who come unto him for remission of sin, that they take on his yoke upon them, and bring forth works of new obedience, Matth. 11:29, and this is the order which the Apostle doth prescribe, Tit. 3:8. This is a faithful saying, and these things I will thou affirm constantly, that they which have believed in God, might be careful to maintain good works: these things are good and profitable unto men.

6. The moral precepts of the law are so to be pressed, that the hearers, whether un-converted or converted, may, by them, whether in some measure obeyed or disobeyed, be driven to Christ, that the law may ever, in some sort, be a pedagogue unto Christ: for, before conversion, sin must be made manifest by the law, and the merit of sin committed, must be shown forth, that the man to be converted may see himself in a lost condition, and that he must certainly perish, except he flee for refuge to Christ the Redeemer, that by him he may have remission of sin.

And after a man's conversion, the believer must, by the precepts of the law, be convinced of his duty and inability to perform obedience, except, by grace, power be communicated unto him from Christ both to will and to do. And when he hath gotten grace to give obedience in some measure, yet must he examine his best works by the rule of the commands, and acknowledge the imperfection of his service, that he may be more and more humbled in himself, and glory only in the imputed righteousness of Christ, and withal give unto Christ the glory of any good thing which he hath in any measure done well.

7. The threatening's also all of them, must so be applied in general, as both converted and un-converted may be forced to run to Christ, who only can deliver the un-converted from guiltiness and wrath, and death eternal deserved by sin; and who only can deliver those who are converted from the deserved punishment of their sins, and from the execution of the sentence which the law pronounceth; and who only can make them eschew and hold off the way which God hath cursed.

And it is easy to judge how much cause of humiliation the godly shall have, by daily comparing their actings with the law, and how dear and precious Christ must be to them, who giveth unto them, as many deliverances from death, as they commit sins, and do fail of their obliged obedience to God.

8. A sinner already convicted of sin and impenitency, and hardness of his own heart, and who is grieved for the same, must not be scared nor deterred from going unto Christ, till first he attain such a prescribed measure of contrition as he conceiveth his sins do call for; which measure, un-skillful Physicians do rigidly exact of sinners, who are desirous of repentance, pretending for their rigidity, their fear, lest if such sinners should be so easily admitted unto Christ, the work of repentance should be marred in them, and presumption should have way and be fostered in them: this fear is needless, because it belongs to Christ alone to give repentance, and he came to call sinners (convicted of sin and destitute of repentance in their own estimation and sense) unto repentance, that he may give them repentance. We grant that there is a danger, lest a sinner, lightly

touched with the sting of the conscience, do not well weigh the weight of his sin and the merit of it, and that he go to Christ with his lips only when his heart is far from him; but, on the other hand, there is no less hazard, left he who is destitute of repentance in his own sense, and not permitted to go to Christ to have it, may either be driven to despair, or conceive, that by his own pains on his own heart, repentance must be wrought before he go to Christ, whom God hath exalted with his right hand, to be a Prince and a Savior, for to give repentance unto Israel and remission of sins, Act. 5:31.

We must be wary therefore, lest a burdened conscience in any measure, being excluded from going to Christ till he be in such and such a measure humbled, set himself so upon bodily exercise of ordinances, without daring to go to Christ, as that he put some merit in effect, upon his bodily exercise which he useth, to bring himself unto contrition, or else turn desperately careless, and leave off all using of means.

We need not fear, that instantly upon a sinners coming to Christ, he shall find too soon consolation, and so not be humbled as need were: for, Christ is only wise, and can prudently deal with the sinner coming unto him; he hath eye-salve to give his proud merchant, to let him see his blindness, poverty and misery, as well as gold and garments to the poor and naked: but if any be proud and rich in their own conceit, and approach toward him without sense of sin, he can suspend them from comfort, till first he rebuke and chasten them, and keep them off from felt access a while, till they be truly humbled, and thirst in earnest after pardon and imputed righteousness.

9. As the narrow way to the kingdom of heaven must not be made straighter than God hath made it, So neither must the way be made broader then God hath made it, and reins loosed to men's lusts,

as if believers sins were either none, or but light ones: for, God is not a favorer of sin, and whosoever do turn the grace of God into wantonness, undoubtedly they are ignorant both of the Law and of the Gospel. Wherefore the Law and the Gospel must be so tempered, that on the one hand, none who would be at Christ, and through him at mortification of their sinful nature, be discouraged; and on the other hand, that no man, boasting of his profession of faith, be strengthened in his iniquity: for, this is the true sense and intent of God, both in his threatening's and promises, that none despair, hearing threatening's, but repent and live; and that none presume to sin, upon hearing his gracious promises, but walk in fear before him, Ezek. 33:10-12, to v. 20, and Christ doth blot out from the number of the saved, all them who break off and make void any of the precepts, and do teach men so to do, Matth. 5:19.

10. Because God doth make use of the same arguments in his Word, both for moral suasion and for effectual operation of saving faith, and bringing forth fruits of new obedience; therefore the force of God's arguments and inducements (as occasion is offered) must so be opened up, and sharpened and pressed, that the hearers, being soundly convinced of the holiness, equity verity and necessity of the Lord's commands, may at least be morally persuaded to yield unto them. And to this end, that hearers must be exhorted, that they call to mind and weigh such and such arguments unto duties, that by reasoning with themselves, they may prevail by God's blessing to believe the Word of God; So did Paul, directing his speech to the governor Felix, brash the castle of his conscience with this engine, that he near by took it in, Act. 24:25, and so did he deal with Agrippa, whom he near-by persuaded to become a Christian, Act. 26:28, and this was his endeavor to persuade all his hearers to believe the

truth he taught, 2 Cor. 5:11. Knowing therefore (saith he) the terror of the Lord, we persuade men. And the same Apostle hath taught all Christ's disciples to exercise the faculty of reasoning, in the matter of strengthening their faith and purpose of obedience, that having set before them the arguments which the Word of God doth furnish they may sum up the truth in conclusions drawn there-from, and by holy reasoning, tie themselves to believe and obey the Word of God, Rom. 6:11. Like ways (saith he) by reasoning, reckon ye yourselves to be dead unto sin, but alive unto God through Jesus Christ our Lord. And giveth an example of this reasoning, 2 Cor. 5:14,15. The love of God constraineth us, because we thus judge, &c.

11. Because the Lord divers ways, according to his own wisdom, exerciseth men, that sometime by his longsuffering patience he leads them unto repentance, sometime also by his word and rods, he doth drive them thereunto; therefore let the use of all exercises, all temptations and afflictions, and the use of all benefits and divine dispensations of providence, be carefully made use of, that men may so look upon God's bounty and longsuffering on the one hand, and upon their own sins and ill deserving's on the other hand, as they may be led and constrained in love to seek after so gracious a God, and to flee for refuge unto Christ, mourning for their provoking of justice so oft against themselves; and in whatsoever condition, of prosperity or adversity, to submit themselves to God, however he shall be pleased to dispose of them.

12. The doctrine of reprobation must not be determinately applied to any particular person, how wicked soever he shall for the present appear; neither must the suspicion which any man may have of his own reprobation be fostered, because particular reprobation of this or that person, is among the secrets of the Lord, not to be meddled

with, whereof a man may not give out sentence before the Lord hath revealed his own decree. But on the contrary, all the hearers must be warned and pressed to be wary to entertain any hostile thought of God, or to foster suspicions of him, as implacable, but rather think of him as their faithful Creator; just indeed, yet merciful, longsuffering and bountiful, both to the kind and the un-kind, as they shall find, if they will seek him: for, Satan will press this temptation hard enough, and foster the suspicion which he hath suggested against God, in the minds of them whom God hath afflicted, albeit he get no assistance by any imprudent and un-just application of the Lord's Word, unto this or that particular person to conclude their reprobation.

13. The scope of all doctrine must be this, that sinners may be humbled in the sense of their unrighteousness, indigence, infirmity and unworthiness; and being humbled, may be led unto Christ, believe in him, and be more and more glued unto him, and grow in the love of him, and rest their souls upon him, as God, one with the Father and holy Spirit, worshiping him in spirit and truth, endeavoring according to their vocation to advance his Kingdom in themselves and others. And to this end, let neither on the one hand his incarnation, nor humiliation in the days of his flesh, wherein he was in paying the promised price of our Redemption, derogate anything to the estimation of his person, who is one God with the Father and holy Spirit, God over all blessed forever; Nor on the other hand, his Majesty make sinners stand off, or be afraid to make their address to him; but, by the contrary, that the personal union of the divine and human nature in him, and his clothing himself with the offices of Prophet, Priest and King, may allure all sinners, who hear of him, to come to him as Media-tour, who will not deal with them who come unto him as a judge against them, but as an advocate, Surety, and intercessor for

them, and who will save to the uttermost everyone that come unto
God through him, Heb. 7:25.

14. For trial of a man's regeneration and coming rightly to Christ,
and growing in grace, the exercise of these three duties are necessarily required, to wit, 1. The exercise of repentance, or the entertaining
in himself of the sense of his natural sinfulness and infirmity to do
good, and of the power of inherent corruptions, whereby he may be
made more and more to renounce all confidence in himself, and walk
humbly before God.

2. The exercise of faith, or the daily renewed employing of Christ
for grace, and actual help in all things, as his case requireth.

3. The exercise of love, or the endeavor of new obedience, flowing
from love to God and his neighbor, through Christ.

CHAP. IX. - Of the more special application of divine covenants, for removing the impediments of regeneration.

WE HAVE SPOKEN OF the prudent application of divine covenants in general, it followeth that we speak of the curing of the sicknesses of the conscience concerning regeneration more specially. Some of these sicknesses, do tend to hinder regeneration, that it be not wrought at all, whereof we shall speak God willing in the rest of this first book. Other sicknesses, do tend to obscure the work of regeneration begun, and to foster questions in the regenerate man and make him doubt whether he be regenerate or not? Or whether he be in the state of grace or not? And of these we shall speak somewhat in the second book. And last of all, some cases and sicknesses of the conscience, do tend toward the deceiving of the regenerate man about his present condition, wherein he is, without calling his state in question at the first, and of these we shall speak in the third book.

2. As for the first sort, these cases which impede and altogether mar regeneration, cannot easily be numbered, because of the multitude of deceits, whereby the unregenerate are deluded; but it shall suffice for our purpose, to name some of them only for examples cause; in handling whereof the way of curing other like cases may be observed.

In handling of these cases, it is not to be expected we should follow any exact method, or accurate distinction of one case from another; partly, because many faults may be variously interwoven one with another; partly, because in all these cases, the same faults are found after divers ways to put forth their poison. We therefore, that we may follow the easiest course, shall divide all unregenerate men, impeding their own regeneration, in three ranks. The first rank shall be of those who eschew so far as they can all examination of their own conscience, least it should pronounce sentence of their state and disquiet them. The second rank shall be of those who do judge themselves indeed according to the law of God, but after examination do despair of any remedy. The third rank shall be of those, who make a slight examination of themselves, and upon some slight pretense give our sentence of absolution of themselves which God will not allow.

3. As to the first rank, to wit, of those that eschew all examination of their own conscience, we shall name only seven sicknesses, or impediments hindering their self-examination and passing sentence on themselves. The first is gross ignorance of their natural sin and misery, and of deliverance to be had through Christ, and of the duty required of them that are delivered by Christ. The second is a false religion, or damnable error in judgment about the matters of salvation, and God's worship: In which error, so long as a sinner doth lie, he

cannot be humbled for the damnable course he is in, or put question about his way. The third is dissembled unbelief and atheism, covered over with gross hypocrisy, which under hand doth reject the rule of examination. The fourth is the brutish stupidity of the cauterized conscience. The fifth is a vain pretense of fear to examine themselves, least it drive them to desperation. The sixth is a lazy delaying of examination from day today. The seventh is immoderate care for things of this life.

4. Concerning all these impediments hindering self-examination, these three things are observable in general, 1. albeit all or some of these evils may fall upon the reprobate, yet are they not their proper maladies; for, some of the elect before their regeneration, may lie for a time under one or more of these evils. Wherefore the Pastor, hoping the best of all, because he knoweth not the marks of reprobation, must deal with all his hearers to guard them against all these evils; that the elect, whom God will bless with the faith and obedience of his commands, may be saved.

Secondly, we must distinguish between a voluntary examination of the conscience, whereunto the godly do in their best condition set themselves daily, and a forced examination and wakening up of the conscience whether the sinner will or not. This sort of examination, may come either by preaching of the Word, an example whereof we have in Felix the Governor, who at the hearing Paul's discourse of virtues and vices, fell a trembling, Act. 24:25. Or this wakening of the conscience may come by affliction, whereof we have an example of Joseph 's brethren, whose consciences did lie sleeping securely under the guilt of distressing their brother Joseph, but by affliction at length were wakened, Gen. 42:21. The Pastors part here is, not only to exhort men to a voluntary examination of themselves, but also by the sword of the spirit, must labor to open the apostums of proud sinners, discovering unto them, as occasion serveth, their wickedness, and denouncing the wrath of God against them, if possibly the Lord shall give them repentance, as he did to the hearers of Peter, Act. 2:37.

Thirdly, let not a Preacher be too solicit and anxious about the success of his labors, when he hath to do with obstinate sinners, whose consciences cannot be wakened, neither by challenges nor threatening's, nor exhortations: But after he hath used means publicly and privately, let him commit the matter unto God, who will have mercy on whom he will have mercy, and whom he will he hardeneth. It may suffice him, that all Christ's sheep will at length hear his voice. Only let not the Pastor despair utterly of any man, but even toward those that are excommunicate, let him follow such a course as may reduce them unto repentance, as the Apostle giveth direction, 2 Thess. 3:14,15.

For removing of the first impediment of self-examination.

But that we may speak more particularly of the cure of these seven evil diseases, for removing of the first impediment, to wit, gross ignorance; it is not needful to say much of catechetic instruction: seeing in all Churches, it is presupposed there is some form of a Catechize, wherein the rudiments of saving knowledge are set down, by way of question and answer, for the use of children, and of the ruder sort come to years. Only, we offer to those that intend the holy ministry, this overture, for disposing and preparing people, for a more easy up-taking of some formed Catechize: Because most part of formed Catechizes, are somewhat larger then they can be read at one time, or being read can be explicate any other way then by parcels, so many questions and answers at one time, and so many at another time, which how hardly it can be all explicate to the whole congregation, in a long time, experience may bear witness; therefore it may serve to good purpose, if so many of the ruder and ignorant sort, as may well be gathered together into one place at one time, the Pastor should profess before them all, that he purposeth to hold forth unto them a short sum of saving doctrine in six or seven heads of doctrine, so that in the space of an hour or thereby, before they dissolve their meeting, they may, if they be attentive and willing to learn, have some measure of found light and understanding of the grounds of true religion.

After which preface used, let him so shortly or plainly as he is able, speak something, first, of the creation of the world by God the Father, God the Son, and God the holy Ghost, the only one true God in three persons; and something also of the creation of Adam and Eve our first parents, according to God's Image, in wisdom, holiness and happiness; and something of the covenant of works made between God and them, including their posterity, the sum of which covenant is this, Do this and live, but if thou sin, thou shalt die.

Secondly, let him speak somewhat of the breach of the covenant of works by our first parents, in whose loins we are all made guilty of death according to the tenor of that covenant.

Thirdly, let him speak of the remedy provided in the counsel of God, before time, but revealed timeously after the fall of our first parents, to wit, the covenant of Redemption, between God and God the Son designed Mediator, Christ Jesus our Lord, the sum whereof is, Gen. 3:15, the seed of the woman shall tread down the head of the serpent, &c. That is to say, it is agreed in the counsel of God, that the second person shall be born of a woman, and suffer for the sins of the elect, and destroy sin and death, the works of the devil.

Fourthly, let him speak of the covenant of grace and reconciliation between God and believers in Christ, the sum whereof is this, whosoever do acknowledge their sin and fly to Jesus Christ for relief from sin and wrath, shall not perish, but have eternal life.

Fifthly, let him speak of the two seals of this covenant, to wit, Baptism and the Lord's Supper, whereby the covenant, with the benefits held out therein to all believers, is sealed.

Sixthly, let him speak of the necessity of amendment of life and bringing forth of good works for glorifying God, and probation of the sincerity of their faith.

Last of all, let him speak of the day of Judgment when Christ shall come in the clouds, and perfect to all his elect and believers in him, all his promises of righteousness and eternal life, and cast all the wicked and unreconciled into the fire of hell. The same course may be taken with ruder ignorants in private, whose conscience is wakened with terror. After that about the space of an hour the Pastor hath spoken to all these heads shortly, and repeated again, and inculcate at some other few meetings, till the people have somewhat understood the business, then he may draw forth these seven heads in some few questions, taking answer of the people in their own words as they have conceived the purpose.

These grounds being laid, the Pastor shall find by God's blessing some desire and appetite raised in the people after more knowledge of these grounds, and hope put in them to overtake a formed Catechize, and to have it by heart as may be: To which end, the people must be encouraged by promises on the one hand, and stirred up by threatening's on the other hand, such as are, John 17:3, and, 2 Thess. 1:7,8, and other like places.

Now when the people or any ignorant before, is begun to understand these seven grounds, they must be pressed to make use thereof; and that, 1. they should acknowledge their sins and deserved judgment, according to the covenant of works, which curseth every sinner for every sin. 2. That they should fly for refuge to Christ according to the covenant of grace. And, 3. that everyone who is fled to Christ for grace and mercy, must take on his yoke and endeavor new obedience of his holy commands, by his grace and furniture.

For removing of the second impediment.

The second impediment of self-examination, which is an unrenewed man's infection with some deadly error in religion, and this is not easily removed: for, the conscience that is deceived by error, absolveth the sinner from the crime, whereof the error maketh him guilty, how grievous soever it be, and therefore so long as he lieth in the error, he securely contemneth all accusations and threatening's for his error and erroneous practice, till he be convinced of his error. And usually four causes do concur to obdurate him in his error. The first is the cunningness and malice of the devil, who when he cannot altogether obscure and suppress all the articles of saving doctrine, nor banish the Scripture out of the world, he useth by his emissaries (of old destinate to this damnation) to spread doctrines of devils in the visible Church, whereby so far as he can he may detain men in their sins.

The second cause is, the wisdom of the flesh, which is enmity to God, and therefore very bent to defend every lust whereunto men are inclined, and to sight against the truth of God contrary to their lusts.

The third cause is, the multitude of these who consent with the perverted conscience, and avouch the same error.

The fourth is, the righteous judgment of God, who upon such as receive not the truth in love, sendeth powerful delusions, and efficacy of error, that they may believe a lie, and so be damned, who have not received the truth in love, but have pleasure in unrighteousness.

2. But because the Pastor cannot know any man's reprobation in particular, and therefore must take the best course he can for every man's salvation, who is under his charge, if the erroneous person cannot be content to fall upon Christian conference, in private with the Pastor, it seemeth not expedient to fall flat at the first upon the error wherewith he is infected, but to hold upon agreed unto principles, and from these grounds, lay open the merit of these sins, whereof the erroneous party will grant himself no less guilty, then other men will be found to be, and labor to convince him that for these common sins, no ransom can satisfy God's justice save the perfect obedience which Christ gave to the Father, even to the death of the cross, in name of all that flee unto him for the benefit of Redemption. If the erroneous party can condescend to cast himself wholly on Christ's mercy, offered in the Gospel for pardon of acknowledged sin, then at another time the conference may be further followed, and the danger of the error may be laid out before the erroneous, and he no more urged for the time, but that he would consider what hath been told him, and that he would by prayer for Christ's cause, beg light from God in the point questioned; And so go on with him in all meekness and evidence of love to his soul, as the Lord openeth a door for using of all means that may reclaim the party erroneous.

3. But if the error be likely to infect the flock, let the Pastor openly refute the error or heresy, and that not only by hinting at some arguments against it, but of set purpose once at least, solidly showing how contrary it is to the word of God, and what are the fearful consequences thereof, that it may become in the sight of the judicious, no less vile and odious then gross transgressions against the second table of the law; which sort of sins is more hated of natural reasonable men, then sins against the first table: for, natures light is sharper

sighted in the mutual duties of man to man, then in the matters of God and Religion, wherein a man hath no light at all in special, save that which is by revelation of Scripture. The true intent and meaning whereof, if a man be ignorant of it, or shall mistake it, the conscience runneth headlong (without the least secret check) after the error and darkness which men naturally love more than truth and light.

For removing the third impediment.

The third impediment of self-examination, to wit, infidelity, dissembled and covered with gross hypocrisy, whereof the man himself is conscious, and studieth to hide, and delighteth himself in his cheating of others, of all evils is most hardly cured: Of this sort of hypocrites are they, who think they can give a reason of all their ways to any man. And because they respect the laws of the kingdom, wherein they live, more than the Scripture, therefore they cover over all their avarice and cruelty with practice of law, that beholders, think what they please, can say nothing against their following of the civil law: for, such men fear not God, and are not afraid for his judgment. And albeit they largely commend the piety of holy men, before some auditors to whom they conceive their speech will be plausible, yet under hand, and among such as themselves are, they do but laugh and scorn all such piety, as puts men in hazard of any worldly inconvenience: for, in those men's eyes the simplicity of the godly is foolishness, and their faith in God, in their estimation, is madness, especially if for defense of the truth of Religion they suffer persecution. These hypocrites the Psalmist calleth unwise and foolish, Psal. 14:1. The fool hath said in his heart, there is no God; and, verse. 6. You have shamed the counsel of the poor, because the Lord is his refuge. Such men as these, albeit they fain themselves to be holy, yet in heart they are haters of all true saints, in whom the sparks of grace and

solid Religion doth appear: for, so saith the Lord of them, Psal. 14:4.
They eat up my people as they eat bread, and call not upon the Lord.
They have a form of godliness, but in their deeds they deny the power
of it; for, they believe never a word of what is preached of things
spiritual, revealed in the word of God: No wonder therefore that they
will not examine themselves, nor receive any accusation from their
own consciences for any sin of this sort, which concerneth godliness.

2. The causes of such men's hardening of their heart, may be four;
the first is, the measure of worldly wisdom granted to them and others like themselves, above common people, with the conceit whereof
they are so puffed up, that they care for nothing save this present
world, they acknowledge no other holiness, but civil observance of
human laws, as if Scripture and all Religious exercises were to be
referred to this only end, that men, living according to the laws and
customs received, into the Societies they live into, should study to
make the best they can of this present world. And this worldly and
carnal wisdom, is called, Psal. 1, the counsel of the ungodly, because
all ungodly persons do think it shall be more safe to walk in the ways
of their wisdom, then to be hemmed in by the laws of God.

The second cause of their obduration, is carnal confidence in their
worldly prosperity, which they hope always to enjoy, and that by the
principles of their own wisdom, Psal. 10:6, he hath said in his heart, I
shall never be moved, I shall never be in adversity.

The third cause, is the stumbling block of the cross and affliction,
wherewith they perceive the godly usually to be exercised. Upon
which offense they stumble the more readily because they judge, that
the greatest part of the affliction of the godly proceeds from their
own imprudency, and do ascribe their own prosperity to their own
wisdom, wherein they are so lifted up in their own estimation, that

they despise all men in comparison of themselves, Psal. 10:5. As for his enemies, he puffeth at them.

The fourth cause is, the not observing, the slighting and despising of God's Judgments, concerning which they do not give credit unto God when he speaketh, and therefore do not make use of the operation of his hands, Psal. 10:5. Thy judgments are far above out of his sight.

3. Albeit there be very small hope of the conversion of any such, because they cannot abide free dealing from any man in private, for to give them any admonition, is to them a reproach, and they cannot endure it, and nothing can cut them at the heart more than that any man should suspect them of hypocrisy and atheism; yet because no Pastor may despair of any man or judge him a reprobate, so long as the longsuffering patience of God inviteth him to repentance, therefore the Pastor must deal with such men in the general in his sermons, that from the Scripture he may convince them of their ignorance of God's ways and of their atheism.

To which end and purpose, first, he must point such men forth in their colors as the Scripture doth describe them, yet so as he hold himself in general in dealing with all such persons without particular description of any man by particular circumstances, whereby such a man one or more of the auditors may appear to be picked out and shot at.

Secondly, he must denounce gravely and with compassion the heavy Judgments of God against them.

Thirdly, he must pull the mask of civil honesty off their face, and let them know the righteousness of Christ imputed to humble sinners flying to him, to be the only garment to hide nakedness, if possibly the hearer may conceive hope he may be forgiven his former hypocrisy, and be allured unto Christ.

Fourthly, let him often against such persons make use of the Apostles admonition, 1 Cor. 3:18,19. Let no man deceive himself, if any man among you seemeth to be wise in this world, let him become a fool that he may be wise, for the wisdom of this world is foolishness with God: for, it is written, he taketh the wise in their own craftiness.

Fifthly, let the Pastor observe the occasion, if at any time it shall please God to lay calamity on such a man; and then let him wisely labor with all meekness and tenderness to awaken up his conscience to take notice of the sparks of wrath, least he perish in God's displeasure, if he do not humble himself before God and draw in to Christ; upon which condition let him make the fairest offers of grace and mercy that the Gospel can yield to him, if possibly the Lord may give him repentance and faith in our Lord Jesus Christ.

For removing the fourth impediment.

The fourth impediment of self-examination, is the stupidity and senselessness of the conscience, past feeling, as it were, burnt with a hot iron. This disease may be seen in besotted Epicures, given to their brutish lusts, who are so carried on after their furious beastly affections, that they have no more power over themselves then beasts, and such monsters of men by frequent sinning have extinguished all sense of sin; for, albeit by nature there is some remainder of light in fallen man, whereby the work of the law may be found written in their heart, as far as to make them inexcusable, when they do contrary to it; and albeit there is left in the natural man some natural power of the conscience to vex him that rebelleth against it, to restrain him thereafter from doing the like, yet some have so sold themselves to the lust and wantonness of their flesh, that they will not hear any admonition or check of the conscience which might make any remorse, but do run madly after all sort of uncleanness, corrupting themselves as brute beasts.

The like disposition may be seen in openly profane persons, who not only in their deeds have denied the power of godliness, but also renounce the profession of all form of godliness, and shamelessly foam forth their ungodliness, as an open rotten grave casts forth the stink thereof. Of this sort are these, who when they do blaspheme, will not be reproved. Psal. 12:4. Our tongues are our own, who is Lord over us? And who as dogs do trample under-foot all holy things and rent them who reprove them, and who insult over the godly in their affliction, saying with David's enemies, where is their God? And who openly scorn all religion like these desperate scoffers, 2 Pet. 3:4, saying, where is the promise of his coming. Such as these are practically atheists, and in some sort also in their minds; for, albeit they have some natural principles of a Godhead imprinted on them, yet they smother all knowledge of God and belch out their own shame against God and religion and all the godly.

2. Of men's falling unto such a fearful abomination, four causes may be rendered. The first is, the man's violence used against his conscience frequently in committing of grievous sins wittingly, and from the slighting of the admonitions of the conscience arising up to the contempt of all accusations which the conscience can lay in against him, and at last boldly rising up against the conscience, as it were, to be avenged of it, for rebuking him, by committing these same sins most frequently, for which he hath been oftnest reproved by his conscience. The second cause may we reckon the devil, who thinketh it too little to allure men to sin, and harden their heart in it, and spoil them of all sense of their sin, except he also draw them to renounce

God and bark against him, and become like the devil himself, so far as he can drive them. The third cause we make the holy justice of God, giving over the man who contemneth the light and checks of his conscience, unto a reprobate sense, that being deprived of common use of reason and judgment, he may run mad in his sin like the devil: for, if God did punish the heathen so for this sort of sinning, Rom. 1:28, what wonder he punish, seven times more, them, who thus rebel against the light of holy Scripture? Yea, these that do not come to this height are punished, by giving them over to strong delusions, 2 Thess. 2:11. The last, but sinless, cause, is the deep wisdom of God, who suffering such wretches to fill up such a measure of sin, doth make manifest to all beholders, the power and poison of in-born sin in man, and draweth forth to light the natural enmity of man against God, the seeds whereof is in all men, and could hardly be believed to be incident to men, except it were by experience seen and found in some men.

For remedy of this evil, it is too little that such a monster should be driven from all Church-society, and given over to Satan; it is the part of the Magistrate to bind beasts and mad devils, and punish them as it becometh the bearer of the sword to do for avenging of evil-doers. But, if the Magistrate do not his part, yet, let the Pastor do what in him lieth; for, albeit the Scripture giveth small hope of the recovery of such vile monsters because of the stupidity of their conscience, that cannot be wrought upon by man, yet seeing such evils have been found, even in some elect, as Manasseh and some of the Corinthians before their conversion, 1 Cor. 6:9-11, and because experience hath often found, that some of this sort going to public execution by the Magistrate, have been converted and saved by faith in Jesus Christ; a Pastor should not altogether despair of such vile men, but essay what may be done by conference, especially when God sends calamity on them, or the Magistrate executes justice on them for any crime, if possibly such miscreants, being convinced of their perverseness, may repent and fly to Christ, the Redeemer of such as fly unto him.

For removing the fifth impediment.

1. The fifth impediment of self-examination, is a false fear of no small danger to their souls, if they should ripe up their conscience for by-gones; for, seeing, they feel themselves quiet, they think it were unprofitable and dangerous to trouble their own peace. Such persons will tell you, that their faith is surely set on God, and that they never had any doubt or suspicion of God's love to them, and therefore dare not trouble themselves with self-examination, first, because all Sermons bid them firmly trust in God. Secondly, because they know, if they should trouble themselves with self-examination, they might soon weaken their faith, as they conceive. Thirdly, because they know the subtlety of Satan, as they say, to whom if a door were opened by search of their old ways, they fear he should over-charge them with accusations, and drive them to desperation, as (say they) it hath befallen sundry, who after wakening their consciences, never rested till they put hand in themselves, not being able to bear the torment of their conscience.

There are other some, who, nill they will they, are drawn before the tribunal of God's Judgment, and their conscience beginneth to stir against them, which so soon as they do perceive, incontinent they interrupt the process. Such a one was the heathen Governor Felix, Act. 24:25, who after hearing, for a little, Paul's discourse of righteousness, temperance and judgment to come, did tremble, and therefore desired Paul to forbear for the time. Of this sort also are they who do with-draw themselves from Church-meetings, and hearing of public Sermons, lest they should be troubled with the serious speeches of a faithful Pastor. Some are also of this sort, who take the course that King Saul did take, and call for a minstrel, or for merry company to suppress the voice of their barking conscience, or do by some such way divert their conscience from entering in judgment with them.

2. The causes of this evil in the un-regenerate man, may be found these four, (besides others more particular) First, ignorance of the duty of self-examination prescribed of God, Psal. 4:4, or a voluntary mis-kenning that such a duty is required of all. The second cause is a fixed purpose to go on securely in their old ways. The third cause is, the sense of the sweetness they imagine they do find, and have found of a long time in the carnal rest and sleep of their conscience. The fourth cause is a persuasion, that they could not rid themselves out of the grips of their conscience, nor endure the blind blows, which conscience, set down on the tribunal, should inflict on them; which sorrow and vexation they conceive they cannot other ways eschew, but by throwing down their conscience from the bench that he enter in no process against them.

3. When the Pastor hath to do with such a man, his first care must be, that this blind fear may be drawn forth to the light, by showing him, that this his flying from the light and hiding himself in darkness, is to no purpose, and that there is no place for him to fly unto and hide himself from God. Secondly, let him press the decree of God, that all men must once die, and then come to judgment: wherein he cannot miss perpetual condemnation and endless torment from an angry Judge; except he now judge and condemn himself, and fly to Christ the Mediator while it is today, while Christ is exercising his Mediatory-office, and is inviting all sinners to repent, and calling all

weary and heavy loaden to come unto him. Thirdly, let the Pastor show to those fearful persons, that this their tear is groundless; for, if they mind to draw in to God, they need not fear to confess all their sins and fly to his grace, which if they do not, the sleep which they love to lie into is deadly, because God hath said, There is no peace to the wicked, Isa. 48:21. Fourthly, let him press the precepts for self-examination and judging ourselves, Psal. 4:4, and trying whether we be in the faith or not, 2 Cor. 13:5, except they would choose to be judged of God without mercy. But seeing here we speak to Pastors, or to such as aim at the holy Ministry, we need not insist, but with the Apostle, 2 Tim. 2:17, pray the Lord to give his servants wisdom and prudence in all things.

For removing the sixth impediment.

The sixth impediment is, a lazy and sluggish putting off of the duty of self-examination from time to time. And many are guilty of this sinful folly, who will grant, that it is a duty lying on them to set their conscience on work for trial of their state or condition, but like ill debtors, who, promising to pay as oft as they meet with their creditors, do notwithstanding put off time and delay the work from day today; Such men's disposition in spiritual things is well resembled in the description of the sluggard, Prov. 6:10. How long wilt thou sleep, O sluggard? When wilt thou arise out of thy sleep? Yet a little sleep, a little slumber, a little folding of the hands to sleep. So shall thy poverty come as one that travaileth, and thy want as an armed man. And, Prov. 26:14-16. As the door turneth upon his hinges, so doth the slothful man upon his bed. The slothful hideth his hand in his bosom, it grieveth him to bring it again to his mouth. The sluggard is wiser in his own conceit, then seven men that can render a reason. Such are our lazy delayers of examination, of whom we speak, they cannot endure to be at pains to search their ways or commune with their heart: But, so long as God suffereth their conscience to sleep, so long they put off the duty of searching themselves and lie still in security, esteeming it a torture to have their sluggish sleeping any way interrupted by any person.

2. Of this evil disease, five causes may be given; The first is, the abhorring of all pains in spiritual duties, how profitable so ever diligence might prove. The second cause is, the bewitching sense of sweetness they conceive they feel in this their idle carriage. The third is, the deceit of the sluggard's heart, still promising to follow his purpose of amendment of life from day to day, and yet, albeit deceived a thousand times, he doth give credit to his own false heart. The fourth is, a false opinion which the sluggard entertains of his own spiritual abilities, as if he were sure he could repent at any time; and that if any sickness or appearance of death should befall him, he would then undoubtedly make his reckoning with God and crave pardon, and so be saved, and in such pleasant dreams he counteth himself a much wiser man then many who do put themselves to daily toiling and vexation, by keeping their conscience on the rack-stock, when with less misery they might follow his sluggish way of it. The fifth, but sinless, cause, is the Lord's lengthening of prosperity to the sluggard, which although it should lead him to repentance, yet he becomes hereby more and more drunken, and lulleth himself over in a deeper sleep.

3. This sickness is not easily cured, except the Lord take up a rod and rouse the sluggard out of his sleep. But, as for the Pastors part, he shall do well in private if the sluggard confess his fault, and howsoever, to set an edge on the law in public, that all such sluggards may apprehend the real danger their soul is into by delaying their

repentance, because the endurance of this brittle and frail life is most uncertain; for, the fool knoweth not whether the very next following night after admonition is given to him, his soul shall be taken from him. Secondly, he must know, that the longer he delay, the number of his sins and the hardness of his heart, and the wrath of God against him, do daily grow to a higher measure. Let the sluggard then be convinced of his madness, if he shall delay for an hour, by acknowledgment of his sin and flying to Christ, to vomit up the deadly poison of his sweetest sins, and to have the hot burning wrath of God against him extinguished. Thirdly, let the deceits wherewith he beguileth himself be laid open and refuted, and an offer be made unto him, whether he will choose, that his conscience be tormented forever in the society of unclean devils, after a short while sleep in sin in this life, rather than while he hath time, while Christ offereth himself Mediator in his Gospel, while he may have the sweet fellowship of the Saints, he will choose to put his conscience to it, and acknowledge his sins and fly to Christ, that he may have peace with God and so be saved for ever.

For removing the seventh impediment.

The seventh impediment of self-examination, is the too earnest care for earthly things, and the man's involving himself in the affairs of this life: for, there are many who do not refuse the duty of trying their own spiritual state and condition, who notwithstanding of this conviction of their duty, do spend all their time in the businesses of this world, wherein they are so involved and carried head-long, that they pass perfunctoriously all exercises of religion, and do neither wait for the direction of God's Word, or of their own conscience, about what they have to do, nor call themselves to account for what is past, done or not done. Of this sort are these, of whom Christ doth speak, Luke 14:18, who being invited to a free supper, answered, some of them, I have bought land, another, I have married a wife, another, I have bought a yoke of oxen, &c. and so sought to be excused, for their not coming to the marriage, all pretending their earthly affairs, as a just reason of their slipping of the invitation given them. Of this sort of men speaketh Christ, Math. 13:22. He that received seed among the thorns, is he that heareth the Word, and the cares of this world, and the deceitfulness of riches chock the word, and he becometh unfruitful. This sort of men are complained of, Jer. 8:6. I hearkened and beard, but they spoke not aright, no man repented him of his wickedness, saying, what have I done? Everyone turned to his course, as the horse rusheth into the battle.

2. Of this evil, four causes among others may be given, first, inordinate concupiscence of earthly things, which eateth up all the time and travel, which the love of things spiritual doth call for, and, as it were, spurreth the man to the immoderate pursuing of things temporal. The second cause is, the beguiling of the conscience under the pretense of seeking what is lawful and necessary for a man's well-being in this life, as if a man's spending of his care and pains, and time in earthly business, in itself lawful, were sufficient excuse for neglecting things spiritual and heavenly; or, as if it were not required of all men that hear the Word of God pointing out the way of men's salvation, to prefer that one thing necessary before all commodities of this earth; for, what can it avail a man to gain the whole earth, if he lose his own soul? The third cause is, the deceitfulness of riches, which every man naturally is inclined to pursue too eagerly, and which many pragmatic busy men do attain: for, God useth to recompense every man's diligence in a lawful occupation with a sort of external reward of the same kind with his work: This success and

rewarding of men's industry and pains, by increasing busy men's riches, earthly-minded men, do interpret to be the special blessing of God, and an approbation of their immoderate pursuing after things earthly, wherein they are much mistaken; for God never ordained any man's civil calling to be a hindrance of the spiritual welfare of his soul, and if any man neglect his soul and pursue worldly riches, if he obtain them, what can be said? But verily he hath his reward, and cannot look after the fruit of pains taking in spiritual matters which he neglected. The fourth cause is, a light estimation of the Word of God, and of matters concerning salvation which by reason they fall not under sense and present possession, but are offered to us in promises, and are not bestowed for the present, therefore many are less careful for things promised after this life, and do follow the more eagerly after such things whereof they can take hold in this life.

3. The way to cure this malady, so far as pertaineth to a Pastor, is, that both in public sermons and private conferences, he give unto things lawful and to the following of a man's civil calling the own room and time, and wisely let men know the subordination of all civil affairs unto the welfare of their souls, and so to lay open the peril of men's souls, when they are following too too eagerly their civil vocation, as in the meantime he do not condemn men's diligence in their callings, but that he give directions for such a wise moderation of every man's care about things of this world, that the precious excellency of the soul, and the infinite worth of eternal life be first and above all earthly things provided for, and that in the using or conqueshing of riches no prejudice do come to his own salvation, which is not possible a man shall do, if he do not daily examine his own conscience carefully, and keep it in a tender disposition, resorting to Christ upon all occasions for pardon of daily sin and keeping

him, that if riches increase, he may not set his heart thereon, but may be forth-coming to the duties of charity towards others as his power shall be, and opportunities shall be offered.

CHAP. X. - Concerning them that are like to despair.

WE HAVE SPOKEN OF the first sort of them who do hinder their own regeneration by abhorring, declining, delaying and shifting off of the examination of their consciences. The second sort or rank of those who hinder their own conversion, is of such as after the wakening of their own consciences, whether voluntary or by compulsion, do despair of all remedy offered unto them in the Gospel of grace in Christ, and renouncing the counsel of God, do follow the counsel of Satan and their own heart.

2. We distinguish a voluntary examination of the conscience from a compelled and enforced examination thereof, as was hinted at in the former Section; for, it is one thing to say of a man, he hath voluntarily examined himself and found out his ditty and deserved judgment, and to say of him, he is forced to examine himself and in himself to receive sentence according as his ways have been: for, there are many who will not judge themselves, yet after are forced unto it against their will: These are said to judge themselves voluntarily, who, by a free act of their will, do enter themselves to be judged of their own conscience, and do go about the work either slightly and perfunctoriously, or strictly and exactly according to their knowledge

of the rule: But a compelled examination is ever more exact and strict and joined with the chastisement of the sinner for neglecting or slighting or delaying of examination, Psal. 50:21. This distinction is holden forth to as by the Apostle, 1 Cor. 11:31,32. If we would judge ourselves, we should not be judged: But when we are judged, we are chastened of the Lord, that we should not be condemned with the world. Both these sorts of examination have a blessing following upon them when Christ is fled unto after examination: but if Christ be not fled unto, then desperation may follow upon both slight and serious examination, both upon voluntary and enforced examination.

3. We do not take desperation here for every dissidence of God's performing of promises, or of God's making good of his gracious offers, but for diffidence to obtain reconciliation with God, or to find mercy through Christ the Mediator. Neither do we call by the name of desperation every diffidence to obtain mercy and reconciliation, cast in man's mind by the tempter Satan, and yielded unto for a time under the sense of God's wrath; for, at some sits, the diffidence will be found in renewed Saints, as in Jonah, chap. 2:4. Heman the Ezrahite. Psal. 88:16. David, Psal. 116:11, who seemed to themselves for the time to be cast off, but did swim out of this deep by faith. Neither do we take desperation for every short or long eclipse of hope, wherein a distressed soul seems to its self to despair, yea, and may possibly utter and profess they do despair, and in the meantime will not renounce the use of the means, whereby they do get, or recover hope: Such was the condition of Heman the Ezrahite, Psal. 88:14,15,16. Lord why casts thou off my soul? Why hidest thou thy face from me? I am afflicted and ready to die from my youth up, while I suffer thy terrors, I am distracted. He thought he was cast off, yet for all that he went on

daily praying for the sense of mercy and found it, and was directed by God to acquaint the Church unto all generations with his long and sad exercise. But we take desperation for a prevalent impression made by Satan upon the spirit of a man, that God will not show him mercy, and so fixed in him, as the man resolveth not to deal with God anymore for mercy.

4. Of this properly called desperation, there are two sorts, one which we may call careless and secure desperation, another which we may call anxious and tormenting desperation. Cain's desperation in his last resolution, was of the first sort, and Judas desperation was of the other sort. We call that a careless secure desperation, when a sinner, being convinced of his gross and many sins, either believeth not God's Word or conceiveth God implacable and irreconcilable, and to have destinate him to destruction according to the sentence of the law, pronounced against such sinners as he knoweth himself to be, and so doth harden and obdured himself against all threatening's, and goeth on in his own ways, resolved to take ease and pleasure in the world, so long as he liveth, and not to make himself miserable before the time; Such was the desperation of carnal Israelites, Isa. 22:13, who, hearing the threatening's of the Prophets concerning the just Judgments of God to come upon them, when they should have humbled themselves in prayer and fasting, in sackcloth and ashes, and sought mercy from God, they did set themselves to make good cheer, and to feast one another, saying, Let us eat and drink, for tomorrow we shall die. Of this sort were also these in Ezekiel's time, chap. 33:10. Thus ye speak, saying, If our sins and transgressions be upon us, and we pine away in them, how shall we then live? They do not deny that they are loadened with iniquity, they doubt nothing of the righteousness of the threatened Judgment; but, comparing

the justice of God's Judgment with their sins, and laying aside all thought of a remedy from God's mercy, they flatly despair, as if there had been no remedy provided in the Word of God for them, or as if the threatening's had been pronounced, as sentences pronounced absolutely, without exception of their repentance.

5. The causes of this evil, are specially these three; the first, is gross misbelief of God's Word, contemning all threatening's, as but the words of an angry prophet stirred up to vent his passions against people. The second, is the perverseness of corrupt nature, so hardened with the custom of sinning, that the conscience not being terrified with God's threatening's, is nothing moved with inward accusations, which they know to be just; whereupon they resolve neither to seek for mercy, nor care for reconciliation with God, not to shed with their carnal pleasures and sinful lusts, but will go on in their own ways, and take their hazard. The third, is a false persuasion, that it is impossible they can be reconciled to God, arising partly, from the vileness of their former life and grossness of their sins, partly, from the ignorance of the Gospel, and of the rich grace of God offered to the worst of sinners, who shall forsake their former ways and fly unto Christ; and partly, arising from the ignorance of the scope and end of the law, which is appointed to be a pedagogue to lead and draw men unto Christ, after their conviction of sin by the law, how grievous soever their sins have been.

6. The remedy of this sort of secure desperation is very hard, and in some incurable, namely these, who do not believe the threatening's and go on still in unbelief; or, do believe the threatening's, but are so wedded to their lusts, that they will not change their course and manner of sinful carriage, come what may come, but resolve to eat and drink and be merry while they live: Concerning whom the

Prophet Isaiah saith, chap. 22:14. It was revealed in mine ears by the Lord of hosts, surely this iniquity shall not be purged from you, till ye die, saith the Lord of hosts. The best ground of hope is of such, who, through ignorance of the end of the law and offer of the Gospel, have taken up a false persuasion of their desperate estate. Now because the Pastor hath no warrant to read the decree of any man's reprobation in particular, his care must be in private and public, to waken epicures, and all besotted in their sins, out of their deadly sleep; laying before them, from Scripture, the unextinguishable fire of hell, and the torments of the damned to be endured forever by the impenitent and unbelieving sinner on the one hand; and on the other hand, making offer of remission of sin and reconciliation to all who shall forsake their former vicious ways, and be content to embrace Christ Jesus for their righteousness, sanctification and salvation. And to this end, let him certify all his hearers, that threatening's are not intended of God to drive any man to desperation, but to lead all to repentance, that they may be saved, and that the exception of repentance and faith in the Redeemer, is to be understood in every threatening, for so the Lord hath made a plain commentary upon all his threatening's and all his promises also, that he be not forever mistaken, which is this in sum, that by his threatening's he doth not intend to make any man to despair, but to repent and turn to God; and that by his promises he doth not intend, that any man should presume to sin, or turn his grace into wantonness, as is at large set down, Ezek. 33, from ver. 10 to ver. 21, and, chap. 18, from ver. 21 to the end.

Of anxious tormenting desperation.

Anxious and tormenting desperation is when a sinner, from the apprehension of his guiltiness of irremissible sins, and fear of inextricable woeful misery, wherein he hath thrown himself, doth cast away all hope of relief to be had, and so is tortured and vexed within himself without rest. In this sort of desperation, the miserable man having wrestled a while, doth either turn himself to a carnal temporary consolation in this world, and maketh choice of a careless and secure desperation, that he may be rid of present anxiety, or else he resolveth to dispatch himself by some sort of self-murder, counting it more easy to die by his own hand, than to live and endure the tormenting vexation of his own mind.

2. As for that sort of anxious desperation, which after the sore biting of the conscience once wakened, falleth back again in carnal security, it is most perilous, and giveth very small hope to the Pastor, or faithful friends who perceive the man after fearful wakening of his conscience, to have fallen back to his old ways, and turned careless of the means of salvation: for, such a man, is of set purpose and resolvedly wicked. Such was the desperation of Cain, who, after a whiles lamentation and howling for the curse pronounced upon him by God, plucked up his heart, departed from the society of the Church, where God giveth his presence, and goeth into the land of Nod, or voluntary banishment, and giveth himself over to building of Cities, Gen. 4:13,14. Such also was the desperation of Esau, who, when he saw he was excluded from the spiritual blessing of the birthright, laments a little, and then turned himself toward the earthly blessing, and sought all his consolation in it, Gen. 27:34,38, yet such men must be dealt with, if God possibly may bless the means.

3. As for the other sort of anxious desperation, except it be cured by God's blessing of the means used, it draweth on voluntary and deliberate self-murder. We put a difference between brute self-murder, and voluntary or deliberate self-murder: for this beastly brute self-murder, may befall mad persons, furious, melancholious, dis-

tracted persons, or such as are beset by some evil spirit, in whom the faculty of reasoning is so impeded, that without the use of reason, or common sense, they are carried to destroy themselves some way. Such persons can hardly be called voluntary and deliberate self-murderers, because they are neither able to observe and discern their own condition, nor their danger, wherein they are, nor any circumstances which might hinder them from the mischief; and therefore it cannot properly in this case be called desperation, because the miserable person is not so much capable of reason as to consider the grounds and motives of hope or despair.

But voluntary self-murder, proceedeth from properly called desperation, because the wretch, after deliberation, how to escape from misery lying on and coming on, when all reason of hope seemeth to fail him, he casts away any further inquisition after the remedy; and out of apprehension, that he can be in no worse case after his death, then he presently feeleth, and that he can no other way be rid of his present torment then by death, wittingly and willingly putteth hand in himself: In this voluntary self-murder, sometime the sense of wrath for sin committed, doth predominate, as in Judas the traitor, his desperation and self-murder: sometime the apprehension of more worldly misery, more bitter then death, doth predominate, as in King Saul, who chose rather to fall on his own sword, then fall alive into the hands of the Philistines, 1 Sam. 31:4, and in Ahithophel's hanging himself, when he foresaw what misery should come upon himself, when his counsel was not embraced by Absalom, 2 Sam. 17:23.

4. To speak of self-murder in general, requireth a Treatise larger than our purpose doth permit; it sufficeth us to speak a little to it, as the temptation thereunto, and desperation of finding God's mercy is

a hindrance of regeneration. To this end, where any fear or suspicion of any intention toward this fearful sin, doth appear, all meekness should be used by all that have interest in the person suspected, that may serve to save the vexed party from such a mischief; God must be in-called and requested for relief unto the patient: Physicians should be called, and more Pastors then one, if they can be had, the soul in danger must by friends, be watched and waited on, in a prudent manner night and day, that he never be alone. If the person be capable of reason, he must be dealt with freely to confess his temptation and purpose toward this sin, the causes moving him must be inquired after; and if they be other than sense of sin and fear, or feeling of God's wrath, then course must be taken to make the party sensible of sin and to fear God's wrath, and to consider, that if they give way to that sin they are tempted unto, they do no less, in effect, then cast themselves in hell, where the justice and wrath of God shall lie upon them without hope of ease or ending of their everlasting torment, from which fearful destruction, they may be preserved both in soul and body, if they shall acknowledge their sin, and fly to God in Christ offering grace and pardon of sin and delivery from hell, and right unto heaven, promised to all and everyone who shall embrace Jesus Christ for their redemption. And for these, whose vexation is mainly from the conscience of heinous sins, and felt wrath of God pursuing them, the grace offered in the Gospel must be cleared unto them and inculcated; if they can be moved to give reasons of their fear and to propone their doubts, who knoweth what blessing may follow on their free dealing, and from faithful answers from Scripture returned unto them? Conferences of experimented Christians may with profit be made use of in the patient's audience, whereby the party may receive both increase of knowledge and some beginnings of comfort. Among other means, godly persons, who have in their own exercise had experience of such temptations, and have gotten victory by flying unto Christ, may serve much by their conference to encourage them. In some of those tempted souls, tokens of good hope will shortly appear; in others, it may be, none can conjecture what shall be the event, till the time declare it, whether justice or mercy was intended of God; for, both in the elect, who are cured of this disease, and in the reprobate who perish in their sin, the same symptoms may appear; if the anxiety and expressions of the one and the other be compared. Therefore, care must be had of everyone under such temptations, whatsoever the event may be and the Lord's blessing waited for in the use of the means. Scripture showeth us how hard exercises God's dear children have been under. Beside many other Saints, we shall only name two witnesses, the one is Heman the Ezrahite, that precious soul, not much inferior to Solomon in wisdom, 1 King. 4:31, of whom no man could say he was a weak brain and hypochondriac or melancholious person, whose sad exercise stands registrated (Psal. 88) for many man's comfort. The other witness shall be Job. whose perplexities we read in his dispute with his friends, and how he tasted of this bitter temptation also, Job 7:13,14,15. When I say my bed shall comfort me, my couch shall ease my complaint, then thou scarest me with dreams and terrifies me with visions, so that my soul chooseth strangling. Behold there is a very sad exercise of the most holy and righteous man on earth; there is a sore temptation even unto self-murder, but how is this temptation over-come? First, he doth not hide his temptation, but openeth it up in the worst shape: this giveth the temptation vent, he will not conceal it, nor be Satan's secretar in this; and this is one mean to weaken the temptation. Then he presenteth it before God, and poureth out his complaint unto the Lord, and this giveth him the victory. So let all souls tempted unto desperation do, and cleave to God in Christ, and they shall be victorious also.

CHAP. XI. - Concerning them that absolve themselves without warrant.

THE THIRD RANK OF those that impede their own regeneration, remaineth to be spoken of. Of this kind are all they, who, after they have slightly examined themselves, and are convinced of sin and of deserved death, if they were dealt with in rigor of justice, do unwarrantably absolve themselves, deceiving their own conscience by a fallacy, false syllogism or captious reasoning, and from the conscience, as from a blinded or seduced Judge, do draw forth a sentence of absolution to themselves which God doth not allow. All such persons do either lay down some false principle or ground for absolution of sinners; or, if they lay down a true ground, they make wrong application of that ground to themselves, and so beguile themselves miserably.

The first sort.

Some do grant themselves to be sinners, but do persuade themselves, that God is so merciful as he will not destroy any man for sin: which principle being once laid down, no wonder such men go on in their own way and sing a requiem to their own souls. Of this sort of

men the Lord doth speak, Deut. 29:18,19, showing, that he makes his
covenant with his people, lest there should be among you, saith he,
a root that beareth gall and wormwood. And it come to pass, when
he heareth the words of this curse, that he bless himself in his heart,
saying, I shall have peace, though I walk in the imagination of my
own heart, to add drunkenness to thirst. It is possible, few shall be
found so impudent, as that they dare, in express terms, profess this
their mis-belief of God's justice; yet, they are not a few who foster this
error in their heart, who having, as it were, made a Covenant with
death and hell, are far from fearing to perish in their sins. In this sort
are all they to be ranked, who conceive, that all the threatening's in
the Scripture are given forth, to the intent, that men, being bridled
by terrors, might compose themselves to a more human and social
life among others; who, lest they should seem Atheists in word, do
cry up God's mercy, bounty and love to man, so as they make small
reckoning of the Lord's truth and justice, even as if the justice of God
in punishing rebels, could not consist with his mercy to the penitent,
or as if the end of creating man, could not be obtained, if obstinate
sinners be destroyed.

2. The main cause of such error, is an obstinate purpose to walk
after the counsel and imagination of their own heart; and because
they cannot quiet their conscience in following their own ways, except in promising to themselves impunity in their sinning, they presume confidently to go on in their own ways against all threatening's,
and so do blow their consciences blind. Such profane presumption,
although it deserveth to be beaten with a rod, rather than to be rea-
soned with, yet let the Pastor deal with the presumer, as he ought to
do with other desperate like sinners; and in the first place, let him
propose for remedy of this evil, what the Lord doth speak against

such a person, Deut. 29:20. The Lord will not spare him, but then the anger of the Lord and his jealousy shall smoke against that man, and all the curses that are written in this book shall lie upon him, and the Lord shall blot out his name from under heaven. And as he findeth this work upon him, So let him deal with him.

2. Some are near of kindred to such persons, who do not reject all threatening's, yet do think in their heart that none are in danger except gross flagitious and notorious sinners; but as to themselves, they conceive because they are not the worst of men, they are without the reach of divine justice, especially if their conversation be according to human laws so regulated as they have the reputation of honest neighbors. With such men Christ dealeth (Luk. 13:1,2,5) when word came concerning the Galileans whose blood Pilate mixed with their sacrifices, Christ saith to them, Suppose ye that these Galileans were sinners above all Galileans, because they suffered these things? I tell you, nay, but except ye repent you shall all likewise perish. This is the remedy prescribed by Christ to such men.

3. Some there are who hope to be absolved before God, and do absolve themselves in their own conscience, by their good works and obedience done to the law: Of this sort was Paul before his conversion, who, till the time that the spiritual light of the law brake in upon his mind and killed the conceit of his own inherent righteousness, was no mean man in his own eyes. Rom. 7:9. Such was the rich young man in the Gospel, who said to Christ, that he had keeped all the commands from his youth up, till Christ did prove him a covetous Idolater, who put a higher price on his riches then upon Christ and the kingdom of heaven: Such were the Pharisees, who, by their obedience to the law (such as it was) doubted nothing to absolve themselves, and that God should absolve them also. But that

the meet-yard should be no longer then their clothe, or the law of further extent then their imagined possible practice, they admitted no metonymy or figurative speech in the law, whereby under one branch of a duty commanded, all duties of that kind are comprehended, and all faults contrary to the duty are forbidden. As for example, they counted not the sixth command to be violate, except the man did take away his neighbor's life, nor the seventh command broken, except by gross adultery and violation of the marriage-bed; nor the eighth command transgressed, except another man's goods were openly or privately taken away, whose mistake Christ doth correct, Matth. chap. 5 and 6.

2. Such men as those are far from repentance, far from humbling themselves before God and seeking remission of sin through Christ; for, they are ignorant of the righteousness of the Gospel by faith in Jesus Christ, and of the way of coming to ability for doing any acceptable work by faith in Christ, and therefore they go about to establish their own righteousness, Rom. 10:3, and 9:31,32. The false ground which they do lay for their own absolution, is this, they think to be justified by their works, against which ground, the Apostle hath pronounced condemnatory sentence, Rom. 3:20. By the deeds of the law, shall no flesh be justified in God's sight; for, by the law is the knowledge of sin.

3. With this sort we may join these, who not only come short of the obedience due to the law, but also are in conscience convicted of many transgressions of the Lord's law; yet, they conceive that God will not exact of them, or of any man who is about to obey his law, more than the man can in the common infirmity of flesh overtake, and do persuade themselves, that God will be satisfied with all them, in whom is a willingness to obey the law: their false ground which

they lay, is this, that God will accept a man's will for the deed: And to this purpose they do abuse the Scriptures, Isa. 1:19, If you be willing and obedient, you shall eat the good things of the land, And, 2 Cor. 8:12. If there be first a willing mind, it is accepted, according to that a man hath, and not according to that he hath not.

4. But here is their error, whereupon they purchase from their conscience mis-informed an unwarrantable absolution; first, they lay down for a ground that they must be justified by works. 2. Because they know they do come, and shall come short in obedience, they turn the condition of the covenant of works, into other terms then God hath appointed, and make the will of a man to obey the law so far as he is able, to be the condition of the covenant, which God disclaimeth. 3. They deceive themselves in this, that what is spoken to converted believers in Jesus Christ, already justified by faith, aiming at new obedience, they do apply to themselves, lying under the curse and covenant of works: for, it is true indeed, when God is dealing with those that are already justified by faith in Jesus, and have renounced all confidence in their own works, and fled unto Christ, and have taken on his yoke, the Lord doth take in good part the first fruits of the new creature, and doth much esteem the tender fruits of the spirit, as the places cited (Isa. 1, and 2 Cor. 8) do show. But when the Lord hath to do with the proud natural man, the unrenewed man, the man that is not humbled for violation of the covenant of works, he dealeth with him according to the rigor of the law, according to the condition of the covenant of works, pronouncing his curse against that man, for every sin, till the sinner be humbled and sly to Christ.

5. With the former we may join all these, who believe they may wash away their sins, partly by bearing such afflictions as are laid on them by God in this life; partly, by their tears, prayers, fasting's,

pilgrimages penances and scourging of themselves; and partly, by their alms-deeds and other good works, do believe they shall make amends for all their misdeeds; and what they cannot perfect in this life for the matter of good works, they will take assignation to the supererogation and superfluity of the merits of Saints, made over unto them by the Pope; And what for the matter of suffering is not endured in this life, they will take upon them to endure in an imaginary purgatory and place of hell after this life, and so (poor souls) they think they may absolve themselves at least from the sentence of everlasting condemnation by such poor shifts as those. But the truth is, so long as they rely upon their own sufferings and satisfactions they deny both the necessity and the worth of Christ's sufferings; and so long as they have confidence in their own works, or works of other men, they reject and disclaim the covenant of grace, and yet, behold how proud they prove themselves to be, Isa. 58:3, when they plead with God, saying, wherefore have we fasted, and thou seest not? Wherefore have we afflicted our soul, and thou takest no knowledge?

6. Last of all, unto the former sort we join these who please themselves in the composition of righteousness by works and righteousness by faith, thinking to save themselves under the shelter of the one righteousness, or of the other, however God shall deal with them. Such were the Seducers and seduced amongst the Galatians: for refuting of whole error, the Apostle (as it were) travelled in birth till he brought them to take up the right frame of Christ's way of salvation,

7. The cause of all such men's deceiving of themselves in a false absolution of their conscience, is their ignorance both of the righteousness of the law and of the righteousness by faith: for, such as think their sins are so few and light, or their lives so innocent, or

their good works they have done so weighty, and their purpose to do yet more good works, to be so holy, or their pains taken in religion so considerable, or their sufferings resolved upon, so great, and thereupon do absolve themselves, consider not that the law, or covenant of works, doth require perfect, personal obedience to all God's law, under the pain of God's curse, growing in Items as the law is oftener transgressed, till they fly in to the perfect ransom of Christ's obedience. And as for the righteousness of faith in Jesus, they consider not, that his righteousness will not be bestowed upon any who do not renounce all confidence in their own or others works, and betake themselves altogether to the only grace of Christ; they consider not, that if the worth of any work be relied upon, the bargain of free grace is spoiled, and clear marred; for, if it he by works, it is no more of grace; and if it be of grace, it is no more of works; for, these two are so opposite one to another in the matter of man's election and justification, that they can no more consist together as causes procuring or moving God, then contradictory sentences can be both true, as Paul teacheth, Rom. 11:6.

3. A third sort of self-deceivers and unwarranted self-absolvers, we reckon all persons poisoned with deadly heresies, who, being drawn away from the doctrine of Christ, set down in the holy Scriptures turn after some false christ and false religion of men's or their own devising, giving unto their Idol, what worship, what service, what employment, what power they please, and making their own conditions of peace with God as they think good; some denying the eternity of the Godhead of the true Christ; some the reality of his assumed human nature; some evacuating so far as they can his three offices, and the fruit of his execution thereof; all of them promising to themselves salvation in another, then in the true Christ described to us in

Scripture, who is Creator, up-holder and Governor of all things, very coeternal God with the Father and holy Spirit, in the fullness of time made man, ever-living Prophet, Priest and King to his Church, both before his incarnation and constantly since, the way, the truth and the life, made of God unto true believers in him, wisdom, righteousness, sanctification and redemption, who walk, among the golden candle-sticks, and searches the ways and hearts of every man, as he holdeth forth himself in these Epistles unto the seven Churches of Asia, Rev. chap. 2, and 3. Of this danger of mistaking the true Christ, and embracing a false in his room, he himself doth carefully fore-warn his Disciples, Math. 24:4,5,24-26, Take heed that no man deceive you: for many shall come in my name, saying, I am Christ, and shall deceive many.

The proper remedy of this evil, is this, let everyone that hath an ear, hear what the spirit speaketh to the Churches, not only in these seven Epistles, but also in all the rest of the holy Scriptures, which are the expressions of the holy Spirit; but, if any man receive not the truth in love, set down by the Lord's Spirit in the Scripture, his punishment is set down by the Apostle, 2 Thess, 2:11, and for this cause, to wit, because they received not the love of the truth that they might be saved, God shall send them strong delusion, that they should believe a lie, that they all might be damned who believed not the truth, but had pleasure in unrighteousness.

1. The fourth sort of absolvers of themselves without God's warrant, are these who pretend unto true religion, and deny the power of it; of whom some are convinced of their duty to repent their sins and to forsake their lusts, and to endeavor a reformation of their life; and this they do promise to themselves, and purpose seriously to do (as they think) only they cannot presently, and at once, break off the

course they are upon, but do hope by little and little to come forward, and at length that they shall wholly give themselves to religious exercises, and a holy life; mean time they conceive, they may come in among the true converts and young beginners, albeit they come not up the length which they intend, but are under the power of some beloved lusts, which they cannot rid themselves of, but do hope they shall betime overcome them. Such men do miserably mistake the matter, first, in that they think their purpose of repentance and a new life bred in them by conviction of their duty, to be the very grace of regeneration and begun sanctification. Secondly, they conceive that the lusts which do reign in themselves are common to them and all other regenerate persons, of whom few or none (think they) want their own gross faults. Thirdly, they conceive they can repent more seriously when they please, and will repent after a whiles following of their beloved lusts, as if repentance were not a saving grace of the holy Spirit, whom they do daily provoke by their vileness, but a work in the power of every man's free-will, being once convinced of his sin. Fourthly, they do not consider, that by the delay of repenting and turning from all sin unto God, their heart is daily more and more in God's Judgment, hardened, and God provoked to punish their voluntary impenitence with judicial hardness of heart, that they shall never repent. Such men our Lord compareth to the disobedient Son, who promised to his Father he would go work in his vineyard, and went not, Math. 21:30. Such men are they, who know the well of the Lord, but do it not, and therefore worthy of double punishment, Math 12:47. The remedy of this evil Christ giveth. Luk. 13:24-26. Strive to enter at the strait gate; for many, I say unto you, will seek to enter in, and shall not be able, Men know not how soon God may shut the door, therefore men had need while it is today, not to harden their hearts. Psal. 95:8.

2. Other some are, who being of a civil life, profess and do persuade themselves, that they indeed do repent and believe in Christ, and by faith in him do certainly expect salvation freely of his grace. If you pose any such men, whether they do indeed believe in Christ, they shall presently answer, that they firmly do believe in him, and that they never doubted but he is their sweet Savior who died for them. If you press them to speak in earnest from their heart, they shall presently be ill pleased with the question, and ask, what cause of suspecting the sincerity of their faith and repentance can be justly alleged? Or, what cause hath any man to suspect them, or doubt of God's favor toward them in Christ? In whom should we believe (say they) if not in Christ? Is there any other Savior of sinners beside him? If a man please to try the truth of their faith by their repentance, they shall forthwith affirm, that they repent day and night, and have just cause so to do; for, in many things we sin all, and why then should we not always repent? If they be asked of their love to God and their neighbor, they shall answer after the same manner. Such men are these, of whom Christ speaketh, that they will confidently come to him and call him Lord, Lord, and yet be found no ways careful to do the Lord's will, but servants to their own lusts.

3. Such men do deceive themselves, first, by framing to themselves such carnal notions of faith and repentance, and of the love of God and of saving hope, and other spiritual graces, as in their fantasy they conceive they do practice, which conceptions are not grounded upon the Word of God. Secondly, they esteem the assent of their mind unto the truth, commending these duties unto men, as good as the performance of them: and they do take the sentence of their

conscience concerning the equity of such duties, for the sentence of their conscience bearing witness of their practice and obedience of these duties; and while their conscience saith why should not I do so? They take that for as good, as if it had said I do so: but saving graces go deeper then civil carriage, and to commend the duties of repentance and faith in Christ is not enough, except they be put in practice also, in daily sorrow for sin and hatred of it, and flying to Christ daily to be washen and more and more sanctified.

4. Some there are, who, when they have heard that a man is justi-fied by faith in Christ only, without the works of the law, do imagine a faith, which needeth not to bring forth any good works at all; and so they take off the justified man from all necessity of following good works, as far as they take off good works from being the cause of justification, and do open a door to themselves to live after their own will in the lusts of their flesh, conceiving, that they who believe in Christ are freed, not only from the covenant of the law, but also from the command of the law, against whom our Lord doth speak, and doth cut off such libertines and turners of the grace of God into wantonness, from the kingdom of heaven, Matth. 5:17-19. And the Apostle, to guard against this self-deceit, (Heb. 12:14) commandeth to follow holiness, without which no man shall see the Lord.

5. Some there are, who pretending to esteem well of the offer of the Gospel, and of the duty of following the means of making them partaker of the marriage-supper, do yet think themselves excusable, when they have much ado in their worldly callings, albeit they pre-fer the care of their family and provision for their things out-ward, unto the main work of their entertaining communion with God; yea, they conceive, that God will allow them in so doing, as Christ doth insinuate in the parable of the guests invited to the feast, answering

the invitation with I pray have me excused, Luke 14:18,19. This is a rise evil in great personages, rich persons and such as are much employed in earthly affairs; such men deceive themselves, first, in laying down this ground with themselves, that their earthly affairs, the necessity whereof doth, first, and most sensibly appear, must in the first room be cared-for, and that the one thing necessary may be followed after, as their civil and earthly affairs may permit. Secondly, they reckon gain to be godliness, 1 Tim. 6:5, for, they cannot be persuaded when gain may be had, that God requireth of any man to slip the occasion, or to put his worldly goods in hazard, by defending or following matters of religion. Thirdly, they think themselves so wise, as they can well enough serve two Masters, God and covetousness, albeit when it cometh to the proof, they will be found to serve, not God, but their own lusts. This error our Lord refuteth and giveth warning to beware of it, Matth. 6:24. And, Luke 21:34. Take heed to your selves, lest at any time your hearts be over-charged with surfeiting and drunkenness and cares of this life. No wonder then, that such men profit not by the Word of God, but remain fruitless, because they are by our Lord compared to the ground that receiveth the seed among thorns, Matth. 13:22. He heareth the word, but the cares of this world, and the deceitfulness of riches, chokes the word, and he remaineth unfruitful.

6. Some there are, who, having received a sufficient measure of gifts, whereby they may promove the kingdom of Christ, and be profitable to the society they live in by making use of their gifts, do pack up all their duties in a sequestration of themselves from all business, conceiving this way to be fittest both for God's service and their own salvation. Whereupon, they betake themselves to a private life in some obscure corner, choosing rather to live as Monks and Eremites,

then to appear in public and make use of their gifts, with the hazard of toiling themselves and tossing of their estimation among beholders of them. And this their resolution is backed with a pretended purpose, to spend their time in reading and prayers, without provoking any man to hatred or emulation against them; thus they conceive they shall provide best for their own ease and safety: and if withal, they apprehend that they are not fitted with gifts, which may be profitable to others, and do think, what they have bestowed upon them by God, to be scarce sufficient for the carrying of themselves on in the course that tendeth to happiness, then they conceive they are well excused, if they let all public works alone, without putting forth their finger to help what they see amiss. We do not deny, but sundry godly persons, in the heat of persecution, have been forced to lurk in a wilderness among wild beasts during the time of the danger, of whose fellowship the world was not worthy; neither do we deny, that age and infirmity of body may make men unfit for all public employment; But, the fault we tax is of such men, as being able, in Church or State, to do service to God and the society they live in, do, for the love of their own ease, hide their talent, and not make use thereof for the benefit of others; for, if a narrow search be made of such men's resolution, the fear of outward trouble in the world, a declining to fight the fight of faith, impatience to be at any pains, and a desire to keep the estimation of their parts from the hazard of men's censure, and love of their own fleshly ease, will be found the fountain of their resolution. But, here we deal with none but such as the Apostle and Christ doth speak against, to wit, such as in some honest employment, for the common utility, refuse to be at pains and work, and therefore are not worthy of their bread, 2 Thess. 3:10. And let us hearken to Christ's judgment of such men, whom the world admireth for most holy Monks in the parable of the talents, he taketh up the lazy lubbart, of whom we speak, under the reckoning of a knavish servant, who because he had but one talent (which amounteth to no small sum) went away and hid it in the earth, Matth. 25:26. Thou wicked and slothful servant, saith he &c. and, ver. 30, cast the unprofitable servant into outer darkness, there shall be weeping and gnashing of teeth.

The remedy is, that men of parts and abilities do not yield unto their lazy humor nor to their discouragements, which may foster their temptations to idleness, but study rather to live in the sense of their obligations to God, and to improve all that they have received from him, for his honor and the well-fare of his people: and to this end, it is fit they should hearken to the counsel of judicious friends, rather than lean to their own judgment over-swayed with temptations, lest the Lord decipher them, and lead them forth with the workers of iniquity, Psal. 125:5.

7. Some are very like, in all externals, to the true converts, so far as can be observed by beholders: for, they profess the true religion with others, they seem to have consecrate themselves unto Christ, they associate themselves unto, and haunt the company of these who are in best esteem, and join themselves always with the reputed godly, they seem ready prepared to bear Christ's cross, and to go forth out of the city after him bearing his reproach, and to be waiters upon his second coming, yet inwardly they were never renewed, they are not troubled with the sense of sin and sinfulness, they do not in earnest, or seriously, seek after Christ's righteousness and remission of sin through him, nor worship God in their spirit. These are described to us in the parable of the foolish and wise Virgins. Matth. 25, the foolish were in company and outward fellowship of religion with the

wise, their outward conversation was without scandal, as was the behavior of the wise; they had lamps of profession as the wise, and were not suspected by themselves or others to be unsound, they went forth in profession waiting for the coming of the Lord, as the wise did; and last of all, no other infirmities were found in them, then such as the wise Virgins were subject unto also, they all fell asleep now and then, nothing could be outwardly found to difference them from the wise Virgins; which external likeness, as it deceived the beholders of these foolish Virgins, So also it deceived themselves; neither shall this personal difference be openly manifested, till the Judge, the searcher of hearts, shall come and separate the goats from the sheep, and the hypocrites from the unfeigned believers. The remedy is, that everyone who pretend unto holiness externally, search their own hearts, and inward sinfulness, daily, and fly to Christ in earnest, that their nakedness may be covered and their affections made spiritual, seeking after things above, and that by faith in Christ they may be filled with the unction of the holy spirit, for bringing forth true fruits of faith.

8. Unto the former, we may join such, as for their eminent gifts above the common sort of pious people, and their abilities to confer, discourse and dispute of matters of religion, seem to themselves and to beholders also, eminent Saints, especially if they appear sharp censurers of others, and zealous against every least degree of sin in others, but most of all, if they, for their enduements, be fitted, and called to pray in public and preach the Gospel to others, and withal do live without scandal, they doubt nothing but they are high in God's estimation, as they are set up in reputation among the godly in the visible Church. Now that such gifted men may deceive themselves, and pass sentence in their own favors for their own absolution from

any challenge, which may condemn them, our Lord doth fore-warn us, Matth. 7:21,22, telling us, that not only many private professors of the Christian Religion, and seeming zealous worshipers, crying Lord, Lord, may deceive themselves and miss heaven, but also Preachers of the Gospel, yea and Prophets, yea and men endued with the gift of doing miracles and casting out of devils in Christ's name, not a few shall be disclaimed by Christ and condemned by him in the day of judgment. If it be asked, what can be their mistake, and the cause of Christ's rejecting of them? We answer, Such men deceive themselves, 1. because both they and beholders also think them holier, then they who are inferior in place and gifts unto them. 2. They compare themselves with those they live among and not with the law of God. 3. They put not due difference between common gifts and saving graces. 4. They consider not, that to whom much is given, much will be required of them; and therefore, after trial they will be found puffed up with the estimation of gifts, enduements, employment and success which they have had, as if these were the undoubted evidences of their regeneration, and of God's special love towards them; they will be found men void of repentance and far from humble walking. In the sense of their natural, habitual and actual sins; they will be found void of all fear of wrath, which might drive them, in the acknowledgment of their blindness, poverty and misery, unto Christ the Redeemer and justifier of sinners; and they will be found void of all care of, and endeavor after, new obedience, conceiving, that the exercise of their gifts and success in their employments, are sufficient holiness and evidence of the holy Ghosts dwelling in them and working by them; for, other ways, Christ will never disclaim them who have fled to him in the sense of their sin, and haunted him as their refuge, in the fear of deserved wrath, and studied by faith in him to be furnished to bring forth the fruits of the Spirit, which he hath promised to them that abide in him.

It is one thing to be justified before God, another thing to be reputed righteous by men, and esteemed so by a man's own self; it is one thing to be endued with the knowledge of divine mysteries, another thing savingly to believe them and have them written in their heart; it is one thing to teach others the way of salvation, whereby the hearers may be saved, another thing to apply saving doctrine to themselves and make right use of it; it is one thing to cleanse the outer side of the plater, and reform the man's outward carriage, another thing to be inwardly renewed; it is one thing to teach repentance and mortification of lusts, another thing by the Spirit of Christ to mortify in-bred pride, and the love of the world, vain glory and other carnal lusts. The course which Paul followed, is the only safe way, though he was a man most laborious in the work of the Lord, yet he lived most sensible of his natural corruption and the body of death; he did not trust in his holy life but in Jesus Christ, Rom. 7:24,25, he so made use of faith in Christ, as he did not neglect the means of mortification of his sinful nature, 1 Cor. 9:27. I keep under my body, and bring it under subjection, lest that by any means, when I have preached to others, I myself should be a cast-away.

The fifth and last sort of self-deceivers, by absolving of themselves without the Lord's allowance or approbation, are temporizers, who, for their temporary believing, temporary repenting, temporary motions of their affections, and temporary amendment of their manners, do seem to themselves and others also, true believers. This sort, however it be in sundry cases coincident with one or more of the former four self-absolvers, yet, because our Lord, in the parable of the sower of seed, (Matth. 13:21, and Luke 4:17) doth put a difference between the stony ground and the other sorts of ground, we shall give it a room by itself, specially because it may have the own proper considerations.

Temporizers then, we call such, as upon temporary motives, from temporary principles for temporary ends, do embrace the Word of the Lord readily, but slightly, and do as readily and lightly pass from it upon temporary motives, in special, when persecution ariseth for the Word, Mark 4:16, when they have heard the Word immediately, they receive it with gladness, and afterward, when affliction or persecution arises for the Words sake, immediately they are offended. Lightly they take up truth delivered, and lightly do they pass from it again; they have no root in themselves or solid believing of the truth, for the truths cause; but what pleaseth others, pleaseth them, and what displeaseth others, doth displease them, in the matters of religion; the way of God set down in Scripture, when they hear it, they can say nothing against it, yea, they think it good to hear the Gospel, and the largeness of God's grace, and because it showeth unto them, a possibility of their salvation, they receive it with a sort of natural gladness, which sort of believing doth endure for a time, to wit, so long as the way of others among whom they live, and the laws of the country, and prosperity and good estimation with others goeth along with the profession of the truth received; but when the wind of another doctrine bloweth, and doth carry with it power to trouble and persecute them who will not receive it, by and by they are offended, and renounce the truth controverted, because it draweth trouble with the profession of it: for, such persons suppose, that gain, ease and applause are very godliness. It is true, sometime the true believer may be surprised with a sudden temptation to renounce the profession of truth in some point, for fear of death, as Peters example doth show us; but true faith recovereth strength, and ariseth after a fall, and endureth persecution for that truth, as temporary belief doth not, but faileth altogether: And the temporizers repentance faileth also, because it ariseth from natural principles, and is for natural motives and ends. Such was the repentance of Saul in weeping and justifying David for sparing his life, 1 Sam. 27:21. Such was the repentance of the carnal Israelites Psal. 78:36, and the humiliation of Ahab; and such is, their amendment of life, all nothing but temporary, and which doth not continue, as Hosea (chap. 6:4) showeth, O Ephraim! What shall I do unto thee? O Judah! What shall I do unto thee? For thy goodness is like the morning cloud and like the early dew that passeth soon away.

Neither is it any wonder, that unrenewed men may attain to something like unto faith and repentance and outward amendment of manners, if we consider that human writings find so much credit with men as not to be called in question, but believed to be true; for experience testifieth, that their affections are moved sometime with delight, and sometime with indignation and pity, not only when they read Histories, but also when they read very Fables and feigned Romances which they know to be such, and yet they cannot command their affections in reading of them: May not then an unrenewed man give as much credit to holy Scripture, and be affected with the holy history thereof, without any change made of his perverse nature, the wisdom whereof is enmity against God, and cannot subject itself either to his law or Gospel? Secondly, if we consider what the power of a natural conscience can work upon the affections, by just accusations, or excusations, for raising grief and joy therein, whereof not only Scripture, but also heathen writers do bear witness, we need not doubt, but the natural conscience may have the same power in a temporary believer. Thirdly, if we consider what the precepts of moral Philosophy hath wrought upon the Scholars of Socrates and Aristotle and other heathen Masters, for the outward framing of them unto seeming virtues, we need not doubt what the precepts of the moral law may work upon a temporary believer, for putting a luster on his life as was to be found in sundry Pharisees without conversion and renovation of the inner man toward God. Fourthly, if we consider what delight is found by Scholars in the contemplation of these things which Philosophy doth treat of, we may easily persuade ourselves, that more delight may be had in contemplation of what holy Scripture doth hold forth, without making the man a new creature. But when unto the natural man's foresaid seeming perfections, knowledge of the mysteries of religion and the gifts of preaching and prophesying are superadded, which are but movable gifts, common to renewed and unrenewed men, and far from being saving graces, what wonder the natural man and temporary believer be puffed up with a high estimation of his own worth and hope of being received by Christ the Judge, and yet be found at last to have deceived himself, and unwarrantably absolved himself by his own deluded conscience, as Christ giveth warning, Matth. 7:21.

Quest. But, what? Can a temporary believer want coming up all the length that is now spoken of and supposed to be endued with so many seeming good things, whereunto many saved Saints do not attain?

Ans. Every saved Saint is beaten out of self-estimation, for anything in himself, beaten out of confidence in anything he doth or can do, and is humbled in his heart by the law, the spiritual perfection whereof being understood, killeth his natural pride, Rom. 7:9.

2. Every saved Saint is chased for refuge to fly to Christ, to his right-eousness and the riches of grace holden forth in him, and every saved Saint is a new creature aiming more and more to follow the course of new obedience and drawing virtue from Christ by faith to please God and worship him in spirit, Phil. 3:3. So that his purpose and endeavor in some measure, is like unto that of David, Psal. 71:10,15,16, saying, I will hope continually, and I will praise thee more and more, my mouth shall show forth thy righteousness and thy salvation all the day; for I know not the numbers thereof, I will walk in the strength of the Lord God, I will make mention of thy righteousness, even of thine only. But the temporary believer, reckoneth not for his debt and deserving's with the law, he is not humbled in the sense of his sins and sinfulness, and inability to satisfy the law by himself, he hath not the root of repentance in him; for immediately upon the hearing of the Gospel, he receiveth the Word with joy, without godly sorrow for his sins, Luk. 8:13. The temporary believer, is ignorant of the righteousness of God by faith in Jesus Christ, and goeth about to establish his own righteousness, upon the bottom of his own blame-less conversation, privileges of the visible Church, common gifts of the Spirit, and success with prosperity: all which, because he is not justified by faith in Christ, do not advance him above the state of the workers of iniquity, Matth. 7:21-23.

The symptoms and ordinary signs of this malady of unwarrantable self-absolution, are these, 1. all of this sort, are well pleased with their own ways, they are not daily humbled in the sense of short-com-ing in duties, and chased to Christ's righteousness, which may hide their nakedness. 2. They are all secure and fear no wrath, but put the evil day far from them. 3. They cannot be induced to any accu-rate examination of their own life, ways, condition or estate. If any man insinuate any suspicion of hypocrisy in them, or if their own conscience begin to question their sincerity, they cannot endure it. 4. Albeit they say unto Christ Lord, Lord, yet they make little use of his office of mediation, of his power and virtue for illumination, humiliation, healing and helping on to salvation. 5. They look more to the seeming good things in themselves for strengthening their carnal confidence, then they take notice of the evil of a body of death in themselves to drive them to Christ, the only deliverer from it. 6. Yea, they all serve some Idol, lurking in their heart, they yield obedience to some reigning lust which they will not forsake, for which cause Christ foretells, that he will declare them to be but workers of iniquity, Matth. 7:23.

The causes of this evil, are, 1. the ignorance of the law and the utter inability, yea, averseness of nature to be subject to it; the knowledge whereof might make men live all their days in a loathing of themselves and cut off all hope of obtaining righteousness by the law. 2. The ignorance of that dear-bought righteousness of Christ, and of the riches of his grace, offering to impute his satisfaction to every self-condemned sinner who shall fly to him and accept his offer. 3, The ignorance of the necessity of the bringing forth the fruits of faith, in love, and study of new obedience and sanctification, by the furniture of Christ, without which no man shall see God. 4. The taking of a presumptuous dead faith, instead of that true justifying faith which layeth hold on Christ and worketh by love. The taking of a vain groundless hope for that lively hope, which purifieth both the heart and external conversation also. 5. The comparing of themselves either with the worst sort of vile sinners, or with such as are like to themselves, or with the Saints in their gross failings not judging themselves according to the law.

The use to be made of this doctrine is, first, to stir us up to take notice of that power of the soul called conscience, which God hath put in every man to observe all the man's words, deeds and intentions, and to compare them with the law and will of God, so far as it is informed and to accuse or excuse, condemn or absolve, smite or comfort the man as it findeth cause, that we suffer not our own conscience to sleep, but set it on work whilst it is time, that we may know how all matters do stand between God and us.

Secondly, that we inform the conscience well from the Scripture, not only concerning the law and covenant of works, whereby we may know how guilty we are of manifold sins, and how impossible it is for us to be justified by our works, or to escape condemnation, but also concerning the Gospel and covenant of gracious reconciliation by faith in Jesus Christ and concerning the covenant of redemption, whereupon the covenant of grace offered in Christ is grounded

Thirdly, that we make due and orderly application of these covenants, that the conscience may always be furnished with matter of humiliation, and held on in the exercise of repentance, and not only keeped from desperation, but also may be furnished with grounds of good hope to be saved, through the grace of our Lord Jesus who hath purchased remission of sins and imputation of his righteousness to every humbled sinner flying to him for grace.

Fourthly, that being engrafted in Christ by faith, we, by way of thankfulness, study in the furniture of his Spirit, to live holily, justly and soberly; and that whatsoever measure of sanctification we attain unto, we beware to fall back to that deadly error of seeking justification before God by our works, whereunto we are naturally inclined: for, upon this rock the flour and most shining professors in Israel after the flesh, made shipwreck of their salvation, Rom, 9:32. Israel which

followed after the law of righteousness, hath not attained unto the
law of righteousness, wherefore because they sought it not by faith,
but as it were by the works of the law. And, Rom. 10:3, for they being
ignorant of God's righteousness, and going about to establish their
own righteousness, have not submitted themselves to the righteousness of God. Unto this error of seeking righteousness by our works,
after entering in the way of justification by grace, we are all naturally inclined; for, the covenant of works is so engraven in all Adams
children, do this and live, that hardly can we renounce this way of
justification, and howsoever it be impossible to attain righteousness
this way, yet hardly can we submit ourselves to the righteousness
by faith in Christ, which not only the experience of Israel after the
flesh maketh manifest, but also the experience of the Galatians lets
us see; for, they having once outwardly renounced justification by
works, and embraced the covenant of gracious reconciliation by faith
in Jesus, did turn about for a time, to seek justification by the works
of the law, and were on the way of falling from grace and communion
with Christ. And the experience of Papists doth show the same; for,
whatsoever they profess concerning faith in Christ, yet they abhor
justification by Christ's imputed righteousness and do blaspheme
that way as a mere conceit of men and an assumed or only imaginary
righteousness, and do seek to establish their own righteousness, and
to be justified, not only before men, but also before God, by the merits
of their own and other men's works and sufferings; the imputation
whereof they can tell for money, in the midst of their blaspheming
the imputation of Christ's righteousness. What can be said for a thief,
condemned to die for his faults, and redeemed by a potent man, upon
condition that he should be the domestic servant of the redeemer, to
work his work all his life-time, and live upon his allowance, and so

never be necessitated to steal anymore? If the ransomed thief should after steal his Masters goods, and make himself a stock-purse whereupon he thought he might live, and loose himself from his redeemers grace and live upon his own finding, were he not worthy, upon the finding out of his thefts and other faults, to be left in the hands of justice, to die according to his deserving's? And what could be said for a tenant, laboring a parcel of ground of his Lands-lord, for a yearly farm-duty, by his own miscarriage falling to beggary, if he should be taken in to the free table of his Lands-lord, and trusted with the same parcel of ground to be labored for his Masters use, if he should misuse the fruits of that ground, and being weary of his Masters bounty and grace, should seek to be fired of his Masters service, and to labor the ground for himself, for payment of rent? If upon the finding out of his theft, and not payment of his rent, he should be cast in prison, did he not deserve to be dealt with according to justice, who would not live by grace? So may be said of the man, who shall turn from justification by free grace, to seek justification by his works.

The fifth and last use of this doctrine is, that to the intent we may not absolve ourselves without God's allowance, we study to make our calling and election sure, by endeavoring to walk in the sense of our unworthiness and ill-deserving, and renouncing all confidence in anything without Christ, to rely on him for righteousness and life-eternal, and by faith in him draw spirit and life from him, for furnishing us unto new obedience: for, he is the justified man, approven of God, who hath no confidence in the flesh, and rejoiceth in Jesus Christ, and worshippeth God in the spirit, Philip. 3:3.

CHAP. I. - Of considerations to be premised.

HITHERTO THE SICKNESSES OF the Conscience of the un-regenerate man are spoken to, and this was needful, to the end, that we might show how Regeneration is either altogether kept off, or hindered from growing where it is begun. And because many of these sicknesses, which destroy many of the sons of Adam, cleave to the regenerate man, and though they do not reign, nor altogether prevail over him, yet do molest and vex him, and hinder his comfortable walking toward his everlasting blessedness: Now we come to speak, first, in this Book, of these cases of the conscience of the man regenerate, which do brangle, and bring in question his state in grace, and make him doubt whether he be a man translated out of the state of nature, out of the kingdom of Satan, or not. And next, of these cases that concern his condition in the state of grace in the following Book.

As to the first sort of cases, which concern the regenerate man's state, some considerations must be premised, for making particulars afterwards more clear.

1. In the question of this, or that man's regeneration or his being in the state of grace, it is all one to question whether he be born again, or be effectually called, or endued with saving faith, or be a justified man, or be reconciled to God, or be an adopted child? And in the

answer of this question, let it be proven, that he is any of these, and it is proven also, that he is all these: for, albeit these denominations, in their formal conceptions in the abstract, may be distinguished, yet upon the matter in the conceit they fall upon the same individual person altogether, because it is impossible to prove a man to be regenerate, but he must be proven also a true believer in Christ, a man reconciled to God, a man justified and an adopted child

2. It is necessary therefore, for proving a man to be regenerate, to know the right description of the regenerate man which is given by the Apostle, Phil. 3:3. We are the circumcision, which worship God in the spirit, and rejoice in Jesus Christ, and have no confidence in the flesh. Wherein the Apostle holdeth forth the truly regenerate circumcised in heart. 1. He is not sinless, but so sensible of his sinfulness, as he hath no confidence in himself, nor anything else in himself. 2. He is not free of accusations or temptations and doubts, but he flyeth to Christ for righteousness. 3. He is not an idle and unfruitful branch, but a worshiper of God in spirit and truth. 1. He is burdened with sin. 2. He cometh to Christ for relief. 3. He puts on Christ's yoke, Math. 11:28,29. If a man have these three properties jointly in him, he is a regenerate man, and may defend his interest (in the state of grace) and right to righteousness and eternal life through Jesus Christ.

3. Divine operations and saving graces which accompany salvation, such as are faith, repentance unto life, hope, Christian love to God and men for God's cause, effectual vocation, justification, reconciliation, adoption, go together in time by God's gift, but one of them goeth before another in order of nature; for, effectual calling goeth before faith, and faith goeth before hope, and before charity or love. Again, these graces which are given to the redeemed child of God jointly, in respect of time, do not show themselves in their

evidence alike soon in time, nor do they equally manifest themselves when they do appear in time. And so the evidences of repentance may be discerned in not a few converts, before faith in Christ do show itself in them clearly. So also love to God and his Saints ofttimes may be discerned in a regenerate man, before he himself dare affirm anything of his faith in Christ.

4. Albeit there be many regenerate persons, who for the present time cannot perceive in themselves any undoubted signs of their conversion; yet it is certain also, that there be many, who, to their own unspeakable comfort, are assured of their regeneration, and that they are translated from death to life, and that they have received the spirit of adoption and earnest of eternal life, as is pointed out in the experience of the Ephesians, chap. 1:14. And this is certain also, that all who are fled to Christ for refuge, should by all means labor to make their calling and election clear and certain to themselves, 2 Pet. 1:10. And to this purpose we are commanded to examine ourselves, and try whether we be in the faith or not, whether Christ by his Spirit be in us or not, 2 Cor. 13:5, for otherwise, except a convert know certainly the blessedness of his own state, and that he standeth in grace and favor with God, it is not possible for him to give hearty thanks to God for the change of his state, from being an enemy, to be made a reconciled subject and child of God. It is not possible for him to rejoice in the Lord, or set cheerfully himself to serve God, or comfortably call on God, as a father to him in Christ: Wherefore, all who in the sense of their sins and fear of deserved wrath are fled for refuge unto Christ, should deal by prayer earnestly with God, that he would graciously grant unto them his Spirit, by whose operation in them, they may know the saving graces which he hath freely bestowed upon them, of which gift of the holy Spirit the Apostle doth speak, 1 Cor. 2:12.

5. The knowledge of a man's own regeneration, hath many degrees of clearness and assurance, by reason of the variety of conditions wherein a man truly converted may be: For, many doubts may arise in the man regenerate, which may darken his sight, and hinder the assurance of saving grace granted unto him, whereof sundry causes may be found, and in special these four among others. 1. In a man illuminate and renewed by the holy Spirit, there remains a great deal of ignorance, much doubting mixed with faith, by reason of unskillfulness of the convert to examine and discern this blessed change made in him, where through that cometh to pass in many young converts, which will be seen in infants, who have a soul indeed, but do not know or perceive that they have a soul till they come to some years of discretion; yea, many sound Christians, are ofttimes at a stand about their regeneration, and know not what to make of their faith or repentance, especially when they feel the power of the body of death, the strength of natural corruption in themselves, and great indisposition for any spiritual exercise; they are forced with the Apostle to cry, miserable man that I am, who shall deliver me? Rom. 7:24, mean time for weakness of their faith, they are not able at the first to wrestle against discouragement, and to come up unto the Apostles thanking God through Christ. 2. By the temptation of Satan ofttimes the persuasion of holy men is darkened, so as they cannot see the evidences of their own regeneration clearly: for, Satan sets himself to vex the Saints who are delivered from his kingdom and bonds, whom albeit he know that he cannot destroy them, yet he will not cease to trouble them, that at least he may make them some way unfit for God's service and mar their cheerfulness in his service; and because he feareth harm from them unto his kingdom, by their dealing with the unconverted to repent their sins, and to turn unto

God, therefore he finds them work at home in their own bosom, and puts them to defend themselves and to forbear to invade his subjects, till they be settled themselves. 3. Ofttimes the Lord is offended by the sins of the regenerate, and specially by their gross transgressions, for which his Spirit being grieved, doth for a time cease from comforting them, and doth not bear witness with their spirits, that they are the children of God, as he hath formerly used to do. 4. Ofttimes the Lord by suffering doubts to arise in their hearts, useth to try and exercise the faith of his children, and thereby to stir them up to the pursuing of the duties of piety and righteousness more vigorously and sincerely, that after victory obtained over these temptations, they may be more confirmed in their faith, and more diligent in his obedience.

6. It may come to pass, that while the true convert doth most doubt of his own regeneration, that the work of God's special grace may be observed in him and clearly seen by others more experienced in the ways of God, and endued with the spirit of discretion. The reason whereof is, because howsoever the weak convert, and child of light, walking in darkness of temptation and desertion, cannot discern his own blessed state, yet there may appear, and be perceived in him, such signs and undoubted evidences of saving grace, that the prudent beholder of him under his sad exercise, may in the judgment of discretion and charity, declare his righteousness, and him for his state to be in grace and favor with God. In these two disciples going to Emmaus, Luk. 24, saving faith was not extinguished, albeit they were driven to suspect themselves to have been mistaken, when they once believed that Christ was the promised Savior; for, in that same time, there appeared in them evident tokens of their unfeigned love to Christ: for, while they are troubled with suspicion of their being mistaken about Christ, they are very sad and sorrowful, and were

regrating the sufferings of Christ, and were gathering what arguments they could for supporting their faith, whereby their dying faith might be supported by conference about this matter, laying forth their doubts and temptations one to another.

7. The precise time of begun regeneration, is not always observed nor known, either by the regenerate man himself, or by beholders of his way, as experience maketh evident in many, who from their infancy are brought up in the exercises of true religion, in whose conversion no notable change can be observed. In those the words of Christ in part are verified, the kingdom of heaven cometh not with observation. Such persons when they begin to examine themselves, whether they be regenerate, whether they be in Christ, and at what time they were converted, they can neither determinately condescend upon the time of their conversion, nor can they confidently speak of their conversion, till after sundry trials and experiences they can gather proofs of their sincerity from such signs, effects and marks of the work of saving grace in them, as may prove that Christ hath dwelt in them of before.

8. Albeit regeneration be of the same kind, specie and definition, in all the regenerate, yet it doth admit sundry accidental differences, when the conversion of such and such persons is compared: for, some do not stay long in the straits of regeneration, or new birth, but within a short space of time they are both wounded and healed, are both casten down and raised up again, are both slain by the Law and quickened by the Gospel: Of this sort we have a past proof in some thousand converts, Act 2, who by one sermon or two were converted to the faith of Christ and fellowship with the Church. On the other hand, experience of many doth show, they have been under the spirit of bondage a long time, before they could receive the consolations of

the Gospel, Heb. 2:15. Some in the beginning of their conversion are
handled very tenderly, and afterward fall in hard exercises of mind, as
we may see in David, who in his youth, while he was keeping his fathers sheep, did pass the time in holy songs, and playing on his harp,
but afterward he was more sharply exercised, and much afflicted
from time to time with the sense of divine wrath. Some in sorrow and
much weeping do follow Christ, and study to promove his kingdom:
such a one was Timothy, whom the Apostle exhorteth to admit a
larger measure of consolation allowed unto him by the Lord, that he
might be the more cheerful and courageous in the warfare whereunto
he was called, 2 Tim. 1:4. Another of this sort was Heman the Ezrahite,
who (Psal. 88) declareth, that from his youth up he was so keeped
under terror, as he was ready to die under discouragement: And in
the experience of this holy man, we have a proof of what was holden
forth in the preceding consideration, to wit, that regeneration may be
begun in a man, and well promoved before either himself or others
can well discern it: for, of them who are keeped under the law and
spirit of bondage, it is hard determinately to judge, before faith in
Christ begin to appear in them, whether their exercise be the special
work of the holy spirit of regeneration, or not: for as it may come to
pass, that the spirit of fear and bondage may for a time work, and
go no further then to convict a man, and not go on to convert him,
So also it may come to pass, that there be some wrestling of faith
lying under-foot in the midst of terrors, not perceived for a while; of
which wrestling none can well give out sentence, that it is a wrestling
of saving faith, before faith get some victory over temptations, and
break forth in some evident effects. In which case it is very needful
warily and circumspectly to apply the doctrine of the Gospel, so as
the afflicted soul may be supported with hopes of a gracious out-gate;

for, the work of the law, humbling the sinner, is a fair call to come to Christ, and a messenger sent by Christ to bring him up, Gal. 3:24.

9. Albeit the regenerate man, in respect of the state of his person, by standing in grace and favor with God, fixed and unmovable as the Apostle doth show us, Rom. 5:1-3, partly, because the love of God manifested to the believer in Christ is unchangeable; and partly, because the covenant of grace through Christ is an everlasting covenant, Isa. 55:3, and partly, because the saving gifts and calling of God are such, as God will never repent him to have bestowed them, Rom. 11:29, yet in respect of his condition the regenerate man, is subject to many changes in his life and conversation, in the disposition of his mind and affections, and in the exercise of his gracious habits, and in the sense and observation of the grace of God in him and favor of God toward him: for, it may come to pass, yea, and ofttimes doth come to pass, that men who are regenerate, and in the state of grace, which is a notable good state, may be in a very evil condition, in a miserable and deplorable disposition of heart, as befell the Church of Ephesus, Sardis and Laodicea. And it may be also, that regenerate persons, after their consciences are wakened, and they do perceive the miserable and sinful condition of their affections and conversation, that no small doubts arise in their hearts whether their state in grace be real or not, which doubts will evanish, when after the renewing of their repentance, their condition is changed to the better: for, Christ pre-occupieth this temptation, speaking, to the Church of Sardis and Laodicea, counseling them to strengthen the thing that remaineth, which was ready to die, and not to doubt of his love toward them, Rev. 2 and 3.

10. These temptations whereby the regenerate man is troubled, and tempted to doubt whether he be in the state of grace, should be

distinguished and discerned from actual doubting; for, there may be a temptation unto doubting, without a yielding unto the temptation, as we see in Christ our Lord, whom the devil durst tempt to doubt, whether he was the Son of God, but his holy heart could not admit such a temptation. And the Apostle (Eph. 6:11,12. &c) doth warn the Saints, that our adversary Satan useth to throw fiery darts at all the children of God; which fiery and poisonable darts, the regenerate man should not meddle with nor finger them, but by the shield of faith, with all speed, quench and extinguish them. But when a probable reason is joined with the temptation, and the temptation doth appear to be very reasonable, and when there is a fear, that the temptation shall be yielded unto, except the scruple be removed, then let the temptation be examined and brought to the form of a reason or syllogism, that the strength of it being tried to be null, it may be rejected; or let the temptation be communicated to a prudent friend or Pastor, who may discover the sophistry of the temptation; for, if the temptation shall be slighted and not discussed, albeit it lie quiet for a time, yet it will return again and raise more trouble and vexation to the conscience, then it did before.

11. In answering of doubts and temptations tending to weaken faith, it is needful to observe and show an usual stratagem of Satan, whereby he doth multiply and heap together a number of doubts; and after he hath suggested one doubt, presently doth suggest on the back of that another, and after that another, whereby he marreth the answering of the first doubt, which from the Word of God, either immediately, or by some faithful Friend or Minister, is offered for solution thereof: by this mean, Satan endeavors that the mind of the afflicted person may, at one time, both be turned off from taking notice of the answer offered, and be taken up wholly with the con-

sideration of the new suggested doubt, So that the answer to the new doubt hath no place, because the afflicted party doth not take heed thereto. In this case, both the party afflicted, and the party offering consolation, must hold to the first doubt, and not suffer any other new doubt to have place, till a satisfactory answer be given to the first doubt, and after that, let every objection, moved by the party afflicted, be answered one after another in order.

12. Seeing every doubt, whereby the regenerate person is troubled, doth tend either to weaken faith in Christ, or to hinder the bringing forth of the fruits of faith, let no answer to any doubt of this kind be esteemed sufficient, except it lead the afflicted person unto Christ, teaching him to humble himself before God; and being brought low in his own eyes, to lay hold by faith on Jesus Christ, the only Redeemer, and relief from sin and misery; and after laying hold on the Physician, to request for the remedy of that evil which hath moved and given strength to the doubt: for, Christ is the end, both of the Law and of every spiritual exercise: for, the enjoining of such and such moral duties, whereby un-skillful Physicians use to over-charge diseased consciences, commanding the afflicted party in the first place, to go about such and such duties, and the exercise of such and such virtues, as may remove the evil which gave ground to the doubt, can never avail the diseased person, except he be led first unto Christ for remission of sin and acceptation of his person, that in him, power to do these duties may be obtained, and by his Spirit, moral precepts may be quickened; for, if these precepts be pressed upon the diseased without Christ, they can do no more but detain the afflicted in self-confidence, and make him hope in vain, that he may or can by his own work over-come the evil felt in him, or that he can by himself, attain to that good which he conceiveth necessary for

loosing of his doubt; but let him go to Christ for remission of sin, and then for strength to go about the duty.

13. Because almost in all cases of conscience which pertain to the state of the regenerate man, some grace or Christian virtue is pitched upon and called in question, whether it be in him or not, heed must be taken that evangelic graces, virtues or actions, be not weighed in the balance of the moral Law and covenant of Works, wherein nothing hath weight which cometh short of absolute perfection of personal obedience; for, in the strict judgment of God and the conscience, according to the law of Works, no mere man, nor any action of man, can stand, Psal. 130:3, for, there are so many imperfections and blemishes in the Saints and their best works, being compared with the perfect rule of righteousness by the Law, that whatsoever luster or appearance of good may be in a work, it is blacked and made to hide its face before the Law: but, let the tender buds of new obedience and fruits of faith, be examined by the grace of the Gospel, which judgeth of the begun obedience of the believer in Christ, according to the sincerity and uprightness of the man aiming at conformity to the Law, how short soever he come of his aim, and of the spiritual perfection of the Law, and it will be taken for new obedience. It is true, the Evangel requireth, that a man fled to Christ for justification, and reconciled to God by faith in Christ, should set himself to work the works prescribed in the moral Law, for the glory of God, and should aim at the exact obedience of all the Commands; yet, the Gospel doth not reject a good work for the defects, imperfections and blemishes thereof, but accepteth and taketh in good part the first fruits and buds of new obedience, and doth foster the tender and small beginnings, that they may grow and increase. And the reason is, because the Gospel doth not teach us to seek the justification of our persons

before God by works, but by faith in Christ, and then teacheth us to seek the justification of our faith before men in our own and others conscience, by the sincere endeavor of new obedience. And therefore,

14. While we are about the cure of the wounds of the conscience and strengthening of faith, we must on the one hand take heed, left we foster presumption, and hinder either the exercise of repentance, or doing diligence in following duties: for, Christian graces do not impede, but help and strengthen one another, if they be real and kindly, because they must flow from the same fountain of the spirit of sanctification, and do run toward the same end, which is the glory of God: and on the other hand, we must take heed lest we press the exercise of repentance, as it were out of our own strength, or the practice of duties, so as we hinder the exercise of faith in Christ, who is that exalted Prince to give repentance, and is the author and finisher of faith. Let us so cry up the imputed righteousness of Christ, that we neglect not to press the regenerate man (freely justified by grace) to bring forth the fruits of faith, and to follow hard after the growth of sanctification, without which, no man shall see the face of God; and let us so extol the covenant of Grace, and freedom of the believer from the covenant of Works, that we neglect not to keep up the authority of the moral Law and the commands thereof, as the perpetual rule of new obedience, the use whereof is very profitable, in the whole course of a Christian life, to hold forth the duty of believers in Christ, and to show unto them, by their short-coming in duties, the poison and power of corruption remaining in the Saints, and to make them sensible of the necessity of flying daily to that imputed righteousness by faith in Christ, and of drawing strength from Christ to bring forth more abundant fruits, whereby Christ shall be more

and more precious in our eyes, and be acknowledged absolutely necessary for our justification, sanctification and salvation.

15. When question is made concerning Christian virtues and operations of the holy Spirit in us, the order of God's working held
forth to us in Scripture, is carefully to be marked by us: which is,
that sense of sin should go before faith in Christ; for, the Law is a
pedagogue to Christ, for, he came not to call the righteous, but sinners to repentance, Matth. 9:13. And faith in Christ goeth before the
fruits of faith, and the fruits of faith before the sensible approbation
of them, and approbation of the fruits by Scripture goeth before the
sensible sealing of the believer, and the quieting of the conscience in
its approbation of what the Scripture approveth; for, after we have
believed, we come to be sealed, Ephes. 1:13. Now, for the not observing this order, many real Christians do make unto themselves
a very un-comfortable life, for, albeit they be convinced of sin, and
humbled in the sense of their own inability to help themselves, and
are fled to Christ for pardon and help, and do lead a life blameless,
yet do they unhappily suspend the acknowledging of the work of
faith bestowed upon them, and do disquiet themselves, so as they
cannot rest on Christ, but do quarrel the reality of their faith, till they
shall feel and perceive, with approbation of their conscience, such
and such fruits of faith in themselves, and that in such a measure as
they have fore-imagined to be the necessary evidences of faith; yea,
and they refuse to account themselves persons justified, because they
cannot perceive such mature fruits in themselves, as they conceive
must not only be, but be acknowledged also to be, in the justified
person, before he can lay hold on justification. Such persons do, in
effect, invert the order which they should observe; for, when it were
their part to fly unto Christ the only Mediator, because they come

short of new obedience, and because they are loaden with sin, that in him they might have God reconciled to them, and by his Spirit, pouring in of his grace in their souls, to make them more holy, they take another and contrary course, by suspending their faith upon their works, and do exact of themselves works before faith, and so do weaken their own faith, and hinder it to bring forth such fruits as they do require. It is reason indeed, to prove our faith by our works, and it is just, that such a faith be accounted dead, which is not accompanied with the purpose and endeavor to live holily, justly and soberly. But it is against all reason and equity to condemn weak faith, accompanied with the purpose of a new life, as if it were no faith, because it hath not as yet brought forth so fair and fully ripe fruits as the weak believer would. It were their wisdom, when they perceive such impotency to do what is good, and such strength of the body of death in them, to fly unto the Redeemer so much the more, and in him to seek remission of sin, and strength to bring forth good fruits, and to be sucking juice and sap out of him, as the true Vine: for, if we come to him and abide in him, we shall bring forth much fruit, Job. 15:4,5. For, faith in Christ, in order of nature, goeth before good works; for only they who come to Christ and abide in him, do bring forth abundant fruit, and not they, who upon the apprehension of their want of fruits, do loose or slacken their grip of faith, and upon discouragement, are ready to depart from the living God.

16. The like wisdom is required in dealing with the consciences of men concerning the preparatory dispositions of such as may confidently come unto Christ to be justified, sanctified and saved; for albeit it be true, that all that come to Christ, ought to come in the sense of their sin and acknowledgment of wrath and death deserved for their sins, ought to come with contrition of heart, with godly

sorrow for their sins, and a humble renunciation of all confidence
in themselves; yet must not such persons, as do not satisfy themselves in the measure or sincerity of such preparatory dispositions
in themselves, be keeped back, or debarred from coming to Christ,
because they not only want, as they conceive, both the humiliation
and sorrow of heart for sin, and fear of wrath, required in such as
have access unto Christ, but also do perceive in themselves such
blindness of mind and vanity thereof, such stupidity of conscience
and stubbornness of a proud heart, as is not fit (as they conceive) to
be received by Christ, or fit to be comforted by him; such persons I say
are not to be forthwith debarred from coming to the throne of grace;
for, ofttimes sincerity of conviction, compunction and humiliation is
to be found in such as are displeased with their own short-coming in
such preparatory dispositions, more than in many others who make
a fairer show and profession of their godly sorrow and humiliation,
and are well pleased with themselves in that respect. We must be
wary also while we require sorrow and humiliation, and other like
preparatory dispositions in them who may come unto Christ, least
we secretly import and insinuate a sort of merit to be in such dispositions, so as if he that doth not perceive himself thus qualified, could
expect no good at Christ's hands, except he have in his hand such
preparatory dispositions as if it were a price of purchasing address
to Christ. But let us hold this fast, that the more poor and empty a
man be in his own eyes, he ought to draw the more near unto the
riches of grace in Christ, because in him only are to be found all the
treasures of every saving grace, and preparatory dispositions for receiving thereof; he is that exalted Prince, who giveth repentance unto
Israel, Act. 5:31, he is the author and finisher of faith, unto whom all
they, who in the sense of their want of repentance and faith, do sigh

in themselves, ought, and safely may come, that they may have from him a more ample measure of faith and repentance. Neither need we in this case be feared, least any such person go or be sent too soon unto Christ, and that the teacher of this doctrine be found to foster presumption, and to offer untimely consolation; for, it is one thing to direct a man to go to Christ, for supply of whatsoever good is wanting in him, and another thing to warrant a secure sinner to lay hold on the consolations of the Gospel, which God hath reserved in his own hand, to be dispensed in due time and order, to the truly humble penitent. The Lord knoweth how to deal with such as come unto him; he can hold an unhumbled supplicant praying and knocking at Heaven's door without giving him a comfortable answer until he be humbled, and so prepare him by humiliation for consolation in due time.

True it is, that many draw near to Christ with their lips while their hearts are far away, and remain senseless of their evil estate and condition, and are far from the earnest desire of the remedy which is to be had in Christ: and therefore it is, not without cause, that Pastors in their sermons require the sight and sense of sin, and hunger and thirst for righteousness in them who come to Christ, and desire to profit by their coming to him: for, albeit it be free to God, without antecedent preparatory exercises, to fall in upon man's heart suddenly, and at one sermon both convince him of sin, and lead him in to Christ, as he hath sometime dealt with a multitude, when Peter was preaching, Act. 2, yet it is not free for men to neglect their duties, when they are advertised that the order of God's working ordinarily, is, to take a time for information of their mind concerning their natural misery, and his gracious way of delivery, and for a time to work on their hearts by the law, before he give them the felt fruits of the Gospel. Mean time this must be remembered, that no man, displeased with his disposition, as not fitted for mercy, and who doth regrate that he is a stupid sinner, and so hard-hearted that he cannot repent: should be keeped off, and debarred from going to Christ, till he discern in himself the contrition and humiliation of heart which he would have: for, this were as much as to say in effect, that before a sinner may go to Christ, he must seek, not from Christ, but out of his own strength and abilities to work up his own heart to the sense of sin and humiliation of heart, and other such like dispositions, as ordinarily go before the act and discerning of saving faith; for, if even Simon Magus, discovered and found out to be in the gall of bitterness and bond of iniquity, was exhorted to pray that God would forgive his sins, and remove the perverseness of his heart and save him from deserved wrath, Act. 8:22. How much more are they to be encouraged to go to Christ for relief from these evils which they feel and fear, in whom not only this gall of bitterness doth not appear, but also some appearances may be marked, by wise beholders, of a begun work of grace in them, albeit the man himself cannot perceive so much for the time?

17. Seeing it is certain, that God doth preveen by grace every converted man's actions, before the man do actually turn himself to God, and that the Lord useth to open the eyes of the man whom he is converting, to see such and such evils in himself before these evils be taken away; and seeing it is God's usual way by preventing, to give some measure of the good to be prayed for, that the man may pray for more good upon the receipt of some measure of that good already bestowed; therefore all they who desire to approach to Christ, must be taught to make, observe and take notice of the least degree of good bestowed upon them, of the smallest beginnings of illumination, of the meanest degrees of conviction for sin, of the least measure of

estimation of Christ and his grace wrought already in themselves, and to thank the Lord for so much eye-salve as hath opened their eyes to discern their own blindness and misery, and Christ to be the remedy of all the evils they do see; and after they have marked what is bestowed already on them, and have blessed God for the gift, they must be exhorted to request the Lord to make out and perfect the begun mercy, that they may be sure of their own real conversion; for so doth the new convert pray, Jer. 31:18. Convert me, and I shall be converted; and the humble soul, Cant. 1:4, draw me after thee, and we will run after thee. And this we speak not, as if any unconverted man could in the sense of his sin and misery sincerely and heartily seek after Christ, or for more grace from him. But because some that are converted, do not perceive that they are converted, we frame our speech to their estimation of themselves, that they may be edified who are brought unto Christ, by the draught of effectual calling, and have not as yet received the gift of the Spirit to perceive these things which are freely bestowed upon them, 1 Cor. 2:12.

18. As it useth to be in the sickness of the body, So it falleth out in the sicknesses of the conscience, that as there are some sicknesses simple, and other some complicate, when more sicknesses concur together; So in the conscience, there are some simple, some complicate ill cases. Simple and single cases of conscience are these, wherein the diseased soul is troubled with one doubt only for the present: as for example, when the party afflicted, is doubtful only of the will of God toward him, and not of his power: such was the case of the Leper, Matth. 8:2. Thou canst make me clean, if thou wilt.

Complicate and involved cases, are, when many evils concur together, and the conscience is troubled with many doubts. In which case many questions may offer themselves in a throng together, which the afflicted party cannot well distinguish, and thereupon is driven to darkness and confusion of mind. In this case the Pastor, or prudent Christian friend, must observe some order, beginning with the most perilous doubt, that it may be first solved: which doubt being answered in the first place, let him fall upon the answering of the rest of the doubts in order. As for example, if the party be afflicted with temptations unto desperation, let him be cleared and led by the hand to see and acknowledge a possibility of salvation by Christ, and then a probability and appearance that it shall be, by an argument taken from his present exercise, which putteth an errand in his hand, and so a warrant, to go to Christ; and so piece and piece let him be dealt with to accept the general offer of grace in Christ and to believe in him. Now that such may be the exercise of the child of God, appeareth, Psal. 42:7. Deep calleth unto deep, at the noise of thy water-spouts, all thy waves and billows are gone over me. And Psal. 77:7,8, will the Lord cast off forever, and will he be favorable no more? Is his grace clean gone forever? And will he be favorable no more? &c. At last he discovereth his duty to believe in God, and concludeth against himself, that his giving so far way to the temptation was his infirmity.

19. We must distinguish worldly sorrow, and hypochondriac-passions and perturbations of mind, from cases of conscience, and spiritual exercise in the wrestling's of faith, that for a natural disease and distemper a pertinent remedy may be called for from the bodily Physicians; and to such as are under a spiritual exercise, the doubts of their conscience may be prudently loused. In such a case, when both the bodily distemper and spiritual exercise are joined, circumspection is necessary, that proportionable remedies be used by the Physician and the Pastor or prudent friend, that bodily medicine

and spiritual consolations may be each in their own time and order wisely made use of: and because it useth to fall out, that exercise of conscience and distemper of bodily humors are oftentimes joined one with another, let it be sufficient, that a word is casten in here for advertisement.

20. In curing cases of conscience, it is not sufficient to louse some-one doubt or other, but after satisfaction given to the parties afflicted concerning the present case, which hath troubled them, they must learn to observe other causes, which may trouble them afterward, wherewith for the present they possibly are not troubled, and must be directed to acquaint themselves, with Christ, that in him they may have relief from every sin, and every sort of misery; and to that end and purpose they must consecrate and devout themselves to him, to depend upon him in all things, and at all times, whatsoever way he shall be pleased to exercise them: for, whosoever do come unto Christ, must come of set purpose to abide in him, and never depart from him, but to live in him, and draw grace after grace out of his fullness; grace to mortify sin, grace to renew the acts of faith and repentance daily, according as they find new guiltiness contracted, and weakness in themselves to do commanded duties: for, except the do so, they shall easily slide back from their begun sanctification, and furnish matter to Satan for raising of new doubts in their souls and new temptations unto sins, wherein they have not fallen before: therefore must they keep the habits of faith and repentance in actual exercise daily.

21. In dealing with a troubled conscience, let not the comforter, whether a Pastor or a prudent friend, trust to his abilities, or arrogate to himself above what is due to him, but let him keep his eye upon the Lord and in his heart be praying to God to bless the Word in his

mouth, giving glory to God expressly, if he perceive the afflicted party laying hold on God's Word delivered by him. And let him also teach the afflicted to lift his eyes to the Lord, when the Word of consolation is dispensed to him by the Minister or prudent friend, that God may have the glory in his consolation, and no more ascribed to the instrument then is due: For, the Minister may sow the seed and plant, and water, but God only can give the increase: men are ready to fail in this point and mar the blessing, for God is a jealous God, and will not give his glory to another.

22. In case the expected consolation be not found, or the doubt propounded be not solved so soon as is desired, let the afflicted be exhorted, that he make not hast in seeking comfort, but patiently submit himself to God's will in exercising him for a while, and humble himself under his mighty hand, in meekness waiting for clearness and comfort in due time; for, affliction is sent to work patience, and patience to work experience, and experience to work hope, which shall not make the patient man ashamed: and it is far better for a soul to lie for a time in the bonds of affliction, till it be daunted and subdued, then before patience hath had the perfect work, to seek to have its foolish wishes granted unto it: for if once a soul heartily submit itself to God, or strive to submit, and patiently wait on, consolation will be found not far off.

23. In regard the work of the holy Ghost, working the conversion of a man, may begin before it can be marked, it is the part of him who meddleth with the afflicted conscience, to deal tenderly with the afflicted, and so to temper his speech, as he may both further repentance and faith, pre-supposing the parties exercise may prove a begun work of grace; for, it is better so to judge in charity of God's dispensation, then to foster sinister suspicions of the party afflicted,

which may readily break forth in some unhappy expressions to the hurting of the patient, and hindering his profiting by what may be said beside.

24. Because we have to do in this Book with the weak believers, who, in the sense of sin and deserved wrath, are fled or flying unto Christ, with a purpose of amendment of life, but do fear they are not, or shall not be admitted into that kingdom of our Lord Jesus, for this and that pretended reason: therefore, it will be to purpose in comforting them, to make use, as of other Scriptures, so in special of these two passages; the one, 2 Cor. 5:19, the other, 1 Cor. 1:30, the one serving to convince them, that they are already in the state of grace, and of the number of believers in Christ, how strongly soever they are assaulted with fears, doubts and suspicions, that it is other ways; for, in this passage, 2 Cor. 5:19, the Apostle summeth up the whole Gospel in few words, holding forth, first, that the fullness of God in three persons, was in the second person of the God-head the Mediator Christ Jesus, and is, upon the work of reconciling the world to himself, not imputing their transgressions unto them, that receive the gracious offer of reconciliation tendered through Christ in the Gospel. Secondly, that God in Christ hath committed unto his Ministers the word of reconciliation that they, with authority, may offer reconciliation and friendship with God unto the hearers of the Word of the Gospel. Thirdly, that the Apostles and Ministers of the Gospel, are sent forth and directed as Ambassadors, to exhort and request men, in God's name, and in the name of Christ God Mediator manifested in the flesh, to be reconciled unto God. Fourthly, that so many as do consent unto and embrace the gracious offer of reconciliation, are reckoned to be believers, even all they who do acknowledge their natural enmity and sins against God, and do welcome the message

of reconciliation, (sent by the Ministers of the Gospel) and do engage themselves to hold fast this Covenant, aiming to walk as reconciled children and servants unto God, uprightly laying forth their burdens and desires before him daily: all these (I say) are believers in Christ, and may assure themselves of reconciliation; for there is no more in the Apostles and Ministers commission required, for entering of the humbled sinner into a covenant of friendship, save this, we request you in God's name, and in the name of God incarnate, Jesus Christ the Mediator, we beseech you be reconciled to God, v. 20. Now we judge, that humbled sinners fled to Christ, and purposing to amend their lives by his grace, will not be found unwilling to accept this offer of reconciliation, but will declare their hearty consent to this offer; and so may be convinced, that a covenant is closed between God and them, and that God hath given unto them saving faith, how weak soever it seemeth unto them; for, the consenting unto, and accepting of, this offer, is the condition required for entering in covenant, and the proper act of saving faith. Fifthly, the Apostle hold-eth forth the ground-right of this covenant, and reason whereupon the sinner, fled to Christ, may be assured of justification: because in the covenant of Redemption, past between God in three persons on the one hand, and the second person of the God-head as Mediator and perfect Redeemer by price-paying on the other hand, it is agreed, finally ended and decreed, that Christ's satisfaction, made for the embracer of this offered reconciliation, shall as certainly make the believer judicially righteous and justify him, as Christ was judicially made sin or a sacrifice for the sins of the redeemed: for, God, saith he, v. 21, hath made Christ to be sin for us, who knew no sin, that we might be made the righteousness of God in him. Therefore, as Christ the only Mediator, by accepting the covenant of Redemption, had the sins of the redeemed imputed unto him, (albeit there was no sin at all, nor could be in him) and was punished for them unto the death of the cross; So, the humbled sinner, by flying unto Christ, and accepting the offered covenant of reconciliation, hath Christ's satisfaction imputed unto him, (albeit he can see nothing in himself but a mass of inherent sin) and shall not enter into condemnation, but be brought to life-eternal, through Jesus Christ our Lord. Both the covenant of Redemption made with Christ in the Redeemers name, and the covenant of Reconciliation made with us through Christ, are of God's making, and so must stand, and cannot be dis-annulled forever.

The other place, 1 Cor. 1:30, holdeth forth the right which God hath made to the believer, unto the unsearchable riches of Christ, whereunto the weakest believer, fled from sin and wrath unto Christ, as the refuge and perfect remedy from both, may claim, namely wisdom, righteousness, sanctification and redemption by him: and that by covenant and decree registrate in this and other places of Scripture, as judicially declared and adjudged unto all and every believer in him; So that they may and should make use of Christ, as made unto them wisdom to direct them, justification to justify them, sanctification to perfect them piece and piece in holiness, and redemption to support them under, and deliver them from, all bonds of misery.

For the better understanding of this rich passage, we shall take it up in four sentences pronounced from the holy Spirit by the Apostle; in everyone whereof, these three things are insinuate and imported, first, our need of Christ; 2. his engaged help and supply; and, 3. our duty to lay hold upon and make use of him, according to the right and interest in him, made unto every believer.

The first sentence is this, Christ is made unto us wisdom, which importeth, first, that not only we are by nature blind and ignorant of our sin and misery, blind and ignorant of the way of salvation and right manner of serving God, but also after that we are illuminate by grace, and made in some measure to know our last condition and to fly unto Christ for delivery, we are compassed about with much darkness and foggy mists of doubts, errors and mistakes, and have need to be in every step of our way directed and powerfully taught by Christ's Word and Spirit, to know what is that good and acceptable will of God.

Secondly, it importeth, that as Christ is the treasure of all wisdom and knowledge who hath revealed in the Scriptures the whole counsel of God concerning our salvation; So he is judicially made over unto us as anointed Prophet to his Church, to make known unto us the way of life by his Word and Spirit.

Thirdly, it imports our duty to receive him as the great gift of God, and to give up ourselves to his teaching, to employ him and depend upon him as Prophet appointed to us for direction by his Word, what to believe and how to live before God. Whereupon the weakest believer may trust in him for guiding them in the use of the Scripture and exercise of the means appointed by him unto salvation; because he is made of God unto us wisdom, and intimation thereof is made by his Apostle.

The second sentence is this, Christ is made of God unto us righteousness: which presupponeth, first, that we are by nature destitute of righteousness, condemned as unrighteous by the law, and unable to deliver ourselves from condemnation, and when we are fled to Christ and delivered from condemnation, that we are not able to stand in that state, but by our daily sins wherein we fall, do deserve to be condemned as unrighteous.

Secondly, it imports, that Christ is not only righteous in himself and able to satisfy divine justice for our sins, but also hath undertaken to pay, and actually hath paid the price of our redemption by his obedience unto the Father even to the death of the Cross, and hath taken on him the office of high Priest to apply unto us absolution from our sins, make us accepted and to be dealt with as righteous, and to keep us in that blessed estate by his intercession.

Thirdly, it imports our duty to lay hold on Christ our Cautioner, by virtue of our right and interest in him, granted and intimate unto us, and so to rest on him, that whatsoever Satan, Conscience, or Law violate by us, shall say, we who are fled from sin and wrath to him, may oppose this sentence of our absolution registrate here, Christ is made unto us righteousness judicially, by the decree and decreet of God.

The third sentence is this, Christ is made unto us of God sanctification, which presupponeth, that in the justified believer there are remaining still the relics of sin inherent, from which we are not able of ourselves to deliver ourselves, but have need of divine power to mortify sin in us, and to repair the image of God by increasing holiness in us.

Secondly, it importeth, that Christ the Mediator, the holy one of Israel, hath not only paid the price of our redemption for removing of our guiltiness and saving us from condemnation, but also hath undertaken to the Father to write his law in our heart, and at last to present us perfect without spot or blemish, for which end, he hath taken by appointment the threefold office of Prophet, Priest and King.

Thirdly, it imports, that it is our duty to lay hold upon this rich gift and right intimate unto us judicially from God, and whatsoever commanded duty we are to go about, we do it in the name of Christ, sucking by faith, sap and virtue from him to bring forth good fruits holy and acceptable to God through him: Because Christ, the second person of the God-head incarnate, is made unto us, and judicially intimate from God to us, our sanctification.

The fourth sentence is this, Christ is made of God unto us redemption: which importeth, first, that we who have fled from sin and wrath unto Christ, and are justified by faith, and begun to be sanctified, are yoked in a warfare with our sinful flesh, the world and Satan, being subject to many miseries in this life, and to death natural and the grave. In which warfare we are not of ourselves able to stand, nor to deliver ourselves from the miseries whereunto we are subject, except by divine power we be supported, brought thorough and saved.

Secondly, it imports, that Christ not only hath paid a satisfactory price for our redemption, and is able to deliver us from all sin and misery against the power of whatsoever adversary; but also, that he hath undertaken the work, and hath by compact with the Father, obliged himself to deliver us powerfully from all sin and misery and to overcome to our behoove all our enemies and tread them underfoot, and that he is judicially established in his kingly office, and made over to us for our assurance by decreet intimate to us.

Thirdly, it importeth our duty, that by virtue of the right and gift of Christ God-man, made over unto us by God's decreet now intimate, we should rely by faith on him, as the pledge of perfecting our salvation thoroughly, and fight out our battles, against all adversary powers and all miseries, in his strength, rejoicing in his victory over all our enemies; for, God hath made him unto us redemption.

CHAP. II. - Wherein the regenerate man's doubt of his being in the state of grace, by reason of his felt unworthiness, is answered.

THESE PREMISED CONSIDERATIONS, MAY serve for the more easy solution of doubts and particular cases wherein the regenerate man may be troubled about his being in the state of grace. For which end, it is needful also, by way of example, to propound some usual questions in particular: the answering whereof, may serve to answer all questions, which do arise from the like original: For,

1. Howsoever it be certain from Scripture, that the regenerate shall not perish, and that their state in grace is unchangeable, and that their perseverance in the faith is established by Christ's undertaking to make them persevere according to the charge given unto him from the Father. John 6:39,40, yet, it is true also, that every regenerate man is not clear about his regeneration, and many regenerate persons have only a conjectural opinion that they are regenerate, who are

not come up as yet to an assurance and persuasion of their blessed estate. And the number is not great of these who always, or any long time together, do enjoy that serenity and tranquility of conscience, that they can confidently triumph, and glory with the Apostle, Rom. 5:3-5, because of desertions and temptations, raising doubts in their conscience, concerning their estate, ofttimes holy persons are disquieted. With such persons, while they are in that case, a Pastor or a prudent friend must deal so, as he would deal with the infirm, and with them who think themselves not converted, because the same remedies will serve to strengthen a weak believer and to draw a soul, sensible of sin, and under the pangs of the new birth, unto faith in Christ.

2. But let us come more particularly to examine the doubts of some that are regenerate, and their pretended reasons for their doubting. Some are so sensible of their own unworthiness, that they question if themselves, or any like unto themselves, can be in the state of grace, mean time their carriage is such a, becometh a Christian, blameless: I feel in me(saith one) such strength of inward corruption as doth defile every best action I go about; I see what holiness is required in those that approach unto God, that I do utterly loath myself, as unworthy to be admitted into the fellowship of God or Christ the holy one of Israel: yea (saith another) I think it no small presumption to draw near unto Christ, or count myself among his Saints and followers.

This for a short time was the case of Isaiah, when in a vision he saw the glory of Christ in the Temple, and heard the Seraphim's proclaim him thrice holy, Isa. 6:5. Woe is me (said he) for I am undone, because I am a man of unclean lips, and I dwell in the midst of a people of unclean lips, for mine eyes have seen the King, the Lord of hosts. This also was the case of Peter, who in the sense of his own unworthiness, wakened up by the shining of the glory of Christ's God-head in the miraculous tack of fishes, Luk. 5:8, falling down at Christ's knees, he crieth depart from me, O Lord, for I am a sinful man: which is as much as if he had said, I am utterly unworthy to be admitted unto fellowship with thy holy Majesty. The like also was the case of the Publican in the parable, Luk. 18:13, out of which case, after some wrestling of faith, he cometh forth toward God, yet standing a far off, nor daring to life up his eyes to heaven: wherein is pointed out to us the sense of his unworthiness, hindering him to approach confidently to the throne of grace.

3. For removing of this doubt, five or six considerations may be represented to the party afflicted, with this proviso, that the sense of his unworthiness be not discharged, or diminished, but wisely entertained in him rather; for, it is not to be presupposed, that any man can esteem himself so unworthy and far from meriting any good at God's hand, as he is indeed: But yet his doubt, how he dare or may draw near unto Christ because of his felt unworthiness may be solved. 1. If he consider the nature and offer made of the covenant of grace, whereby these that are sensible of their own unworthiness, are so far from being debarred from the covenant of grace, that the covenant of grace doth not admit any person to be received into it, but such only who do renounce all confidence in their own works and worthiness, and do fly unto the offer of the free grace of God in Christ: for, our Lord hath said, Matth. 9:13. I came not to call the righteous but sinners to repentance: And the promises of the Evangel, are made to the poor in spirit, to the hungry, and thirsty for the righteousness of Christ, which only can satisfy a hungry soul, Matth. 5:3,6, yea, the sense of unworthiness is in effect that self-loathing whereof Ezek.

speaketh, chap. 36:31, which sense of unworthiness, may be seen in Job, as a special act and evidence of his repentance, Job. 42:6.

Secondly, let him consider, that because by reason of sin, no worthiness can be found in us, therefore God hath freely loved the world and provided grace in Christ, that all that fly to him, may out of his fullness receive grace for grace, John 1:16.

Thirdly, the three-fold office of a Mediator, wherewith Christ hath clothed himself, doth obviate and meet the doubts of the humbled soul under the sense of unworthiness: for, albeit he be ignorant and slow to understand and believe the revealed will of God, about men's salvation, and his prescribed service; yet, upon his flying to Christ, he hath Christ offered and given to him for his wisdom, a Prophet able to inform him, to open his eyes, and persuade him to embrace by lively faith all saving doctrine. Albeit he be exceeding sinful and worthy of condemnation, yet he hath Christ as Priest made of God unto him righteousness and sanctification, upon his flying to him for refute from sin and wrath, undertaking also powerfully to sanctify him, by mortifying his corruptions, and perfecting at last the Image of God in him. And albeit he have the world and his own flesh, and the power of all principalities and spiritual wickedness, with many miseries in this life to wrestle with; yet, he hath Christ Jesus as King, made of God unto him redemption, upon his flying to Christ for refuge against all his enemies; So that he may be sure to be found among them whom he hath redeemed by price-paying, and for whom he hath undertaken powerfully to sustain them in all this warfare, whatsoever misery they may be in, and at last to bring them out of all sin and misery to a perfect rest in everlasting glory. And to what end hath our Lord taken on the office of a Mediator and Redeemer, if not to open the eyes of the blind that fly to him for eye-salve, to cover the naked, flying unto him, with the precious garment of his imputed righteousness, and to enrich the poor, needy and unworthy out of the store house of his unsearchable riches of grace? Rev. 3:18.

Fourthly, let him consider the constant course of grace and practical dispensation thereof in all ages toward all the converted. Are not all they to whom the Gospel cometh, in the state of corrupt nature, when God cometh to convert them? For, never was there any person called unto the state of grace, but he was found in his sins and in the state of lost sinners by nature: none but children of wrath and enemies by nature are reconciled; none but they, who, by the law, are condemned, are justified; none but they, that in their own sense are lost, do obtain salvation; for, Christ doth plainly tell us, I came to seek and to save them that are lost. Did he ever reject any that fled unto him, because they were unworthy? No; for it is said, Psal. 9:10. They that know thy name will trust in thee; for thou never forsook them that sought thee. And, (John. 6:37) he saith, These that come unto me, I will in no case cast out. 2 Tim. 1:9. Not according to our works, but according to his own purpose and grace, hath he called us.

Fifthly, let him consider the worthiness of Christ's person and merits, who, (because he being God and man in one person, hath paid a price of infinite value for redemption of sinners who fly unto him) is worthy, for whose cause, the unworthy sinner, flying to the throne of grace, should be received in favor, and made fit for eternal life by the sanctification of his Spirit.

Sixthly, let him consider, that if he stand a-back from Christ, and do not fly unto him, how unworthy soever he think himself, he remains under wrath and the condemnatory sentence of the law, John 1:8, but, let him rather remember, that he is warranted by a command of God the Father, to fly to Christ, 1 John 3:23. This is his commandment, that we should believe on the name of his Son, Jesus Christ, and love one another as he hath commanded us. And therefore, let him say of his own soul with the Centurion, speaking of his servant to Christ, (Luke 7:6,7) I am not worthy that thou should come under my roof; but say the word, and my servant shall be healed. The word is said frequently in Scripture, let the afflicted rest himself on it.

CHAP. III. - Wherein the regenerate man's doubts, arising from the multitude and weight of his sins against the Law and the Gospel, and against the light of his conscience, are answered.

As in the pangs of the new birth, this doubt hath much weight to keep a soul a-back from embracing Christ and receiving pardon through him; So after a man is regenerate, and made quiet in his conscience, when through sad affliction and sore temptation, these wounds of his conscience begin to bleed again, his pardon and peace is called in question. Of this exercise there are three degrees: the first is, when sins against the law are mustered, and led in a host against a soul; which was the case of the afflicted Psalmist for a time, till by faith he over-came the doubt, Psal. 40:12. Innumerable evils have compassed me about, mine iniquities have taken hold on me, so that I am not able to look up: they are more than the hairs of mine head; therefore my heart faileth me.

The second degree is, when beside the man's sins against the Law his sins also against the Gospel, against Christ and the means of salvation, do arise in battle against him, and do drive him to cry out, with these not yet converted sinners, (Act. 2:37) men and brethren, what shall we do?

The third degree is, when the regenerate man, for some gross sins against the light of his conscience, is given up for a time to be scourged with the temptations and accusations of Satan, as if he had sinned against the holy Ghost, and no more mercy were reserved for him; and this was the case of the Prophet Jonah, when being guilty and conscious to his late rebellion against God, he is pursued and apprehended by God, and casten in the sea, he falleth in a fit of desperation till God gave him victory by faith, Jon. 2:4. Then I said, I am cast out of thy sight; yet I will look again to thy holy Temple: which was the trysting place of God with sinners in a Mediator. This was also the case of David for a time, after that his conscience is wakened by the message of God sent unto him in the mouth of Nathan the Prophet, when he found the spirit of consolation with-drawn from him, and the wrath of God breaking his bones and consuming the marrow thereof, Psal. 51:8-12. Make me to hear joy and gladness, that the bones which thou hast broken may rejoice, &c.

2. In answering this doubt, we must proceed suitably to each degree severally. In curing this case in the first degree, let the afflicted admit all the just aggravations of his sins against the Law, which the conscience doth press: for, by extenuation of sin, neither is God's jus-

tice glorified, nor the conscience satisfied; and consolation or hope of remission of sin must not arise from the few number or lightness of sins, but from the multitude and largeness of God's mercy: and therefore, we must not cut short the reckoning with the Lord's law, nor must we diminish the weight and estimation of our evil deserving's; but course must be taken, that by the sense of guiltiness, the judgment of the afflicted person be not so confounded and perplexed, as if his case were desperate, and possibility of salvation were passed; but rather let the afflicted humble himself under the mighty hand of God, who alone can destroy and make alive, and who usually bringeth down to death and brink of hell, and bringeth back again, and who alone doth work wonders.

This doubt then arising from the multitude of sins, may be loosed, first, by a fresh consideration of the infinite excellency and worthiness of Christ Jesus, God manifested in the flesh, and of the incomprehensible value of the price of redemption, paid by him for all who fly unto him: for, the Father hath declared himself satisfied by him in behalf of the redeemed, for whom he did offer himself, Matth. 3:17, saying, This is my well-beloved Son, in whom I am well pleased. And (Heb. 7:25) This is he, who is able to save to the uttermost, all that come to God by him. Secondly, by consideration of the infinite largeness of Gods bounty, grace and mercy, wherein he hath set no bounds to himself in pardoning and abolishing the sins of those that come unto him, how gross and grievous soever they have been, Isa. 44:22. I have blotted out, as a thick cloud, thy transgressions, and as a cloud thy sins, return unto me, for I have redeemed thee. And, (Isa. 1:18) Come now and let us reason together, saith the Lord, though your sins be as scarlet, they shall be as white as snow, though they be red as crimson, they shall be as wool. And (Matth. 11:28) Come unto me saith Christ, all ye that labor and are heavy loaden, and I will give you rest.

Thirdly, by the consideration of the many examples and experiences of the mercy of God manifested in the pardon of heinous sinners, both in the old and New Testament, set down in Scripture, of set purpose to invite such as are troubled with the sense of their manifold sins, to come unto Christ the Mediator, or to God in Christ reconciling the world to himself, by not imputing sins to them who embrace the offer of grace and reconciliation tendered unto them in the Gospel.

As to the second degree wherein the doubt is augmented by the addition of the sins against the Gospel, unto the sins against the Law, by despising or slighting the means of salvation offered in the Gospel; true it is, that the despising or slighting of the offer of grace in Christ, cannot be sufficiently aggreged, because the sins of Sodom and Gomorrah will be found lighter, being laid in the balance with the contempt of the Gospel, Matth. 10:14,15, yet, notwithstanding, when God is entered in reckoning with a sinner, and is begun to challenge him for his sins against the Law and the Gospel also, and hath by his terror humbled the man, there is mercy insinuated unto that person in the bosom of the threatening. Wherefore the soul born down with the sense of ill-deserving by his sins against both Law and Gospel, must be exhorted to humble himself before God, and fly in unto Christ, who of set purpose that he might answer this doubt, hath declared, that whosoever speaketh a word against the Son of man, it shall be forgiven him, to wit, if he repent this injury done to Christ, Matth. 12:32, and he standeth knocking at the door of luke-warm Laodicea, with an offer of coming in to them, and supping with them, that shall open to him, notwithstanding they have slighted him long in their senselessness of sin, nakedness and misery.

As to the third degree, wherein the afflicted doth suspect, that he hath sinned against the holy Ghost, because he hath sinned against the light of his conscience, and ditement of the holy Spirit, let the afflicted consider, that the sinning in actual gross out-breakings against the light of the conscience, is indeed a high provocation of God to his face, for which the offender is to be humbled all the days of his life. Secondly, let him learn to glorify Gods Justice, who hath made a proud rebel to be scourged with scorpions, and sore bitten with the remorse of a slighted and contemned conscience.

Thirdly, let those particular transgressions, objected to be done against the light of the conscience, be examined with their motives and circumstances: and out of the bitter rod of God's correcting the offender, that he should not perish with the world, let the afflicted take up the Lord's love in judging him, that he may not be condemned. As also let the Pastor, or the prudent friend, who goeth about to comfort the afflicted, carefully observe if the afflicted be grieved for grieving of the holy Spirit, if he desire and long after the consolation of God, whom he hath offended, if he purpose to walk more circumspectly afterward, and eschew the snare he hath taken into, or what other evidences of repentance can be seen in him, whereof use may be made to assure the afflicted, that he hath not sinned unto death. Because the sin against the holy Ghost, as it is described unto us in holy Scripture, is either a malicious refusing and opposing wittingly and willfully of Christ Jesus, after that the Spirit of Christ hath convinced the person, that Christ is the Redeemer; and this was the sin of some Pharisees, desperate, professed, and irreconcilable enemies to Christ, Matth. 12:24, to 33, or, it is a total apostasy from Christ after they have known him to be the Redeemer, joined with a malicious oppugning of the Christian Religion, as it is set forth, Heb. 10:26-32, and whosoever falleth in this sin, he neither repents him of it, nor desires to repent or be reconciled with God.

And therefore, let the humbled and afflicted penitent, longing to be reconciled unto God through Christ, and to find the sense of his favor granted or restored, not suspect himself anymore guilty of this sin, but let him make use of the offer of grace in the Gospel and of the example of penitents mentioned in Scripture. Who knoweth how soon the Lord may take the penitent in his fatherly embracement's and comfort him abundantly? Meantime, till the sensible comfort be given unto him, let him hold fast the promises made to them that fly unto Christ.

CHAP. IV. - Wherein is solved the doubt of the regenerate man, raised by his suspicion, whether he be elected or not.

IT COMETH TO PASS sometimes, that a sinner lamenting his sins, and seeking liberation from sin and misery, doth call in question whether he be regenerate, because he hath a deep and fixed suspicion, that he shall possibly be found not among the Elect, and by consequence be found a reprobate: of whom if ye ask a reason why he saith so, he can give no solid answer, only he will tell you he can perceive no certain signs and evidences of his election: yea, that he findeth nothing in himself, but that which may be found in reprobates, and that he is afraid he be found one of that number, and that this suspicion hath taken deep root in him, that he cannot rid himself of this doubt and fear.

2. This case, we must confess, is very dangerous, except it be timeously cured; for, here faith is taken as it were by the throat, and the ground of hope is like to be razed. The suspicion of God's decree is daily fostered and augmented, and the afflicted person, not only

doubteth of God's good-will to him, but is tempted unto desperation: By this means the command of God to believe the promises and consolations of the Gospel, seem to him to be offered to him all in vain: the hope of success, or profiting in the use of the means appointed by God, is undermined, so long as this suspicion is entertained; yea, all the exercises of religion become burthensome, out of a fear he shall follow the exercise thereof to no purpose; and so the duties of religion, are ofttimes left undone, or cast off for a time, if the temptation grow strong, and continue with him without cure or comfort; thus he standeth upon the border and precipice of some sort of desperation, if his fear and suspicion be not removed in some measure.

3. For cure of this case, the Pastor or prudent friend, as in all his conferences with the afflicted, So here in special, must seriously pray to God, that he would bless the means of information and consolation, which he is about to use for the satisfying of the afflicted.

To this end therefore, first, let all the reasons whereby the afflicted pretendeth to make his reprobation probable, be resumed and refuted as frivolous all of them. And certainly, they cannot but be found frivolous, because God hath not given any certain evidence or sign of reprobation, so long as a man is alive, except that sin unto death, the sin against the holy Ghost, in a malicious refusing, rejecting and hostile opposing of Jesus Christ wittingly and willingly: for, as to final unbelief and impenitency, no man can pass sentence upon any person, that hath heard anything of the Gospel, so long as breath is in him; for, God can convert a soul to himself in the pangs of imminent death, as he did the thief on the cross.

All the evil which the afflicted can say of himself, cannot prove him a reprobate, the height which his reckoning can rise unto to fortify his own suspicion of himself, is only to give appearance that he is not regenerate; meantime we presuppose the afflicted person under this temptation, to labor under the sense of manyfold sins (which do furnish strength unto the temptation) and to be hungry and thirsty for righteousness, and to be desirous to draw near to God in Christ, if he could be delivered of his suspicion of God's purpose and affection towards him. And therefore his Christian friends are bound in charity to expound this his hunger for righteousness, and thirsty desire of reconciliation through Christ, to be a begun work of gracious regeneration, and so also a hopeful sign that he is elected.

Secondly, after refutation of his pretended reasons for his suspicion and fear, this suspicion must be set before him as a strong temptation of Satan, and a soul-murdering lie, thrown as a fiery dart at him, (such as the Apostle, Ephes. 6, maketh mention of) of set purpose to beat the shield of faith out of his hand: Wherefore he must be exhorted to resist the Tempter, and that so much the more, as Satan out of envy and malice doth slander God, and the begun work of grace in the man, and all to vex the soul of him whom he cannot keep in his snare.

Thirdly, the giving so much way to this wicked suggestion, must be represented to the patient as an act of ignorance and folly, yea an act of iniquity and injury unto God, and to his own soul: for, what a madness is it to pry in upon the secret counsel of God, and to neglect his revealed will set down in Scripture? What presumption to intrude ourselves upon his secret decrees, and to cast behind our back his open commands given to us? To refuse obedience to God's ordinances given to us for our salvation, except he shall first tell us what is his purpose about us in particular? To open our ears to the false suggestions of the devil a liar, and murderer from the beginning, and stop our ears from hearing the voice of God speaking to us in

Scripture? Wherefore, let the afflicted under this temptations take heed to what is said, Deut. 29:29. The secret things belong unto the Lord our God, but these things that are revealed belong unto us and our children forever, that we may do all the words of this Law. Let the Lord's Command be first obeyed, and then the decree of God concerning the believer in him, shall be timeously revealed: for, his promises are agreeable with his decrees, and his promises are offered to us, that thereby his decrees may be brought on unto a just and gracious execution.

Fourthly, let the afflicted call to mind, what benefits the Lord hath bestowed upon him from his infancy, and in special, that he hath offered, and doth continue to offer, Christ Jesus unto him, if he will receive him for wisdom, righteousness, sanctification and redemption; and upon this ground he is bound to give unto God a good construction in every sort of dispensation toward him, and look upon God as his friend and father.

CHAP. V. - Wherein the regenerate man's doubting of his regeneration, because he findeth no power in himself to believe in Christ, is answered.

SOMETIME IT COMETH TO pass, that the renewed man, after a long time standing in the state of grace, falleth in doubt about the work of grace in himself, because when God doth change his dispensation toward him, and bringeth him to trial by trouble, wherein he is found weaker than he expected, he beginneth to suspect whether the former work of grace hath been found or not, and his reason is, because he findeth by experience often repeated, that in straits and difficulties when he would most exercise faith and believe in Christ, he is found least able to do it; yea, he findeth it no less impossible to observe the whole moral Law, then solidly to believe in Christ: hence ariseth anxiety in the soul of the afflicted, while he neither dare depart from Christ, nor yet is able to approach unto him confidently. In this case many new doubts and temptations do arise, which weaken his faith yet more, and hinder him in the exercise of religion and discharge of duties, not a little.

That this sometime may be the case of some converted, the experience of the Saints, set down in Scripture, maketh evident, Psal. 30:7. Lord, saith David, by thy favor thou hast made my mountain to stand strong; thou didst hide thy face and I was troubled. And in his prayer, (Psal. 61:2) while his mind was overwhelmed in him with perplexing thoughts, he findeth in himself no strength or ability to deliver himself or put forth acts of faith on the Mediator, as he would have done, but prayeth, that while he is now exiled and driven far off from the tabernacle and ark of the Covenant, he may be raised up to believe in him who was signified by these types, to wit, Christ the Rock of all Salvation: which Rock of salvation, he perceiveth to be a higher mystery then he can discover or ascend upon, without the hand of divine power. And therefore saith, from the end of the earth, will I cry unto thee, when my heart is overwhelmed, lead me to the rock that is higher then I. Yea, the godly afflicted Hebrews fell in this sickness, whom the Apostle exhorteth to take courage unto them, Heb. 12:12,13. Wherefore lift up your hands which hang down, and the feeble knees, and make straight paths for your feet.

2. For answering of this doubt, the afflicted person must be convinced of his infirmity and sinful dissidence, because being called of God to the exercise and trial of his faith in Christ by whatsoever sort of trouble, he hath been discouraged and fainted, which did not become a soldier of Christ, and that for no other pretended reason but this, that he could not give such a proof of his faith as he should have given and hoped to give, before he was put to trial.

Secondly, he must consider how far he is mistaken in leaning to his own strength, in the exercise of his faith; of which self-confidence, the more a man is emptied, the more speedily he shall be furnished, if being emptied he fly to Christ for supply. This was the experience of the Apostle, 2 Cor. 9:10, who was made weak in himself, that the strength of Christ might be made perfect in his weakness; and therefore he resolved to make use of the strength of Christ in all his felt infirmities, and that he did, with good success. For when I am weak, saith he, then am I strong. Whose example we must resolve to follow.

Thirdly, after search, it will be found, that the person afflicted, under the notion and expression of I cannot believe, hath, in effect, this meaning, I cannot find such a full assurance of faith as I would be at; or, I cannot find such a sense of the approbation of my faith as can satisfy me and persuade me that I do believe really in Christ. And so it is another thing, and another gift of the Spirit he is seeking, then what he pretendeth to seek: for, the sense and feeling of approven faith, and full assurance of faith, is not given to every believer, but to him that sights the fight of faith, and in his trials, adhereth closely to Christ and to his truth, when he is tempted to sin, as the clause in the close of the seven Epistles to the Churches of Asia doth teach us, Rev. 2:3. To him that overcometh, I will give to eat of the tree of life, to eat of that hid manna; I will give him that white stone, and a new name written thereon, which no man knoweth, save he that receiveth it.

Fourthly, the afflicted must be instructed or put in mind to distinguish between believing in Christ, and the knowing that he doth believe in Christ, as may be learned from 1 John 5:13. These things I write to you, that believe on the name of the Son of God, that you may know, that you have eternal life; and that ye may believe on the name of the Son of God. He must distinguish between true (though weak) saying faith and strong faith. True saving faith is in that person, who, being pursued by the Law, doth fly for refuge to lay hold upon Christ the hope set before us. The man that dwelleth in this city of Christ, and maketh use of Christ as the only remedy against sin and misery, as he is offered to us in the Gospel, hath right unto that strong and well-grounded consolation spoken of, Heb. 6:17-19. True and saving faith is in that person, who acknowledging himself a child of wrath, heartily receiveth the Lord Jesus Christ, as he offereth himself to us in the Gospel; for, such a person hath the right and privilege of a child of God, and may reckon himself among believers in Christ, John 1:12. As many as received Christ, to them gave he power to become the Sons of God, even to them that believe in his name. True and saving faith is in that person, who, being convinced of his enmity against God, doth answer the request of God in Christ, in the mouth of his Ministers, with a hearty consent unto the covenant of grace and reconciliation offered to all that hear the Gospel, 2 Cor. 5:19,20. God was in Christ, reconciling the world unto himself, not imputing their trespasses unto them; and hath committed unto us the word of reconciliation. Now then, we are Ambassadors, for Christ, as though God did beseech you by us, we pray you in Christ's stead be ye reconciled unto God: for he hath made him (that is, Christ) to be sin for us, who knew no sin, that we might be made the righteousness of God in him. Therefore, let the afflicted answer thus. I receive the offer, and do consent, upon these terms, to be reconciled to God, Lord help my unbelief; for, thou hast said, seek ye my face; and my soul answereth Thy face, O Lord, will I seek, hide not thy face from me, Psal. 27:8,9. He that upon these terms, doth fly to Christ, and resolveth to adhere unto him, needeth not doubt but he is received in the state of grace: for confirmation whereof, let the fruits of faith

outward and inward, which may be observed by the afflicted himself,
or by his comforter, be called to mind, and let him rest and go on in
the course of obedience of the Gospel.

CHAP. VI. - Wherein the doubt of the regenerate man, concerning his being in the state of grace, arising from his apprehended defect of humiliation and sorrow for sin, is answered.

SOME REGENERATE PERSONS WILL be found, who mourn indeed for their sin, and do acknowledge, that they deserve death for their sins, do confess they stand in need of Christ, do thirst for his righteousness, do desire earnestly, to be united unto him by faith, do follow the exercise of Religion, and do endeavor to keep their consciences undefiled in all things; and yet for all this, do not only doubt whether they be renewed, but also do esteem it a presumptuous rashness in them to approach unto Christ, or to cast themselves over on him by faith, before they be more seriously humbled, before they feel a more hearty sorrow and grief, before they feel the pangs of the new birth more sharp, before they be more pressed with the burden of their sins, and do feel in themselves the spirit of fear and trembling and bondage in a higher measure.

From whom, if you ask a reason of their doubt, they shall answer, that they are not yet called to come unto Christ, because these are only called to come unto Christ who are weary and loaden in the superlative degree, and are so born down with the weight of sin, as they cannot be more, and not despair; for so do they interpret that saying of Christ, Matth. 11:28. Christ is sent only to the contrite and broken in heart, who sit in the dust, under the spirit of bondage, that is to say, as they take it, to them who are under grief unspeakable, as they expound, Isa. 61:1-3. So in their opinion, Christ came to save only those who in their own sense are lost, that is, who are on the brink of desperation: wherefore, in respect they are not gone down deep enough as they think into this gulf and hell of anguish and sorrow, they dare not approach or look toward Christ.

Mean time they lie daily mourning and weeping, and will not grant that their grief is worthy of the name of grief; which sorrow they cannot dissemble or hide, but do bewray it in their countenance, habit, walking and frequent sighing, and will profess, that they can hardly think they have right to eat or drink of God's creatures, and were it not for fear of adding yet more sin to the former, they would not eat or drink at all: ofttimes they chatter as swallows and sigh as the turtle dove, and ofttimes their bowels sound out as if their parents or children or nearest relations were dead, and yet for all this do not satisfy themselves in sorrow, but do complain that they are stupid and senseless of their sinful and miserable condition, wherein they do lie bound: and though they do confess, that sometimes they mourn, yet they allege their mourning is but like the early dew, or morning cloud, that goeth soon away. All the while it is in vain to offer to the afflicted consolation in Christ, because (saith he) I am not one of the mourners in Zion whom he will comfort: and in this their mistake, they do confirm themselves by another error, saying, that the measure of repentance and sorrow should answer unto the measure of sin; my sins, saith he, go far beyond the sins of others.

This and the like objections they cast in, whereby they do obstruct their own way unto Christ and keep themselves aback from him, till they be satisfied with their own prescribed measure of sorrow; which case indeed deserveth much compassion: for, who would not commiserate their case, who, being in a very miserable condition, dare not seek relief from their own misery which they do feel, and all because they are not yet more miserable? And when they are asked, cannot determine what measure of affected humiliation they would stand at as sufficient:

2. In the cure of this case, as much must be yielded to the afflicted, as reasonably can be: and first, it must be confessed, that it is the duty of all who approach unto Christ, to come in the sense of sin, and acknowledgment of their miserable condition, and that the due deserving of their sin, is everlasting death.

It must be confessed also, that the measure of compunction, contrition and lamentation for sin, may possibly be exceeding great, as we see in the experience of Heman the Ezrahite, Psal. 88:11. I am afflicted and ready to die from my youth up; while I suffer thy terrors, I am distracted. And David, Psal. 38.

This also further must be yielded unto him, that the operation of the spirit of conviction by the law, doth ordinarily and of its own nature go before the spirit of adoption or the operation of the spirit of the Gospel, according to the covenant of grace, so that no man can in earnest embrace Christ as a Physician, as Mediator and Savior of his soul, except he be sensible of his disease, acknowledge his natural enmity against God, and his own lost condition, being by nature under the curse of the Law.

Secondly, when these things are agreed upon, the afflicted person may be posed concerning the measure of the sorrow for sin, whether it must be the same in every convert, to wit, in that extremity and superlative degree, which he doth miss and desiderate in himself, and how long that sorrow in this eminent measure must continue? By this question he cannot choose but be at a stand, and unable to answer with Scripture-warrant; for, the Scripture doth indeed require serious repentance, but the measure of sorrow and sadness, it doth not prescribe: for, Matth. 3:2-6, many upon the hearing of John the Baptist preaching, were convicted of their sins, and did confess their sins in the general, and forthwith were baptized by him. And, Act. 2:37,41, three thousand souls at the hearing of one sermon of Peter, were convinced of their sin, pricked at the heart, repented, and fled to Christ for grace; were converted, baptized and entered members of the Christian Church, all in one day. Again, the afflicted may be posed with another question, seeing he desiderates such a measure of sound hearty sorrow in himself before he can make his address unto Christ, out of what fountain mindeth he to draw this sorrow? Of himself he hath it not, and from Christ by his grounds he cannot seek it: for he saith, for want of his imagined measure of sorrow for sin, he dare not approach unto Christ, because as he alledgeth none are called to come unto Christ, except such only as are in a superlative degree weary and loaden, and so full of the spirit of heaviness, that he must be at the point of desperation near-by. But the Scripture doth teach us, that Christ is that exalted Prince to give repentance unto Israel, in what measure of sorrow he pleaseth; and that therefore, such as are convinced of and in any measure sorrowful for offending God, should run unto Christ, that he may give them a better measure of repentance.

Thirdly, the evils and danger which accompany and follow upon this practical error, may be represented unto the afflicted; for, first, by this his error he giveth way to Satan's temptation, who when he perceiveth the sense of sin begun in the afflicted by God's mercy, and that the afflicted cannot now be hindered from repentance, nor be keeped in his former snare, doth change himself as if he were an angel of light, and setteth all at naught the measure of sorrow which the afflicted hath already, and shows unto him, how unanswerable the proportion of his sorrow is unto the multitude and heinousness of his sins, and so spurreth him on to mourn more and more, that if it be possible he may distemper and distract him, or make him pine away and perish in his sorrow, without faith or consolation in Christ: this is one evil.

Another evil is this, the affectation of such a degree of sorrow, smelleth of seeking some sort of expiation of sin, and compensation of the pleasure taken in sin, by suitable sorrow for it: unto which practical error, we are by nature too too prone: for as by nature we strive to be justified by works according to the covenant of works, written in the children of Adam; so when we see ourselves come short of the righteousness of works, we go about (as is to be seen in Papists) to supply the defect of works, by someone sort or other of our sufferings and satisfactions for sin, in special, that by sorrow and tears in abundance, we may wash away the guilt and pollution we have contracted by sin. And in this course we run on naturally, after wakening of the conscience, to exact penance and punishment on ourselves, till the deluded heart say, it is enough. And then, as if all were well, the deceived sinner resteth himself: which deceit of the heart, the oftener it hath place and prevaileth, without being observed, it is the more dangerous.

A third evil, following on this practical error, is, by it the free grace of God and merits of Christ, are greatly obscured, and both the man's consolation and sanctification are marred: the loss that the afflicted sustaineth on the one hand, and the drawing on of new guiltiness by such a course on the other hand, is covered under the vizard of humiliation.

A fourth evil followeth this error, which is this, the afflicted person, so long as he continueth in this mistake, he giveth way to the temptation, and doth of set purpose foster his own misbelief, that he may thereby foster and augment his own sorrow, and affright himself with dreadful imaginations what shall become of him, that he may augment his affected heaviness of spirit, and make the fountain of his tears run the more abundantly.

A fifth evil is, the afflicted so long as he suspends his going to Christ, because he hath not mourned sufficiently for sin, he fosters another fault unawares, to wit, a purpose to lay down anymore sorrowing for sin, if once he had overtaken his imagined measure of sorrow, and had his access so made unto Christ. This deceit of the heart, is brought to light in the practice of some Antinomians, who allow themselves once to mourn for sin, that their mourning may make way for faith in Christ; but after they apprehend they have once repented, and casten their burden on Christ, and do number themselves among believers, they scorn to mourn anymore for sin, they harden themselves against all remorse of conscience, and do reject secret challenges as groundless, and make themselves merry with their own fancy, and reckon all penitents to be under the spirit of bondage: which evils, if the afflicted person would perceive to follow upon his error, which as a net is spread before his feet to keep him from going to Christ, and following the course and exercise of repentance all the days of his life, he would take heed better to his steps.

4. The afflicted must be informed, or called to mind concerning sorrow for sin, that it is not commended from the quantity or measure of it, but from the quality or sincerity of it. Now sincere sorrow for sin, is best discerned by the hatred which the mourner hath against sin, by the mourners humiliation of himself before God, by his abhorring himself both for his sin, and for the hardness of his heart under sin, by his purpose to strive against all sin, by his flying in unto Christ for relief from sin, by his entertaining and renewing of godly sorrow after he hath believed in Christ according as he findeth the inherent roots of sin to be springing up in him. This is indeed sincere and godly sorrow, which causeth repentance never to be repented of.

5. Fifthly and last of all, the afflicted must be exhorted not to linger anymore but fly to Christ, and let him be humbled so much the more as he is not so humbled as he should and would be; let him call to mind, that Christ came not only to comfort mourners for sin, but also to call sinners unto repentance: for, Christ hath not put such a measure of sorrow, whereof we are speaking, to be the condition of the covenant of Grace, he doth not fell his precious wares, nor his gifts of grace, for the price of men's tears; but let him remember, that whosoever is so destitute in his own sense of all good, as he

finds neither the sense of sin, nor repentance nor faith, nor any other good thing in himself, which may commend him to God, but by the contrary, much evil of all sorts, and yet cometh to Christ, is no doubt the poor in spirit, whom Christ hath pronounced blessed, Matth. 5:3, and that the sense of his sin and misery, in the measure which he hath of it, is the evidence of eye-salve already bestowed upon him, to encourage him to buy of Christ all the riches which he holdeth forth to the poor in spirit, Rev. 3:18.

CHAP. VII. - Wherein the Christians doubt, whether he be regenerate, because he findeth not his righteousness exceeding the righteousness of the Scribes and Pharisees, is answered.

THERE ARE SOME REGENERATE persons, who, in the sense of their sins and acknowledgment of their unworthiness, and inability to help themselves, are fled unto Christ, and have given over themselves to him by faith, and are endeavoring to bring forth fruits suitable to repentance, who for all this, fall a doubting whether they be renewed, whether their faith be true and saving faith; and the reason which they give of their doubting, is, because the reformation of their life, whereunto they have attained, appeareth unto them not to exceed the righteousness which may be found in some Pagans, or in Scribes and Pharisees, of whom Christ hath said in the Evangel. Matth. 5:20. I say unto you, that except your righteousness exceed the righteousness of the Scribes and Pharisees, ye shall in no case enter into the kingdom of heaven.

This doubt is followed with grief, anxiety of mind, and fear least all virtues in them be found nothing but counterfeit: and this case, except it be speedily cured, cannot choose but draw after it heavy and hard consequences.

For curing whereof, we must confess, that many Pagans and Infidels may be found in human Histories, who from the principles of nature and civil education, have led a more innocent and blameless life, than many who glory in their Christian profession, for whose conviction and condemnation, Pagans and Infidels shall arise in the day of judgment, and be brought forth for a witness against many called Christians, and who shall be beaten with fewer stripes, than many who are counterfeit Christians, and do disgrace the profession of Christian Religion.

But we have here to do with these that are indeed regenerate, and endued with saving faith, who endeavor to be holy, and do lament their imperfections, and do not give over the use of the means, whereby they may profit in holiness, albeit with grief and fear they go on heavily, suspecting they meet at last with disappointment, and be excluded from the kingdom of heaven, for their coming short of Scribes and Pharisees in the point of righteousness.

2. In this case, first, the complaint of the afflicted, concerning the imperfections of his life and fruits of faith, in as far as it is true and just, must be admitted, granted and confirmed, and the afflicted must be taught upon this consideration to be seriously humbled in the presence of God, that he may profit in self-denial, and more and more renounce all confidence in his own works or inherent righteousness. To which purpose, let him consider yet more the body of death and original sin, not yet thoroughly mortified in him; let him look upon and acknowledge, in his present case, the bitter roots of infidelity, and inclination to depart away from the living God, even then when he is most called, and hath most need to draw near and adhere unto him: upon the sight and consideration whereof, he shall perceive a necessity daily to renew the acts of repentance and faith in Christ.

Secondly, let the necessity and timeous use-making of the imputed righteousness of Christ, be showed unto him: which righteousness, if the Lord had not set before us for a refuge, what should become of us in the examination of our works, and felt imperfection of our inherent righteousness? And here the afflicted must be exhorted, in the sense of his own unrighteousness, to run always toward Christ, to have his nakedness, hid by the garment of Christ's imputed righteousness, and exhorted to apply and embrace more and more straitly the righteousness of Christ our Cautioner, who is judicially by the Father adjudged to the believer fled unto him, for righteousness, 1 Cor. 1:30: But of him are ye in Christ Jesus, who is made unto us wisdom and righteousness, and sanctification, and redemption. And here let the friend, comforter of the afflicted, insist, that he may consider the value of the ransom paid for us, and of the righteousness purchased unto us, for the only garment able to hide our nakedness.

Thirdly, let the afflicted person understand, that it is righteousness with God to be displeased with his children, when they esteem little and make little use of the dear bought righteousness which Christ hath purchased, and that in wisdom and righteousness, Christ doth not increase the inherent righteousness of those who slight him in the matter of his imputed righteousness; for, we are not justified by the perfection of inherent righteousness, which in this life is impossible, but by the perfection of Christ's righteousness imputed unto the believer in him.

Fourthly, when the Pastor or prudent friend perceiveth the afflicted now convicted of his mistake and error, and to be brought to acknowledge, that the justification of a sinner doth come by the imputation of the righteousness of Christ alone, without respect to the works of the law; and that the justified man must set himself to bring forth good fruits in the gracious furniture which Christ hath promised to the believer. Now, I say, let him enter upon the comparison of the righteousness of the penitent believer in Christ, with the righteousness of the Scribes and Pharisees, and then shall it be clear to the afflicted person, that the righteousness of the weak Christian shall far exceed the righteousness, not only of Pagans, but also of Scribes and Pharisees of the highest pitch, and that for three reasons; the first is this, the Pharisee cutteth short the interpretation of the law, unto the measure of his own external obedience, lest the law whereby he seeketh justification should condemn him; but the Christian acknowledgeth in all things the spirituality and perfection of the Law, and doth not reject any duty which the Law doth command, but finds himself bound to obey the Law in all things, and to aim to be perfect as his heavenly Father is perfect. The second reason is, because the works which the Pharisee or Scribe doth, are all counterfeit and corrupt, in regard they arise from the strength of the natural man, and are done for his own glory and carnal ends, and not for the glory of God; but the works of the Christian, exercising faith in Christ, proceed from the power of the spirit of Christ in him, and are done to the glory of God by him. The third reason is, because the righteousness of works which the Scribes and Pharisees did affectate, is altogether impossible, and maketh void the grace of God: for, if righteousness be by works, it is no more of grace, it overturns that heavenly way of justification by faith in Christ: for, the righteousness of the Pharisee by works, cannot consist with the righteousness which is by faith of grace; but the righteousness and justification of the Christian by faith in Christ, is possible and ready at hand, to everyone who renounceth all confidence in his own worthiness, and flyeth unto Christ for grace: and this is a most perfect way of righteousness, which dependeth upon the obedience and satisfaction of Christ imputed to the believer in him. Which righteousness only can stand in the judgment of God as perfect, which only doth open the fountain whereby the power of the holy Ghost runneth down upon the man justified by faith in Christ, to enable him to bring forth the acceptable fruits of new obedience.

By this comparison, it doth easily appear, that the righteousness of the weak believer in Christ, doth far exceed the righteousness of the Scribes and Pharisees: and thus may the afflicted be solved of his doubt, arising from comparison of his righteousness with the righteousness of the Pharisees.

3. If these grounds of satisfaction, laid before the afflicted, do not satisfy, but his wounds do break up and bleed afresh, let us examine his reasons. O! saith he, what I have been aiming at in the way of new obedience, I suspect is not accepted of God, because I find not these

fruits of the Spirit, which the Apostle speaketh of as evidences of a new creature, Gal. 5:22, love, joy, peace, longsuffering, gentleness, goodness, faith, meekness and temperance; the defect and little feeling of these fruits, doth argue, that God doth not approve my works.

For answering of this doubt, let us remember, that it is pre-supposed and found by experience, that some that are afflicted with this doubt and suspicion, do not cease to follow duties howbeit heartlessly, do live blameless in an evil world, and so are not idle nor unfruitful: only this doth trouble them, that they find not the peace of conscience which they did expect, they miss joy in God, consolation in their prayers, patience in affections, cheerfulness and alacrity in following their calling; they do not find sensible approbation of their work from God, as they did promise to themselves and did expect. Hence flow their tears, lamentations and complaints of themselves, and suspicions of the reality and sincerity of their faith, and all without just cause: for, as in bodily sicknesses, sometime more maladies than one are complicate, and to each of them respect must be had for perfecting the cure; So in this case, more practical errors do concur, and each of them must be deciphered and removed. We shall condescend upon four; The first practical error of the afflicted, is the suspending of his faith upon a tacit condition, that such and such effects be produced, and that God's sensible approbation of his diligence and works be felt, as if there were no warrantable act of faith for laying hold on Christ, except after a certain time and trial taken whether it shall produce such or such fruits or not. And here three deceits do concur; The first is, a faith with a secret reservation, if such fruits follow, is by suggestion of the tempter, thrust in, in the place of absolute believing without reservation, and in effect, is a trying of God, instead of trusting, in him; for through temptation, the afflicted tacitly craveth a condition to be performed by God, that when God performeth the prescribed condition, then the man's faith after that may rest upon him, other ways not: for when a sinner cometh to Christ, he should speak to this sense.

O Lord, my God, seeing it hath pleased thee to reveal thyself to me, a blind impotent sinner, running toward hell, and hast offered thyself to me for a Savior, in whom I may have wisdom, righteousness, sanctification and redemption. Behold, O Lord, I heartily receive the grace offered, I embrace thy Word, and thy Self offered to me in thy Word, and do give up myself wholly to thy government, that thou may repair in me the lost Image of God, and powerfully carry me on unto salvation.

Instead of saying thus, and closing absolutely the bargain with God in Christ reconciling the world to himself, the tempter would have the poor afflicted man to speak, as it were, to this sense.

O Lord, the condition whereupon thou dost offer to be my God and Savior, doth please me well, but because I fear I may deceive myself in performing that condition, I require another condition of thee, that thou wouldst, first, let me see the fruits of faith in me, which if I shall find within sometime hence, then will I count myself a believer, and will rest on thee: but if I find not such fruits as may evidence true faith in me, I must pronounce my faith, either no faith or a dead faith, which hath a name of faith, but neither power nor life in it.

For, faith without works is dead, as James saith, ch. 2:26.

Now, what is this else in effect, then to make a new condition in the covenant of Grace, and to promise upon this condition, to believe on Christ, if God shall do as the sinner giveth him direction? That is, if God shall make him bring forth the fruits of faith first, when it became him absolutely to embrace Christ, that he might both be forgiven of sin, and enabled to bring forth fruits of faith?

Another fault is here also, which is this, the afflicted person doth require mature fruits from a weak faith, from a faith that is not settled and fixed, but suspended on a condition, which is no less unreasonable, then if a foolish Gardner should require fruits of a young tree lately planted, yea before the roots of it were well settled in the ground; yea, and would not let it stand in his garden, except, it should first bring forth fruits, whereby it might evidence itself worthy of pains taking on it.

A third fault is this, that the afflicted, in this case, doth pre-suppose, that true faith is posterior to the fruits of true faith, both in nature and time: for, if he will not believe in Christ, till after he perceive and feel in himself the fruits of faith, upon this ground he can never believe till he first find the fruits of faith in himself, which is nothing else in effect, then to imagine, that the effect must go before its cause.

Unto this threefold self-deceit, we offer this one remedy in general, that the afflicted person in the foresaid case, humble himself before God in the sense of his barrenness, and so much the more as he findeth small or no fruits in himself, let him fly to Christ and fasten himself the more on his imputed righteousness, and cleave unto him by faith, without delay, that he may draw virtue and furniture from him to bring forth good fruits; for, this is the only way to make him bring forth fruits in abundance, as Christ doth teach us, John 15:5. He that abideth in me, and I in him, the same bringeth forth much fruit: for without me, ye can do nothing. He, and he only, can make a good tree of an evil imp, and cause it bring forth fruits answerable to the nature of the true vine wherein it is engrafted. And seeing Christ in the Canticle, ch. 2:13, doth make no small account of the green figs and tender grapes, let not the afflicted despise the day of small things.

4. The second practical error in the afflicteds foresaid case, is this, the afflicted person hath imagined in himself, that such and such fruits would presently follow upon his receiving the offer of Christ, as that he should forthwith be skillful in the knowledge of the mysteries of salvation, able to pray eloquently, made cheerful in singing songs of praise unto God, ready and expedite to every good work, and that he should feel constantly an un-interrupted peace in his conscience, and joy in the holy Ghost; but after that by experience he hath found, that he cannot so much as enter upon any good work without a fight with Satan and with his own corrupt nature, and other impediments, and withal he doth feel the peace of his conscience and the joy of the holy Ghost with-drawn, hereupon he begins to suspect the whole work of God's grace in himself, and that he remaineth in the state of nature unrenewed.

5. For removing of this error, let the afflicted know, that the hopes which he hath conceived at the hearing of the Gospel, shall not be disappointed (albeit according to his childish fore-conception they come not to pass) for in a time due and acceptable, God shall perform all his promises and bring the believer (fled unto him) on upon his way, till he put him in full possession of freedom from all sin and misery. But yet this felicity is brought about, not all at once, but piece and piece, and not without conflict with the enemies of our salvation, and not without use of the means appointed of God. Wherefore let the afflicted be exhorted to take courage unto him, as becometh a soldier of Christ, and let him go on in the ways of the Lord in hope and patience, being assured that whatsoever God hath promised, he

will surely perform, in that manner, measure, order and time, and by his own appointed means as he hath set down in his holy Scriptures.

6. The third practical error of the afflicted in the foresaid case, is, that he doth not judge rightly of his own faith, nor of the fruits thereof: for of his own faith he judgeth no other ways than of the faith of another man, while as there is a diverse way to judge of my own faith then of another man's faith; for because I cannot reach to the internal acts of the soul of another man, therefore I must judge only by the outward effects, according to the rule that James giveth, chap. 2, ver. 10. Show me thy faith without thy works, and I will show thee my faith by my works. Yet of my own faith I may judge, not only by the external effects of it (which in the first closing with Christ, are not yet observable possibly) but also by the internal act of faith which the holy Spirit who knows the heart doth reveal unto me, by making me not only heartily to embrace Christ offered in the Gospel, and love him, but also can make me reflect and turn back mine eye upon his own gift and grace in me, according to that of the Apostle, 1 Cor. 2:12, we have received the Spirit of God, that we might know the things freely given to us of God.

Again the afflicted doth not judge rightly of his own fruits of faith, according as the truth is, and as the Lord in his Word doth judge; he should distinguish between the sincerity of the work and the perfection of it (a work may be done uprightly, and yet be imperfect) he should distinguish what is God's part in the work, from that which is wrong and corrupt, flowing from the remainder of sin in him. These things he doth confound, and doth so fix his eyes upon the defects and imperfection of his work, that he seeth nothing but what is wrong, when it is his duty both to observe what is wrong, that he may be humbled, and cast away all confidence in his work, and to observe also what is good and right in his work, proceeding from the grace of God in him, and so praise and thank God for it in Christ, who will not quench the smoking flax, Isa. 42:3.

7. For remedy therefore of this error, let the afflicted, first, look upon the acts of his faith both internal and external, both on the elicit acts of faith and the imperate acts (as they are called in the Schools) and let him judge of both according to what is right and equitable, that whatsoever be the measure of new obedience, it may be differenced from the mixture of infirmity, defects, or corruption. And let him not judge of his work according to the suggestions and calumnies of Satan, who always condemneth so far as he can, what is good in God's children; or if he cannot condemn it, doth labor to have it abused.

Secondly, let the afflicted observe the due order both in doing his duties and in judging thereof: for of necessity he must, first, put forth an act of faith and love on Christ, before he can pass judgment on it, and let him first do the work commanded to the believer, and then pass sentence, that he may be strengthened to do more duties, and so to present them to God to be washen, accepted and amended in his following service.

Thirdly, let him carefully look unto the end which he should propose to himself in judging of his acts of faith and obedience: for the end of judging ourselves and our works, should be to confirm our faith in Christ, when we find anything done according to the rule, and to fly to Christ for pardon and grace if we conceive all is wrong after we have examined matters.

6. The fourth practical error, is, that the afflicted first suffereth his faith to be wounded and weakened by Satan's temptation, and then to be drawn forth to the field to give a proof of the strength of his

faith in some difficile duty, before the wound of faith be bound up or healed; for, it is a great disadvantage to enter the lists with Satan about the fruits of faith, whether they be sincere or not, when faith is wounded, yea, fainteth, and is brought in question whether it be true faith or not. Now this is a special stratagem and wile of Satan, by whatsoever mean he can to hurt the faith of God's children, that he may by that mar communion-keeping with God, and cut off, if he can, the conduit whereby the power of Christ is conveyed to the believer for making him give acceptable obedience unto God. And certainly, it is no less difficile, when faith is wrested, and for a time out of joint, to set about acceptable service, then it is to make a man to set upon his work when his arms are out of joint.

Therefore, for remedy of this error, let the afflicted, so soon as he findeth his faith wounded, incontinent set himself down before God humbly, and acknowledge his foolishness, want of watching, un-worthiness and inability, either to know how he hath grieved God's Spirit, and made open a door for the Tempter to fall in upon him, or to repent the sins which he knoweth might have provoked God so to exercise him; and next, let him look unto God in Christ reconciling the world to himself, and lay hold on the horns of the altar, on the throne of grace for strengthening his faith, that he may find help for the present need, and thereafter also to walk more wisely: for, this is the counsel which Christ doth give to the corrupt Church of Sardis, Rev. 3:2. Strengthen the thing which remaineth and is ready to die. Thus may the afflicted recover strength of faith and ability to resist Satan, and furniture for bringing forth unquestionable fruits of faith.

CHAP. VIII. - Wherein the regenerate man's doubt, whether he be in the state of grace, arising from his unquietness of spirit, is answered.

THIS CASE IS INCIDENT to many dear children of God, and may befall Champions in time of sad affliction, as we see in the Prophet, Psal. 42:11, and 43:5, why art thou cast down, O my soul? And why art thou disquieted within me? But even in time of outward prosperity, or when no great affliction bodily lieth on, many, who in the sense of their sinfulness have fled to Jesus Christ, and have taken his yoke upon them, are troubled with doubting's, whether they be of the number of true believers, whether they have rightly come unto Christ, whether they have been well accepted of him; and for their doubting they can give no other reason, save this, I cannot be quiet, nor rest in assurance, that I am in the state of grace; if they be interrogate, what they think of the evident signs of their regeneration which have been and are to be seen in their conversation since they began in earnest to seek the face of God in Christ? They will possibly not altogether deny God's work in them; but yet dare not lean weight upon these signs, because they do find these signs also brought in question, whether they have been or are kindly and sincere; mean time they are about to do that which is acceptable to God in the course of their calling, albeit with more heaviness and less alacrity then becometh persons reconciled to God in Christ.

2. This disease will be found complicate and made up of more mistakes and errors then one: and therefore is to be the more narrowly considered: because it is no small hindrance of a comfortable Christian conversation, which God doth allow on his children; for in the party troubled with unquietness, we presuppone, 1. There is a serious sense of sin, and purpose to do better. 2. An unfeigned embracing of the covenant of grace and reconciliation in Christ Jesus. And, 3. an honest, though weak, endeavor to bring forth the fruits of new obedience: and yet notwithstanding the person is not quiet, but walketh heavily and is discouraged, by reason of his uncertainty, whether he be in the state of grace or not: yea, he is cast down and disquieted, because he is disquieted, and cannot get a reasonable answer from his conscience when he asketh of it, why are thou cast down and disquieted within me?

3. The mistakes and errors, whence this dissatisfaction and unquietness doth flow are many; but we shall condescend upon eight or nine only. The first error, and cause of unquietness is, or may be this, that the party afflicted, albeit he have the habits of saving grace in him, and doth by God's grace put forth these habits in actual exercise, yet he doth not reflect upon, nor turn his eye to observe, the

operations of God's holy Spirit in himself, nor the acts of saving grace, which the holy Spirit hath made him put forth, of which if he take not notice, they are to him for the time as if they were not; and so no wonder he be disquiet, while he perceiveth not in himself that which might make him quiet: For example, when the sense of sin is raised up in a man's spirit by the holy Ghost, if he do not observe that this is one of the operations of the holy Spirit convincing the world of sin, or if he do not turn back his eye on this operation, and upon his own act, stirred up thereby, to subscribe the sentence of the law against himself, no wonder that he doubt of his conversion, till he see the foot-steps of God the converter of him, from the love and approbation of sin, unto the hatred of it; and when he is fled to Christ the only Redeemer from sin and misery, and hath laid hold on him according to the covenant of grace offered in him, if he do not look back on this operation of God drawing him to Christ, and upon his own act of coming unto Christ, by the draught of God's Spirit, what wonder he do not reckon himself among believers, albeit he be in God's account one of that number? And when the holy Spirit hath kindled in him not only a purpose of new obedience, but also a begun endeavor to live holily, justly and soberly, if he do not observe and acknowledge these operations of God's Spirit making him to bring forth these acts, what wonder that this mistake and inconsideration do open a door to disquietness and doubting, whether he be in the state of grace or not?

4. For removing this cause of disquietness, the afflicted person must beware that he pass not sentence of God's dispensation towards him, according to the temptations and suggestions of Satan, nor yet according to the opinion which his Pastor or friend may have of him, judging somewhat uncharitably of him, upon sinister suspi-

cions: neither let him stand to the suspicions of his own incredulous heart; but let him consider what the Word of the Lord hath said of the person in whom these three graces do concur, to wit, 1. the sense of sin and inability to help ourselves; 2. flying unto Christ for relief from sin and misery; and, 3. some measure of upright purpose and endeavor to serve God in new obedience; for of such saith the Apostle, Phil. 3:3 We are the Circumcision or true Israelites, who have no confidence in the flesh, but rejoice in Jesus Christ, and worship God in the spirit. Let him therefore esteem the discovery of his sinful and wretched estate in himself to be the very fruit of the eye-salve and work of the Spirit bestowed on him by Christ, and let him esteem his hearty consent given to the covenant of grace and reconciliation, to be the undoubted act of saving faith. For, hearty consent to the offer of grace in Jesus Christ, presupposes, first, that the person sees no standing for him by the law or covenant of works, but is beaten from all confidence in himself, and made to believe and subscribe the righteous sentence of the law against himself to the praise of God's truth and justice. Secondly, it imports the man's believing the testimony which God hath given of Christ Jesus, to wit, that God hath made a gift of life eternal to the soul that hungereth and thristeth for righteousness, and that this life is in his Son; yea it imports the man's receiving and embracing of Christ offered in the Gospel. Thirdly, it importeth, that the consenter to the covenant of grace as he hath renounced confidence in his own works, So he hath given up himself to God, to live by the grace of Jesus Christ unto eternal life. Now if the afflicted shall reflect upon these two operations of the holy Ghost, making him humble in the sense of sin, heartily to receive Christ Jesus for his relief, and withal do observe an unfeigned purpose and begun endeavor to live more holily and fruitfully by the grace and furniture of Christ, howsoever he labor under many infirmities, not only is he undoubtedly a new creature, but also by observing the foresaid evidence thereof, may conclude, that God hath begun a good work of grace in him, and so shall this first cause of disquietness be removed.

5. Another cause of disquietness is, or may be this, if the afflicted, after examination of the work of grace in himself, being convinced of his blessed estate and confirmed by present sense of God's love shed abroad in his heart, do not hold fast his estimation of God's work in himself longer then the sensible comfort thereof remaineth with him, but either doth retreat his judgment of his blessed estate, or doth not defend his right, doth not resist Satan by being steadfast in the faith, no wonder his disquietness and dejection of courage return upon him.

6. For removing of this cause of disquietness, let the afflicted consider, that spiritual consolation, and sensible feeling of God's favor, is granted to God's children to make them steadfast in the faith of God's grace toward them, when sensible comfort is with-drawn, and when they are put to the trial and exercise of their faith, under trouble and temptations. And therefore, when the afflicted, once being made clear of his interest in Christ, and of his keeping on him the yoke of Christ, doth find a change in his condition, let him presently humble himself before God, in acknowledgment of the power of the body of sin in himself, and of whatsoever evil fruit it hath brought forth, whereby he hath procured the change of his own comfortable condition; and let him renew the acts of his repentance and of his faith in Christ, striving against all temptations for the faith once given to him, and disputing for his right and interest unto God's grace in Christ, that he may with patience obtain the victory over his temptation, and be able, not only with David to charge his own soul

to trust in God, the help and health of his countenance, Psal. 42, and 43, but also to glory with the Apostle, and to say, 2 Tim. 1:22. I know whom I have believed, and I am persuaded, that he is able to keep that which I have committed unto him against that day. And so may the second cause of disquietness be removed.

7. A third cause of disquietness is, or may be, this, if a sincere convert, finding himself come short both of his purpose and hope of making progress in the course of new obedience and reformation of heart and conversation, shall, instead of being more humbled and beaten more out of confidence in his own strength and works and instead of laying faster hold on the imputed righteousness of Christ, yield unto discouragement, and so open a door for calling his own conversion in question. In this case, the disquietness of the true convert is augmented, by reason of the conscience of his sincerity in his conversion, wherein he renounced the love and service of all sin, renounced all confidence in his own worth or works, did fly unto the grace offered in Christ, and received him heartily, and purposed honestly to serve God thereafter in newness of life, which maketh him say in himself, I can never put repentance from dead works, and faith in Christ, and purpose of new obedience more sincerely in exercise, then I have done; and now, seeing I come short of my purpose and hope of profiting and can never more sincerely repent of sin or believe in Christ then I have done, have I not just cause of doubting of my estate and of discouragement and disquietness.

8. For removing this cause of disquietness, let the afflicted consider first, that there is a great difference between purpose and practice. A holy and sincere purpose ofttimes cometh short in practice; for, the Apostle saith, Rom. 7 18. To will is present with me, but how to

perform that which is good, I find not. The inlake here is of strength to perform, and not in the sincerity of the will and purpose.

Secondly, let him consider, that there is a difference between the consent of a well-informed conscience to the discharge of holy duties, and the practical coming up of the not well-reformed heart, unto the actual discharge of those duties; for ofttimes the heart is like a deceitful bow, that disappointeth the archer; therefore, let not the afflicted deny the sincerity of his purpose, but let him be humbled for the corruption of his heart, which hath not answered his purpose and expectation.

Thirdly, let not the afflicted think, that he hath so fully renounced all confidence in his own works as he conceived: we may be clearly convinced not to lean to our own righteousness, and so more easily in our judgment renounce all confidence in our good behavior; but the dregs of the sin of misbelieving Jews is not easily purged out of us, wherein they went about to establish their own righteousness, and did not submit themselves to the righteousness of faith, Rom. 9, and 10:3. As he therefore, who denieth, that he leaneth his weight on his staff and yet falleth to the ground when his staff doth slide, is found to have leaned more weight on his staff then he pretended; So he is found to have leaned too much weight upon his own works, who is cast down, because his performances are not answerable to his purpose and hopes. Humbled indeed he ought to be, and to lament his misery under the body of death, but not be so dejected and discouraged, as to loose or slacken his grips of the covenant of Grace; especially when he doth consider, that the Lord, by this experience of his own weakness, is teaching him thereafter to have a more high estimation, and make better use, of Christ's imputed righteousness, and to lean less to his own purposes, and promises, and inherent righteousness, that so he may draw more ability from Christ by faith, to bring forth better fruits: for without me, saith Christ, you can do nothing, Joh. 15:5.

Last of all, let him neither say nor think, that he cannot put forth any act of repentance or faith, or purpose of amendment of life, more sincerely then he hath done; for, no man hath attained such a measure of sincerity in the discharge of any act of saving grace, but there is room for him to receive a greater measure both of activity and sincerity in acting, then he hath attained already: but rather let him examine more narrowly, and find out the corrupt inclination of the heart to lean to its own inherent righteousness, and difficulty of subjecting itself wholly to the righteousness of faith, and sanctification through faith in Christ; for, this doth the Apostle teach us to do, Philip. 3:12-14, he did not think himself already perfect, but reached himself forth to those things which were before him, pressing toward the mark for the prize of the high calling of God in Christ Jesus. And the end of the pressing of the Law is, that sin may be the more clearly discovered; that as sin hath reigned unto death, even so might grace reign through Christ Jesus our Lord, Rom. 5:20,21.

9. The fourth cause of disquietness is, or may be, this, if the true convert, being frequently convinced of the manifold deceits of the heart, for this cause shall begin to call in question all the work of grace in himself: which inconvenience doth flow from his not putting difference between the true consent of the heart unto the covenant of Grace and acts of holiness, in so far as the heart is renewed on the one hand, and the doubting or hesitation of the heart, in as far as it is not purged from the relicts of incredulity and backwardness unto godliness on the other hand; or, because he puts no difference between the effects of renewing grace, and the effects of in-dwelling

sin in himself, both of them putting forth their power in the self-same actions: for, if this difference shall not be observed, and sentence so given, as that which is in the renewed man be absolved and commended, and that which flows from indwelling sin be disallowed and condemned, without prejudice to any good, which shall be found in the renewed man, it is impossible that the conscience can be quiet, or that any good action of the Saints can be approven, by reason of sin in us; for, the evil which we would not, shall be found in us, as is clear in the Apostles censure of himself, Rom. 7:15 to 20.

10. For removing this fourth cause of disquietness, let the afflicted learn so to observe the inlakes and sinful imperfections and pollutions of his best works, as he observe also that which is good in his actions, that of the good he may make thankful confession unto God, and pray for the increase thereof; and of the inlakes and pollutions of his works, he may make confession also, and be humbled for them, and fly to the unspotted righteousness of Christ, and to the fountain opened up in his house for sin and uncleanness, Zech. 13:1. This wisdom is taught us in the example of the father of the child possessed with a dumb and deaf spirit, crying out and saying with tears, Lord, I believe, help thou my unbelief, Mark, 9:24, he maintains the begun work of faith in himself, and confesseth the evil he found in himself, and flyeth by prayer to Christ to help him.

11. The fifth cause of disquietness is, or may be this, if the true convert suspend the absolution of his own faith and fruits thereof from being hypocritical and counterfeit, until he find himself freed from disquietness, and do enjoy peace and tranquility of mind, which he doth apprehend should always accompany sound, sincere and unfeigned faith, and on this ground he esteemeth that faith only to be true faith, which hath overcome all doubting's, and now be-

ing victorious, bringeth peace and quietness with it; and that faith
which is tossed, or troubled with doubting's, he thinketh may justly
be suspected of unsoundness, as if temptation to doubting, were a
sufficient reason to make a question of the sincerity of believing: or
as if it were a sufficient reason for a man to call his faith in question,
whether it be true faith or not, because Satan calleth it in question: for
if this were a sufficient reason to question a work or act of grace in a
man, no work of grace, nor no point of true religion, should be holden
for sound and true, because Satan never ceaseth to calumniate and
quarrel the truth, both of God's Word and working, for he was so
malicious and impudent as to question Christ, If thou be the Son of
God, Matth. 4:3.

12. For removing of this cause of disquietness, let the afflicted
consider, first, that the assaults of the enemy do neither diminish
the worth, nor the estimation of faith; for, faith fighting, is no less
solid and sound in the time of battle, then it is after victory, standing victorious. 2. Let him consider that we are called to a warfare,
not only against flesh and blood, but also against principalities and
powers and spiritual wickedness's Ephes. 6, and that we may not
promise to ourselves, freedom or exemption from Satan's throwing
fiery darts at us, so long as we live, as the Apostle doth warn us, Ephes.
5. Let him consider thirdly, that objections and questions, moved
against the converts faith, are rather a token of the sincerity thereof,
then a reason for bringing it in question: for, the Pirate Satan can
discern well enough between an empty vessel and a ship loadened
with precious wares, and useth to set upon the rich ship, that he may
spoil it, if he can, of that most precious faith, and not trouble himself
to molest a secure presumptuous person, lest he should waken him,
by such means, out of his dream, and chase him unto God. But as

for a man that is already fled from him and turned to God by faith in Christ, he will not fail to follow the chase, that if he cannot bring him back, yet he may vex him and dog him at the heels till his entry in heaven. Fourthly, let him consider, that the Lord useth to suffer Satan to trouble the believer with suggestions to waken his faith, of set purpose to teach the believer to fight his battles, and by frequent exercises to be purified more and more, like gold or silver put ofttimes in the furnace, yea, and that the wrestler may be made valiant in fight, Heb. 11:34, whereupon the afflicted must be exhorted not only to take courage and to despise the malice of the adversary, but also to rejoice when he doth meet with manifold temptations (as we are charged, Jam. 1:2) because of the fruit following by God's blessing on such exercise. And to this end, let him put on the whole armor of God, that when he hath resisted and overcome one temptation, he may stand and resist another, Ephes. 6.

13. The sixth cause of disquietness, is, or may be this, if the true convert do not distinguish, but confound, the peace he hath with God, and the peace he hath in his conscience; if he do not distinguish but confound peace with God and rest from assaults of the adversary; if he do not distinguish, but confound, peace of mind, and peace of conscience; if he do not distinguish and put a due difference between these sorts of peace, he cannot choose but be disquieted, by suspecting his peace with God, because he hath not rest nor peace from Satan's assaults; he cannot eschew disquietness, when he conceives that his peace with God is dissolved, when trouble ariseth in his own conscience. And no wonder he be disquieted when he apprehendeth every perturbation of his mind to be a breach of peace with God, or with his own conscience.

14. For removing of this cause of disquietness, the afflicted must consider, first, that peace with God, doth follow immediately upon an humbled sinners flying to Christ, and embracing the offer of reconciliation with God in Christ, when, in the meantime, the conscience possibly may be going on pursuing the convert with challenges for all sort of sin and guiltiness; for he that is fled to Christ by faith, is justified, and being justified by faith, he hath peace with God, granted, decreed, pronounced in his favors, and registrate in the Court-book of the Evangel, albeit possibly the absolved convert, hath not drawn forth the extract of the decreet, nor considered it, when he hath read it, nor applied the same to himself according as the general sentence giveth him warrant.

Therefore, the humbled sinner, fled unto Christ, and engaged heartily to his service, must not take heed so much to what his sickly, and not clearly informed conscience doth say, as to what God, who is greater than the conscience, and giveth order and rule to the conscience, doth say to such a poor soul fled unto Christ.

Secondly, let him consider, that his peace is not marred with God, by Satan's warring against him; for, peace with God, standeth well with war against all spiritual enemies: and therefore the less rest he hath from Satan's trouble and molestation, let him be the more confident of his peace with God, whose battles he is fighting against Satan.

Thirdly, let him consider, that perturbation of mind, doth neither hinder peace with God, nor peace of conscience: for the mind and thoughts of a man, for many reasons may be troubled and disquieted, when peace with God and peace of conscience are settled and established: for, when the mind is troubled, and tempted to anxiety, the Apostle showeth how to remove the perturbation of the mind, and settle the peace of conscience also, Phil. 4:6,7. Be careful, saith he, or anxious, for nothing, but in everything by prayer and supplication with thanks giving, let your requests be made manifest to God, and the peace of God which passes all understanding shall keep your hearts and minds through Christ Jesus. And in his own experience he lets us see the difference of perturbation of mind, from peace with God and the conscience also, 2 Cor. 7:5,6. When we were come into Macedonia, our flesh had no rest, but we were troubled on every side, without were fighting's, within were fears; nevertheless, God that comforteth these that are cast down, comforted us in the coming of Titus: So also, 2 Cor. 2:12-14.

15. The seventh cause of disquietness, is, or may be this, if the true convert be either ignorant or forgetful of the way of obtaining, maintaining, repairing and recovering the true peace of God in himself, and of the change of God's dispensation toward his children which is common; through many tribulations God doth bring his own to heaven. Sometime he shows them his countenance in a comfortable providence, sometime he hides his face, but doth not change his love toward them, Psal. 30:7. Thou hidest thy face, saith David, and I was troubled, but here was his wisdom, he went the straight way to recover his peace, I cried to thee, O Lord, and unto the Lord made I my supplication, and his mourning was turned into dancing, Psal. 30:7,8, to the end. But many weak converts are not so wise, who by their inconsiderate courses do cast themselves in fears, jealousies and suspicions, both of God's love to them and of their own interest in him: when they miss felt consolations they fall to quarrel their right. And if they resolve to have their condition helped, they prescribe their own time, way and measure, and nothing can satisfy them till they recover possession of lost sense, with the Spouse, Cant. 2:5. Stay me

with flagons, comfort me with apples (saith she) for I am sick of love. It is true, sometime God doth condescend to their passionate put suit of comfort, but their not believing, in the meantime, and their hasting to have their condition altered, before patience hath wrought the perfect work, is not to be commended or approven.

16. For removing this cause of disquietness, let the afflicted consider, first, that the Lord neither showeth his loving countenance to the weak disciple, nor hideth it from him, but out of love; he neither corrrecteth nor comforteth him, but out of love; I am the Lord and change not (saith he) Mal. 3:6, Therefore you sons of Jacob are not consumed. If he give consolation sensibly, it is to confirm their weak faith, by sensible experience of the fruit of believing in him, and if he withdraw his consolation, it is that he may exercise their faith, and train them to believe his Word without a sensible pawn for it: And therefore, for removing, this cause of disquietness, by all means let the afflicted beware to mis-construct the Lord's dealing, but let him strive against all suggestions of Satan, or his own misbelieving heart, and entertain friendly thoughts of God; for a true friend, or father among men, will take it for no small injury to be suspected of his friendly or fatherly affection to his friend or child, yea, even Physicians and Surgeons find a good exposition from their Patients, when they give them bitter potions, when they cut, and carve, and burn their flesh, still they are exponed to aim at the patients good; much more should every man, whatsoever dispensation of God he meet with, give a good construction of his working.

Secondly, let him consider, that the Lord hath his own way and order of working; first, he discovereth sin and misery and weakness in the creature, and after that he discovereth his grace, mercy and power in Christ to relieve; first, he humbleth, and then lifteth up;

first, he woundeth, and then he healeth; first, he smiteth, and then bindeth up; first he bringeth down to death, and then restoreth unto life, Hos. 6:1, and, Psal. 9:3, and therefore, let the afflicted be humbled under the sense of apprehended causes of his disquietness, and seek of God the restoring of what is lost or wanting, and the healing of the wound inflicted, in due order. Now God's order is this, he will first, have the Law magnified, and his Justice acknowledged by all afflicted sinners, even by them who are in the state of Grace, and are not under the covenant or curse of the Law, to whom notwithstanding the Law must still be a pedagogue to lead them to Christ; and when the Lord's Justice is acknowledged, and all fretting and murmuring against his dealing stopped, then comes, in the next place, the discovery of grace in Christ: for, since the fall of Adam, God hath always been in Christ, going about to reconcile the world to himself not imputing their transgressions to them, 2 Cor. 5:19. And when God hath drawn the sinner by faith to the Mediator Christ, God incarnate, then there is a matrimonial contract made betwixt God in Christ reconciled and the believer, and an union between Christ and the believer in a judicial manner; and so the believer is made to have a right unto Christ's person, according to that of the Spouse, Cant. 2:16. My beloved is mine, and I am his. And by this means also, the believer is made to have right unto Christ's purchase and benefits, and to communion with him and his Saints, as the Apostle teacheth us, Rom. 8:32. He that spared not his own Son, but delivered him up for us all, how shall he not with him also freely give us all things? And after right given to the believer, in due time the Lord giveth and reneweth the earnest-penny of the inheritance, Ephes. 1:13. In whom also ye were sealed with that holy spirit of promise, who really reneweth the believer and giveth him peace, joy, consolation, strength and other gifts of grace, with an ebbing and flowing thereof in the sense and feeling of the believer, as may best serve the good of the believer, and glory of Gods gracious dispensation: and therefore,

Thirdly, let the afflicted person, whatsoever cross-dispensation he meet with, whatsoever distemper of soul he fall into, whatsoever grace or measure of grace he misseth or cometh short of, seek his relief in God's order; that is to say, let him justify the Lord's wisdom and justice, humble himself under his mighty hand, renew the acts of repentance in humility, turn his face toward Christ by the renewed acts of faith in him, lay hold on his right unto Christ's person and benefits, that he may come to the sensible feeling of what he hath right unto by the covenant of Grace. And whatsoever defects, transgressions, temptations unto discouragement and disbelief, do brangle his confidence, let them humble himself indeed, but so as they do not drive him from that Covenant, but be made use of as spurs, and forcible motives to lay the faster hold on Christ and his infinite grace contracted in that Covenant.

17. The eight cause of disquietness, is, or may be this, if the true convert, daily lamenting his own sinfulness, and daily troubled with suspicion of his own blessed estate, by reason of his felt manifold corruptions shall meet either with the calumnies of men, or comforters like Job's friends, who instead of healing his wounds in his affliction, shall foster his suspicion of his estate by uncharitable censure of the poor man's complaint of himself; in this case, if the afflicted do not maintain his righteousness by faith in Christ, as Job did, and his upright endeavor to please God, which is manifest by his daily godly grief for his short coming in his aimed-at holiness, no wonder he be disquieted.

18. For removing of this cause, let the afflicted consider and distinguish what is right in him, and what is wrong, and beware to confound these. For example, 1. This is right, that he doth not lean to the worth of his own works, nor is puffed up with a vain conceit of himself before God. 2. That he is sensible of his sinful imperfections and corruptions, and of the bitter root of original sin in him. 3. It is right in him also, that he aimeth toward perfection, forgetting what is behind, and pressing toward the mark and prize of his calling. But this is wrong in him, 1. that he fostereth suspicions unjustly of his own blessed estate. 2. That he doth not observe the work of God's grace in himself so carefully as he observeth his imperfections and corruptions. 3. That he doth not so much the more make use of Christ's imputed righteousness, as he findeth the imperfection of his own inherent righteousness. 4. That he measureth God's estimation of him, according to the estimation he hath of himself, when indeed God in Scripture doth show no less approbation of him in his wrestling, then he doth in the time of his victory and quiet condition. 5. That he doth not observe the difference of the way he doth walk into which is good, from the sliding's, imperfections, errors and mistakes in particular actions and passages in that way. 6. That he doth lay more weight ofttimes upon the judgment of mistaking spectators of his course, then he hath reason to do, and doth not take heed to the sentence of the Lord in the Gospel, concerning the poor in spirit, the contrite, the meek and lowly disciple. These things let the afflicted consider and make good use thereof, for his encouragement in the way of new obedience.

19. The ninth cause of disquietness is, or may be, this, if the true convert be not acquainted with living by faith; for there are many honest and tender-hearted converts, who, in the sense of their sins,

are fled unto Christ, resolved never to depart from him, and careful
to lead a blameless life, who notwithstanding, whensoever they meet
with changes of dispensation, with variety of temptations, fresh feeling of the power of sin in themselves, or any cross bodily or spiritual,
are disquieted and cast in suspicion of their state: and albeit they
neither will give over to follow after Christ, nor will God suffer them
to perish, yet they make themselves an uncomfortable and miserable
life, by their leaning to present sense and feeling, when they should
remember the saying of the Apostle (2 Cor. 5:7, we walk not by sight
but by faith) they are cast down, do mourn and complain, because
it is not with them as they would, and are most part male-content
with their lot, frequently regrating unto God their wants and imperfections, and seldom are they praising or thanking God for what they
have gotten of him.

20. For removing this cause, let the afflicted, first, consider what
the Apostle speaketh to the afflicted Hebrews, Heb. 10:36, ye have
need of patience, that when ye have done the will of God ye may
receive the promise; for yet a little while, and he that will come, shall
come, and will not tarry. Now, the just man shall live by faith, saith
he.

Secondly, let him consider, that to live by faith, doth require these
six duties, 1. That we renounce our own corrupt reason and sense,
lest we count that to be our life which may be seen or felt, or that
which may be altered and changed, but reckon that to be our life,
which is hid with God in Christ, and shall be revealed at the glorious
coming of our Lord. 2. That the covenant of grace, and rich promises
of the Gospel be esteemed of us as our meet and drink, whereby our
hearts may be sustained in all adversity, and our hope upholden in
patience through the comfort of the Scriptures. 3. That we make use

of all God's benefits bestowed upon us by virtue of that new right made unto us in Christ for being partakers thereof. 4. That in all our actions we implore and seek our strength from Christ, and give him thanks for the measure whatsoever he bestoweth. So did the Apostle live, Gal. 2:20. The life which I now live in the flesh, I live by the faith of the Son of God. 5. That we rejoice and glory more in Christ Jesus in the midst of trouble, then we grieve for our troubles whatsoever, whereby as with a sharp pencil, he is drawing in us the lineaments of his own Image and conformity with himself; So did the Saints, Rom. 5:3,4,5. Last of all, to live by faith, requireth that in every condition we should keep faith and a good conscience in Christ Jesus, and esteem ourselves blessed of the Lord, albeit we be tossed with troubles immediately sent from God to exercise us, albeit we do fall in manifold temptations, be assaulted with doubting's, and persecuted unjustly by men: for, it should and may suffice a believer in Christ, if he be not distressed, albeit he be troubled on every side; he must not despair albeit he be perplexed; he shall not be forsaken, albeit he be persecuted; he shall not be destroyed, albeit he be cast down, 2 Cor. 4:8,9. Upon these and the like grounds, the Apostle lived a comfortable life, Phil. 4:12. I know both how to be abased, and I know how to abound, everywhere and in all things I am instructed, both to be full, and to be hungry, both to abound and suffer need; I can do all things through Christ who strengthens me. Thus must Christian soldiers live in the midst of their toiling, in warfare, in want of many things, in watching and running hazard of life, in hope of victory and promised glory, holding up their hearts by faith in Christ.

And these things which we have spoken in explication of this case, are not intended to hinder the tender hearted believer from praying, and endeavoring by all means, that the face of the Lord may shine upon him, and that he may be filled with the joy of his Spirit; for we are charged to seek his face and strength continually, Psal. 105:4. But all our speech doth drive at this mainly, that the afflicted in his discouragement and unquietness, meekly submit himself to the will of God, howsoever he be exercised, always going on in the way of God according to his vocation, through honor and dishonor, through good report and evil report, looking unto the promises which are made to him that endureth to the end. And what is spoken here of living by faith, must not be abused to softer negligence in well doing or bringing forth fruits of faith in every condition, or to hinder the daily exercise of repentance, or to require of a Christian a stoical stupidity under trouble; but the thing we aim at, is, that the Christian in all cross dispensations and vexations, endeavor by faith to be of good courage in the Lord, and endeavor to draw virtue from Christ to bring forth fruits, giving glory to him, whatsoever measure he shall bestow more or less, because it is Christ who is made unto us wisdom and righteousness, sanctification and redemption, and in him alone shall the soul of the afflicted have rest, Matth. 11:24.

CHAP. IX. - Wherein the converts doubt, arising from his uncertainty as what time he was converted, is solved.

THERE ARE SOME TRUE converts, who after they have passed a good part of their journey to heaven, begin to halt and make slow progress, by doubting whether they be walking in the true converts foot-steps, or whether they be converted at all, or not. The reason of their doubting, ariseth from this, that in conference with sundry of the Saints of their acquaintance, they have observed, that every one of them could design the time of their conversion, and from that time can reckon their age in Christ: Or, from this is their doubt arisen, that in the Treatise of some modern Writer, they have read, or from the Sermon of some well esteemed Preacher they have heard some such doctrine, whereupon the true convert falleth out with himself in saying, I was bred and brought up in a godly family, I have followed the exercises of religion; after hearing the heads and sum of Christian Religion, I have embraced the truth; I seemed to myself to believe in Christ, and en-tertain the exercise of repentance, and to endeavor the amendment of my life; I love these whom I see to live holily, and I do hate the ways of the profane, but because I cannot tell when or what day or year I was really converted, as I know sundry of the godly of my acquaintance can do; therefore I doubt whether my conversion be begun or not, but mean time, though I will not turn off the way I have been following, yet I go on halting and heartless till I be cleared of my doubt.

2. For removing this doubt, we must yield this far to the afflicted, that many indeed deceive themselves, who being civilly educated, and from their child-age accustomed with the exercises of religion; are nothing beyond the foolish virgins, and do rest satisfied with their own and others opinion of themselves. If such persons be questioned, when they began to repent, or believe in Christ; it is true, they cannot design the time when they were unconverted, but have still been pleased, and are pleased, with their own estate, and in effect were never converted. But it is no less true on the other hand, that there are some who indeed are renewed, in whom, piece and piece, without any notable change, faith and repentance, and a holy conversation, have grown with the growing knowledge of the Gospel, and will of God therein; of whom it may be truly said, the kingdom of heaven cometh not with observation; of whom it is said, Mark. 4:26. So is the kingdom of God, as if a man should cast seed into the ground, and should sleep, and rise night and day, and the seed should spring and grow up, he knoweth not how.

But to solve the doubt, it matters not whether a man know or not know the day of his conversion, provided he be indeed regenerate and made a new creature. Wherefore the afflicted may be of good courage, if after serious examination of his own conscience, he be humbled frequently in the sense, not only of his actual sins and short-coming of his duty, but also in the sense of his original and in-dwelling corruption or body of death; if, as he doth indeed loath himself, and renounce all confidence in his best works, so he seriously embrace the imputed righteousness of Christ, and in his strength, by faith in him, doth endeavor to live holily, righteously and soberly, (albeit joined with many imperfections) he may conclude, he is regenerate: for, if these three be joined in him in any measure of honesty, he needeth not be anxious what day, month or year the holy Spirit began to work these things in him. Only let him give all diligence to grow in humility, faith and new obedience, and to hold on this way, whatsoever doubts or impediments he shall meet with; for, the Apostle exempteth such a man from the number of hypocrites and unconverted, Phil. 3:3. We, saith he, are the circumcision, or the Christian converts, who worship God in the spirit, and rejoice in Christ Jesus, and have no confidence in the flesh.

CHAP. X. - Wherein is solved the converts doubt of his regeneration, arising from his apprehension, that the beginning of the change of his life, was not from the sincere love of God, but either from terror or self-love, which he conceiveth to be but carnal.

SOME TRUE CONVERTS ARE, who can design the time of the change of their way from sin to Christ, and to a holy life, whereof they have not only the Church they live in, but also their own conscience witnesses; yet after a considerable time, do fall in suspicion, whether that time of their change was the time of their effectual calling; some of them bringing no other reason of their doubting, save this, that they were never much troubled with the terrors of the Law, but most part allured to draw near to God, and to eschew the way of sinning by the love of eternal life. Other some, doubting of the soundness of their conversion, because the terror of God and fear of condemnation and hell prevailed more with them, for changing their course, then the love of God and true holiness did; and both the one sort and the other do conceive the chief rise of their change to have been natural or carnal, self-love, fearing harm, and loving life.

2. For removing of this doubt, we grant, that there are many, who after some notable delivery from death, or some notable benefit received, or after some sharp rod of chastisement for their sin, have changed their outward way of living, left off gross vices, and led a more civil and blameless outward life, and yet have neither seriously repented them of sin, nor seriously fled in unto the grace of Jesus Christ offered in the Gospel, neither knowing what saving faith is, nor careful to know it; but of such we do not speak here, for we are speaking of the true convert and renewed man, who in the sense of sin is fled to Christ, in the sense of his unworthiness maketh the grace offered his refuge, and in the sense of indigence, looketh up to Christ and seeketh supply of him in all things, and by the holy Spirit is striving against sin, endeavoring in some measure of sincerity to bring forth the fruits of faith and repentance; and yet for all this, he doubteth of the sincerity of his own conversion, for the reasons

foresaid. To this soldier and wrestler we say (as before we said to him that doubteth of his conversion, because he cannot design the time of his conversion) it is not material by what way, or means or motives, a man is brought unto Christ, provided he doth come and indeed adhere to Christ; it is all one whether the rise of the man's turning from sin to God, was love alluring, or terror driving him, whether a benefit or a sharp rod, whether fear or hope did at the first beginning of his change, move him to seek God; provided, God manifested in the flesh Christ Jesus the Redeemer of sinners, be now his beloved Lord, and precious in his eyes: for, he that is most sweetly allured to come to God, and without much fear is converted, who possibly after serious conviction of sin and deserved death, is not kept long at the door of mercy, but forthwith is admitted to the throne of grace, and tenderly entertained by the Spirit of consolation, may fall in hard exercises afterward. This is evident in the experience of the Prophet David, in whom his brethren, living in the same family with him, did not perceive any signs of a sorrowful or heavy heart, as his brother Eliab's words do show, 1 Sam. 17:28. I know thy pride, and the naughtiness of thy heart. Thus did Eliab judge of David's cheerful carriage, whereof also we have some evidence, that David was of a ruddy and beautiful countenance, and for some years of his youth, did pass the time pleasantly, serving God with his songs and harp while he was feeding his sheep in the wilderness: now none can justly question his conversion all this time, or his sincerity in this service, yet afterward he was other ways exercised: for ofttimes he felt the power of the Law upon his spirit, and was tossed with the terror thereof, and made to mourn and weep heavily. Such doth Job's condition seem to be in his youth, as it is described, Job 29, but afterward in the trial of his faith, what a conflict with temptation he had, the sacred History doth testify. Therefore, there is no reason why any, in whom these evidences of a true Israelite are found in any measure, should suspect the sincerity of his regeneration, because he hath been gently handled in his conversion: for it may come to pass, that the same person may fall in fiery trials and so hard temptations, as he may fall in doubt of his conversion, in regard of the sad afflictions inward and outward whereby he is exercised. In which case he will be found to be mistaken no less than he was mistaken in the former case and condition; for, some dear children of God may possibly, both in their conversion and most part of their life, be exercised with the terrors of the Law, and yet retain fast hold by faith on Christ's grace in their deepest afflictions: For instance, we offer that precious soul Heman the Ezrahite, who came near unto Solomon in the point of wisdom, 1 King. 4:31, and yet how bitter his afflictions of spirit were, the 88th Psalm beareth witness, specially. v. 13-15. But unto thee have I cried, O Lord, and in the morning shall my prayer prevent thee. And why castest thou off my soul? Why hidest thou thy face from me? I am afflicted and ready to die from my youth up: while I suffer thy terrors, I am distracted, &c. And therefore, there is no just cause, that any, in whom the evidences of faith and repentance may be found, should call the sincerity of his own conversion in question, how hardly soever he seem to be handled of God: for whosoever is joined to the Lord Jesus, and will neither suffer himself to be driven from him, nor yet will endure sin to remain in himself uncontrolled, is certainly a true convert. As for these, who for some temporal cause, are come to Christ (as many did come in the days of his flesh) that they might be delivered from some temporal evil, or obtain some temporal benefit, and for that cause do doubt of their conversion or sincerity thereof; they need not dispute much about the occasions of their first seeking after God, provided that they have learned what Christ's grace is, and do seek righteousness and salvation in him; for, we read in the Evangel, that sundry, that they might be cured of leprosy, palsy, blindness, &c. came unto Christ, who afterward came and adhered to him by faith, as the only Redeemer and Savior of their souls from sin and misery. Wherefore, in such doubting's, let not the afflicted trouble himself, nor call his conversion in question; but let him give all diligence to strengthen his faith, and to increase in holiness, making his calling and election sure by well-doing: for, if he do this, he shall neither be found idle, nor unfruitful in the knowledge of our Lord Jesus, as the Apostle promiseth, 2 Pet. 1:8.

CHAP. XI. - Wherein the converts doubt of his being in the state of grace, arising from heavy afflictions and grievous temptations, is solved.

SOME TRUE CONVERTS SOMETIME fall into great suspicions of their regeneration, of their effectual calling, and of the love of God unto them, and that because they meet with sore outward afflictions, and are assaulted also possibly with horrible inward temptations which do befall them unexpectedly, and are ready to swallow them up; for whereas, after divers conflicts in their conversion, and peace of conscience following after these sad exercises of mind, they hoped to have enjoyed God's peace still after, they do meet possibly with sad calamities which they did not foresee nor fear, and being yoked in conflict with more fearful temptations than ever before, which they find themselves unable to overcome, they seem to themselves, to have just cause to call in question all the former work of grace in themselves, and to doubt of their regeneration, and of their reconciliation with God. Of this sort, some who lived in great wealth and outward prosperity, do fall in so deep poverty, that they are neither able to sustain themselves nor their families, but are forced to live on the private charity of others, or openly to beg. Other some do fall in heavy sicknesses, yea, in uncouth diseases, which but rarely do befall any, which seem to be evidences of the wrath of God. Other some do fall in horrible temptations, and are troubled with blasphemous suggestions against God and the holy Scripture, and the way of the Saints, which as fiery darts do stick fast unto them, and disquiet them continually. Other some are tempted unto heinous sins and to such wickedness against themselves or others, as nature doth abhor, to which acts of wickedness they find themselves so powerfully solicited, as they fear God hath decreed to give them over, and that they shall be overcome with the temptations; some after one way, some after another way, by one sort or other of vexation, are tossed, so as they suspect God is pursuing them in wrath and dealing with them other ways then with any of his children. Whereupon ofttimes they break forth in sad complaints, and misbelieving suspicions, saying, if God loved me he would not deal thus and thus with me; if I were a true convert, and reconciled with God, he would not thus pursue me; my case is not the case of the children of God, for anything I know, and other such like regrates and lamentations are uttered by them.

2. For solving this doubt, we neither esteem such exercises, and temptations proper to the regenerate man, or a token of regeneration; neither do we deny, that such exercises may befall true converts: for,

all sorts of afflictions and calamities are common to the good and evil, to the godly and the wicked, so that by those troubles and miseries neither the love or hatred of God can be certainly concluded; but thus much may be said in reason, if these calamities do befall a man, while he is walking in his own sinful ways, then are they undoubtedly to be interpret as evidences of God's wrath, at least fatherly anger, against the afflicted, and to be esteemed as forewarnings of more and more heavy calamities to come upon him, yea, and final perdition also, if he do not repent.

3. In which case the afflicted shall do well to humble himself before God, and give a good construction of God's purpose in sending on him such calamities, in regard when he might forthwith have destroyed the sinner, he hath sent forth these sad afflictions to waken his conscience, and to warn him to fly from the wrath to come, least he perish utterly.

4. He shall do well also to consider with himself, and to acknowledge, that such a bitter potion was necessary, in so deadly and desperate-like disease, as his soul was lying into: for, what should the Lord do unto those who despise the worth of their own souls and of eternal life, and do seek their felicity in vain and perishing pleasure, profit and honor? What shall he do with those whom he will not suffer to perish with this evil world, but break their Idols in pieces and put themselves to grief, who vex his holy Spirit?

Wherefore let the afflicted read his sin in the rod wherewith he is beaten; if he be deprived of temporal goods, or earthly comforts, which he hath abused to the hazard of his own soul, let God have the glory of his justice and mercy also, in that he by cutting off earthly things from him, is sending him to seek things spiritual and everlasting in heaven, where Christ is at the right hand of the Father, Col. 3:2.

If he be vexed with temptations unto blasphemies, and such horrid fearful sins which even nature doth abhor, let him consider, that misbelief of threatening's and promises are no less in effect, than real asserting of blasphemies, and that entertaining of sinful lusts which fight against his soul, is in effect a defiling and destroying of his own soul; by which afflictions and temptations, if the afflicted take not warning and repent, he may justly fear these calamities and tormenting temptations are but the beginnings of sorrows.

But if these calamities and fearful temptations befall a man walking in the ways of God, who is a believer in Christ, who hath casten his anchor within the veil, and studieth in any measure of uprightness to please God, let not such a man be afraid; for, God is not pursuing him in wrath, as Satan his adversary suggesteth, but as a most wise and loving father is trying, and training his faith, and bringing forth the evidence of grace bestowed upon him, to the praise of his own name, shaming of Satan and edifying all beholders of this man's exercise: Wherefore let the afflicted comfort himself in the Lord, and be strong in the faith of holy Scripture, which is granted to the Church for upholding of believers in patience and hope of the promised reward: for even Job, the holiest man on earth in his generation, was both suddenly surprised with a multitude of concurring calamities, and also deprived of all consolation from God and man for a season; for at once he was spoiled of all his goods, deprived of all his children, tempted by his wife to despair, despised by his servants, judged to be a hypocrite by his most entire godly friends, stricken by Satan with an unusual plague of botch-biles; and how far the Lord did hide all comfort for a time, the history of his complaints make evident. Yea, our blessed Lord Jesus Christ, hath sanctified in his own person, the hardest exercises of this sort which his children can fall into; for albeit he could not be defiled with sin, yet he was tempted of Satan unto most abominable sins, in special he was tempted to cast himself down from the pinnacle of the Temple, which was to kill himself; he was tempted to fall down and worship the devil, which O how horrible blasphemy is it? Yea, for a time power was given to Satan, albeit not to hurt Christ, yet to carry his body from one place to another, as we read in Matth. 4, and therefore let this be for consolation to such of God's children as are vexed with vile and blasphemous temptations, and solicitations to abominable sins, Heb. 2:18, for in that our Lord himself hath suffered, being tempted, he is able to succor them that are tempted.

4. But if the afflicted insist and say he is so put to it by Satan's temptations to commit sin against his light, and is ready to succumb, because he neither hath strength in himself to resist and stand out, nor is their appearance or hope of God's assisting him in his conflict, because God seemeth to have not only deserted him, but also to have given him over in the hands of an unclean spirit to be vexed.

Unto this temptation we answer, first, that the dearest of God's children have been exercised after this manner, for even to the Apostle Paul (2 Cor. 12:7) there was given to him a thorn in the flesh, the messenger of Satan to buffet him, to keep him from pride: which temptation was so strong and violent, that he could not resist it by any strength in himself, but was forced to fly unto God by prayer and beg strength from Christ to bear him out against the temptation and to be delivered from the power of it.

Secondly, let the afflicted under this exercise put a difference between the sin of Satan the tempter of him, and his own sin under the temptation; for, the fiery darts of Satan, and suggested blasphemies are Satan's sins, and not properly the sins of the afflicted to whom these wicked temptations are not pleasant, but are his greatest affliction. It is true indeed, that temptations unto sin in some measure draw on some degree of pollution ofttimes in sinful men, because it is not with us as it was with Christ; for when the prince of this world came to tempt him, he had no stuff of his own in Christ to work upon; but when he cometh to sinners, he findeth our corrupt nature and inclination to yield to his temptations, as his own materials to work upon, ready to be kindled by his fiery darts; and yet must we still distinguish the sin of Satan suggesting and tempting, from the suffering of the poor afflicted child of God, who is vexed, with the temptation: for if the afflicted shall own the temptation as his own sin, and confound Satan's part, and his own part in that exercise, he is in danger to be swallowed up in the sense of the sin which is not his own but Satan's.

Thirdly, the afflicted must put difference between sin and troublesome exercise: for God is the author of trouble, whereby he is about to try, exercise and train the faith of his child, to reach him patience, and hope under his trouble; but Satan is the author of the sin, whereunto he doth tempt the afflicted, and shall be punished for it.

Fourthly, let the afflicted wisely observe Satan's drift, and wiles to drive him unto sin one way or other by these his horrid and bitter temptations; for though he prevail not with his grosser temptations, to cause the afflicted commit or consent unto that wickedness which he suggesteth by his fiery darts, yet he in some measure prevaileth ofttimes by new temptations following on the back of the other; for when he hath troubled the soul of the afflicted child of God with these terrible temptations, then he beareth in upon the mind of the afflicted, that he hath acted or consented to these vile blasphemies, and soliciteth him to impatience, under this trouble, and to doubt of

God's love to him, and of his being in the state of grace, and to suspect he is not one of the elect, and to fear that God will not deliver him from these evils whereunto he is tempted. Now, these latter temptations ofttimes prevail so far with the afflicted, as he hearkens unto them, yields unto them in some measure and suspects Satan's false allegiance to be too true. And so these acts of unbelief, impatience and discouragement, become indeed the sins of the afflicted, because they are not so resisted, disclaimed, abhorred and sorrowed for, as the first sort of temptations were, which do most vex the afflicted. These wiles of Satan the afflicted must beware of, least he continue in, or foster these ordinary sins, whereinto, that Satan might cast and catch him, he did lay his net in these extraordinary temptations.

Fifthly, let the afflicted after he hath perceived Satan's wiles and malice, and his own foolishness and weakness, look upon the Lord's wise purpose, who by suffering his child so to be exercised, is calling him to a deeper acknowledgment of his original sin, that he may be humbled yet more before God, and loath himself yet more, and have Christ's righteousness imputed to the believer in higher estimation. Upon which consideration, let him so press the removing of the troublesome temptation, as in the meantime he submit himself unto God, and patiently endure the trouble, and put repentance and faith, hope and love to God in exercise, following his external vocation as he is able, least Satan take advantage of him if he be idle; and withal let him have such a care of his bodily health as he may be fitted the better for God's service in his calling: for we are not our own, but Christ's, who hath bought us with a price, and are bound to glorify God both in our bodies and spirits, which are the Lord's, 2 Cor. 6:19,20, and therefore, whether we eat or drink, or whatsoever else we are about, which is lawful, we ought to do it in his name, and so to glorify him, 1 Cor. 10:30.

CHAP. XII. - Wherein is solved, the converts doubt of his conversion, arising from the power of his corruption manifesting itself more after his entry upon the course of new obedience, then it did before he began to repent.

SOME CONVERTS BEING YET but young soldiers in the Christian warfare, when they find the corruption of their nature breaking forth more powerfully than it did before they did engage their heart to serve the Lord, do readily fall in deep discouragement and sad suspicion, that the renewing grace of God was never bestowed upon them, whatsoever were their purposes, promises, and beginnings to mortify their lusts and affections. And we must confess, that this is no small temptation: for, they who have renounced the service of their lusts, and have consecrate their life to God's service, when they find their lusts prevail, and like to reign in them, no wonder they suspect their state in grace; for (2 Pet. 2:20) it is told to us, If men after they have escaped the pollutions of the world, through the knowledge of the Lord and Savior Jesus Christ, they are again entangled therein, and overcome, the latter end is worse with them then the beginning: for, it had been better for them, not to have known the way of righteousness, then after they have known it, to turn from the holy commandment delivered unto them. But it is happened unto them, according to the true proverb, the dog is turned to his own vomit again, and the sow that was washed to her wallowing in the mire.

2. This condition indeed is perilous, when after profession of repentance, sin doth recover its strength again, and prevail over the whole man, and show forth its victory over him in the gross pollution of the external man: But most of all is it perilous, when the overcome and enslaved sinner, lieth still in his sin, senseless and secure, and doth please himself in his pollutions; for, whatsoever he may be, the holy Ghost points him forth among the unregenerate as a dog or sow. If such a man after a time shall repent and bewail his condition, and set himself to the seeking of God in Christ, and to draw grace out of Christ to mortify his lusts we shall not pronounce or determine of his former estate, whether he was before that time regenerate or not, but for the present case of his repenting, he is on the way to evidence

his regeneration more clearly than before: only let him take heed to humble himself in earnest before God, and to repent more seriously, that so he may confirm himself, and go on in the course of faith and obedience of the Evangel, strengthening his brethren as Peter was commanded to do by our Lord, Luk. 22:22.

3. But if corruption of nature do not break forth to defile the whole man, but inwardly stirreth and striveth to bring its old servant into bondage again; unto which temptations albeit the afflicted do not succumb, yet he is shaken and staggers in his faith, doubting of his state, and of the sincerity of his conversion, because he findeth the power of sin in him more vigorous, then he had found it before the change of his old conversation. We do not deny, but this case is readily incident unto such as are lately converted, from formality in religion, and fair civil carriage before men, to true repentance and inward holiness beseeming Christians. This case because it may have sundry causes, doth require also sundry cures.

4. First, this case may befall a young convert, who because he hath not as yet gotten the experience of his own weakness, is somewhat puffed up in the conceit of his own strength, and is more confident than he hath reason, that the sincerity of his purpose, shall bear down and overcome all his spiritual enemies, so oft as they shall oppose his holy resolution. In this case, what wonder is it, that the Lord by a new proof of the man's weakness, let him see, that it is not in him that willeth or in him that runneth, but in God that hath mercy? To the intent his pride may be broken down, and that he being humbled in himself, may learn not to trust any more to himself, but to God, to Christ who by his Spirit maketh his children to mortify sin in themselves, as the Apostle teacheth us, Rom. 8:13, saying, if ye mortify the deeds of the flesh by the Spirit, ye shall live.

Therefore the afflicted in this case, must beware to fret, or murmur, or entertain suspicions of God's grace in himself, but rather let him, after experience of his own weakness, humble himself and renew the exercise of repentance, and resolve in the use of the means to lean to the strength of Christ who doth help his soldiers in their conflict against sin and Satan, either by giving them the victory quickly, or else sustaining them in the conflict by his grace, as he did the Apostle, 2 Cor. 12:7, to whom Christ did not grant the victory, till he, despairing of his own ability to stand out against the messenger of Satan, did humbly beg deliverance from the temptation, and then he gave him assurance, that the assistance of his grace should prove sufficient to sustain him in the conflict, and to deliver him in due time.

Secondly, this case may fall out by the mere malice of Satan, who doth set himself to vex the young and tender convert, lately taken out of his dominion, to the intent he may make him repent his coming out of Egypt, if it be possible, and by leading out against him a new army of temptations, may move him to despair of the victory, and so bring him back to the flesh pots, and taking on again the yoke of bondage if he can.

2. And here consideration must be had, of God's wise and holy permission, who suffereth Satan to put a young convert to so hard trials, that in the weakness of his own child, he may make evident his great power, in upholding his young soldier against the forest assaults of Satan; and his wisdom, in breaking by this mean the strength of in-born corruption, raging against the work of grace in his child.

In this case, let the afflicted remember he is called to give a proof of his faith and sincerity, that he may acquit himself manfully, and not be afraid of the power of temptations but bear out stoutly, resisting

Satan, being confident of the victory and of tramping Satan under his feet shortly; yea, pre-suppose with inward temptations, external persecution be joined, let the Lord's soldier follow the example of the godly Hebrews, whom the Apostle doth exhort to prepare themselves, after spoliation of their goods, to meet with grievous affliction, under hope to overcome, Heb. 10:32,36, and 12:4.

3. This case may fall out, not so much from the growing power of corruption, as from the growing light of grace, discovering sin more clearly than before regeneration: for he, who before regeneration, was lying dead in sin, did not feel the weight of sin at all, or was sensible only of gross out-breakings, but when the clearer light of the Law doth come, opening up the dens and caves of natures corruption, out of which come forth legions of sinful motions, and amongst these, sundry monsters of unperceived wickedness, are discovered to the young convert, what wonder he be afraid, and cast in many doubts and suspicions? For, if even the Apostle Paul himself, out of the sense of inherent sin, and of the bonds thereof, where-with he did find himself bound, was compelled with tears to cry out, Miserable man that I am, who shall deliver me from the body of this death? Rom. 7:24, what wonder is it that a novice in Religion do tremble when he seeth and smelleth the dunghill and filthy stable of his own unclean heart?

In this case, all the comforts which the Gospel doth furnish are to be ministered to the afflicted, hope is to be fostered in him of victory over all those evils; the wisdom of God is to be set forth before his eyes under this exercise, wherein the Lord hath brought to light the latent corruption of nature, of set purpose, that he might yoke his young soldier in combat with it, and give him the victory by the holy Ghost, over not only those evils which do trouble him for the time, but also all other sins, and so promoveth the mortification and abolition of the whole body of corruption in him.

4. The fourth cause is, or may be this, that the afflicted hath not such estimation of the imputed righteousness of Christ as is requisite, but with the slighting of Christ's satisfaction and righteousness purchased to the believer by Christ, goeth about to establish his own righteousness, whereupon the Lord discovereth his short-coming in sanctification, which in this life is imperfect, and should indeed be followed after carefully, but not be rested upon. It is indeed natural unto us, to seek to have perfection in ourselves, for our own glory, and not to follow the way prescribed to us of God, for perfecting of us unto the glory of God, as may be seen in the flower of Israel after the flesh, Rom. 9 and 10. Now the order of God is, that we should be first justified by faith in Christ without the works of the law, that is, God will have us in the first place to confess unto him our sins, and renounce all confidence in our own works before, in, and after our conversion, and to renounce all confidence in our own worthiness or our own strength, and betake us to that righteousness, which by the obedience and satisfaction of Christ is purchased unto us, and offered in the Gospel to be accounted ours of mere free grace: In the second place, God will have us, being clothed with Christ's imputed righteousness, to approach unto the throne of grace, that by faith in Christ, we may receive the power of the holy Spirit in a larger and larger measure for increasing our sanctification more and more. And in the third place, he will have us, as we profit and grow in holiness, to give the thanks and praise and glory thereof unto God in Jesus Christ, who both justifieth us and sanctifieth us by his own Spirit; and in as far as we come short in the measure of sanctification which we aim at, he will have us to be humbled in ourselves, and lay faster

hold on Christ who justifieth us, that he, by his Spirit, may more and more sanctify us,, and that because Christ is made of God unto us, not only our righteousness, but also our sanctification, as the Apostle teacheth us, 1 Cor. 1:30. Now, when any man breaks this order, and seeketh justification by Christ, but sanctification by himself, as it were; and when he findeth sanctification not to grow as he hoped it should, doth not fly in to the garment of Christ's imputed righteousness, which alone is able to hide his nakedness, Rev. 3:18, but instead of humbling himself in the exercise of repentance, is ready to call his justification and conversion in question, and to cast it away, as it were, what wonder is it, that God, being justly offended, because the righteousness of Christ is not in due estimation and precious in that man's eyes, doth not grant unto him a better measure of sanctification, especially while he is contending to have his own prescribed measure of sanctification, with the prejudice of that divine righteousness which is by faith in Jesus Christ, and will not, as a humble penitent, hold grip of Christ's righteousness, except he obtain such a measure of sanctification and freedom from wrestling with sin, as he hath resolved to find in himself before he can stand to his interest in Christ for justification? What wonder is it, that God suffer sin in the afflicted to put forth its power more than before, that he may teach his young convert and soldier, ignorant of his duty and of God's order of proceeding with his children, to be more wise, and to adhere more closely under the sense of his sinfulness, unto the righteousness of Christ, unto which he did fly and was forced to fly in his conversion? As also, that he may teach his child, that sanctification must be drawn out of no other fountain then Christ, out of whose fullness we must receive grace for grace, and who by faith applieth to his redeemed ones his imputed righteousness, and by faith applieth and worketh in them sanctification purchased unto them in the covenant of Redemption?

5. Wherefore, for remedy of this mistake, first, let the afflicted, when he perceiveth and feeleth the power of sin to be more then he conceived he should have found in himself after his conversion, let him (I say) forthwith humble himself before God, acknowledge his natural uncleanness, and utter inability by his own strength to resist sin, and being humbled at the heart, let him bless God, who of his free grace hath prepared and freely granted unto him a righteousness purchased by Christ, 2 Cor. 5:21, with which being clothed, he may stand before the Tribunal of grace absolved. Next, let him earnestly and daily pray, that he may both hold fast grips of that righteousness of Christ by faith, and out of the same fountain of God's glorious grace in Christ, study to increase in sanctification, and piece and piece to mortify and abolish the corruption of nature. Thirdly, let the afflicted use the ordinances and means appointed of God for mortifying of sin and reparation of the Image of God in him. And fourthly, let the afflicted, in the use of appointed means and ordinances of God by faith look unto Christ, that out of him he may suck sap, and the furniture of his Spirit, to bring forth good fruits: for, without him we can do nothing; but if we abide in him, we shall bring forth abundant fruits, Joh. 15:5.

CHAP. XIII. - Wherein is solved the converts doubt, whether he be in the state of grace, arising from his comparing of himself with the hypocrite and unregenerate in those perfections they may attain unto.

SOMETIME A TRUE CONVERT, when he perceiveth how far specious hypocrites may make progress in the way of righteousness, with how many virtues they may be endued, with how many gifts they may be adorned, how-like the foolish virgins may be unto the wise, and how far temporary faith may carry a man, especially when it is busked with spiritual common gifts, how many glorious professors of the true Christian Religion have made apostasy, how many ways men do deceive themselves and may possibly further and further deceive themselves (of which self-deceiving's somewhat is spoken in the end of the former book) what wonder is it, the weak convert stagger, and fear least he also deceive himself, especially when he seeth nothing in himself which may not be counterfeit?

2. For lousing of this doubt, wherein many have been puzzled, we must yield to the afflicted, that there are many indeed, who do deceive and destroy themselves with their vain thoughts; which because it doth very frequently come to pass, it should stir up all men to be circumspect and wary least they deceive themselves in the matter of their salvation, and for that intent to examine themselves whether they be in the faith, 2 Cor. 13, least they be beguiled, and so perish. And because tender faith is easily hurt, all their fear must be turned into a holy carefulness, to be found sincere and serious in the use of the Lord's ordinances, least Satan beguile them on the right hand or on the left. And for this end, we offer advice to the afflicted to discern things that differ, and first to distinguish gifts, common to hypocrites and true converts, from saving graces or benefits accompanying salvation: for, learning, and skill to govern great matters, and eloquence and understanding of deep mysteries, and revelation of things to come, and the gift of working miracles, and the gift of preaching the Gospel, may be granted unto the unregenerate for the use and edification of the Church. The observing of this difference shall teach the afflicted to esteem well of all the gifts of God, which may serve for human society, or to edify the Church, but not to look upon them as evidences of regeneration, for they are nothing in comparison of saving graces; for, if he shall study to humility and repentance toward God and faith toward Jesus Christ, and love to God and his Saints, and

to a holy life by the grace of Christ, in any measure, let him esteem more of them, then of all these common gifts how glorious soever they seem. As also let him put a difference betwixt the judgment of charity concerning other men's estate, which contents itself with probabilities, and the judgment of certainty and real verity, concerning his own estate, which proceeds from the operation of the holy Spirit, bearing witness to our spirits, that we are the children of God, and revealing unto us what things are freely given to us of God, to wit, among other gifts, giving unto us eye-salve to make us know, that we are blind, poor, naked and miserable, with grace leading us to buy without money or price from Christ, gold tried in the fire, and garments to hide our nakedness, which is the righteousness of Christ imputed unto us. In the judgment of charity concerning other men's estate, we see nothing save what is outward, and cannot pierce into their hearts, which God only can and doth search; but concerning our own estate, we may know certainly, if we search well, 1 Cor. 2:10-12. Wherefore that the afflicted may overcome this doubt, let him leave unto God the judgment of the hearts of these hypocrites and apostates, which were never humbled in the sense of sin, nor seriously believed in Christ; but to satisfy himself concerning his own estate, let him study to discern the power of sin in himself more and more, and daily be humbled before God in the sense of it. And the more he discern the loathsomeness of sin in himself, let him the more heartily embrace Christ offered in the Gospel and consecrate himself wholly unto him, that in his furniture, drawn by faith out of Christ, he may bring forth good fruits and add one virtue to another, and so shall he be sure, that he hath passed the perfection of the unregenerate, and is a true subject of the kingdom of God effectually called, and elected of God unto eternal life, 2 Pet. 1:5-8.

CHAP. XIV. - Wherein is solved the doubt of the true convert, whether he be in the state of grace, because some godly persons look upon him as a hypocrite.

SOME TRUE CONVERTS, DO suspect themselves not to be true converts, because some of the godly of their acquaintance (whose judgment other ways is not to be lightly rejected) not only do suspect them to be hypocrites, but by words spoken of them and behavior toward them, declare their judgment of them.

2. This temptation doth not a little afflict the weak in faith, who of themselves are ready to call in question their own conversion, and when they perceive their own suspicion of themselves to be as it were confirmed by the suspicion and testimony of some Saints (howsoev-

er rashly judging other men's hearts) no wonder the temptation of Satan, questioning whether they be the children of God, grow strong against them.

By this stratagem Satan useth to assault the strongest in faith, and to vex them at least, as we may see in the exercise of Job, whose faith was mightily assaulted when his godly friends mistook his affliction, and condemned him as a wicked hypocrite. The like we see in the exercise of the Prophet, Psal. 38:11, when his friends stood aloof from his plague.

3. For strengthening the afflicted under this temptation; first, let him examine himself so much the more accurately, because of the suspicion that the godly have of him: after which examination, if he find any measure of sorrow for sin in himself, and of faith flying to Christ for relief, and of endeavor to live holily, righteously and soberly, albeit joined with much infirmity and manifold imperfections, let him not cast away his confidence, but rather strengthen what he findeth of the Lord's gracious work in him, although it seem to him ready to die.

Secondly, let him consider whether this exercise and affliction be a correction from God, chastising him for his rash judgment of others, whom possibly he hath wounded with such rash suspicions of them; but whether he find this or not, let him not despise this exercise, but be humbled before God in the acknowledgment of the relics of hypocrisy in our corrupt nature, and fly unto Christ (in whose mouth there was no guile) that he may be clothed with his righteousness head and feet; and let him study unto more and more sincerity, that he may approve himself to God, and to discreet Judges of his conversation, and let him not alienate himself altogether so far as in him lieth from them, by whose suspicions his faith and good name hath been wounded, but in humility and charity toward them, in the constant following of piety toward God and righteousness toward men, labor to commend himself to all men's consciences.

And in so doing he needeth not stand for the rash judgment of any man: for by so doing Job was victorious over this temptation in his conflict with his friends: and it is sure, that men may be deceived in their judgment of other men's estate; for, first, the ignorance of another man's heart, maketh the Judge to judge what he knoweth not. It is true, God hath granted unto his children liberty according to his Word to judge of the actions of other men, and from their actions to judge of their condition and temper in relation to those actions; but to judge of their state who outwardly do what is right, doth not belong to men, but to God who hath reserved to himself the searching of every man's heart, and only knoweth who is the upright and who is the hypocrite, who is the wise and who is the foolish virgin, the outward conversation of both being like one to another. Again, to know another man's manners, engine, inclination and way of his life, doth require long conversing with him, comparison of his actions one with another, and a prudent conjunction of all signs of his inward disposition, before a discreet charitable judgment can be had of him. And whosoever do judge rashly of other men's hearts, do not well know their own heart, or of what spirit they are in judging: for many presume too much to justify their own condition and state, and make themselves to be as rules and patterns unto others, and so become too too rigid censurers and severe judges of other men's conditions and state, except they find it like to their own. And if there be any dissimilitude of manners or discrepancy of judgment, or contention about any matter, then partiality hindereth a right judgment one of another, and affection marreth reason many times that it cannot discern what is right.

Therefore let the person afflicted with this temptation, turn himself to God who searcheth the reins, and let him humble himself in his sight, renewing the exercise of repentance and faith in Christ, and let him apply to himself what the Scripture doth pronounce of these who in the sense of their sin do fly to Christ Jesus, that in him they may have remission of sin and amendment of their life: for so did the Prophet in the whole Psal. 17, when he had to do with his uncharitable friends and kinsfolk, and so let the afflicted do.

CHAP. XV. - Wherein the converts doubting of his being in the state of grace, so oft as he doth not feel the sense of his reconciliation with God, is examined and answered.

SOME TRUE CONVERTS ARE, who indeed are endued with the saving graces of faith, hope and charity, and give evident proof of the in-dwelling of the holy Spirit in them, and do rejoice now and then in God their Savior, when his love to them is shed abroad in their heart, but when a cloud cometh over their eyes, and they do not feel the warm beams of the Sun of righteousness shining in their soul as they before have felt, they are assaulted with doubting if any saving grace be in them at all, and do entertain these temptations ofttimes, so far as to suspect and

express in words, that there is no solid faith in themselves, no lively
hope, no Christian charity, no mortification of sin, no purity of heart,
and such like; if when they are thus tempted and tossed they lay hold
on Christ, as in their first conversion, and find the sensible comfort
of the holy Spirit by the word of the Gospel applied unto them, then
all is well, their doubting is overcome for the time, they rejoice and
praise God: But if the Lord shall delay, for his own wise ends, to renew
their sensible consolations, and to renew the earnest-penny of their
inheritance, forthwith they begin to doubt again, and to hearken to
Satan's suggestions, and to suspect that their former feelings were
but temporary, and not the special operations of the holy Spirit, and
at length break forth in many sad complaints. And, in a word, they
do not maintain the work of saving grace in themselves longer then
the sun shine of spiritual felt consolations abideth with them. And
albeit their exercise be no ways so hard as was the Prophets, Psal. 77,
yet they fall out in the same complaint which the Prophet expresseth,
ver. 7,8,9. Will the Lord cast off forever? And will he be favorable
no more? Is his mercy clean gone forever? Doth his promise fail for
evermore? Hath God forgotten to be gracious? Hath he in anger shut
up his tender mercies.

2. For clearing of this case, two diseases may be perceived in the
afflicted which is here described. The one is this, the afflicted setteth
himself to live rather by sense then by faith, and doth put his faith
on work of set purpose that he may obtain or recover consolation
shortly; but if his desire be not shortly granted, he maketh not use of
the formerly felt consolations to strengthen his own faith when consolation is withdrawn: The other sickness is this, the afflicted doth
not take up the nature of saving graces, nor perceive the beauty thereof, except in the sun-shine of sensible divine approbation thereof, he

doth not take up the right definition or description of saving graces: for, faith is to him nothing, if it be not a full persuasion; except he can pour forth tears always, he thinks he doth not repent; except he find a joyful expectation of Christ's coming in glory, he thinks his hope not lively; and so of charity and patience, temperance, righteousness and holiness, if he do not find them in some eminent measure as they may near-by stand before the law, the afflicted of whom we are now speaking, thinketh he hath nothing of saving grace in him. We grant, that this sickness is very rare, and few they are that are troubled with it; yet where it appeareth, it must be speedily cured, but with great circumspection cured; for the earnest desire he hath of feeling the sweet sense of the joy of the holy Ghost, must not be disallowed, but commended to him, and he taught to cry as it is said, Cant. 2:5. Stay me with flagons, comfort me with apples, for I am sick of love, yet with holy submission unto God's will for time, manner and measure. 2. He is also to be commended, that in his trouble he goeth to God in Christ, not altogether without faith which he putteth forth in active exercise thereof by confession of sin, by supplication and other ways; but here is he to be reproved, that while he is actually exercising faith, love, hope, &c. he reckoneth all he doeth to be nothing, no faith, no hope, &c. because it is not in such a measure as he would. 3. He is to be commended, that he doth aim at the highest degrees of faith, love, hope, patience, mortification of sin, and practice of holiness, and all commanded virtues; but here he faileth, that he counteth all as naught, when consolation and sensible approbation of what he hath is not felt; for here he despiseth the day of small things, and unthankfully mis-regardeth the lower degrees of these saving graces, which notwithstanding are bought to the redeemed by the same price wherewith the highest degrees are bought, to wit, with the precious blood of Jesus Christ.

3. Wherefore let the afflicted consider, first, that the will of God revealed, requireth of us, that we walk by faith, and under the sense of our sinfulness and afflictions whatsoever, hold fast the covenant of grace in Christ Jesus, and by adhering unto him hold up our heart, and entertain spiritual life in us. Secondly, let him consider, that this way of living by faith and dependence on the word of God's grace, doth please the Lord well; for, without faith it is impossible to please him; and thus living by faith in him, doth give more glory of truth, grace, mercy and constancy unto God then when we suspend the glorifying of him, till we find the sense of consolation from him: for if we believe in God, only because we find the consolations of his Spirit, our faith in that case is weak, and leaneth more upon the pledge and sensible evidence of his truth bestowed upon us, then upon his promise without a pledge: for, no man will refuse to give credit to a man upon a pawn, but God is worthy to be credited upon his word without a pawn, yea, when his dispensation seemeth contrary to his promise. Thirdly, let him consider, that the Lord useth to give sensible consolations not only to help our faith, in the time of consolation, but also to help our faith when the consolations are withdrawn from us, and we are put to hard exercise: wherein it is our duty to glorify our God for his truth and grace, whereof we have sometime had confirmations by felt consolation, and patiently to wait till he restore unto us the joy of his Spirit: for if in the want of sensible consolation we shall put aspersions upon the Lord's work and graces bestowed upon us, and call them in question, we shall be found in so doing more careful of self-satisfaction then to do the duties which God requireth of us. Fourthly, let the afflicted learn so to describe and define every

saving grace of faith, repentance, hope, love and mortification of sin, as the description may take in the meanest measure of those graces; for, it is hard to say, that there is no sound faith where there is not a full persuasion; for the hungry looking of a trembling sinner unto Christ, must not be excluded from being an act of faith; it is hard to restrain the exercise of repentance to the shedding of tears, for many other signs of repentance may be found where these are seldom, such as is the hatred of sin striving against all temptations unto it, and flying from all occasions which may ensnare the believer in Christ in trespasses. Fifthly, let the afflicted distinguish between faith and sense of joy, both are God's gifts, but the grounds of faith whereupon we are commanded to rest ourselves should be rested on constantly, whatsoever dispensation of joy or grief we shall meet with: and this is our perpetual duty, but sense is at God's free dispensation to give and withdraw and restore at his pleasure, and is a movable benefit, which, the Lord, as his wisdom seeth expedient for our good, doth give and continue, withdraw and restore, diminish or augment. And therefore the afflicted is bound by duty still to believe and rejoice in believing. And to have the joy of sense also he may lawfully study, but ought not to suffer his faith to be weakened by the want of it, as the Prophet doth teach us, Psal. 42:11, and, 43:5, and 88. Last of all, let the afflicted be posed upon his conscience if he dare condemn his flying to Christ in the sense of his sins as no act of faith, or if he dare deny his hunger after renewed consolation, and beholding of God with joy as reconciled in Christ, to be an act of love to God and of communion with him? Therefore, let him confess with the Psalmist, Psal. 77:10. This my doubting is my infirmity, I will remember the years of the right hand of the Lord.

CHAP. XVI. - Wherein is solved the true converts doubt of his regeneration, because he seemeth to himself not to grow in grace by the use of the means appointed for his growth.

SOME TRUE CONVERTS ARE brought to suspect their own regeneration, because in the using of the means leading to sanctification and salvation, sundry complain and say, I do not perceive the Lord's blessing on my pains and diligence; I grow not in the knowledge of things spiritual; my faith doth not grow by hearing nor reading of the Word of God, nor by meditation of it; I do not prevail in wrestling against my in-bred sin and corrupt nature, neither by prayer nor fasting: and therefore, what shall I judge of my state, but that it is like I am not converted and renewed? For, if I were indeed converted and reconciled with God, I conceive it should fair other ways with me then it doth.

2. In this case the true convert is in hazard of growing slack and careless in the use of the means, and to grieve the holy Spirit, by prescribing unto him and limiting of him unto such a measure of profiting in the use of the means, and making him know how far he had profited and advanced in the course of sanctification. Yea, there is danger, lest in this case the convert not only become cold-rife in the exercises of piety, but also turn loose in his conversation, and follow the allurements of the world, having so far hearkened to the temptation, as to think it in vain that he hath washen his hands in innocence; as (Psal. 73) befell the Prophet.

3. For removing of this doubt, the afflicted hath reason to check himself for hearkening so far unto the temptation, as to join with hypocrites in his complaint, Isa. 58:5. Wherefore have we fasted (say they) and thou seest not? Wherefore have we afflicted our souls, and thou takest no knowledge?

But because nothing doth more trouble the afflicted then his suspicion of his own hypocrisy, let the causes be searched from which his suspicion doth arise. One of them may be this, that in the use of the means, the eyes of the afflicted are more and more opened to perceive the power and poison of his natural corruption more clearly than he perceived before. And this deciphering of sin more and more, doth hinder him to see the growth of his light and the growth of his hatred against manifested sin, joined with the overturning of his own high imaginations and native pride. Another cause may be this, that the true convert hath promised unto himself, in the use of the means, more and greater benefits spiritual from God, then he doth by experience find, which because he doth not find, he thinketh he hath not profited. A third cause may be this, that the Lord is about the purging of him from practical errors, such as are the high estimation of his own diligence in the use of the means, as if there were some sort of merit annexed unto the works prescribed to the convert by the Lord, or as if the use of the means had in them some force and efficacy in producing such effects in him as the convert hath expected; or, as if the Lord had obliged himself to bless, sensibly, diligence in the use of the means, to the diligent man's satisfaction.

4. Therefore, first, let the afflicted continue in his diligence, and beware of the foresaid practical errors; let him humble himself before Christ, that he may draw more virtue out of him by faith, and by so much the more as he findeth sin himself, and not profiting in the use of the means, let him lay the faster hold on the covenant of grace, and on Christ offered therein, for giving righteousness and sanctification. Secondly, let him set upon the exercise of every duty with prayer, that he may follow the duty in Christ's name with his eye fixed on God's grace; and after the discharge of the duty, let him look to Christ, that from him, he may have the blessing: for, without Christ we can do nothing acceptably, nor with profit. Last of all, let him not esteem lightly of the effects of his diligence, as if he did no ways profit; but when he hath rightly considered matters, if he find the least fruit following his using of the means, let him give the glory of it to God in Christ the giver thereof, and humbly put up his lamentation for his short-coming in duties unto God by prayer: for, this is the way to make progress in faith and repentance, and humility and submission

of his will unto God in the use of the means, and let him thank the Lord, that from day today he is keeped from scandalous out-breaking.

CHAP. XVII. - Wherein is solved the converts doubt, whether he be regenerate, because he seemeth to himself to follow religion and righteousness from the common operation of God's working by moral suasion, and not from the special operation and

impulsion of the holy Spirit.

THERE ARE SOME TRUE converts, who have profited so far in the amendment of their life, and conforming their conversation unto the rule of God's Word, that the yoke of Christ is become easy to them, and their delight is to be frequently about the exercises of religion and works of righteousness, and yet sometime they are troubled with suspicion, whether the work of regeneration in them be solid, because anything they do, may be done, as they conceive, by temporary believers, in whom no sound renovation of corrupt nature will be found. I find nothing in me (saith one) of the effectual motion of the holy Spirit, but all by way of moral suasion, by imitation of others, by education, as may be found in the unrenewed disciples of moral philosophy: for as they by frequent actions do acquire habits, wherewith being endued, they discharge moral duties more easily and with delight; So, I by discharging acts of religion, and acquainting myself with them daily, do seem to myself to have acquired a facility and delectation in religious actions and works of righteousness toward my neighbors.

2. This case we grant is very perilous, and subtly colored by Satan to deceive and weaken the true convert; for, it is true, what power hath been seen in moral philosophy among Pagans, to put a luster on men's civil conversation, must be also granted to Theology among professed Christians, because divine threatening's and promises, for procuring outward reformation of a man's life, are more apt to prevail

with a man, then all moral philosophy; and it is true also, that education by parents, and imitation of good men, is of great force morally to persuade a man to the following of the outward duties of religion, and to a civil conversation. Wherefore it is no wonder to see a true convert doubt of his own regeneration, when he compareth external duties discharged by himself, with the external duties discharged by others whose heart he cannot see, but must judge charitably of them, and yet can neither be clear determinately to affirm all such to be true converts, nor to affirm himself to be a true convert, so long as he suspecteth, that as some others reformation, So also his own reformation, may prove no better than from moral suasion, which may be found in a man unregenerate.

3. For lousing of this doubt and strengthening of the faith of the true convert, let him examine himself, whether in the conscience of his natural sinfulness, and sense of his own unworthiness and inability to deliver himself from the power of sin, wrath and misery, he hath fled, and from time to time doth fly to Christ according to the tenor of the covenant of grace, to be justified, sanctified and saved by him, and doth follow the exercises of religion and righteousness in obedience to the commands of God. If his conscience answer him, that so he doth, then, first, let him look upon his doubting of his state, as the subtle temptation of Satan; and that he may be strong against this temptation, let him renew the acknowledgment of his sins and sinfulness, of his weakness and unworthiness and renew also his consent to the covenant of grace in Jesus Christ and his purpose to obey the commandments of God in the strength of Christ: for, by this means he shall gain the entry into his refuge where-from Satan was drawing him, by furnishing doubts and weakening his faith. Secondly, having casten his anchor within the veil, and settled his faith on

Christ Jesus, let him now maintain his former course, so far as truth will suffer, that his former course of life, in following with delight the exercise of religion and righteousness, did proceed from the holy Spirit; and let him consider, that it is not a sufficient reason to call in question the infused habits of saving grace, because supernatural habits, infused immediately by the Spirit of Christ, are entertained, augmented and confirmed by frequent acts and daily exercise, no less then natural or moral habits are, which are acquired by exercise: And this is clear from Scripture, wherein are many exhortations to put faith, love, repentance, patience, &c. in frequent exercise, that these gracious habits may grow strong, as the Apostle Peter doth speak, 2nd Epist., 1st chap., ver. 5,6. &c. Thirdly, let him put a difference in judging of his own conversation and the conversation of others, of whose principles and ends of outward godly carriage, he cannot judge, as he can do of his own: for, a man in nature unregenerate, or a temporary believer, may make profession of true religion, and outwardly go on in a blameless conversation, with this opinion, that by his works he shall please God, and procure salvation to himself. But the true convert shall be found a renouncer of confidence in his own works, a man sensible of his own sinfulness and imperfections, who hath fled and resolveth still to adhere to Christ for righteousness and salvation through him; the finding whereof in any measure after examination, may solve the converts doubt: for, a man in nature, cannot so hate sin and follow holiness, as to renounce confidence in his holiness, and fly unto Christ for righteousness. Fourthly, let the afflicted convert consider, that the Lord's dealing with his children both by moral motives, and by effectual persuasion unto the obedience of faith, may and doth very well concur and agree together, neither is the special operation of the holy Spirit with any reason to be suspected, because he sweetly leadeth on his child, by way of counsel, (without the child's observation of any notable impulse) making him to overcome strong temptations unto sin, whereunto he is naturally inclined: for, the more victorious grace is over corruption, the efficacy of the Lord's grace is the more conspicuous, and that obedience is most pleasant to God wherein corrupt nature maketh most opposition. Therefore in this case here presupposed, let him stand to the defense of his faith in Christ, and go on cheerfully in the way of righteousness against Satan's temptation soliciting him to doubting and discouragement; which counsel if he follow, he shall find by experience, that he hath made use of the shield of faith, and gotten the victory not without the special operation and impulse of the holy Spirit.

CHAP. XVIII. - Wherein is solved the true converts doubt, whether he be regenerate, because he findeth not self-denial in the measure which is requisite in converts.

SOME TRUE CONVERTS ARE found, who having for a time enjoyed peace of conscience, have called their conversion in question by occasion of hearing or reading some sermon of some zealous Preacher pressing the marks of true and sincere conversion, and making self-denial and loving of God for himself, the main marks of conversion, and without circumspect and wise difference put by him betwixt legal perfection and evangelical sincerity, pressing self-denial and the loving of God abstractly, further than any Saint doth attain unto in this life. Where-upon some tender souls, do fall in question with themselves, whether they be among the true and sincere converts, because they know that our Lord requireth self-denial in every person who will follow him, and doth condemn them all for unbelievers who seek glory of men, and not the glory which is of God: And because the Preacher possibly hath made the loving of God for his benefits, to be too too mercenary, and hath pressed without respect to benefits, that God must be loved for himself, therefore the weak convert beginneth to be troubled, as if he were not a true convert at all, saying, what shall I think of myself and of my following of Christ, seeing I feel so little of self-denial in me, seeing I have loved Christ for my own good, and many a time in my best actions I have sought the commendation of men in my heart, and I have been ill pleased when I did not obtain it?

2. For solving of this doubt, we grant that every man who will follow Christ, is bound to deny himself: And true it is, there is nothing more difficile than to forsake our own carnal wisdom, and estimation of our own worth, works and abilities how small soever. Neither is there any more dangerous evil, then in the discharge of Christian duties, to seek or accept our own glory and the applause of men: for he that in this point doth foster his natural corruption, certainly doth not in so far favor these things which are God's, but serveth his own flesh. Therefore, because the relics of this and all other sin do remain in the regenerate, the Lord by variety of exercises setteth his children daily to learn this lesson over and over for mortifying their corrupt lusts. It is their duty therefore, when any spark of this evil of self-seeking doth appear, to cast themselves down humbly at Christ's feet and confess the sin, lest some spark of wrath break forth upon them from the Lord. For, the end of this exercise, yea, and the reason of the Lord's not removing fully in-dwelling sin, is to humble us, and send us to Christ, least if he should other ways deal with us,

we should grow proud, and not make such use as becometh us of God's free grace and Christ's righteousness imputed to the believer; mean time we must not yield to Satan's temptation, colored with pretense of Scripture, as if Christ had discharged us to seek any good from him to ourselves. Or to love him for the good which he hath purchased to us, and which he from time to time bestoweth on us: for, when Christ requireth of us to deny ourselves, he requireth indeed the renunciation of our own carnal and corrupt lusts, and confidence in our own wisdom, worth and works. But he doth not require of us to renounce the sanctified love of our own well-being, or the seeking our sanctification, consolation and salvation in him alone; for, the love of God and of his glory, is the main end of all our desires; and the seeking that God would glorify his own grace and truth in his promises to us by sanctifying, comforting and saving us, is a subordinate mean unto God's glory: yea, the more we seek our righteousness, consolation and salvation in God, through Christ, the more we glorify God, and do say in substance of God, that he is the fountain of all felicity, and that he is good and faithful to grant all good things to such as believe in him and do seek grace for grace from him.

3. It is true, that we should love God above all things, and love him more than ourselves, and love him though he should slay us; but it is true also, that the more we love him for any cause, the more we esteem of him, the more we magnify and glorify him; and what is love to, and seeking of, God, but the acknowledgement of our own emptiness and his all-sufficiency? And what is our seeking communion with him, but a refounding of ourselves into the fountain whence we have our being, that he may be glorified in our being, and fully well-being? And so our spiritual love of God for himself and for the goodness which is let forth in doing good to us, is not mercenary love,

but is the acknowledgement of his perfections and of his grace to us, to whom he will be our God in Christ, even all in all to us in him. As for seeking of men's applause, whensoever, whether upon receiving of any benefit, or discharge of any duty, the corrupt lust of vain glory doth mix itself (which cannot but obscure and hinder the shining of his glory, which should be aimed at in all things by us) incontinent upon the first motion of this our sinful corruption perceived, let out sin be humbly acknowledged and confessed unto God, the searcher of the heart, and let supplication in our spirit be made unto him, to pardon our sin, and mortify the bitter root of this and all other evils in us.

CHAP. XIX. - Wherein is solved the doubt of the true convert, whether he be indeed converted, arising from this, that he knoweth no child of God so hardly exercised as he is.

SOME CONVERTS ARE, WHO by the light of the Law of God are brought to the acknowledgment of their sin and misery, and by the doctrine of the Gospel are brought to seek their relief in Christ, and have taken on his yoke and submitted themselves to his discipline, and yet fall in question, whether they be converted, because they do find such inequality in their conversation, and such changes in their condition, and variety of temptations, as they can find no example of the like in Scripture; and where it pleaseth them to be free with their Pastor or confident Christian friend, do fall out in questions, if ever they have read in Scripture any like unto them, in such and such particulars as they please to condescend upon; and if their Pastor or Christian friend shall give them some example in the Scripture, of God's children so exercised, they are ready to find such differences between the case of the godly in Scripture, and their case, as they cannot receive satisfaction. And if possibly it be told them, that their case is not singular, but such as hath befallen sundry of their Christian acquaintance in this present age, yet they cannot receive satisfaction for all this, but still do insist, that their case is not like to any of the godly. Whereupon they foster the suspicion of their not being converted.

2. This ground of judging of men's conversion by the manner of God's exercising of them, so as other converted Saints have been exercised before them, and of judging the man to be unregenerate, who is other ways exercised then they know any convert to have been exercised, did deceive the friends of Job, who in Job's face avowed this their error, Job, 5:1. Call now, say they, if their be any that will answer thee, and unto which of the Saints wilt thou turn? That is, name any example of any upright man who hath been dealt with by God as thou art? And what Saint or holy man can thou name, to whom thou can compare thyself and say, such a man hath suffered such things as I do?

This doubt doth arise from this error and mistake; the afflicted doth without ground suppose, that express examples of every particular case of the Saints is set down in Scripture. It is true, there are examples of many cases which may befall the godly; but it is not to be expected that we shall find examples of every particular exercise of mind, wherein the Saints may fall: For as the Evangelist saith, if all particulars were written, the world could not hold or make use thereof. It is sufficient that the Scripture hath set down rules whereunto the Saints should labor to conform themselves, and that it hath opened up the causes and remedies of all spiritual diseases, and hath given so many examples as may clear the rule. It is also a mistake to make the experience of the most exercised soldier a rule for every Saints exercises, or to think that any man can know the variety of cases which befall the Saints: for, there are many whose cases are not revealed to any, but laid open unto God only, by prayer, and are helped by faith in Christ.

3. Wherefore the afflicted must walk by rules set down in Scripture, whether he find the practices thereof in Scripture or not. Now this is the rule, that whatsoever evil condition we fall into, whatsoever temptation, whatsoever pollution hath defiled our consciences, we must humble ourselves before God, and fly unto Christ for remission of the guiltiness, for washing away the filthiness thereof, for breaking down the power of corruption, and pulling out the roots thereof; withal praising and thanking Christ, who hath discovered unto us these evils and hath made them our affliction, and not suffered them to break forth to the scandal of others. And whatsoever calamity or temporal misery we shall fall into, the Scripture hath given order unto us, humbly to submit ourselves to God's dispensation, and to make a good construction of God's love and wisdom in exercising us so: for, by this rule Job did walk, defending his faith in Christ, his living and loving Redeemer, against Satan's temptations, and his friends uncharitable wrangling disputations, when the question was about his state, whether he had ever been converted or not, whether he was a wicked hypocrite or not? And by so doing, he over-came the temptation whereof we are now speaking.

And let not the afflicted lay it for a ground that by his hearing of the exercise of another, like unto his condition, he can be cured: because no example of the exercise of another can be found so quadrant unto his condition, as he could thereby take satisfaction. For, as in comparing of men's faces one with another, (such is the incomprehensible variety of the riches of God's wisdom in framing them) some difference and dissimilitude will be found betwixt face and face; So, in comparing of the cases of the Saints, none of them can be found in all things so like one to another, but some dissimilitude shall be found between them. Wherefore, the afflicted shall do well, in every condition, to draw near God, and pour out his heart before him at all times: for, God is a refuge for us in all cases, Psal. 62:8.

CHAP. XX. - Wherein is solved the converts doubt, whether he be converted, because he doth not find in himself the infallible marks of regeneration.

SOME TRUE CONVERTS SOMETIME are in suspense, doubting whether they be indeed converted, because they do not discern in themselves the unquestionable evidences of their conversion; and albeit they have the undoubted marks of regeneration, to wit, the daily conviction and acknowledgement of their sins, and do fly daily by faith unto Jesus Christ, and are endeavoring in some measure of sincerity to bring forth the fruits of new obedience, with respect to all the Commandments concerning love to God and the brethren, yet they dare not defend the sincerity of these evidences, because of the discerned imperfection thereof: for, when they do compare these marks of the new creature with the rule, they find much halting and short-coming therein. In special, they find their sense of sin to be but weak, their faith in Christ to be weak, and their failings and short-comings in the love of God and their neighbors, to be many, So that they scarcely dare allow these begun saving graces, the name of saving graces. And among other defects, they reckon their not feeling of the spirit of Adoption, whereof the Apostle speaketh to the converted Galatians, Gal. 4:6. Because ye are Sons, saith he, God hath sent forth the Spirit of his Son into your hearts, crying, Abba, Father. And, Ephes. 1:13. In whom after you believed, ye were sealed with the holy Spirit of promise. Which Spirit of promise and of adoption, sealing believers, they conceived was known and discerned in the Apostles time by every believers feeling in himself.

2. For solving of this doubt, something is spoken before concerning the imperfect fruits of faith, the buddings and blossoming whereof are not despised by Christ, Cant. 2:13, and, 6:12. But that this doubt may be more fully answered, let us take up the causes thereof, 1. One cause is or may be this, that the afflicted, albeit, together with the endeavor to lead a blameless life, he be endued with the grace of prayer, and looketh on God as his father; yet he doth not take up this work of God in him, to be the work of the Spirit of Christ, illuminating his mind about duties, framing his will and affections unto new obedience, stirring him up to prayer and helping him in prayer, but in the earnest desire he hath to find the operations of the Spirit in a larger measure of evidence, he doth not mark the present operation, but doth slight it as nothing, or doth not esteem of it as becometh, and so in his advertence raiseth and fostereth doubts in himself, which do keep his faith in chains: for removing of which

cause, let the afflicted observe the operation of the Spirit of Christ in the meanest degree, for the confirmation of his own faith, and comfort and thanksgiving unto God, as narrowly as he doth observe in himself the first motions of sin and stirrings of corruption, for his own humiliation and exercise of repentance; for wrong judgment under pretext of humility, doth not please God. Now it is an act of injustice not to give unto God the praise of every good thing in a man, especially when the man is found to be cast down in himself, and to be thirsting in his soul for a more intimate communion with Christ, as is presupposed in this case.

3. The second cause is or may be this, that the afflicted, albeit he hath had oft times sweet and sensible consolation, and confirmation of the promises of the Gospel, and hath thereby been put out of doubt of his adoption for the time, yet when new temptations do arise (according to what was expedient for the exercise of his faith) because the same sweetness is not felt, but heaviness for the while, 1 Pet. 1:6,7, he forgetteth the consolations he hath had, or suffereth them to be called in question. For removing whereof, whensoever the afflicted is cut short in the point of sense or sensible consolation, let him then strive to abound in the work of the Lord, and not slacken his hand in the exercise of religion and of his lawful calling, and his endeavor to please God in all things: for, seeing the covenant of grace embraced, is a firm and solid ground for faith to fix upon, albeit full persuasion and victorious consolation were neither at all, or but very rarely felt in this life; the afflicted (whom we have to speak to here) hath no cause to stumble, but reason to bless God, who hath in any measure, at any time, comforted him by the Gospel: for, that condition which the afflicted wisheth for, is reserved unto us in heaven. And presuppose the afflicted should have what he wisheth, consolations always running

like a river, where were place for trying, exercising and training of him in his faith? But let him work and wrestle on, and among hands he shall have as much peace as may suffice a pilgrim.

4. The third cause is, or may be this, that the afflicted hath grieved the Spirit of God, either by ascribing his gracious operations to some other cause then grace, or counting his consolations to be but flashes, and like unto delusions; or, that the afflicted by corrupt communication, or gross offenses, hath provoked God to anger, as befell David, Psal. 51. For removing of this cause, whether the sin of the afflicted hath been more or less provoking, let him with David (Psal. 51) renew the exercise of repentance and faith in God's mercy, who only can renew a right spirit in him, or rather restore him to the formerly-felt consolation and joy of his Spirit, and let him walk more warily hereafter, that he provoke not to wrath so merciful a father.

5. The fourth cause is, or may be this, that the afflicted, albeit he hath consented to the covenant of grace, and hath embraced Christ Jesus offered in the Evangel, yet he doth not set to his seal to the truth of God without an hink, or fear and suspicion of his right to apply the grace offered; in which case so long as he doubts, and doth not rest his sinful soul on the Word of God, offering grace to every soul sensible of sin, who shall fly to Jesus Christ, what wonder the holy Spirit doth with-hold the sealing of the man's faith? For this is God's order holden forth, Ephes. 1:13, that a sinner should first six his faith on Christ offered in the Gospel, and after he hath believed (not before he do believe) wait for the sealing of the holy Spirit.

For removing this cause, 1. Let the afflicted acknowledge that his hesitation, doubting and suspicion, is justly chastised of God, because he hath not firmly adhered to the covenant embraced by him, and because he hath not given unto God the glory of his truth without a pawn, and yet doth in effect quarrel and complain, that he doth not find these consolations which are given and but rarely, it may be even to the sound and strong in the faith. 2. Let him for the confirmation of his faith, hereafter consider well, how strong and solid a foundation faith hath to lean unto, even God's promise and oath given unto all that do fly to Christ for refuge and relief from sin and misery, Heb. 6:17,18, that the afflicted may with the Psalmist, Psal. 56:10, sing in God I will praise his Word. 3. Let the afflicted study to be so fast glued unto Christ in every condition and case he findeth himself, and go about the exercise of repentance and faith and new obedience in his calling, submitting himself to the will of God in every dispensation: which direction if he shall aim to follow, he shall not want the fruit of his faith, and honest endeavor to please God: for, Psal. 97:11. Light is sown for the righteous, and joy for the upright in heart.

CHAP. XXI. - Wherein is solved the doubt of the true convert, whether he be indeed converted, because he cannot confidently apply to himself the promises of the Gospel.

THERE ARE SOME TRUE converts, who albeit for fear of the wrath of God for their sins, are already fled unto Christ, and have hid themselves under the wings of the propitiatory in the shadow of the Almighty Mediator, and are already begun in earnest to give new obedience to the law of God; yet from time to time they fall in fear and trembling suspicion that all be not a sound work of grace in them; and that partly because they cannot confidently apply to themselves the promises of the Gospel, whether absolute, such as are made to the Elect, Jer. 31:31, or conditional, such as are made to believers in Christ offered in the Gospel; or qualified promises, such as are made to the meek and merciful, Matth. 5, which qualified promises they look upon as conditional, excluding them (as they conceive) who do not find in themselves such qualifications: and partly because they are not clear about their right to receive the offer of the Gospel, because they want, as they conceive, fitness in themselves to receive the same, and thus are they ofttimes vexed with doubts whether they be in the state of grace or not,

2. For lousing of this doubt, sundry things are already said, by the way, in answering other doubtful cases. But because many do meet with this difficulty, we shall speak a little more particularly to the case; and, first, it is needful, that the afflicted be confirmed about that which is right in him, that the thing which remaineth and is ready to die, may be strengthened: To this intent we commend the afflicted, that being sensible of sin, and feared for-wrath, he hath fled unto Christ for refuge; next we commend him, that he hath begun to give new obedience to God's Law, and doth purpose to follow on as he shall be enabled; and thirdly, we commend him, that albeit he cannot attain that near conjunction with Christ, which he would, yet he neither will, nor dare forsake Christ, nor put himself out of the number of weak believers in Christ, for he hath said in his heart with Peter, Joh. 6:68. To whom shall I go? For Christ hath the words of eternal life. Hitherto all is right, and the afflicted must resolve to cleave close to this foundation, because Christ hath said, John 6:37. These that come unto me I will in no case cast out.

3. For his doubt arising from the nature of the promises absolute, conditional and qualified, looked upon by him as if they were conditional, we answer. 1. That these qualified promises, having some mark in them of true believers, are not exclusive of these believers

who find in themselves a defect of the qualification, but they are inductive unto all believers, to study the attaining of that qualification, and are corroborative of these believers who find in any sensible measure these qualifications: For example, promises made to the merciful, to the peace-makers, to the upright in heart, do not exclude these who find themselves short in these graces, and yet are hungry and thirsty for righteousness, yet are poor and indigent of all good in themselves and daily beggars at the throne of grace for what they want, Matth. 5, for, these qualifications, sound in a weak believer, are signs and effects of sound faith in them. And we must grant, that of these graces, specified in these qualified promises, some of them are more eminent in some of the Saints, and other some of them more eminently seen and felt in other some of the Saints. And in the same person, one of these qualifications may sometime shine more clearly, and at another time by some temptation, or mistake, be over-clouded, and not shine so clearly as before, yet the qualifications are comfortable to all them who find the same in themselves, and are inductive to make every believer to aim to excel in these graces, and so to confirm their own faith more and more, as (2 Pet. 1:4-7) we are exhorted. Again, these qualifications, are signs of a believer already entered in the covenant of grace by faith in Christ, and begun to bring forth good fruits, but they are not the conditions of entering into the covenant; for then none could enter in covenant till first these qualifications in exercise were sound in them, and that were to dis-annul the covenant of grace, and to set up a sort of covenant of works; for there is not another condition of entering in the covenant but faith in Christ only, whereby the humbled sinner, renouncing all confidence in any good in himself, or from himself, doth betake himself wholly to the grace offered in Jesus Christ in whom perfect

righteousness is to be found. Now unto the man who shall believe in
Christ, all the promises of the Gospel are made, upon this condition,
that he do believe in Jesus Christ; which condition of faith in Christ,
when it is now performed, and by the grace of God, the man made a
believer in Christ, then the absolute promises of making a new heart,
and of writing the Law of the Lord therein, (Jer. 31:31, and Ezek. 11:19.)
and all the promises of saving graces set down in holy Scripture, do
all of them belong to the believer in Christ, in whom all the promises
are yea and amen, as if his name were set down.

4. As to his doubt, arising from his weak and infirm application
of the promises, let the afflicted consider what God hath already
wrought and is a working in him by way of application: for, first,
God hath granted to him the use of the means with others in the
visible Kirk, so that it may be said unto him in this respect, as it is,
Isa. 5:4, what could be done in outward means and offer-making of
grace which is not done? Secondly, God hath drawn more near unto
him, and hath illuminate his mind about his sinful state in nature,
and about the way of delivery by faith in Christ, and yet more, hath
inclined his heart to accept of the offer of Christ and make answer to
the call, as David did: When thou saidst, seek my face, my soul answered, thy face O Lord will I seek, Psal. 27:8. Thus God hath applied
Christ and the promises of the Gospel to the afflicted, and hath made
the afflicted to fly unto Christ offered in the Gospel and to apply him
unto himself, that hitherto the afflicted hath no reason to complain
of not application of Christ and his promises, on God's part, nor
yet of begun-application on the afflicted's part. Where is the in-lake
then? I answer, the defect is, first, in the afflicted, who hath not duly
considered the passages of God's gracious approaching to him, and
drawing of the man to himself in Christ; another defect is, that the

afflicted upon groundless mistakes, doth not lay claim to Christ and to all the promises of grace for righteousness and salvation in him, and that because he is not so clear of his right unto, and interest in, Christ, as he can lay claim confidently unto the same.

5. For clearing of the afflicted in this his right and warrant, confidently to apply Christ and all the promises of the Gospel, let him consider, first, the dreadful sentence of the curse and condemnation of all them that do not believe on Christ, John 3:18. He that believeth in Christ, is not condemned; but he that believeth not, is condemned already, because he hath not believed in the only begotten Son of God. Secondly, let him consider the largeness of the Gospel, wherein grace is offered to all and every believer, John 3:16. God so loved the world, that he gave his only begotten Son, that whosoever believeth in him should not perish, but have everlasting life. He saith whosoever, without exception, lest any man who desireth to believe in Christ, should doubt that he shall be received and made welcome. Thirdly, let him mediate upon the wonderful mystery of the incarnation of the Son of God, who, that he might ransom and redeem his people from sin and misery, hath assumed human nature into the union of person with his divine nature, and given a perpetual pawn and pledge of his hearty willingness to reconcile, justify, sanctify and save to the uttermost everyone who shall come unto God through him: whereunto his mediatory Office, and clothing himself with most sweet relations of Prophet, Priest and King to all his followers, doth hear abundant witness. Fourthly, let him hearken to the quickening and comfortable invitations which by his Spirit, speaking in Scripture, he uttereth in the ears of all to whom the Gospel cometh with a joyful sound; Ho, everyone that thirsteth! Isa. 55:1-10. Come unto me all ye that labor and are heavy loaden, Matth. 11:28. We are Ambassadors for Christ, as

though God did beseech you by us, we pray you, in Christ's stead, be ye reconciled to God, 2 Cor. 5:20. And whosoever will, let him take the water of life freely. Rev. 22:17. Fifthly, let the afflicted consider what answer he will give to the express command of God, 1 John 3:23. This is his commandment, that we should believe in the name of his Son Jesus Christ, and love one another as he hath commanded us. For, this commandment being directed to all the hearers of the Gospel, chargeth everyone without exception, first to examine seriously their life by the rule of God's Law, that thereby they may be convinced of their damnable state in nature, and made to acknowledge their sin and misery, and inability to help themselves: Secondly, having examined and acknowledged their natural lost condition they are commanded to fly to Jesus Christ, that by faith in him they may be delivered. Thirdly, that having fled to Christ, they should evidence their faith by love to Christ or God in Christ, and their neighbors, especially such as are of the household of faith. In which command-ment, both the order of applying Law and Gospel, is set down, and the necessity of believing in Christ, upon the warrant of this clear command; so that whosoever is a hearer of the Gospel, and doth not in this order fly unto Christ, he is inexcusable, even the wicked and worst of men. And much less excusable is the afflicted convert of whom we are now speaking, who already hath acknowledged his lost condition without Christ, and knoweth that there is no hope of relief, except by faith in Jesus, and hath fled to Christ, and dare not depart from him, if this man shall stand here and not rely on Christ and rest his soul upon him confidently, what excuse can he make? If he do object, that his name is not written in this command, 1 John 3:23, it hath no force to impede his faith, for neither is his name written in any of the ten commands of the moral Law, and yet he findeth himself tied to the obedience of every one of them, and why is he not tied also to this sweet command of the Gospel of grace, as well as to other commands? This command being given forth as the last declaration of God's will, for relief of them who acknowledge that they by the law are condemned? Wherefore let not the afflicted anymore pretend the difficulty of applying Christ and his graces offered in the Gospel, seeing it is presupposed he hath fled to Christ, and dare neither depart from him, nor for the pretended scruple draw confidently in unto him; but let him check and chide himself for not haunting Christ, and conversing with him in heaven in that humility and confidence which the Word of the Lord doth allow unto him and commandeth him to take up and hold fast.

CHAP. XXII. - Wherein is solved the doubt of the true convert concerning his conversion, arising from the observation in himself of presumption and security in his prosperity and of his misbelief in adversity.

THERE ARE SOME TRUE converts, who albeit they are neither idle nor unfruitful in the work of the Lord, and in acknowledging of Christ, yet are frequently called in question about their state in grace; for when their conscience is quiet, they fall in suspicion that their faith is but presumption, and when through temptation in adversity they are put to wrestling, their suspicion is, that then felt weakness of faith in wrestling is but misbelief. And when the frequent perturbations of their mind, do make them indisposed for any exercise of religion, a suspicion is raised, that the faith which they seemed to have, is but dead, because when there is most need of bringing forth fruits they are altogether unfit and unable to bring forth any fruits. What shall I think of my estate, faith the afflicted, who when an enemy doth not appear am secure, and when I must enter the combat with the adversary, I faint, and ofttimes when I am called to the exercise of religion, I am confounded, I am stupid and impotent to discharge any duty therein?

2. That this doubt may be solved, the three causes of his doubting must be removed. As to the first, which is the suspicion, that his faith is presumption, we do not deny that carnal confidence in prosperity useth to assume to itself the name of true faith, and that even true converts, do sometime deceive themselves concerning the measure of their faith, both on the right hand and on the left, by judging faith not questioned, to be strong faith, and faith in wrestling to be weak or none at all. We grant also, that some mixture of presumption will be found joined with true faith, and of misbelief also. Which evils do lurk and hide their power, till the man be put to some trial. Wherefor the afflicted hath need of discretion, that he may have a right esteem both of the operation of the holy Spirit, and of the power of native corruption in himself, for faith must not be condemned for the imperfections of it, or for the mixture of presumption and misbelief with it. And to help his judgment, let him observe the nature of prevalent

presumption, and the nature of true faith, which differ one from another in these four respects, first, presumption is founded upon a false imagination without any warrant of God's Word; but faith taketh heed to the Scripture, that from the Word it may give a reason of believing. 2. Presumption is negligent and idle in the discharge of duties, but faith taketh head to the commands of God, and is diligent and serious in the use of the means. 3. The presumptuous man doth not make question of his estate, but blesseth himself, when his way is to be hated, for he doth not examine himself, that he may know certainly in what condition he is, but he that puts his faith in exercise, doth carefully examine his carriage and condition, lest he deceive himself. 4. The presumptuous man in all his ways and actions is well pleased with himself, but the believer, because of the sinfulness he findeth in all his actions, is ill pleased with himself in his best actions many times, and renounceth all confidence in his works, that he may wholly depend on the grace of God.

3. Let the afflicted therefore who so doth look to the Gospel, as he also maketh use of the Law, both in prosperity and adversity, maketh conscience of the exercise of religion and duties of his calling in some measure, and is never so well pleased with himself but he observeth the power of corruption in himself, let him (I say) not reckon himself among the presumptuous, let him not esteem his quietness in believing to be presumption.

4. As for his suspicion, that his faith is null, because it proveth weak in conflict, let the afflicted beware lest he help and strengthen Satan's temptations against his faith, albeit he find his faith weak in trials and assaults, and not answerable either to his own hope or others expectation of him; yet let him not quench the smoking flax, nor break the bruised reed, but let him follow Christ, humbling himself

before God because of his defects, and going about to strengthen that which is remaining. 2. Albeit in some fit of temptation he slide, as Peter did, and find that he hath presumed too much of his own strength and honest purpose as Peter also did, yet let him not think that his faith is null, but let him weep with Peter, and turn again by repentance, and watch better over his own heart for time to come.

5. As for the suspicion he hath, that his faith is dead or idle, because when fruits are chiefly called for, he finds himself utterly indisposed, unfit and unable to discharge any work of religion, as cometh to pass in the time of passions, perturbations of mind, and pollution of the conscience: for clearing whereof, we do acknowledge, that wrath and contention do hinder prayer and other exercises of religion, as the Apostle doth insinuate, 1 Pet. 3:7, where he commandeth husbands to carry themselves discreetly toward their wives, least their prayers in the family or in secret be hindered; and, 1 Tim. 2:8, the Apostle commandeth men to pray everywhere, lifting up pure hands without wrath or doubting. We acknowledge also, that not only wrath, or any other passion or action which defileth the conscience, are able to hinder the exercise of religion, and discharge of Christian duties at a time, but also it is found by experience, that any perturbation of mind, albeit it do not defile or concern the conscience, may in some part hinder the discharge of a religious exercise, as may be seen when any person is surprised with the report of some notable damage, or is possibly wounded by some accident, or terrified by the sight of imminent danger; yet for all this, none of these things can prove faith to be dead, but doth show the infirmity of a man's mind, the use of whose reason may be hindered for a time by perturbations and sudden passions; and at the most, the presupposed cases may prove the weakness of faith, and the interruption of it in the putting forth

itself vigorously for the time, but cannot prove the deadness or nullity of faith, which after such passions are past, doth set forward to bring forth fruits in better measure: wherefore let not the afflicted halt in his way for such temptations, but let him make straight steps to himself, least that which is halting be turned out of the way; let him reject these fiery darts and temptations tending to weaken his confidence, let him humble himself in the sense of inherent corruption, and wash frequently his conscience at the fountain, which is opened up in the house of David for purging away sin and uncleanness; let him carry himself the more circumspectly in all things, because of his frequent experience of Satan's malice, of the power of sin, and of his own infirmities.

CHAP. XXIII. - Wherein is solved the doubt of a true converts regeneration, arising from some false rule applied without reason to himself.

SOME TRUE CONVERTS, JUDGING their state by some false rule, do not only torment themselves, but also (so far as in them lieth) by pronouncing false sentences of their own state, go about to extinguish the spunk of piety which is in them. The false rule whereby they do judge themselves, is strengthened by a groundless persuasion, that it is a true and sure rule, and ordinarily when they think or speak of it, they prefix no reason for it, but some confident asseveration, such as without doubt, it is most certain, and I am persuaded of it, and such like. If I were regenerate and truly converted, without doubt, I should be in a better disposition then I am, I should love the Lord more fervently, I should understand the mysteries of God's

Word more clearly, I should not be so little affected with the sense of God's benefits bestowed on me, I should not go so lightly under the conviction of so many sins against God as I feel in me, I should be more diligent in the work of the Lord, in my calling I should walk more humbly and circumspectly in all my conversation, and such like many expressions. The same course doth the afflicted follow in his examination of the operations of the holy Spirit, and of every Christian virtue in himself: without doubt, saith he, if this were truly as a Christian virtue in me, there would not be such a disposition as I find in me, my condition should be such and such as became a new creature, which because I do not find in me, I have just reason to call in question my conversion. And here is a port opened for Satan to enter at, and to throw all his fiery darts at the miserable soul of the weak convert, whence many complaints do break forth, and thanksgiving for mercies received and for the time enjoyed, is broken off and ceaseth: And partly through diffidence, partly through murmuring, the Spirit of the Lord is provoked to wrath.

2. We grant, that this is a dangerous evil not only to the person afflicted, but also to such as are familiarly acquainted with his condition, because this disease readily doth infect others, as it came to pass in the camp of Israel, where the murmuring of some, set the body of the army on a mutiny against God: for, one that is weak in the faith, when he heareth such complaints in the mouth of one whom he judgeth to be holier than himself, incontinent he falleth on complaining of his own state, saying, that he hath more weighty reason to suspect the soundness of his conversion, then the person hath whom he hath heard suspecting his being in the state of grace.

3. Wherefore let the afflicted before he shall vent his suspicion of his state, examine the rule whereby he hath passed sentence on

himself, whether he can make it good from the Scripture: for, it is not sufficient to say, without doubt, and I am persuaded it is true, except it can be confirmed by the infallible warrant of God's Word; and let his friend who shall hear his complaint, expressly require a reason of his confidence, that such a rule is clear from Scripture, and that the application thereof is made righteously. Which if he cannot prove other ways then Satan doth enforce his temptations, that is, either without Scripture, or by abusing Scripture contrary to the intent thereof, let him acknowledge his readiness to misbelieve and disobey the Word of the Lord, and to hearken to Satan's temptations to the weakening of his own faith, and hindering of his cheerful obedience to the Lord's commands: and because such question-making of being in the state of grace, is ofttimes very inconsiderately uttered, even before them who do not allow the complainers misconstruction of his state, or if they should allow it, and say to the complainer, that they believed that suspicion of his state were very just, it should grieve the complainer more than the doubt itself: Therefore let the afflicted neither hearken to the suspicion, nor vent it when it is strongly suggested; but let him humble himself before Christ, because of these defects and wants of such evidences of saving grace as he would have; and in the sense of these wants, let him cleave close to Christ for covering his nakedness, and earnestly endeavor by faith in Christ to be made more and more conform to the exemplar of holiness holden forth in the Scripture.

CHAP. XXIV. - Wherein is solved the converts doubt of his own conversion, because he hath found the deceitfulness of his own heart, and dare not trust it anymore.

SOME SINCERE CONVERTS, WHO uprightly do serve Christ, and adhere unto him by faith, when they consider the doctrine of the deceitfulness of the heart of man, and how many are deceived by trusting to the testimony of their own heart, concerning their regeneration and justification, do begin to call in question all the work of their own conversion, and do fear least they be found in the number of the finer sort of hypocrites, who deceive both themselves and others, having nothing in them but a civil life and form of religion, without the power of godliness, and do sleep to death in security: of which sort our

Lord Jesus forewarneth, that not only private persons, but also many preachers shall be found, Matth. 7:22, of whom we may suppose, that they were not conscious of open and gross wickedness, but were of a blameless carriage before the world, professing the Christian faith, and teaching others to believe in Christ, and doubted nothing but Christ should judge of them as real Saints; to whom for all that, Christ shall one day say, depart from me ye workers of iniquity, I never knew you. It is certain that such men have been deceived by their own heart: which when the afflicted doth consider, he standeth astonished and trembleth for fear, saying with himself, what shall I think of my former opinion of my blessed state, I fear my heart hath deceived me, as others of greater gifts and better life, have been deceived by their own heart.

2. This is a doubt which hath need to be solved; but neither this nor any other doubt can be solidly and effectually solved by any mean, except the holy Spirit give a blessing to the means: for, it is certain, that there are many, who being religiously educate and free from gross vices, do not repent of their sins, are not touched with the sense of their original sin and corrupt lusts, but without taking any burden on their consciences for these, do pass by their time, well pleased with their own estate. Some also there are, who having fallen in gross and scandalous sins, do find for some time remorse of conscience for these gross sins, but for their other sins beside those, and for their in-born corruptions, are not careful, thinking it sufficient if thereafter they do not fall in such gross faults: The first sort of men, do deceive themselves, thinking they have little to repent of, in regard they are free of gross out-breakings. This last sort deceive themselves also, because they esteem their natural sorrow for such sins as are gross and scandalous, to be true repentance, albeit they be not humbled

for the fountain of these out-breakings, to wit, their in-born corruption of nature and filthy concupiscence, and the daily out-breakings thereof, to the polluting of their spirits, whereof they do take little or no notice. Many also there are who deceive themselves, esteeming the outward exercises of religion, and some works (in themselves commendable) to be sufficient fruits and evidences of their faith in Christ and of their regeneration, albeit they have not as yet fled to Christ sincerely, neither ever put a right estimation upon the imputed righteousness of Christ. Such men, when they should renounce all confidence in their own works, and in the sense of their sinfulness fly unto the covenant of grace offered in Christ, that in him they might have remission of sin, and from him by faith draw strength and ability to bring forth good works, they run a contrary course; for in the confidence of their own strength they go about sundry duties toward men, and exercises of religion toward God, trusting in those works, as if by works they were to be justified. Therefore justly shall Christ say unto them, depart from me ye workers of iniquity, I never knew you. Such were many of the Israelites, who being ignorant of the righteousness of God, went about to establish their own righteousness. These things when one, weak in faith doth consider, no wonder he be troubled and be afraid lest he deceive himself and perish as others have done.

3. This is a dangerous disease, and so long as it is not cured, it hinders much the tender beginnings of the new creature, that it cannot come up to manly strength, First therefore, let the afflicted wisely examine the course of his by-gone life, lest he either absolve, or condemn himself, rashly; and let him beware lest he esteem the worse of the evidences of a new creature, and the fruits of faith, because these that look to be justified by their works, can produce the like works.

Secondly, let the afflicted call to mind whether in the beginning of the reformation of his life, the Law as a Pedagogy did lead him unto Christ; and whether since that time, the law did daily put him on, and force him to fly to Christ, and to embrace Christ and his righteousness, and hath made him to study obedience to the law, out of love to God, so much the more carefully, as he perceived himself obliged thankfully to acknowledge grace granted in Christ to him; for if any measure of the daily exercise of repentance, if any measure of love to Christ, and any measure of endeavor of new obedience, be found after examination in the person afflicted, out of doubt the ground is laid solidly of his salvation, out of doubt he hath an evidence of the work of grace by the operation of the holy Spirit in himself.

4. If in this examination the afflicted be not clear, but the doubt doth yet stick, because of the suspicion he hath of the felt deceitfulness of his own heart, we offer unto him this counsel, that he quickly humble himself before God, and do ingenuously acknowledge the native perverseness and deceitfulness of his heart; and for that very reason, let him embrace Christ the Redeemer in the arms of faith, offering himself to every condemned sinner; and let him thank God who hath deciphered unto him this deceitfulness of his heart, and offered Christ unto him for the true remedy of this and every other sinful malady. And in the meantime, let him put a difference between himself and an hypocrite, in whom the deceit of the heart is neither acknowledged nor seen, but fostered and defended: for, a close hypocrite, after hearing of the doctrine of the deceitfulness of the heart, will stand to the defending of his own sincerity, and will take it hardly if any man labor to convince him of any measure of hypocrisy: but a true convert, or regenerate person, will not deny but much hypocrisy may be found in him; and albeit he be sorrowful,

that this deceitfulness of heart hath had lodging in him and lurked too long, yet is he willing and glad to have this evil more and more discovered unto him, and heartily doth he deliver up this traitor to Christ, to be mortified and abolished by his Spirit.

5. But if the afflicted cannot be quiet and satisfied, still fearing and suspecting he be found a man unrenewed, and that for the running issue of this filthy boil, opened up to him by the sword of the Spirit, let him beware that he pass not peremptory sentence against himself, that he do not conclude himself to be a man altogether in the bond of iniquity; but let him suspend for a time, the disputation, and do that which is allowed unto every self-condemned man in the beginning of his conversion, that is, quickly let him fly unto Christ for remission of sin, let him lay hold on that righteousness purchased by him; and the more he feareth to find God a severe judge, let him the more firmly lay hold on Jesus Christ the Mediator, who justifieth the ungodly by faith: this is the only solid way to persevere in faith, to overcome Satan, to solve doubts, to resist temptations, and to cure the wound made by Satan's fiery darts; for, unto that man, who in the sense of his sins and ill deserving, and inability to help himself, doth fly unto Christ, it shall never be said by Christ, depart from me, I never knew thee.

6. Now when the person afflicted hath of new laid hold on Christ and guarded the fortress of faith, and repulsed the tempter, who by all means, and specially by quarreling and questioning the by-past work of grace in him, had labored to weaken and overturn his faith for by-gones, and for the present also, lest it should convalesce and grow stronger for time to come; now (I say) let the afflicted after victory return to the dispute and to the examination of his state in grace, of his faith in Christ and of his regeneration, and he shall see all the begun

saving graces which were darkened by temptations clearly appear, and shall perceive the several steps and degrees of God's grace toward him in former times, more evidently then he could discern them in the hour of darkness and temptation. And so he shall return from this battle stronger in faith then he was before, and more persuaded of the work of the holy Spirit in him, then he was before the temptation.

CHAP. XXV. - Wherein is solved the doubt of the true converts conversion, arising from his breach of the covenant of Grace, as he conceiveth.

THERE ARE SOME SINCERE converts, who, albeit they do not doubt but penitents, flying to Christ, are received in favor with God, are justified from their sins, and do obtain right unto all the privileges of the Saints; yet, they doubt whether every sincere convert shall remain in the covenant of Grace, if possibly they have so far abused grace, as to defile themselves again with the pollutions which they seemed to repent of before. And this erroneous opinion of the instability of the covenant of grace, they do apply to themselves; for, when they have found by experience, the power of sin, as it were not only raging, but in appearance reigning in them, as the conscience of their relapsing in their old sins beareth witness. And when they know their nature so corrupt and ready to sin yet more, they doubt if this condition can stand with being in the covenant of Grace; and whatsoever they have found of their being in this covenant, they now fear that they be fallen from grace, because they have, as they conceive, broken the covenant of Grace on their part, therefore they apprehend also, that God in justice, being provoked ofttimes by them, hath now at last dissolved the covenant of Grace on his part: for (say they) it is no reason that God should be tied unto them in covenant, who so many ways have violated that covenant; but as Adam, by sinning, excluded himself from all benefit of the covenant of Works, So is it reason, that everyone who have violated the covenant of Grace as I have done, should be excluded from the covenant of Grace. And here the afflicted doth stand as a miserable man, uncertain what to do: in which condition, horrible temptations and heavy suspicions of their state do arise, namely, that they are in the condition and case wherein Esau was, who when he had sold his birth-right for a mess of pottage, found no place for repentance, albeit he sought the blessing with tears. Now what torment may be in the conscience of the afflicted in this case, it is easy (for them who at any time have felt the wrath of God) to conjecture. And this doubt doth vex the man most, who is conscious of his often abuse of the grace of God: for, what shall I do, saith he? Shall I defile myself and go and wash, and again defile myself and go and wash, and by this means augment my own guiltiness from day today? What is, if this be not, to abuse the grace of God?

2. That this evil may be removed, we must confess that there are many, who after some remorse for some sins, raised by a natural and unrenewed conscience, do weep now and then (as Saul did for his injust persecution of David) and do think, that by their tears they have

washen away their sin, and attained to some sort of quietness in their conscience for a time, who yet do not cease from their wickedness, but remain in their natural state strangers from God and Christ. We must also acknowledge, that some of the regenerate in their carnal security, falling back in their old sins, ordinarily are sharply chastised by God; and indeed no wonder is, that such as have once attained to peace with God, do meet with broken bones, after they have abused the grace of God, in giving way to their sinful lusts, which was the case of David, Psal. 51.

3. As for those who fall in open gross scandalous sins which defile the whole man, soul and body both, it is safest for them (whether they were before that time converted or not) to let alone long disputation, whether they were regenerate or not before their fearful fall, and to stir up themselves to a deep search of the wickedness of their nature, that they may be humbled before God, and in the sense of their in-born sin and gross actual out-breakings, fly unto Christ for pardon and grace to bring forth better fruits then they have done.

4. As for these who have not fallen in grievous open transgressions, but in their wrestling against sin, not obtaining the victory they would, or hoped to have, do find themselves polluted in their spirits, and put to the worse in their conflict against their sinful lusts and passions, and that very frequently; and thereupon they apprehend, that either they were never in the state of grace, or if they were in it, that they have abused and broken the covenant of grace; To these we answer, that every transgression of the commands, albeit it be a violation of the covenant of works, yet is not a dissolution of the covenant of grace: for, it is one thing to fail in a duty, which the covenanted party should have done; another thing to break or dissolve the covenant of grace; for, it is provided in the covenant of

grace as a special article, that God will forgive the sin of his confederate people, when they confess their faults, and sue for pardon according to the promise of mercy to the covenanted, Jer. 31:32: and lest any humble sinner should be discouraged and not receive this solution of his doubt, let him consider the words of the Apostle, Gal. 6:1, expressly set down for their comfort, who, having resolved to live holily, justly and temperately, are overtaken in an offense, and are not purposed to abuse mercy, or turn the grace of God into lasciviousness; and, 1 Joh. 2:1. These things I write unto you (to wit, believers in Christ, careful to live holily) that ye sin not; but if any man sin, we have an advocate with the father, Jesus Christ the just one. And this article of the covenant, for granting daily remission according to the necessity of the Saints, maketh the covenant of grace perpetual, and to be daily made use of, as we are directed in the Lord's prayer. And in this doth the covenant of grace differ from the covenant of works, which by any one sin is so violate, as the curse doth follow, till the sinner run in to the covenant of grace in Jesus Christ: And by this doctrine a door is not opened unto sinning, but the door only is closed to keep in the true convert from desperation, and running away from Christ, and to help him out of the mire of discouragement wherein he is fallen, lest he sink in it and despair. Neither is the study of holiness hindered by this way, or the diligence of the convert slackened in the duties of new obedience and pleasing of God, but only servile fear in the manner of serving God, is taken away, and the obligation of love to God (who is found to be so merciful) is more strictly tied upon us: which love (as it is augmented daily by new confirmations of faith, and fresh experiences of his grace to us) doth cast out servile fear, as the Apostle teacheth, 1 John 4:18.

As for the afflicted convert, his fear that he be like Saul, who though he felt remorse and shame, when all the beholders in his army saw him so confounded by David's loyal carriage toward him, yet did he not repent this sin at all, nor amend his life at all; there is no ground to suspect himself to be like unto him, or to Esau who was solicitous only for an earthly blessing; and when he could not have the first place in his fathers blessing, contented himself with what portion in the earth he could have beside. Therefore let the afflicted labor to understand well the nature of the covenant of grace and the several articles thereof; and let him consider, that there is no advantage to be had by excluding of himself from that covenant, but that if he will be saved, in every condition he must draw near to Christ, and lay hold on him for remission of sin, and fresh furniture of grace for every duty: for, it is good always to draw near to him, because he will destroy all them that depart far from him, Psal. 73:27.

CHAP. XXVI. - Wherein is solved the true converts doubt, whether he be regenerate, because he findeth himself not only far from the measure of holiness which he observeth to have been in the Saints commended in Scripture; but also short of the measure which some

# of his acquaintance have attained unto.

SOME TRUE CONVERTS ARE, who in the time wherein they are about to strengthen their faith by all means, do fall in comparison of themselves with other converts in the matter of their faith, love, endeavor and attainment of an holy conversation; and finding themselves very short of that measure which not only Saints commended in Scripture have attained unto, but also short of what sundry of their acquaintance have gained and given proof of, suddenly are overtaken with a sad suspicion, that they may be found none of the number of true converts: as for example, when they read what David saith of himself in the Psalms, and namely in the hundred and nineteen Psalm, they seem to themselves so unlike the copy he hath cast unto them, so far short of that affection to the Word of God, of that faith, of that diligence, of that sincerity, of that patience, of that fortitude in afflictions, and delectation in God, which the practice of this servant of God doth hold forth, that they are ashamed to assume the name of a visible Saint, or faithful servant of God. And for the same reason, do forbear under this exercise to apply unto themselves the precious promises made to the faithful servants of God in the Scripture. What am I (saith the afflicted) that I should presume to intrude myself in the number of the Saints? What am I, that I should apply to myself what is promised to true converts and sincere servants of God? Were I such a one as this person, or that person is, I might then, for my consolation, apply promises made unto such Saints; but now I cannot apply their privileges, except for conviction of my conscience, that I am justly for my unlikeness unto them, secluded from the promises made unto them, and those that are like unto them.

2. For lousing of this doubt, we must acknowledge, that the comparison of ourselves with the rule of perfection holden forth in the Scripture, is to be aimed at by all; and the comparison of ourselves with the eminent servants of God, who have attained a great measure of growth in holiness, is very profitable if it be prudently managed: For, the first comparison teacheth us what we should endeavor to attain, and the other teacheth us what may be by the grace of God attained unto even in this life.

Again, both these comparisons do serve to humble us before God, when we perceive ourselves not only short of perfection, which cannot be fully attained unto in this life, but also short of these degrees which may be attained, and have been attained by others in this life, we cannot choose but think the more meanly of ourselves, and put down the sails of self-estimation.

Thirdly, this sort of comparison is profitable to make us more uprightly renounce all confidence in our own inherent righteousness, and fly for refuge to the righteousness of Christ obedience and satisfaction imputed unto all that believe in him, according as the example of the Apostle Paul who renounced all confidence in his privileges, performances, sufferings and inherent righteousness, counting them all but dung, that he might win Christ and be found in him, not having his own righteousness which is of the law, but that which is through the faith of Christ; the righteousness which is of God by faith, Phil. 3:8,9.

3. But this sort of comparison is dangerous and hurtful, when it tendeth to discouragement, when it maketh us think little of the measure of God's grace granted unto us, when it makes us heartless in the course of obedience, and hopeless that we shall attain unto the measure whereunto the Saints have attained.

4. Wherefore let the afflicted strengthen the thing which remaineth and is ready to die, Rev. 3:2, let him beware lest he quench the smoking flax, or break the bruised reed, wherein he hath Christ's help to look unto, Isa. 42:3. Again, let the afflicted consider, that there are divers degrees of saving faith, divers degrees of the measure of sanctification and growth in grace; for, some are old men, some young, and strong men, and some babes in Christ, and that the same duties in the same measure, are not to be expected from the tender and weak beginner, which are required of the strong and experimented soldier. 3. Let the afflicted remember, that nothing is given, nor promised, nor done unto the Saints in Scripture or in latter ages for any merit or worthiness in them, but altogether of free grace: and so much the more should this be remembered, as this doubting of the afflicted, arising from comparison of his condition with the measure of sanctification in others, doth presuppose the contrary, as if God did deal with his children according to the worthiness of their persons and merit of their good works, which is a false supposition; for, why doth the afflicted cast down his courage and weaken his faith and confidence in God, but for this very cause, that he counteth himself a much more unworthy man, and of less merit before God then those Saints were, or are, with whom he hath compared himself? 4. Let the afflicted by so much as he doth perceive himself more unworthy, and more sinful then those Saints with whom he hath compared himself, thrust himself the more into the bosom of

rich grace; let him so much the more lay hold on the imputation of Christ's righteousness, and cover his nakedness therewith, and employ Christ by faith so much the more, that out of his fullness he may receive grace for grace, and be made able by his Spirit to bring forth more abundant fruits, and come up nearer unto conformity with Christ, and the examples of renowned Saints. 5. Let the afflicted consider, that we must live by rules set down in Scripture, aiming sincerely at obedience of holy precepts, albeit we have not yet come up unto the practice of the rule in that measure, which others have attained unto.

CHAP. XXVII. - Wherein is solved the true converts doubt, whether he be in the blessed state of grace, because he findeth himself frequently in an evil condition.

EXPERIENCE TEACHETH, THAT SUNDRY true converts, because they, feeling themselves ofttimes in an ill condition, do call in question their being in the blessed state of grace, not considering, that the condition of a man, whether in the state of nature unrenewed, or in the state of grace, may be comparatively in better or worse condition, and yet his state remain the same. The multitude of the misbelieving Hebrews, were in an evil condition, at the one side of the red Sea, when they repented their coming out of Egypt, but in a better condition when they did sing praises unto God on the other side of the Sea, and yet for their state, some were, yea most part, still in nature unrenewed: Moses and Aaron were in an evil condition when their passion offended God at the smiting of the rock; but when they did intercede with God for the people, when wrath was kindled against the host, they were in a better condition: and both in the one time and in the other they were in the state of grace, true Saints in God's estimation. This mistake of the weak in faith, not putting difference between their present disposition and their state, maketh them judge of themselves to be in the state of grace when their condition is good, and to be in the state of nature unrenewed when they feel themselves in an evil condition: when they observe their heart enlarged to run the way of God's commandments, then they esteem themselves truly regenerate, and when they feel themselves sluggish in the work of the Lord, dull in hearing the Word, flow to believe what the Scripture speaketh, when they esteem their ordinary service to be after a form of godliness, without affection and power, and what service they do, to proceed from fear of wrath, rather than from the new and right principles of a regenerate man, then they question all the works of grace in themselves. What shall I think, saith the afflicted, concerning my state in grace, when I find my condition so frequently not only short of what it should be, but also polluted with divers sorts of sins?

2. For answer, we must grant, that the external duties of religion, may be discharged from fleshly and corrupt principles; for, many do perform commanded external duties, that they may eschew the reproach of impiety, or that they may insinuate themselves in the good estimation and favor of the godly, or for some base earthly ends for which gross hypocrites do whatsoever they do in religion.

Like unto these are all self-deceiving hypocrites, who go about to establish their own righteousness, mistaking that righteousness which is of God by faith, as if God could be obliged to take their performance for a full, satisfaction for their former sins, and would look upon their works as meritorious of eternal life; and therefore because men may deceive themselves, 1. the afflicted shall do well to examine himself whether he hath renounced all confidence in the flesh, or his own works, Phil. 3:8,9, and fled unto Christ for righteousness, with some measure of honest endeavoring to worship and serve God in his spirit; which if his conscience can witness unto him to be his way wherein he is walking, then may he be assured that he is a true convert. 2. And albeit it be true that the imperfections of the regenerate man do many times obscure his state in grace, yet can they not extinguish the spark of regeneration begun in him, or prove the work of grace in him not to be at all. 3. We grant that the condition of a true convert at sometimes may be so bad by reason of sinful distemper and fleshly carriage, that many unrenewed men's conversation shall be found far more commendable, then the present condition and carriage of the renewed man in his sinful condition: In which case neither God nor his own conscience, nor any that feareth God can speak anything but wrath to him, till he repent and turn to God for mercy in Christ; yet the afflicted penitent convert, lamenting his bad condition, is in better case then any unrenewed man can be into: for, the very grief and perplexity which he findeth because his condition is so oft ill and sinful, proveth his good affection toward God, and his earnest desire to walk before God unto all well-pleasing, in all things and at all times.

3. But if the afflicted shall insist and object, that the fear of God's wrath and judgments, ordinarily is a main motive which setteth him on to do the duties and service which God requireth of him, and not the love of God, the felt in-lake whereof, doth make him go on

halting and heavy in the ways of God. We answer, that albeit the fear of God's wrath and judgments looked upon alone, doth not prove regeneration, yet it may well consist with regeneration: because God doth not for naught join with his precepts, fearful threatening's of judgments against those who shall transgress his commands, that they may be as a spur in his children's sides to press them to their duties, and as a bridle to curb and check their vicious inclination unto sin, which lodgeth in all men by nature. And this motive is evident in the experience of the Prophet, Psal. 119:120. My flesh trembleth for fear of thee, and I am afraid of thy judgments. 2. It may be that the afflicted, lately converted unto God, be not free as yet from the spirit of bondage, but be keeped in some measure under the bonds of servile fear, God so disposing, for the humbling, exercising and training of his child lately entered in his holy warfare; in which condition his fear is commendable, when it ariseth from the conscience of his sinful short-coming in God's service, and of the prevailing of his corruption against the begun work of renovation. Wherefore, let the afflicted go about the discharge of commanded duties in his Christian calling, and particular station wherein God hath placed him, in what condition soever he shall find himself. 2. Let him compare his present condition, which he doth count an ill condition, with the by-gone better conditions whereof he hath had possibly experience frequently; and when he calleth to mind the comforts he hath had, and the enlargement of heart to run in the way of God's commandment, in hope of a change of his present condition to the better, in hope of finding renewed blinks of the Lord's countenance, let him humbly wait on God in the use of the means appointed, till the day-star arise in his heart, praying with the Psalmist, that God would quicken him according to his loving kindness. 3. Let him cleave the more closely to the covenant of grace and the righteousness which is by faith in Jesus Christ, withal giving thanks unto God for the grace bestowed on him, for the giving unto him eye-salve to see his blindness, nakedness and misery, and for making sin odious and grievous unto him in any measure, and for drawing him to Christ to be his refuge in his worst condition.

CHAP. XXVIII. - Wherein is solved the doubt of the true convert concerning his regeneration, because he findeth the power of the body of death in the pollution of the imaginations of his heart, vigorous and powerful.

THERE ARE SOME TRUE converts, who albeit they be cleansed from the pollutions that are in the world, and have their conversation blameless and without giving scandal unto them they live among, yet frequently are troubled with doubting of their state in grace, because they feel in themselves such a power of in-bred corruption of their hearts, as can hardly consist (as they conceive) with regeneration and saving faith, because, James 3:11, maketh the question thus, doth a fountain send forth at the same place sweet water and bitter? &c. unto the end of the Chapter. This doubt the afflicted wrestles with, and saith with himself, what shall I think of myself, whose heart is so polluted, that it casteth forth continually dirt and mire? How shall I reckon myself among the Saints? How shall I intrude myself among the justified, who find so little evidence of the work of sanctification in me? For, faith should purify the heart from this pollution, whereof I do justly complain.

2. For solving of this doubt, many things are already spoken which serve for the curing of this case, and comforting the afflicted in this condition; but because one and the same doubt, doth diversely present itself now in one shape, then in another, and doth vex the afflicted in sundry ways, we shall answer this doubt proposed as it is set down.

First therefore, let the afflicted examine himself whether he may with some measure of honesty say with the Psalmist, Psal. 66:18. I do not regard iniquity-in my heart. I do not so delight in sin, but that sin is still my affliction and my daily grief. Secondly, let him examine himself, whether the power of corruption doth break forth in words and deeds or not, or if it do burst out in some passionate fits, whether he doth open the sluice and give it way, or whether he sets himself to oppose the out-breaking of sin, and is humbled for what doth break forth. Thirdly, let him examine whether he flyeth to Christ to wash him, and help him against the power of sin, or not. If after examination he can in any measure of honesty join with the Apostle in his lamentation, and recourse unto Christ for delivery,

Rom. 7:24,25, he may be assured, he is in the state of grace: For, there is a vast difference between a man's being sold unto sin by his native corruption captivating him, and a man's setting of himself unto sin, as a voluntary servant of sin; for, a renewed man may be in sundry cases a captive to sin, and is a fighter against sin; But a man selling himself to sin, is a slave voluntarily suffering sin to reign in his mortal body.

Let the afflicted therefore comfort himself, because in him there is a perpetual conflict between the flesh and the spirit, between his native inclination to sin, and the new creature, or inclination to holiness. Neither let him by mis-understood Scripture formerly cited, vex himself; for, his faith is indeed upon the work, and the way of purifying his heart; first, because he doth fly to the blood of Christ, which cleanseth him from all sin, in respect of remission granted. Secondly, there is a constant endeavor to be more and more holy, and to draw virtue by faith from Christ to bring forth good fruits, well-pleasing unto God. Thirdly, he is about to mortify his lusts by the Spirit of Christ, and to purge out the leaven of all filthiness of flesh and spirit, albeit he cannot purge it out all at once, or wholly in in this life. And fourthly, because albeit his doubting of his estate in grace be not allowable, yet it doth bear witness that the remainder of pollution in him is his grief, affliction and vexation. So also that other Scripture, James 3:11, which faith, that out of the same fountain proceedeth not salt water and sweet, is not to be understood so as if no rotten speech could possibly proceed out of the mouth of a regenerate man at any time; for James doth witness, that in many things we sin all, in thought, word and deed: But the meaning is, that he that bridleth not his tongue, his religion is vain, and nothing but a presumptuous boasting of that which is not real and in truth, and that it is inconsistent with regeneration, that out of a man's mouth, pretending to bless God, cursing of men who are made after the similitude of God, should flow forth as waters flow forth from a running fountain without controlment.

CHAP. XXIX. - Showing how to quench the fiery darts of Satan, and resist his sinful suggestions whether of shorter endurance or of longer continuance.

SOMETIME ON A SUDDEN Satan casteth a fiery dart of temptation unto some sin, as his messenger seeking to prepare the lodging for him: which temptation he doth so furiously press, as if he would not be refused, or could not be resisted; and possibly may so bear-in his temptation, as the convert may be afraid that Satan shall prevail, finding himself, as it were, over-powered and unable to bear out in such a case, as the Apostle had experience of, 2 Cor. 12:7-9, who found himself, as it were, buffeted and abused by the messenger of Satan, and unable of himself to resist him. The remedy whereof is, that the afflicted with the Apostle be humbled in himself, in the sense of his in-born sinfulness and inability to overcome temptations. 2. That he fly to Christ the captain of militant soldiers, and do pray unto him instantly to help to bear out in the conflict, and to be rid of the Tempter. 3. Let him hold fast the faith of promised grace, and wrestle on so long as it shall please God to exercise him so.

With such a temptation Job also was exercised, which so far prevailed as to make carnal and corrupt nature speak for it. The temptation was very fearful, and no less then self-murder, Job, 7:13-15. When I say my couch shall ease my complaint, then thou scarest me with dreams, and terrifiest me with night-visions, so that my soul chooseth strangling and death rather than life. The remedy whereof is, with Job to fly to the Redeemer, and fix faith upon him, and to present the temptation unto God by prayer and humble lamentation, striving against the suggestion, and never to give over relying on God, as he did.

2. Sometime Satan when he cannot find instruments to charge the convert with hypocrisy, and a course of wickedness, as he found in Job's trial, by his uncharitable friends, he useth immediately to fall a railing against the whole course of the work of grace in the convert, and charge him falsely with deep guiltiness, as calumniators use to do in their furious flyting and slandering of such as they hate, hoping how false and groundless soever the calumnies be, that yet something shall prove likely and probable, and so fasten something upon the innocent. In which case, let the afflicted lift up his mind to the Lord, and pray him to rebuke Satan. 2. Let him humble himself in acknowledgment of his natural corruption, and having fled to Christ for righteousness, let him take the shield of faith for quenching that dart. 3. Let him as he is enabled contemn these devilish slanders of

Satan, and set his mind on some better employment then to dispute with so impudent and restless an adversary; for we have other business to go about, then to take notice of the dogs barking at us: but if it please God to continue that exercise from day today, let the afflicted in patience submit himself to God, and direct his speech and thoughts unto God only, not answering directly such a Shimei at all. It is not safe to direct our speech to Satan at all, but let us say to God, the Lord rebuke Satan.

3. Sometime Satan falleth on with suggestions, blasphemous against God and all the grounds of religion, and fathers all these blasphemies on the afflicted as his proper sins. In which case, let the afflicted be humbled before God, because of original sin, whereof Satan maketh use, as of something of his own in us. 2. Let him renew the grips of faith on Christ the Mediator in whom the fullness of the Godhead dwelleth, reconciling the elect world to himself, not imputing their sins unto them. 3. Let not the afflicted look upon these blasphemies other ways then as Satan's malice against God, for so they are indeed, and not the sins of the poor soul vexed with such suggestions. 4. Let the afflicted beware of discouragements, misbelief or weakening of his faith in God, of impatiency and fretting under this sad exercise: for, there is more cause of fear from Satan's second subtle temptations then from his gross suggestions, whereby at the back of the former gross blasphemies, he goeth about to draw the afflicted to the suspicion of the former work of grace in him, and of God's love unto him. His wiles in this case are much more dangerous than his violence in his furious lion-like assaults: for he may more easily get the consent of the afflicted to some sits of misbelief and impatience or some other sins, then to admit or consent unto any of these gross blasphemies suggested.

4. Sometime when the young and tender convert, is reading or hearing in Sermon, the sad sentences of God against such and such sins, which do reign in the wicked, Satan flyeth on him with a false application, saying, thou art the man, and doth not a little disquiet the weak in faith. In which case, let the afflicted consider, that whatsoever is spoken in or from Scripture of the maledictions of the law, are spoken against them that are under the curse of the law and covenant of works, 1 Tim. 1:8, who have not repented their sins, nor fled to Christ, nor are aiming at reformation of life and sanctification, but these curses are not spoken against the righteous, that is to say, against such as in the sense of their sinfulness do loath themselves and are fled to Christ for refuge, and have taken on his yoke upon them, already justified, and begun to be sanctified.

5. Sometime Satan doth abuse the Scripture and put a wrong sense upon it, that thereby he may wound these that are weak in the faith: For example, it is written, Rom. 14:23, whosoever doubteth, is damned if he eat. But thou (saith Satan to the young and weak convert) hast done many things whereof thou didst doubt whether they were lawful or not, yea thou hast eaten the Supper of the Lord with doubting: therefore thou art damned. Again it is written, 1 Cor. 11:29. He that eateth the sacramental bread of the Lord, or drinketh of the cup of the Lord unworthily, eateth and drinketh his own condemnation: but thou, saith Satan hast eaten the bread and drunken the cup of the Lord unworthily, for thou knowest thou art very unworthy: therefore thou hast eaten and drunken thy own condemnation. In this case and such other like, let the afflicted convert inquire of the Pastor, or some faithful Christian better acquaint with Scripture, concerning the sense of the words of Scripture, which seem to make against him, that the words being well understood, the doubt may

be dissolved. As for example, these foresaid abused Scriptures, do only declare the sentence of the law against him that doth what he doubteth to be lawful, but doth not exclude him from mercy upon the acknowledgment of his sin, and flying to the mercy offered in Christ Jesus. And by eating and drinking unworthily, we must not understand that everyone, who finding himself unworthy, flyeth to the grace offered and sealed in the Supper of the Lord, eateth unworthily, for, so no man should eat worthily, for all worthy communicants, in the sense of their unworthiness, must and do fly to free grace offered in Christ; but the meaning is, that these do eat and drink unworthily, who profane the Sacrament, and put no difference betwixt this holy banquet of the Lord, and a common supper; yea and even this sin of not discerning the Lord's Body, doth not exclude the man from mercy: for, the Apostle, for remedy of this sin, exhorteth these who are guilty to judge themselves, that so they may not be judged by God, who pardoneth the penitent, 1 Cor. 11:31. And so let the afflicted, for strengthening of his faith, know, that every Scripture which speaketh against sin, doth drive the guilty man unto repentance and faith in Christ, without whose grace, sought after and embraced, there is no salvation.

6. Sometime Satan, the adversary of all converts, doth assault the faith of God's children, when he findeth them under some present guiltiness lately contracted, or under trial of their faith, as under desertion and disconsolation, or some miserable condition, whereof he taketh advantage to suggest to the child of God, that his faith is but fantasy, that God neither loveth him, nor can love the like of him. In which case, let the afflicted humble himself before God, and fly to him in Christ offering reconciliation; let him, 1. resolve firmly to adhere to the covenant of grace offered to self-condemned sinners

through Christ. 2. Let him observe his present condition to be the day of his visitation, trial and probation what use he will make of Christ in his difficulties and straits. 3. Let him in the use of God's worship wait for the day-star of divine consolation promised to those that wait on the Lord, Isa. 49:10,11, and Hos. 6:3, and Isa. 40:31. And last of all (lest we insist too long in reckoning the innumerable wiles of the crafty serpent) let every convert consider, that there is no time while we dwell in the tabernacle of this body of death, wherein we may be secure from Satan's insinuations and crafty suggestions, or his more discovered and open assaults; that there is no business we can go about wherein this crafty hunter shall not dig a pit or lay a snare to entrap us, no affliction nor difficulty, wherein he shall not study to keep us back from making Christ our refuge, our helper and deliverer: and that therefore we must take heed to obey the warning of the Apostle, Ephes. 6:10-13. Finally, my brethren, be strong in the Lord and in the power of his might; put on the whole armor of God, that ye may be able to stand against the wiles of the devil, and so forth to the end of the Chapter.

CHAP. XXX. - Wherein are some mixed cases spoken of, whereunto the true convert is subject, and so may fall to doubt of his conversion or interest in Christ.

THERE ARE, BESIDE THE cases whereof we have given some examples and instances, other cases also, which we may call mixed cases, the causes whereof are partly natural, partly spiritual, wherein the true convert may be afflicted with both bodily and spiritual distempers; melancholious humors abounding in the body, and Satan, busy to stir himself in these distempers to the weakening the faith of the convert, may take advantage to vex the child of God.

2. These bodily distempers are common both to the unrenewed and to the regenerate: for, God hath not exempted his children from

diseases of the body; for, the righteous and the wise, and their works, are in the hand of God; no man knoweth either love or hatred by all that is before him: all things come alike to all, there is one event, (or accident which may befall) to the righteous and to the wicked, to the good and to the clean, and to the unclean; to him that sacrificeth, and to him that sacrificeth not; as is the good, so is the sinner, and he that sweareth, as he that feareth an oath, Eccles. 9:1,2. Saul the King of Israel in his melancholious fit, may (by the instigation of an unclean spirit, changing himself into an angel of light) fall on prophesying in the midst of his house, while he is about to murder David, 1 Sam: 18:10, and experience hath showed, that some lying in gross sins, who while they were themselves and in their wits, were found very rude and ignorant in matters of religion and things divine; but sometimes suddenly falling in a melancholious ecstasy and rapture, they could rehearse a number of passages of Scripture, and seemed to pray, and to bring a number of arguments in their praying, as if they had been wrestling with God for mercy, of which Scriptures or words of prayer, they had neither sense nor memory, when they came to themselves, after the melancholious ecstasy was over, which sit lasted sometimes an hour, sometimes two or thereby; all which time they neither did hear nor see the witnesses sitting by, and beholding the spectacle. On the other hand, experience hath showed how far Satan may abuse and hath abused the fantasy of some holy persons, in the height of sharp fevers and frenzies; and what speeches against God and their own souls, by his instigation they have uttered. We have an example in Job, who in his hot fever and painful boils, like a man distracted, cried out, that God was turned an enemy to him, that he did shoot all his arrows against him, whereupon in his distemper he cried for death, and cursed the day of his birth most bitterly. Of which expressions when he is challenged by his uncharitable friends, and judged to be nothing but a wicked hypocrite, he excuseth himself, that when he spoke these words he was not himself, but in a roving distemper, Job. 6:26. Do ye imagine to reprove words, and the speeches of one that is desperate, which are as wind?

3. But our purpose here is not to discourse of melancholy in general, nor what may befall in common to the godly and the wicked in melancholious fits: for this doth require a larger Treatise, and the concurrence both of Physicians and Divines. We purpose only to speak to what the true convert is obnoxious unto; and when we speak of mixed cases, wherein both the distemper of the body and brain do concur with the temptation of Satan, we do not take notice of any light distemper of body and mind, which suddenly cometh and is soon removed, or which the private diligence of the child of God, in the use of the means may, and useth to overcome. Neither do we meddle with phrensies and madness, which so bereaveth the man of the use of common reason, that he cannot understand or make use of wholesome advice and counsel from the Scripture, or rightly conceive truth when it is told unto him (for in such a case the Physician only is to be called to deal with the diseased, not excluding the prayer of the Pastor and Christian friends for him.) But we are to speak concerning more moderate distempers wherein the afflicted may lay forth his temptations, and propound the reasons which seem to fortify his doubts and to dispute of them and receive reasonable answers to his objections, as they are offered unto him. And in a word, such a condition of the man's mind as maketh him ready to hear and follow the advice, both of the Physician and the Pastor, as his need requireth. Now it is not our, that the imagination of these who are of this middle sort of distemper, doth ordinarily fain to itself sad

and terrible things, and being fired with melancholious humors and temptations of Satan mixed therewith, useth to represent to itself God's hot displeasure, death, condemnation and hell, as it were, before their eyes; so that it is no wonder, that for the time they doubt whether they can possibly be in the state of grace. But in special, this seemeth most heavy unto them, that their conscience in the meantime doth write bitter things against them, and double upon them, the deserved sentence of condemnation, casting up the particular sins (possibly repented of, and pardoned) as meriting rejection from God. And here mainly is the stick.

2. In discerning and curing such cases, there is great need of wise circumspection: For, first, information must be had of the afflicted's condition so far as his friends and familiars can furnish. 2. The cure of his wound must be tenderly gone about, as the Surgeon useth to do, when he is to deal with the apple of a man's eye. 3. Whatsoever seem at the first, it shall be safest for the comforter of the afflicted, not to speak peremptorily of the man's state or condition, yea, nor to judge within themselves determinately about him. 4. But it shall be safest to hear the afflicted patiently, to lay out his own condition more or less confusedly, in more or fewer speeches, as he is able to express it. 5. What is further to be searched after, by prudent interrogations, let it be pumped up so far as conveniently may be. 6. So soon as his condition is clear to the Pastor, or friend who is about to help him, let the speaker unto him, recollect in few words his condition as he conceiveth it, and take up his doubt in a word as shortly as may be, that the afflicted may perceive, that his case is well taken up by the Pastor or Christian friend. For ofttimes here is the cure marred, when the afflicted conceiveth that his case is not rightly apprehended, or what is spoken, is not spoken to purpose. 7. Whatsoever his case seem

to be, Christian compassion must be showed to the afflicted, and his affliction estimate no less than the afflicted conceiveth of it, but made possible for God to cure it. For even our Lord in the resurrection of Lazarus, groaned in his spirit, in compassion toward the mourning friends, before he gave them the full consolation. And surely, compassion doth well become a Physician: for, it is an addition to the affliction of the afflicted, when the beholder cometh to him, to think little of his pain. 8. Whether the afflicted seem to be a convert or not, let him be exhorted by his present exercise to humble himself before God, and confess his original and actual sins to God, and fly to the grace of reconciliation, and remission of sins and consolation holden forth in the Gospel to every self-condemned sinner, through Jesus Christ our Lord; for, Christ is the end of the law for righteousness; when the conscience is burdened, and the rod is heavy, the curse of the law, and the rod of correction do drive the man to fly unto Christ and take his yoke upon him: And this course is wholesome and safe whatsoever be the afflicted man's estate, whether he be converted or not.

5. And as for that special stratagem of Satan, whereby he beareth in the sentence of condemnation on the afflicted, and fireth his fantasy with the continual ingemination, and inculcating of this fiery dart, crying over and over again blasphemous words, charging the afflicted with the sin thereof, and pronouncing sentence against him, saying, thou art condemned, thou art a reprobate, and such like; the afflicted man must be informed, 1. that such peremptory sentences are not from the Lord's Spirit, speaking in the Scripture, but from the false accuser of the brethren; for, God pronounceth not condemnation, but remission of sin to everyone that flyeth to Christ. 2. That he must put difference betwixt Satan's part in the sinful suggestions and

his own part in rejecting of them, abhorring them and grieving for
them. 3. That he must put a great difference between his imagination
(or fantasy) and his conscience, between the voice sounding in his
fantasy, whether he will or not, and the sentence of his well informed
conscience approving, or disallowing what is offered unto it to be
chosen or refused, consented unto, or dis-assented from, by the conscience judging according to the rule of God's Word: for, a sentence
of words may be suggested to the fantasy, repeated and obtruded
upon the fantasy a thousand times, which the conscience may and
should refuse, and reject a thousand times. We know by experience,
that a sentence of words may, by oft repeating in the ears of a parrot
and other birds, take such an impression on the fantasy of the bird,
that it shall repeat vocally the words one by one and pronounce them
distinctly, as if that sentence had been the work of its own invention:
So also we see, that by frequent repetition of any whistle or song,
the fantasy of some birds may be so beaten and informed, that they
shall chant the same song over and over again, and make it as if it
were its own. Now fantasy and imagination being a thing common
to man and beast, it is certain, that the fantasy of a man, may be
wrought upon, and stamped with the like impression. And this much,
as experience teacheth us, doth befall men: for when a certain song
or toon is sung in our audience, and is often repeated, our fantasy
before we be aware, useth to repeat and same song or toon, or quietly
whisper the notes and measure of the song or toon: And after our
judgment hath observed this work of the imagination, we can hardly
stay our imagination or fantasy, while we are about other serious
thoughts from its secret sowthing of the measures and notes of the
song: for, fantasy will not be ruled by the laws of reason, more than
the outward sense of seeing can be hindered from observation of

what it seeth, whether pleasant or displeasant. What wonder is it then, that Satan who hath great influence on men's imagination, doth make so deep impression on it by continual iteration, that the afflicted seems to himself to own those blasphemous suggestions as his own thoughts, and as the voice of his conscience, and yet they are indeed nothing but Satan's whistling, and false sentences pressed on the man's imagination? And put the case, that his deluded mind should take them for the justly deserved sentences of the conscience, yet are they only the voice of the conscience ill informed, not judging of the matter according to the rule of God's Word, which doth not impute Satan's suggestions to the soul afflicted by them, and mourning for them. And so much for solving of the doubts of the true convert concerning his state in grace and regeneration.

CHAP. I. - Concerning some premises.

WE HAVE HANDLED SOME examples of those cases of the conscience of a regenerate man, wherein his state whether he be converted or not, is brought in question. Now, follow some examples of those cases which concern his condition. In which cases, albeit the state of the convert, be not at the first brought in question, yet his conscience may be deceived, and miscarry for a time to his detriment. Of which cases that we may speak the more clearly, some considerations must be premised and taken along with us.

1. A man's state and his condition sometime are taken in a larger sense indifferently for the same thing, as when we say that all the regenerate are in a blessed state or good condition, and that all the unregenerate are in a miserable state or in an evil condition: But when we put difference betwixt these two in a more strict sense, a man's state is that relation of his person wherein he standeth either as a child in grace, or as a child of wrath. In which sense every convert is said to be in the state of grace: and every unregenerate person is said to be in the state of wrath, judicially declared such in Scripture.

But the condition of a man is his present moral disposition in order to his exercising of virtue or vice, better or worse. In which sense the renewed man, or true convert, is said to be in a good condition, when he is going about the duties of religion and righteousness, as becometh a renewed man; and said to be in an ill condition when he is other ways disposed, and exercised for the present. And in this sense an unrenewed man, is said to be in a better or worse condition for the present, in comparison with other unrenewed men, or with himself at another time. In which sense, Mark, 12:34. Christ speaking to the Scribe who answered him in all things discreetly, saith, thou art not far from the kingdom of heaven. The condition for the present of this Scribe, was better than his fellows, and better then his own at another time, and yet his person was in the state of wrath, because he was not entered in the state of grace, or in the kingdom of heaven, howsoever he was not far from it. In this more strict sense the judicial state of the man's person is fixed so long as the judicial sentence of the Judge (binding the unconverted to the curse that is pronounced in the Law, or in the Gospel lousing the converted from the curse) doth stand.

But the moral disposition and the condition of the man, whether in the state of grace or nature, is variable and changeable to the better or worse, in comparison with others, or himself at another time. Whence it is, that one and the same person may be in a better or worse condition, his state remaining the same, to wit, good, if he be renewed, and evil if he be still in nature unrenewed.

2. But here we are about the condition of the renewed man only, which may be better at one time, and worse at another time, as his disposition and carriage, in order to the duties of religion and right-eousness, falleth out to be better or worse, according as his actions and behavior are more or less conform to the revealed will of God, and as his conscience doth its duty more or less commendably. Some-times his conscience upon good grounds speaketh good to him, while

he studieth to walk before God unto all well-pleasing, and then he may say with the Psalmist, Psal. 26:12. My foot standeth in an even place, in the congregation will I bless the Lord.

To this good condition we need not say much, because there is no present disease which calleth for cure of this case. Only it is for the child of God in this case necessary to observe diet and exercise to maintain his good condition, and to watch over his heart and ways, that he may continue and go on therein. All that we have to deal with, is the ill condition of the true convert, when his conscience doth deceive him, or doth not discharge its duty: for, in this case only remedy and cure is called for.

3. As that condition wherein the convert is best pleased with himself, is not always the best; So neither is that condition wherewith he is worst pleased, always the worst: But that is the best condition, wherein the holy Spirit doth most bear down the power of sin, and advance the work of sanctification of the man; and that condition is the worst, wherein sin most prevaileth. And as the goodness of a man's condition, is not to be estimate by any eventual accident, but by its own nature and proper effects. So the illness of a man's condition, is not to be estimate by any eventual accident, but by its own nature and proper effects, as God in the Scripture giveth grounds of judgment of a good or ill condition: for other ways, by the default of the renewed man, the best condition may degenerate in a very ill condition. As when a man doth abuse divine consolations, and after receiving of the renewed earnest of the inheritance, from the holy Spirit, groweth carnally secure, and negligent in his duties, or when after some gross pollution of himself in body or soul, having grieved the holy Spirit, he doth not humble himself as became him, but by Satan's suggestion of wicked thoughts against God and his former

work in him, doth fall in suspicion of all former gracious operations of the holy Spirit in him, and mis-calleth all these former experiences; and in his temptation esteemeth and nameth them, among Satan's delusions, or else at least suspecteth and feareth they shall prove no better than such. On the other hand, the worst conditions of the renewed man, by the wisdom, mercy and power of God may be turned to advantage in order to God's glory, and the renewed man's salvation, as the experience of the Psalmist doth show us, Psal. 116:3,4. &c.

4. An evil condition is so called, either, 1. in respect of the evil which the convert not only feeleth really, but laments it seriously; or, 2. in respect of the converts estimation only, who laments his good condition without cause; or, 3. in respect of a real evil, which the convert lamenteth not at all, but lieth under it securely. Of the first sort is the condition of the convert when he seeth his own blindness, nakedness and misery, the hardness of his own heart and the deceitfulness of it, and doth fly for remedy thereof to Christ the true Physician, to cover and cure all his diseases. This condition is evil only in respect of felt evil, but in respect of the converts making the right use of the discovery of these evils, and flying unto Christ for relief therefrom; it is a good condition, because the diseased convert carrieth himself well and wisely in this exercise. Of the second sort is the converts condition, when his faith is put to trial by manifold afflictions and temptations, and he conceives himself to be in a very evil condition: wherein he ought not to afflict himself, but to judge this condition to be a good condition, according to the Apostles exhortation, Jam. 1:2,3. My brethren, count it all joy, when ye fall in divers temptations, knowing that the trial of your faith worketh patience. Of the third sort is the condition of the convert, who when (for example) he feels

himself unapt and unable to pray, or praise or discharge any duty heartily, doth not trouble himself with this his ill case, but either layeth-by the doing of the duty, or doth the work negligently and perfunctoriously, and pleaseth himself in so doing for a time. This condition is evil indeed, both in respect of his spiritual diseases, and of his sinful slighting the duty of seeking relief thereof.

5. For rectifying the judgment of the conscience in any or all of those conditions, first, let difference be put between the sinful diseases and distempers of our spirit (which are evil indeed) and the discovery thereof unto us, which is a benefit in itself, and a gift of eye-salve bestowed by Christ upon us, and the right use of that discovery by flying unto Christ, which is yet a greater blessing, even the work of God drawing us to the Savior of souls the remedy of every evil. Secondly, let difference be put between temptation, or trial of faith, and yielding to temptation under affliction. The observation of temptation offered to make us depart from the truth in trial, is a matter of joy, but yielding is a sin, and matter of sorrow indeed. Thirdly, let difference be put between grief of mind, or heaviness in affliction, and anguish of conscience for sin committed: For, a man may have a grieved mind, and a quiet conscience at one time. Fourthly, let difference be put between our sinful sickness of indisposition to spiritual duties, for which we should be humbled, and God's dispensation for the time, partly chastising us with a less and more sparing measure of ability for these duties, and partly teaching us thereby to make better use of Christ's offices for pardon of sin, for helping and healing our infirmities, then we have made. Fifthly, let difference be put between God's part and Satan's, the worlds and corrupt nature's part, and the part of the new creature. God's part is ever wise, holy, just and gracious, tending to bring his children

unto a good and better condition; Satan, the worlds and the flesh or corrupt natures part, is to procure and hold on, and make worse an evil condition; and the part of the new creature, is variable, as it falls forth in the battle against the flesh, which lusts against the spirit, and it against the flesh, so that neither of them have the victory always, till the warfare be ended, and grace be crowned with glory, for and through Jesus Christ our Lord: These differences being observed the conscience may discern between a good or evil condition so much the better.

6. One and the same convert may observe in himself, if not all, yet the vicissitude of the most notable changes of a spiritual condition, as may be seen in some, especially of his Ministers, of whose exercises he is to make use for the consolation of his afflicted people; which Ministers may say with the Apostle, 2 Cor. 1:6. Whether we be afflicted, it is for your consolation and salvation, which is effectual in the enduring of the same sufferings, which we also suffer; or, whether we be comforted, it is for your consolation and salvation.

7. Sundry converts may be diversely disposed and exercised about the same evil or spiritual disease: for one, under the observation of his evil case, may wrestle against it, and not call his own blessed state in question; another, under the same disease, may fall in question and doubt, whether he who is in such a condition, may be a true convert or not, and his person in the state of grace or not; yea one and the same convert, in the beginning of his ill condition, while he first entereth in conflict with his evil condition, may for a time look upon himself as a true convert, notwithstanding of his present ill condition; but afterward when he findeth his evil condition to remain, and not likely to be removed, he may fall in doubt about the

state of his person, whether he be a true convert or not. In which case let him make use as is said in the former Book.

8. The variety of changes of the conditions of the true convert, ariseth from the variety of the causes thereof. As for example, 1. sometime in the warfare between the flesh and the spirit, the new creature prevaileth, sometime corrupt nature: and both of them prevail sometime more, sometime less, whence vicissitude of changes of condition cannot but follow. 2. Sometime Satan's temptations, setting on in his assaults more or less furiously, or more or less subtly, do make diversity of conditions, as Satan is more or less wisely resisted. 3. Sometime the Lord hideth his countenance from his child more or less, sometime in adversity, sometime in outward prosperity, as his wisdom findeth it meet for the welfare of his beloved children.

9. Sometime the conscience doth discern an evil condition, and doth give forth a right sentence about it. In which case, let use be made of the ordinary remedy of sin and misery. As, 1. let the afflicted search into the causes which have procured his evil condition, as the Lord after prayer shall furnish light. 2. Let him acknowledge his sin and ill deserving, and the Lord's holy, wise and righteous dispensation. 3. Let him grow in humiliation, and in diffidence of his own wisdom, ability and righteousness. 4. Let him renew the exercise of his faith in Christ for pardon of sin, for mortifying the roots of it, and for letting forth his helping hand for ability to make him watch over his own heart and ways, and to bring forth good fruits.

10. When the converts conscience faileth in right judging of its own ill condition, 1. it either taketh an ill condition to be good, (and in this case it is silent and saith nothing, but lieth secure and well pleased without cause) or, 2. it judgeth a good condition to be altogether bad, or at least not so good as it is indeed; or, 3. it doth not distinguish a

good or ill condition simply, from a condition partly good and partly evil; or, 4. it stands in doubt what to judge of the man's condition, being uncertain what to pronounce of it till light dispel the mist and confusion wherein it lieth for the time. Let us instance some cases and examples in every one of these four kinds.

CHAP. II - Wherein is handled, the case of such as are fallen from their first love, and are well pleased in this case. The first rank shall be of some cases, wherein the conscience of the convert is deceived, by judging the man's evil condition to be good enough.

THE FIRST RANK SHALL be of some cases, wherein the conscience of the convert is deceived, by judging the man's evil condition to be good enough.

It cometh to pass sundry times, that the renewed man seemeth both to himself and others also, to go on in bringing forth external fruits of new obedience, when in the meantime his love to Christ is much abated and cooled toward him, in comparison of the fervency which in his first conversion he had: whence it cometh to pass, that his works in his calling are discharged without that eye and affection toward Christ, which sometime he carried toward him; for, in the beginning of his conversion, when remission of sins, reconciliation with God, and the blessed change made in his state through Christ, was green and fresh in his present sense, how dear Christ was unto him, cannot be expressed; but this fervor ofttimes doth cool, when his wonted estimation of Christ is not entertained, as appeareth in the Galatians, who at their conversion were carried with such a measure of love toward Christ, that if it had been possible, they would have plucked out their own eyes and given them to the Apostle Paul for Christ's cause, Gal. 4:15, and yet this love did soon cool, both toward Christ and the Apostle. It cometh to pass also ofttimes, that the renewed man, contenting himself with the seal of the holy Spirit, and the consolation which once he felt, resolveth to go on in the discharge of Christian duties in his calling, and either doth not observe this cooling of his love to Christ, or layeth it not to heart, but pleaseth himself, in this condition, as sufficient to carry a converted man to heaven. And so usually three faults do concur in this sickness.

The first is a notable defection from aiming at the measure felt in his first love at his conversion: for we speak not here of daily distempers which the convert doth mark and mourn for, and is about to have healed by bringing his wounds unto Christ to be cured in the exercise of faith and repentance daily.

The second is the not observing of this decay of love, or the man's ignorance of his duty to entertain communion with Christ in the sense of his daily sins, wants and wounds; for the removing and curing whereof, Christ is to be loved daily no less then at the man his first conversion.

The third is, the man's being well pleased with this condition so long as his conversation is blameless, whereof we have an instance in the condition of the Ephesians, Rev. 2, whose labor in the work of the Lord, zeal against hypocrites, patience in troubles for Christ's cause is commended by Christ. But he reproveth them, first, because they had left their first love, and did not only come short of the measure of their first love, but did not lay to heart this sin, did not repent it, or take course to have that measure recovered; thou hast left, or laid down, thy first love, that is, 1. thou hast remitted and come short of that measure of love which formerly thou had. 2. Thou hast not been displeased with thyself in this thy defection. 3. Thou hast laid aside the care of recovering the measure of thy former love. This condition is very dangerous, as is manifest in the experience of the Galatians, who falling from their first love, did cast themselves open to superstitions and errors, and in danger to be cut off from Christ, by their defection from the faith of the Gospel once received. The reasons for which we say this defection in love is dangerous, are three; the first is this, the greatest measure of love to Christ and rejoicing in him is less than his excellency and merit at our hands doth deserve. If therefore we shall slide from our duty in aiming to hold up this measure of love to him, which we have once attained and cease to grow therein, (because his new mercies are daily letten forth upon us from day to day) in effect, we judge our first love hath been too too vehement, and so Christ is lightly esteemed of, as if he were not still to be loved withal our mind, heart and strength. The next reason is this, when love to Christ, to his Ordinances and sanctified ones, beginneth to relent and cool, incontinent the external exercises of religion and righteousness begin to fall short of this principle of love, and to go on more and more slowly, and so piece and piece to decay: for, as when a tree is smitten in the root, it may retain for a time green leaves, but after a time it withers, and neither beareth ripe fruits nor leaves: So also in the exercise of piety and righteousness, if love toward God our Redeemer, and delectation in his service and obedience inwardly be diminished, it may readily come to pass, that the very outward works, yea and the profession of duties due to Christ, be taken away also: and this is the judgment wherewith Christ doth threaten Ephesus I will come upon thee, and remove thy candlestick out of his place, except thou repent, Rev. 2:5. The third reason is, because Christ, who is altogether lovely and love itself, the very Son of the Fathers love, is a jealous God, and cannot long endure not to be met with love from them to whom he hath manifested his love. Therefore he doth make hast to correct this slighting of his love, and to manifest his wrath against these that lie still well pleased with themselves under this condition, I will come unto thee quickly (saith he) and remove thy candlestick, Rev. 2:5.

2. That the conscience of the true convert, who is lying in this condition, or is declining from his former measure of love, may discharge its duty more easily and solidly, it is needful that the man, being convinced of his fault, first consider, how reasonable it is that he should return to his first love, or formerly felt measure of it: for, the forgiveness of his manifold sins, wherein he lay before his conversion, for the translating of him from darkness to the glorious light

of Christ's Kingdom, should never be forgotten; the proof which he hath gotten by his conversion, that Christ hath loved him and given himself for him, should be always called to mind with hearty affection; the great need of Christ wherein he standeth for renewed pardon of sins, for furnishing him with his Spirit to mortify the deeds of the flesh, and to bring forth more ripe and abundant fruits of new obedience, should bind him to abide and grow in his love. Secondly, let him consider how useful and profitable unto us, is fresh, green and growing love unto him; for, love to him, makes us frequently to think of him, frequently with delight to speak of him, to seek after more and more near-communion with him, to have our conversation with him in heaven, where he sits at the right hand of the Father, and to live in heaven, where our love is, more than where we sojourn in this world. Love makes us love what he loveth, and hate what he hateth; love sharpens our desires after God in Christ, kindles and enlarges our affection toward him, as the beginning of the 63rd Psalm doth make evident. And if the Lord shall seem to with-draw himself, love makes the true convert follow hard after him. Psal. 63:8. Love makes bold to encounter all difficulties and troubles which may meet us in the course of following after him; much water cannot quench love; in God's service, love keeps a man unwearied, strong and stout against his enemies, in suffering patient, in profession sincere, in pursuing duties constant, in all conditions submissive, and after evidencing of his affection with the Psalmist, (Psal. 116:12) to say with the same Psalmist, What shall I render to the Lord for all his benefits toward me? Psal. 116:12. Thirdly, let the convert who is begun to cool in his love to Christ, call to remembrance what a felicity he felt when he entertained love to Christ, when the loving kindness of the Lord was better to him then his life, and sin was more formidable than death, when God's Commandments were not grievous but the joy of his heart, when God's Word seasoned and sanctified his bitterest afflictions. Fourthly, let him consider at what a loss he is of many spiritual comforts, whereof he hath deprived himself, and in how many sins (of omission at least) he hath fallen, since his declining from his first love, and what miseries he hath drawn upon his own spirit at least, if not also temporal chastisements joined therewith: and after comparison of his condition when his love was servant, with his present condition since his fall from his sometime-measure of love, let him humble himself before Christ and fly in unto his rich grace, as a true penitent, and let the fear of wrath, in case he set not himself to recover what he hath lost, hold him up to his duty; for, this is the remedy which Christ himself doth prescribe, Rev. 2:5,7.

CHAP. III. - Concerning the converts sinful conniving at, and tolerating of, the errors and transgressions of others.

THE LAW OF LOVE toward God and our neighbor, layeth a tie on us to procure and promove the well-fare and good of all men, according to our place and power, and to hinder the provocation of God and sins of our neighbor, according to our place and power. And to this end, the Lord hath said, Lev. 19:17. Thou shalt not hate thy brother in thine heart, thou shalt in any wise rebuke thy neighbor, and not suffer sin upon him. Cains answer to God, saying, Am I my brothers keeper? Doth not beseem the child of God: and yet some of the Lord's renewed children in some cases, do seem to themselves to have done their duty sufficiently, if they for themselves profess the truth, and do in their own personal carriage, what they conceive to be right, albeit they tolerate others to profess, teach and practice what is false and dangerous, and pernicious to themselves and others. This fault may befall not only Magistrates and Pastors, Parents and Masters of families, Children and Servants, but also be found in all and everyone, who do defend or excuse such an ungodly and dangerous toleration which may provoke God to wrath and ensnare many in a course of sin. The pretenses, excuses and deceits whereby men delude themselves in this sin, are the same which the Patrons of loose and licentious toleration of every error in religion do make use of, to wit, that men's consciences must be free in the matter of religion, and no ways be urged to use all means which may give them right information, and restrain their expression and practice which may infect, pervert or ensnare others among whom they live: for, say they, God's people must be a willing people, and God only is Lord of the conscience: and a curbing of men's profession and practice, serves not to make men religious, but hypocrites also, and such like other pretenses; but no excuse of this sort can justly hinder any, who is in any place of authority, or power, or relation, to be active or concur to extinguish the incendiary fire which may devour the house of God, and Kingdom wherein they live: for, whosoever have power over others, and do not put forth their power to curb and repress those who lay a stumbling block before others, do not only not impede the growing contagion and infection of the body wherein they live, but also in effect do countenance, protect and promove the spreading of the contagion of error and wickedness which they do tolerate, yea and private persons, who do not lament the sins of such as do destroy themselves and infect others, and do not mourn for the sins of them also who should repress the contagion, do make themselves accessory to these spreading evils. It is true, many excuses might here be alleged, which we leave to those who have answered the objections of ungodly toleration: but the truth is, the fear of worldly inconveniences ofttimes doth more prevail for giving way to licentious toleration, then the fear of sin and wrath of God doth prevail for discharging of duty.

This was the sin of the Church of Pergamos, which did not take order with, and repress the, seducers of the Lord's people and their followers within their jurisdiction, Rev. 2:14,15. I have a few things against thee, because thou hast there them that hold the doctrine of Balaam, who taught Balak to cast a stumbling block before the children of Israel, to eat things sacrificed to idols, and to commit fornication. So hast thou also them that hold the doctrine of the Nicolaitans; which thing I hate. This was the sin which Christ did reprehend in the Church of Thyatira, Rev. 2:20. I have a few things against thee, because thou sufferest that woman Jezebel, which calleth herself a Prophetess, to teach and seduce my servants to commit fornication, and to eat things sacrificed to idols.

2. For remedy against this evil, 1. let us verse ourselves well in the Law of the Lord revealed in holy Scripture, that we may know well what are the duties which God requireth of every man in his station, and what vices he forbids, lest we mistake virtue for a vice, or vice for a virtue. 2. Let us beware of rash censuring and licentious carping at men's infirmities, as the Apostle James giveth commandment; My brethren, be not many Masters, knowing that we shall receive the greater condemnation; for in many things we offend all. 3. Let us earnestly contend for the faith which was once delivered to the Saints, Jude, v. 3, lest seducers draw away the Lord's people from the truth of Christ. 4. Let every one consider his station, place and power given to him, and prudently go about the amending of other men's faults and his own also: for other ways, a good duty may be

marred in a man's hand by imprudent managing thereof. 5. Let a man resolve to meet with difficulties in curbing false doctrine and scandalous practices, and as a wise Warrior to behave himself so, as he may obtain the promises which Christ hath promised to the victorious, Rev. 2:17,26,27. For, it is much better to displease man for his good and others, then to displease Christ, and make ourselves partakers of other men's sin and judgment, and the true convert will easily make the choice.

CHAP. IV. - Concerning the case of the true convert, falling asleep in carnal security under guiltiness of fleshly pollutions, and dreaming himself to be in no ill condition.

SOMETIME THE FLESH SO far prevaileth against the renewed work of the spirit in converts, that not only they are overtaken in a fault (Gal. 6:1) but also are, as it were, taken captive and led away for a time by the lusts of the flesh, and nearby recalled unto the servitude of some wicked concupiscence: In which condition, it is possible they lie sleeping a long time, till God waken them out of their deadly lethargy. And this condition, alas! Is very oft to be found to the dishonor of Christian profession, in these that have begun to live blamelessly, and have fallen back to the filthy puddle of their old conversation, whereby they draw upon themselves and their families God's wrath and sad judgements: Of this disease we find there were not a few to be found in Corinth, 2 Cor. 12:20,21.

2. The causes of this fearful condition are manyfold, and cannot easily be condescended upon: for, many defects and wicked motions of the heart, do usually concur with the neglect of duty, and commission of actual sins, against the direction of the conscience, at least without the remorse of conscience and true repentance, before this fearful condition fix itself on a man; and of this sinful sickness, there are sundry degrees. The first is, when the worship of God and obedience of his precepts is performed perfunctoriously, as when the confession of sin, is without sorrow for sin or remorse of sin in particulars; when prayer is made without earnest desire, to obtain the request; when deprecation of wrath is made without fear of danger; when intercession is made without sympathy and brotherly affection; when thanksgiving is offered without estimation of the benefit received; when singing of psalms is discharged without melody and harmony of the heart, when conference of holy subjects is not entertained, or discharged slightly, and without reverence; when the hearing of the Word is without attention of the mind; when the reading of the Scripture is followed without endeavor to profit thereby, without observation of the will and providence of God for edification; when the profession of religion is without zeal and fruits suitable as occasion doth offer: whosoever doth rest well pleased with himself in this case, he is overtaken by this malady.

The second degree is, when this evil goeth further on, and doth defile the outward man: as when the tongue is not bridled, the man doth not take heed what he speaketh, but lets idle speeches, profane and rotten communication fall out of his mouth, which do not only not serve unto edification, but serve also to corrupt the hearer. And he that pleases himself in this case, declares his religion vain in so far, Jam. 1:26.

The third degree is, when this evil breaks forth in grievous scandalous practices, as in the open profession of some error, in making or fomenting a schism, in contention, emulation, envy, drunkenness, lasciviousness, fornication, or such like: for here, dead works do openly appear, and the garment of Christian profession is openly defiled. This seemeth to be the condition of many in the Church of Sardis, in whom, beside the profession of Christian Religion, little spiritual life was to be found. And therefore Christ, the searcher of hearts, calleth them dead or ready to die, Rev. 3:1,2. Thou hast a name that thou art living, but thou art dead, or in a deadly condition tending to death certainly to follow, if it be continued in, from which condition our Lord doth except some, who had not defiled their garments, but so carried themselves as their conversation was answerable to their holy profession, ver. 4

That this deadly sickness may be cured, 1. it is necessary that the conscience of such a secure sinner, be wakened both by others and by himself, and that by setting his sins before his eyes, together with the merit thereof, and the wrath of God kindled against him, and destruction at hand if he do not speedily repent him. 2. Heed must be taken of Satan's wiles, that the wakened and convicted sinner despair not; for in this case there is no small danger of it, when he who had given his name to Christ, findeth himself to be in Satan's camp and service, and wearing the badge of Satan in giving so public scandal to the people of God. 3. Whatsoever spunk of faith or hope, or repentance, or desire of returning unto God, and setting himself against all sin hereafter, is found in such a person, must be entertained and fostered, lest that little spunk be extinguished which is ready to die. 4. Let him call to mind the Word of God whereby he was first moved to turn unto God, add to consecrate himself to the service of Christ, and let him compare his sometime better conversation, with his late pollutions, that he may be ashamed, and hast himself in unto nearer fellowship with God, from whom he hath so filthily and fearfully made defection. 5. Let him be upon his guard and watch over his heart, lest he be overtaken again by the temptations of Satan, his own corrupt nature, and the enticing example of the world, lest he perish in his transgression, if he shall again provoke the Lord. 6. And last of all, let him set before himself the ample promises which Christ hath made to a victorious wrestler of this kind, Rev. 3:5. He that overcometh the same shall be clothed in white raiment, and I will not blot out his name out of the book of life, &c.

CHAP. V. - Concerning the converts pleasing himself in his luke-warm condition.

IT COMETH TO PASS sometimes, that the true convert, being as he conceiveth sure of his own salvation, becometh negligent in the matter of his sanctification, and worshiping of God in the spirit, and turneth himself about to his own ease and following of what he thinketh lawful: for, because he conceiveth he hath a sure grip of Christ's grace, and of the gifts and benefits flowing from him, so as he needs not now to vex himself in the exercises of religion as sometime he did when he was not sure of his reconciliation with God; therefore he judgeth it sufficient, if he do follow the exercises of religion more coarsely, eschew gross scandalous outbreaking's, do some works of alms and charity, as he hath occasion, and follow the works of his calling blamelessly, giving the rest of his time to be spent in worldly cares, ease of his flesh and lawful recreations. In which condition he pleaseth himself very well, as if he had attained the way of Christian felicity both in soul and body: For he misseth nothing in matters spiritual and necessary to salvation, he is rich and hath need of nothing. Whereupon he troubleth not himself to grow in sanctification, or to set others on work, for adding one virtue to another, if they trouble not the peace of the Church, or do not disgrace religion by a scandalous life: If any man in Christ's matters, will be more earnest then his neighbors, he doth not find fault with it, but let him be as diligent as he pleaseth, for he resolveth not to oppose any man in Christ's service, nor to press any man to mend his pace in Christ's way, and to say the matter in a word, he is a luke-warm man, neither a real and efficient friend to Christ, so long as he lyeth in this condition, nor yet an open adversary of Christ or his ways. In this sickness readily do they fall, who after that the pains of their new birth, and difficulties in their reconciliation are past, do imprudently lay hold upon their liberation from the terrors of the law, and dream of so sweet rest in their conscience flowing from the Gospel (as if now their enemies being all put to flight, and their bonds wherewith they were bound, were all loosed, broken and laid aside) they might compose themselves to security and sleep, when indeed they should stand upon their watch, and upon their guard, least some other way the enemy should set upon them, and catch them in new snares and straits, as the Apostle doth fore-warn, Ephes. 6:13,14. This was the condition wherein some converts in the Church of Laodicea, Rev. 3:15,19, were fallen: for albeit we do not think, that all these who are charged for luke-warmness, were regenerate, yet we cannot judge that all the regenerate and true converts, were free of this sickness, when we see Christ professing his love to the luke-warm, and out of love directing his reproof toward them, whereby he doth invite them to repentance, and to return to that sweet communion with himself, which they did not follow after, for the time. And to make it appear, that true converts might fall in this lukewarmness, he giveth warning to all that have ears to hear, to hearken unto what the Spirit doth speak unto the Churches.

As for remedy of this sickness, this lethargy is hardly cured, except the patient be first casten in a sever (as it were) by the wakening of his conscience. To this end let the luke-warm consider with himself, how the Majesty and excellent worth of Christ hath been flighted by this his lukewarmness, wherein he hath by his fleshly security made no account of the spiritual riches of Christ, who hath redeemed his own from sin and wrath everlasting, that they may with full bent of affection serve him. 2. Let him consider how intolerable this disposition of lukewarmness is unto Christ, who preferreth the open hostility of aliens, to the luke-warm condition of those who profess for him, and hath declared he will not comport with them, but spew them out of his mouth, except they shall speedily repent. 3, Let him consider how many and sad plagues of heart he lieth under if he examine himself well, which may certify him of the flame of God's wrath ready to follow on the smoke of begun spiritual plagues. 4. Let him be speedily humbled before the Lord for his vain gloriation of self-perfections, and supposed need of nothing, when indeed he is blind, naked and miserable. 5. Let him lay hold on Christ's love and care of him in calling him to repentance before further wrath should break forth, and take the offer of renewed, and more intimate communion with him, and enjoying these precious promises, laid up for the victorious wrestler against this sinful disposition: for, this is the proper remedy which the great Physician prescribeth for healing this deadly sickness, Rev. 3:17,18.

CHAP. VI. - Concerning such converts as lean unto the props of carnal confidence and please themselves in this condition.

OFTTIMES IT COMES TO pass, that true converts, while they conceive that they trust in Christ only, are found to lean too much on their own worth and strength, and graces bestowed on them. In which condition, by so much as they are well pleased with themselves, they do in so far displease God, and do provoke him to jealousy, and they who are most overtaken with this sickness are most senseless of it, and are most malcontent, that any man should suspect them, to be in an evil condition; yea, and they conceive, that no man is able to convince them of self-confidence, and here they lie over till God bring them to trial, wherein their mistake is made clear unto them. Their trial ordinarily cometh by some affliction, by some powerful temptation, and by some degree of felt desertion: for, this sickness, as it is contracted by prosperity, So it is fostered, and hid by prosperity, till the prop of their carnal confidence be shaken by unexpected adversity. Of which purpose, that we may speak the more clearly, we shall point forth two sorts of this carnal confidence, and shall show the difference of those two sorts, by the difference of these two pillars whereupon carnal confidence is upholden. The one is the common benefits, which God doth ordinarily bestow on good and bad, renewed and unrenewed persons. The other is, some observable measure of the operations and fruits of the holy Spirit.

As for confidence in the common benefits of God, sometimes true converts fall too much in love with earthly and temporal benefits, do seek too much after them, embrace them greedily when they obtain them, rejoice too much while they enjoy them, fear too much to lose them, and mean time do not perceive the excess of their affection about them; and if they be charged as in any measure guilty in this case, they will not acknowledge their fault, but go about to purge themselves of this sort of failing, saying, we know our duty, that if riches increase we should not set our heart thereon, that we should not love too much our own children, parents, parties, friends and comfortable relations, that we should not delight too much in prosperity nor glory in the common gifts and enduements of the mind, wherein ungodly men may excel, and go far above us; that we should not affect too much the favor of men, or esteem too much of being honored of men. They will also readily confess, that they are not far from the danger of being drunk with prosperity, and falling into the sleep of carnal security, and leaning too much weight on this weak pillar of creature-confidence: But for time by-past they are ready to aver, they have been very cautious, lest they should fall in this fault, and for time to come, that they hope to watch against all snares of this sort, and so they think all is well; but when it doth please God in his wise dispensation to change their outward condition, and to turn their external prosperity in adversity; when God takes away the comfortable benefits which he had bestowed on them, and brings upon them some sad calamity, incontinent they are in the dumps, and sit down astonished, they begin to call God's love in question whereof they boasted before. Thus their faith discovereth its weakness, and the mixture of carnal confidence with their faith doth clearly appear, which before did lurk as dross doth in the gold or silver before it be purified, which doth give the mass a greater bulk without greater worth or price. This infirmity and mistake the Psalmist did observe in himself, Psal. 30:6,7. In my prosperity I said, I shall never be moved; thou didst hide thy face and I was troubled. This infirmity of the convert, and his mistake, shall be yet more manifest, if we shall compare the confidence of the convert in the promises of God for food and raiment so long as God giveth riches, with their confidence when their means do fail and poverty cometh on. The promises of God remain the same in the having and wanting of riches, but there is a great odds between their confidence to be furnished when they have riches and their confidence when means do fail, which confidence now, is very feeble. Wherefrom doth this change come let us see? Certainly it cometh from the removing of the carnal props of their confidence: for when upon the failing of these props and pillars, faith in the promise doth stagger, it is a sure evidence, that they have leaned too much weight on the means, who mis-believe when the means do fail.

3. For curing of this sort of carnal confidence, and leaning too much on temporal benefits, let the convert thus mistaken, after his experience felt, that he hath been carnally confident, not be discouraged, as if his confidence, which he seemed to have placed on God, were altogether vain, and in no degree spiritual: but let him, first, be humbled

before God, and submit himself to the Lord's rod; let him acknowledge the wisdom, justice and mercy of God, who hath removed this
prop of carnal confidence, and reduced him from going astray to depend more on God then he hath done. 2. Let him strengthen his faith
in Christ, according to the tenor of the covenant of Grace, and that
so much the more as he finds his own unrighteousness, in following
and relying on creature-comforts to have been great. 3. Let him set
his affections upon things spiritual, which are above the earth, and
to be found in Jesus Christ, who is at the right hand of the Father, Col.
3:1-3, and to lose his estimation and affection from these things that
are on earth. 4. Because this sickness is not well observed, except in
the time of adversity, let the afflicted person approve himself in the
point of sincerity of adherence unto God, by his trusting in God now,
when he wanteth means and creature-comforts, as Job did, who in
this condition blessed God for the giving of the benefits, and blessed
God at the removing of them from him, Job. 1:21. For, by so doing,
he shall learn both to have and want, and in every condition to be
content, as the Apostle was taught, Phil. 4:12, and this is for the first
sort of carnal confidence.

The other sort of carnal confidence, is that which too much leaneth
to some apparent measure of the operation and fruits of the holy
Spirit, observed by the convert in himself: and this sickness may
be taken up and perceived chiefly by comparison of the converts
stronger confidence of the love of God toward him, so long as he can
find evident signs of his regeneration, and work of the holy Spirit in
himself, with his weaker confidence of the love of God toward him
under the cloud of desertion, or under some powerful temptation,
when these evident signs of his conversion are darkened, or do not
appear so clearly unto himself as they did before. In which case, his

confidence is greatly weakened, and his faith not a little shaken with doubting. In both the one and the other condition, the covenant of Grace standeth fixed, and the promises of the Gospel remain the same, and the convert still adhereth to the covenant and claimeth interest in Christ, more or less confident. Whence cometh then this difference between his former confidence which was strong, and his weaker confidence now in the change of his case, being brought low? Certainly it proceedeth from the smiting of the pillar whereupon his former confidence was too much fixed: for, whensoever the mist is cleared up, and he findeth the liveliness of the work of grace in himself, his confidence convalesceth, and returns to it's former strength, as it seemeth to him; and when his graces are darkened, he falleth in a languishing weakness of faith.

This sickness is so frequently incident to the Saints, that few shall be found who are not again and again overtaken in it: for, how few are they who are not much more confident when they find a heart freely poured forth in prayer, when they enjoy the peace of God in their heart, when the love of God is shed abroad in their heart, when they find the consolations of the holy Spirit, when they observe the fruits of the holy Spirit in themselves, when the candle of the Lord shineth in their soul, and the tokens of God's savor toward them are manifest; and on the other hand, when they find their spiritual condition changed, when darkness falleth on their spirit, when they find themselves unfit for worship and unable to do service, but most of all, when they perceive tokens of fatherly wrath against them super-added unto the foresaid evils; in this case, who is he, that beside the inevitable perturbation of mind incident to those who are strongest in faith, doth not find a diminution of his former confidence, and a conflict with temptations, fears, doubts and difficulties?

Which diminution and abating of his confidence in his trials and inward exercises, doth evidently prove, that in his best condition he hath laid too much weight upon on the mutable disposition of his soul, and hath not so stuck on to the Word of God's grace through Jesus as became him.

2. That this sickness may be the more easily cleared and cured, it is expedient to answer some questions, which being discussed, may inform and edify the afflicted.

Question I.

The first question which the afflicted may propound, is this, Seeing the signs of God's favor, manifested in the bestowing and continuing of common benefits and gifts outward and inward, do certainly serve to confirm a man's faith in God, is it not very reasonable to say, that the signs of God's wrath, manifested in the removing of those benefits, do certainly serve to debilitate and weaken a man's faith?

Ans. 1. Signs of God's favor, and signs of God's wrath, are not inconsistent, because God can carry love and favor to a man, and be angry at him also for the present ill disposition wherein he is; for, love and fatherly wrath, are not opposite and inconsistent, but love and hatred are inconsistent. 2. Let it be granted, that any signs whatsoever of God's favor, may be made use of by the convert for strengthening of his faith; yet it must not be granted, that the taking away of those signs of favor, should be made use of for weakening of a man's faith: For, many things may encourage a man to do his duty, which being removed, must not discourage him, or justly hinder him to do his duty. 3. There is a great difference between the man, who never found any other sign of God's favor beside prosperity in common benefits, and the man who, beside common benefits, hath felt a work of grace upon his spirit, bringing him unto the sense of sin, and chasing him to Christ, and making him to take on his yoke. The first sort of men, can neither from the having nor wanting, or removal of common benefits, conclude eh is loved or hated, for so are we taught, Eccles. 9:1,2, No man knoweth either love or hatred by all that is before him, all things come alike to all, &c. But a man of this sort hath reason to judge, that the sending on him adversity, and wakening of him out of a fleshly and deadly security, doth speak more of God's favor to him, then his prosperity did. And this other sort of men, who have felt a work of special grace on their hearts, may make use both of their prosperity and adversity for confirmation of their faith. 4. Put case that a convert, chased unto Christ in the sense of his sin, and resolved to bear Christ's yoke upon him, shall find common benefits taken back from him in fatherly wrath; yet must he not yield to the weakening of his faith, but rather yet more humble himself, in the sense of his sins which have stirred up wrath against him; and fly in to Christ, and lay hold more closely upon his grace because God, being offended, is not pacified nor pleased, save only by flying in to Jesus Christ.

Quest. II.

Q. But what will you say unto them, whose confidence is weakened whether they will or not, whensoever they apprehend God angry against them, and especially when they feel that God, being provoked justly, removeth gifts and benefits comfortable from them?

Ans. It is not to be doubted, that the confidence of many true converts is shaken and weakened in this case: but the question is, what shall be said unto them? We answer, that they must acknowledge, that they have leaned too much upon these carnal props, the failing whereof maketh them to fall. 2. Let them be humbled yet more because of such sins as have provoked God to change his dispensation toward them, 3. Let them lean more upon the only rock of free grace in Jesus Christ offered in the Gospel, for the comfort and relief of all those, who, in the sense of sin and unworthiness, in the sense of their ill deserving, and of any measure of apparent fatherly wrath, that hereafter, however it fair with them, they may rely upon Jesus Christ, who is the only foundation to build ourselves upon, and whose grace is sufficient to help and uphold them, who have their recourse unto him in every condition, whether it be adversity or prosperity.

Quest. III.

Q. Albeit common benefits are not sufficient evidences of God's favor, yet new obedience of faith and fruits of the spirit, are sure signs of God's special favor bestowed only on the Elect: Seeing then, as these signs when they are present, serve much for the strengthening of faith, so also when they are amissing, have as great force of reason to debilitate faith, yea seeing faith without fruits is dead, may it not be concluded where no fruits are, no faith is?

Ans. If the question be of the universal want of all fruits of faith, such as is to be found in all unrenewed men, whose fruit cannot be good so long as the tree is evil, whose seeming service cannot be acceptable, so long as they remain unreconciled to God through Christ, let the question be yielded unto. But we are speaking of the true convert, in whom there is a missing of the measure of formerly felt fruits, and that in the time present, wherein by some temptation or trial, their faith is sifted and winnowed. And here indeed there is a vast difference between them that were never humbled in the sense of their sins, nor led for relief from sin and misery unto Jesus Christ, and the true convert, who hath renounced the works of darkness, and hath fled unto Christ and consecrated himself to his service, and who is set upon a new course of life, hath brought forth new fruits of repentance, faith, love and hope, and hath felt consolation in this course; and now under exercise of conscience, looketh upon himself as barren ground, doth lament his impotency to bring forth good fruits, and while he is under this exercise, liveth in a sad condition, blameless and free of scandal-giving: great odds between this man, and a man yet in nature. We grant in the unrenewed man, who is a stranger to the life of grace and true godliness, the sentence holds, No fruits no faith; but as for the convert, who hath had comfort in Christ, and brought forth good fruits in some measure, he must not reason from his present dead condition, felt and lamented barrenness, to the denying of true faith in Christ, or to the weakening of his faith, or marring his confidence further, then to acknowledge he hath leaned too much on his formerly felt fruits, and hath not grounded himself wholly on Christ, and the rock of free grace in him, but may and should maintain his faith in Christ against his discouragement, that he may be enabled to bring forth more ripe and abundant fruits.

Quest. IV.

Q. But what shall be said to humbled converts, who looking to the holy Law of God, and finding no fruits, such as should be, do pass sentence in the time of temptation, upon all their works, as unworthy of the name of the fruits of the Spirit, and then do dispute against their own faith by the Apostles words, Jam. 2:20, faith without works, is dead?

Ans. If the conscience do pronounce according to the truth as the matter is indeed, it cannot be denied but faith without works is dead; and God is greater than the conscience and knoweth all things: But when the conscience is misled by a temptation powerfully pressed in by Satan, in the time of some sad affliction, and appearance of God's displeasure, the testimony of the conscience is not a sufficient proof to infer so hard a conclusion: for, it cometh to pass ofttimes, that the convert, who liveth blamelessly, and entertaineth the love and purpose of well-doing in his heart, followeth the exercises of religion constantly, is not negligent in his calling, and is ready upon occasion offered to let forth the fruits of love to his neighbor, for all this sometimes walketh in darkness, and under desertion, seeth no light, as Isaiah 50:10. In this case it may be, he set all his works at naught, as no ways answerable to the Lord's Law. I see nothing (saith he) but sin in me, I see no fruit of true faith in me, I feel no operation of the holy Spirit in me, save the work of convincing me of sin and unrighteousness. In this case we must not give credit to the afflicted, but convince him rather of his error, and in special of his leaning too much weight on his works before this sad exercise fell upon him; for, when a convert maintaineth his faith in Christ, only so oft, and so long as he findeth in himself the fruits of new obedience, but when he hath new experience of the power of the body of death, and findeth the course of good behavior, and bringing forth good fruits to be interrupted in himself, incontinent he resiles from his confidence, such a man certainly giveth evidence, that he hath relied too much on his former felt righteousness an himself: for he doth as if he durst not for sin approach unto Christ, and so he falleth in Peters case, who looking on his own sinfulness and the brightness of Christ's Godhead shining in a recent miracle, crieth out, Luke 5:8, depart from me, O Lord, I am a sinful man: for, Peter in this case did forget Christ's mediatory office, and that he stood so much the more need of Christ's drawing near to him, as he was a man convinced of sinfulness. Another answer we give to this question, the afflicted person must not think, that he wants altogether the fruits of faith, albeit he find them to be short of the perfection which the Law doth require, albeit he find not the fruits whensoever he would exact them, albeit he find them not in that measure as he hath found them before: For as trees are not to be esteemed dead, or barren, which bring forth fruits in due season, albeit they bear not fruit in winter, So faith is not to be esteemed dead, which, as occasion is offered, bringeth forth the fruit, at one time, of mercy, at another time, of justice and equity, at another time, the evidence of zeal, at another time, of love, and other virtues, albeit when occasion or opportunity offereth not, it doth not exercise such and such virtues: yea, albeit sometimes when occasion calleth for the evidencing of such and such gracious virtues, the convert be sometime found inlaking or short of doing duty, or guilty of doing contrary to duty, faith must not be counted dead for all that: Because it may come to pass, that faith may be so wounded, and fall sick and languish, and fall in a swound, that it cannot bring forth fruits till it be recovered of its sickness, as we may see in Jonah, David and Peter, whose faith fainted, but failed not altogether: It is true, they suspected they were cut off, and gone when they were in hard exercise, but after that they did look up to the mercy of God in Christ, draw near unto him, and did show themselves alive in the Lord, and to be in the state of grace. Last of all we answer, that the regrate of the humbled soul of its barrenness and short-coming of bringing forth fruits as it would, is no small evidence of life and sense in the inward man: And of such a disposition it may be said, as it is written, Cant. 2:13. The fig tree putteth forth its green figs, and the vines with the tender grape give a good smell: For he that is fled to Christ, and laments his barrenness, is a lover of doing good works, and of bringing forth the fruits of the Gospel.

Quest. V.

Q. But how can a man maintain his faith in Christ, who after examination findeth no evidence at all of his conversion, and that all his former life hath been spent in the unfruitful course of corrupt nature; and the matter is so indeed, he hath lived after the course of this world, a stranger to the life of God and grace?

Ans. Let such a man's examination and sentence of himself stand, being according to the truth: but this sentence of himself, must not hinder him from believing in Christ or from flying to him for refuge, for remission of sin, for reconciliation, and furniture of grace to bring forth better fruits then he hath brought forth before; he hath proven against himself, that in time bygone he hath not been a regenerate man, hath not been a believer in Christ, but he hath not cut off himself from flying to Christ and believing in him for time to come: for, he must put difference between these two questions, whether I have been of the number of sincere believers in Christ heretofore? And whether I must now fly to Christ for time to come, that I may be found hereafter, and henceforth a true convert believing in Christ? His former want of good fruits altogether, doth prove him not to have been a believer in Christ for time by-past, which is the first question; and the same want of all good fruits heretofore, doth answer the other question for his present duty, and in time to come, to wit, that now except he will perish, he must fly to Christ and believe in him. In proving of this assertion, that I have heretofore for such a space of time been a true convert, I must bring forth the evidence of my faith by my works, as the Apostle James appointeth, show me thy faith by thy works, and I will show thee my faith by my works. But in proving this other assertion, to wit, I must now fly to Christ while the offer is made to me of reconciliation, left I perish; it will suffice to produce, first, my want of good fruits, and next the commandment of the Gospel, charging me to fly to Christ for refuge in time, lest I perish: And so a man must maintain the way of believing in Christ Jesus for time to come, whether he find he hath been a fertile or a barren branch in time by-gone, or not.

Quest. VI.

Q. Seeing the Apostle (2 Pet. 1:10) commands us to make our calling and election sure by well-doing how can it be called carnal confidence which in part doth lean upon good works? For, seeing assurance and certainty of our effectual calling is not attained unto, but by reasoning from our good works, that we are called effectually, and are elected, how do not our works support the assurance of faith concerning our calling and election, and so may be leaned unto?

Ans. A man may make use of his good works for confirmation of his faith, and yet not lean his confidence upon his works, but upon the grace of God, who hath called him of his free grace, and made him embrace the offer of his free grace, and given unto him both to will and to do of his free grace, and made him to be God's workman-ship, created of God's free grace unto good works, wherein he hath made him to walk. Thus grace is by God's word and working cleared up to the believer to rest upon, without laying too much weight upon the man's work: but if a man lay hold on Christ and his free grace, only then, when he observeth in himself such and such fruits of faith, and looseth or slacketh his grips of Christ when he feels deadness and indisposition to good works, justly we may call this a carnal confidence in his works: for when he ought, with Paul, Rom. 7:24,25, so much the more to fly in to Christ and his righteousness, as he findeth the body of death powerful in him, and in-born sin strong to hinder his obedience, he doth contrary ways abate of his confidence, languish and decay in his faith, and look like a departer from Christ, we must say, he putteth carnal confidence in his own works.

Quest. VII.

Q. But seeing it is impossible to persuade me of the truth and sincerity of saving faith in me, except I do observe in me, and can bring forth my good works to prove the reality of faith in me; how is it possible that I should not lean weight on my good works, seeing the proof of my faith is by my works, which proof if I have not, I am at a stand, I cannot prove myself to have been a true believer in Christ, I cannot persuade myself that I have been and am a true believer in Christ?

Ans. 1. The observation of the fruits of faith in me is not the only proof of my believing in Christ; for, the very act of embracing the offer of reconciliation made to me in the Gospel, and flying unto Christ for a refuge, when I am chased by the Law, by the conscience, and felt wrath pursuing me for sin, may be clear to me by its own light and scriptural evidence, albeit (it being possibly the very instant of my conversion) I cannot produce any fruits or evidences of my conversion past; or else what shall be said of malefactors on the scaffold presently to be put to death, and possibly not wakened in conscience before, not fled to Christ before? What shall be said of sick persons near unto death, who being self-condemned, do betake themselves in their last agony unto the grace of God in Christ offered to self-condemned sinners in the Gospel? 2. I must put difference between a reason to prove that I have believed, and a reason why I may and must now believe. The reason to prove that I have believed, is from the effect to prove the cause thereof, to wit, faith to be in me: but the reason why I may now, and must believe, is from the cause to infer the effect that should be in me: the cause of believing in Christ, is God's command to self-condemned sinners; which command I must now obey left I perish, and so if I find fruits, I prove I have believed, because I feel the love of God shed abroad in my heart, and that I love God who hath freely loved me; and here I reason from the effect, to prove that the cause of this fruit, to wit, saving faith, hath preceded and is gone before. Again I prove that I should believe, because the offer of the Gospel and of free grace in Christ's, made to all self-condemned persons, renouncing confidence in their own worth or works, is made to me, with a command to believe in the Son of God, Christ Jesus; for which cause, I may and ought to cast myself upon his grace, who justifieth the ungodly, flying to him, without the works of the Law. 3. I must put difference between my having fruits of faith in me, and my observing and finding these fruits in me: for, a true convert may have both faith and fruits; and for the time, being under trial and temptation, may be so darkened, that he can see nothing in himself but sin, and apparent wrath pursuing him for sin, as may be seen in Jonah in the belly of the fish, Jonah 2:4, and, David, Psal. 51 9,10. 4. I must put difference between my persuasion, that I have been and am a true convert and a sincere believer, and my persuasion, that I have right, reason and good warrant to believe in Christ in my lowest condition: howsoever then I find myself emptied of all signs of saving grace in me for the time, yet my persuasion, that I should in this sad condition fly to Christ and believe in him, doth serve to make me consent heartily unto the offer of the covenant of grace in Christ, doth serve to make way for my justification, and looseth all doubts and objections of Satan tempting me to mis-believe, and to run away from Christ and the offered mercy in him. 5. And last of all, I must put difference between making use of good fruits brought forth by me, for confirmation of my faith, and my putting confidence in, or laying weight on, these good fruits: for, many true converts do here fail, and do not mark the mistakes; for when they find love to God and his Saints, with fear and holy reverence, and such other like signs of grace in their hearts, and outward fruits thereof in their life, then they do believe in Christ and rejoice in him: but when at another time, they find hardness of heart, profanity and perverseness of a wicked nature in themselves, they are like to quite their interest in the covenant of Grace, and to stand aloof from Christ like strangers, when they should most be humbled and creep in to him for remission of sin, and hiding of their nakedness by his imputed righteousness. And what is this in effect else, then in the first place to lean on their works and holy disposition, as if there were merit in them, and then after in the next place to believe in Christ who hath furnished them those fruits? Whereas they should, in the sense of their sin and unworthiness, first, fly to Christ, and firmly adhere to him by faith, that out of his fullness they may receive grace for grace, according as we are taught to do by Christ himself, John 15:5. He that abideth in me, and l in him, the same bringeth forth much fruit; for without me, you can do nothing.

CHAP. VII. - Concerning the case of the convert in some point of doctrine deluded, and pleasing himself in this condition.

TO SPEAK OF DELUSION and bewitching in the general, requireth a large Treatise. It shall suffice our purpose to speak of it, as it hath place in the point of doctrine and practice erroneous: Which we describe thus, Delusion is a powerful operation of a lying Spirit, whereby he obtrudes to men some noisome error in doctrine or practice contrary to true doctrine, fairded over with sophistical deceits, and doth persuade inconsiderate souls effectually to receive the error for truth, and to defend and spread it in their rash zeal: For explication of which description, we say, 1. delusion is a powerful operation of a lying Spirit, wherein Satan in God's judgment is permitted to put forth his power in lying effectually. Therefore in all his effectual delusions, there is a concurring righteous judgment of God in loosing reins to the tempter, that by delusion, one sin in one degree, may be punished

by a following sin in a higher degree. No wonder therefore that a
lying Spirit do work more effectually when he is not restrained by the
powerful hand of God. 2. We say, that delusion is in some dangerous
error tending to the damage of the Church, and hazard of souls. And
this we say not, as if we did think, that any sin doth not draw with it,
the merit of death (for the wages of every sin is death) but because
Satan is not so busy, to spread and foment such errors, as are less
perilous, as he is active in such errors which do most tend to pester
the Church and divert the professors of religion from the path way
of saving doctrine. And to this purpose he essays all means, that he
may obscure and darken the truth, and devise and spread abroad
the most pernicious errors. Mean time he is not idle in sowing and
spreading lesser errors, that he may stir up contention and jangling
in the Church, whereby precious time, which should be spent for
mutual edification, may be idly wasted in needless disputes, and
men's minds may be prepared to receive grosser errors. Thirdly, we
put some difference between errors in doctrine and errors in practice, albeit there cannot be one error in practice, whether it be in
the external worship or government of the Church, or in outward
conversation, which being stiffly maintained, hath not some error of
judgment and doctrine joined with it, or else it should not be contrary
to sound doctrine; yet there may be an error in doctrine and judgment
of the mind, when in the outward practice the error may lie hid,
and men of contrary judgment may consent and agree in the same
practice. Fourthly, we presuppose the errors, whereof we are speaking, to be coloured and covered with fair pretenses, and to be found
deceitful sophistry: For other ways a disciple of Christ could not be
easily ensnared, if the error were seen in its own colors, if it were
demonstrate unto him with sound reason to be contrary to sound

doctrine and pernicious to the welfare of the Church, and to men's souls. For in this case, every ingenuous and honest mind, would keep off from the error as from a deep pit: But Satan setteth forth the error, as if it were no error but most consonant to wholesome doctrine, and profitable for men's souls and the Churches good. And by plausible pretenses, sets out the error so as it may seem lovely and worthy to be defended, and spread abroad by all means. Fifthly, in this delusion we are speaking of, we presuppose, that in the person deluded there is a persuasion (stronger than any probation which he hath) can support: For there the efficacy of error doth specially appear, when the lying Spirit, by probable conjectures, appearance of advantage and sophistical disputation, doth persuade the deluded soul, that the error is as sure as if by divine oracle it were revealed and declared to be a truth. How this can be, and how Satan worketh this persuasion, it is not to our purpose to make inquiry: For, lying Spirits have their own way, unknown to us, whereby they insinuate and suggest their errors unto men. It may suffice us, that the Scripture hath taught us that Satan can form objections against our faith, Ephes. 6:10-12, and throw them at us as fiery darts, and work strong persuasions in unstable or ignorant souls. Such was the persuasion of the Galatians, which the Apostle avoucheth to have been procured not by God who had called them, Gal. 5:8. Sixthly, we presuppose in a powerful delusion a bastard and misled zeal, making the deluded man ardently to defend and promove the error which he hath embraced: For, this is Satan's main endeavor, when he hath leavened with error one or more in a Church, to make all the use of them he can to leaven the Church with the same error.

And to the intent this matter may be the more usefully spoken of, three questions must be answered so briefly as may be. The first

question is, whether such a powerful delusion may befall a true convert? We answer it is possible, and experience proveth it: that it is
possible, we learn from the Apostles fear, 2 Cor. 11:3. I fear least by
any means as the serpent beguiled Eve through his subtility, So your
minds should be corrupted from the simplicity which is in Christ, He
was feared also for the Colossians, lest they should be deluded, Col.
2:4. This I say, lest any man beguile you with enticing words. And
ver. 8. Beware lest any man spoil you through philosophy and vain
deceit, after the traditions of men, after the rudiments of the world,
and not after Christ. Wherein it is clear, that this sort of delusion may
befall the Saints. Now that it hath indeed and in experience befallen
some true converts, it is evident by what Christ saith to the Church
of Thyatira, Rev. 2:20. I have a few things against thee, because thou
sufferest that woman Jezebel, which calleth herself a prophetess to
teach and to seduce my servants to commit fornication and to eat
things sacrificed to Idols. And the Apostle shows the matter evidently
to have befallen the Galatians, Gal. 3:1. O foolish, or mad Galatians,
who hath be witched you, that you should not obey the truth? Secondly, that this delusion drew deep, and was very dangerous, appear,
Gal. 1:6. I marvel that you are so soon turned from him that called
you into the grace of Christ unto another Gospel. And, Gal. 5:2, they
were in danger to lose all benefit by Christ; and, ver. 4, in danger and
on the way to fall from grace. Thirdly, the Galatians did err both in
doctrine and practice; in doctrine, because they sought to be justified
by the works of the Law, Gal, 5:4. In practice they erred, Gal. 4:10,11,
ye observe days and months, and times and years, I am afraid of you,
lest I have bestowed upon you labor in vain. Fourthly, their error
was fairded with the pretense of the truth, which made them greedily embrace the error: for, Gal. 4:9, they turned themselves back to

Mosaical rites and ceremonies now abolished under the pretense of sometime commanded duties. And, ver. 21, they desired to be under the Law, and so run themselves under the curse. Fifthly, their error was not by a light opinion held by them, but by a full persuasion, wrought in them, not by Christ, but by a lying spirit, Gal. 5:8. Sixthly, this bastard, and unhallowed zeal was evidenced both in the seducing teachers, and in the misled Galatians, Gal. 4:17. They zealously affect you, but not well: yea they would exclude you that you might affect them, that is, draw you away from the society of Christ and his true Apostles, that you might be their affectionate disciples. And as for the Galatians, deluded by Satan, by their means, they turned their ardent affection toward the Apostle almost in hatred against him, Gal. 4:15,16. Am I become your enemy because I tell you the truth?

Hence it is clear, that true converts are subject to this evil, and ready to fall in it except they watch carefully, and earnestly deal with God to keep them from deceivers: for, many young converts are like lambs and sheep, very simple, and being lately turned unto the course of holiness, they are easily taken with every appearance of piety, whereof if they do apprehend any seeming signs in seducers, they suspect no guile in wolves clad with sheep's skins, wherethrough they are overtaken unawares, and moved to separate from the society of the Saints by the fleshly authors of division, who by good words and fair speeches deceive the hearts of the simple, Rom. 16:17,18.

Quest. 2. As for the second question what are the effects and marks of such a delusion? We answer, there is a delusion active wherein Satan and his seducing instruments do set themselves on work to delude, and there is a passive delusion in the party deluded by Satan and his instruments. The effects of the deluding or lying spirit, and

the marks of delusion in the party deluded do concur; for, the effects
of Satan's powerful delusion do appear in the party deluded as signs
and evidences of the effectual delusion: These effects and signs albeit
they be many, we shall content ourselves to specify some of them.

The first and chief effect and sign of delusion, is, the rejecting of
a point of true doctrine, and the avouching of a false error contrary
thereto. This we call the first and principal sign, or mark of delusion;
because except this sign be found, other signs albeit they point forth
a perilous condition, yet without this effect and sign be joined, they
do not prove delusion in the strict sense wherein we take it here. This
sign the Apostle doth point at in the Galatians, Gal. 3:1. O foolish
Galatians! Who hath bewitched you, that you should not obey the
truth? Where he challengeth them for rejecting the truth and obedience unto it.

The second effect and mark of delusion, is a bastard persuasion
whereby the person deluded layeth hold on a most false error, as if
it were a most solid truth, and without hink or doubt rests upon it, as
if it were a divine truth: This sort of persuasion we call a bastard and
illegitimate persuasion, 1. because it is not wrought by the Spirit of
Christ: for which cause the Apostle makes the Galatians persuasion
not to be right and legitimate, Gal. 5:8. Secondly, because this persuasion neither leans upon God's Word rightly understood, nor upon
any firm reason deduced reasonably from the Scripture. Thirdly, because this persuasion of the deluded that his tenet is true, is stronger
than his persuasion of many articles of his faith, for which he hath
clear Scripture; and yet this persuasion of the deluded is not so strong
when it cometh to trial, as weak faith well grounded is, which when
the force of temptation and persecution cometh, is more able to bear
out, then the deluded man's persuasion wherein he glorieth. Upon

which ground, the Apostle doth not doubt but the Galatians, being true converts, shall renounce this false persuasion, and return to the truth which they had forsaken. Last of all, we call this a bastard persuasion, because it draweth its original and strength, not from clearness of God's revealed truth, but from the agreement which the error hath with some carnal affection, whereunto this error doth service, for which respect, carnal and corrupt reason is easily drawn to maintain it pertinaciously.

The third effect and sign of delusion, is, the causing division and schism in the visible Church needlessly; and this effect doth readily follow on the former two: for where error in doctrine, and in the rule of practice, getteth up the head, it falleth out inevitably, that the defenders of the truth and spreaders of the error, shall fall in contention and division. In which case, the Apostle doth exhort the Romans, howsoever they should pity the misled multitude, yet carefully to mark the causers of the division, Rom. 16:17. I beseech you brethren, mark them which cause division and offenses, contrary to the doctrine which ye have learned, and avoid them; which presupposeth they deserve excommunication if they be obstinate.

The fourth effect and sign of delusion, is foolishness or a sort of madness, which appeareth partly in the inconsiderate embracing of the error, and partly in the defending and promoving of it: for, if the error in itself be considered, it is a falsehood and deceit; or if we look to the hasty receiving of it, when no sound proof can be had of it, it is foolishness; or if we consider the damage which followeth the defending and spreading of it, which the party deluded did not fore-see and guard against, it is a madness, and cannot but be so: for, a false doctrine, albeit at first it may carry the appearance of piety and prudence, yet when it is compared with Scripture and rule of right reason led by Scripture, it is found nothing but vanity, falsehood, cozening and deceit, as the Apostle doth insinuate concerning the errors which in his time were sprouting forth in the Church, Col. 2:23, which things have a show indeed of wisdom in will-worship and humility, and neglecting of the body, not in any honor, to the satisfying of the flesh, that is, they are not worthy of any estimation, for they serve only to satisfy fleshly corruption of nature, as he observeth in the authors of Angel-worshiping, of whom he averreth, that they intrude themselves into those things which they have not seen, vainly puffed up by their fleshly mind, Col. 2:18. And he calleth the Galatians foolish, or mad, for their embracing of the error, Gal. 3:1, and for hasty embracing of it, Gal. 1:6. I marvel that you are so soon removed from him that called you into the grace of Christ, unto another Gospel: for there are many who after much time spent, and pains taken, upon them by faithful Pastors, do not come up to the understanding of the heads of the doctrine held forth in the Catechize, and proofs given thereof by Scripture, and yet will very readily embrace an error, and seem to themselves so well to understand it, and to be able to argue for defense of it; whose folly and madness may be seen in this, that they do not consider the bitter fruits of their error; to make a schism in the Church they think nothing of it; to rent the body of Christ they care not for it: and for this very cause, the Apostle reproveth the Corinthians, that falling in contest and contention among themselves about the excellency of their teachers, they rent the Church, the body of Christ, did despise his dominion and government, and gave his glory unto men, and did not regard the lamentable consequences of the schism; no not when they were admonished and rebuked by the wiser sort of their brethren, 1 Cor. 1:11, and 2 Cor. 10:2.

The fifth effect and sign of delusion, is the pride of the deluded, and vain gloriation in their error: for, the Corinthians gloried in men, and made it a matter of praise to themselves to have such and such men heads of their schism, 1 Cor. 3:21, and upon this ground did despise and contemn one another. And the Apostle giveth this mark of Schismatics and Sectaries, 2 Tim. 3:2. Men (saith he) shall be lovers of their own selves, covetous, boasters, proud, &c. and the followers of the false Prophetess Jezebel, did despise the Orthodox as ignorant dolts, uncapable of the high mysteries and spiritualities of the Gospel, which indeed were nothing but the deeps of Satan's delusions, Rev. 2:24.

The sixth effect or sign of delusion, is rash, preposterous and bastard zeal: This the Apostle did mark in the mis-believing Jews, Rom. 10:2. They have a zeal of God, but not according to knowledge, saith he. This preposterous and rash zeal is far more fiery and hot then true zeal in the godly: for, the error for which the deluded do strive, is the native brood of corrupt nature; and therefore it hath corrupt reason and affection stout for it, and no wonder that corrupt nature be strong to defend and advance its own birth. But true zeal is much more moderate; partly, because it is carried on with knowledge and prudence, doth fear to offend God by yielding to passions, and hath to strive against corrupt nature which cloggeth and hindereth every grace in the convert, and this amongst the rest. 2. This preposterous and bastard zeal, doth render the deluded person too pertinacious in the defense of the error wherewith he is overtaken, that rather than he will quite his error, he will embrace another error to maintain the former error for which he doth contend. And this cometh to pass, partly, by a sort of necessity, and partly, by corrupt willfulness. Partly of necessity, I say, because one absurd error being received, draweth after it many other errors: for, it is impossible to defend one error in religion, but by broaching and maintaining more errors. I say partly, by corrupt willfulness, because when the deluded person findeth himself in dispute entangled, so as he must either renounce the error which he hath embraced, or receive and maintain another error which followeth thereon, he chooseth rather to embrace the error which followeth upon his first error, wherein he was first ensnared. 3. Holy zeal loveth every truth, yea loveth other points of truth, as much as it loveth that particular doctrine of truth which discovers the error; neither will it suffer a believer, for the defense of any point of doctrine, to pass from another truth; but preposterous and bastard zeal is contrary: for, if many points of truth come in comparison and competition with the error which the deluded man hath drunken in, he will mis-regard them all rather than forsake his error, albeit he profess other truths to be more precious and necessary then his erroneous tenet. A proof of this we have in the Pharisees, who made the great things of the Law of none effect, for upholding of their own traditions, Matth. 15:6. And the same power of delusion may be seen among Papists, who will not so hotly pursue or punish so severely the breach of God's commandments, as they do pursue and punish the neglect of superstitious ceremonies. 4. Preposterous and bastard zeal, is very busy to spread and propagate an error, by all means, venting false doctrine, And such men's speeches do spread as a gangrene, 2 Tim. 2:17, and a little leaven of this kind is ready to leaven the whole lump, Gal. 5:9. In which case Christ advertised and exhorted his disciples to beware of the leaven of the Pharisees, whereby they were about to leaven the whole Church. And this furious zeal, as experience hath taught, doth spare no pains or labor to draw on more and more to the profession of the zealot's errors, as may be observed in Pharisees who compassed sea and land to make proselytes, Math. 23:15. 5. This bastard zeal of deluded persons, carrieth them to have respect unto, and estimation of, them that embrace their error, and to seek respect and estimation from them who are overtaken with their error. This was evident in the schism of the Corinthians, of whom some did choose to be called such men's disciples, other some did choose to be called the disciples of another man, and all did glory in their leaders, 1 Cor. 3:5,21. And on the other hand, the heads of the schism did glory in the multitude and excellency as they conceived of their disciples. This the Apostle observed in the seducers of the Galatians, and in them that were seduced by them, Gal. 4:17. They zealously affect you but not well, yea they would exclude you (from communion with God and us his Apostles) that you might affect them. 6. This bastard zeal of the deluded, doth drive them to disdain and contemn all them who oppugn their error, yea and to hate them, as experience did show among the Corinthians: for so soon as schisms did arise in Corinth, dissensions also did arise, 1 Cor. 3:3, and 2 Cor. 12:20, and of this evil the Apostle doth complain, Gal. 4:16. Am I become your enemy, because I tell you the truth? And this much may serve for our purpose concerning the effect and signs of delusion.

Quest. 3. The third question is, what are the causes of delusion? For answer, the causes are many and various; for some causes are principal causes, some subservient, some meritorious causes, and some promoving and helping forward of this evil: And which causes and instruments, God doth so over-rule in his justice, power and wisdom, that he turneth all to his own glory, and welfare of his Church: This we learn from the Apostle, 1 Tim. 4:1,2. Now (saith he) the Spirit speaketh expressly, that in the latter times some shall depart from the faith, giving head to seducing spirits, and doctrines of devils, speaking lies in hypocrisy, having their conscience seared with an hot iron, forbidding to marry, and to abstain from meats which God hath created to be received, &c. Where, first, he foretells, that there shall be a departing from the doctrine of the Apostles, whereof he giveth an instance of that which might seem furthest from suspicion of delusion, to wit, a putting of a religious restraint upon the use of things lawful in themselves, as marriage and meats. The authors of this delusion, 1. he points forth to be lying spirits, and men seduced by a lying spirit. 2. The way of seduction he foretells, shall be by lies spoken in gross hypocrisy. 3. Left any should wonder how this could come to pass, that any man against his conscience should dare to speak lies, he points at the cause procuring, to wit, the stupidity and senselessness of the conscience, they have their conscience seared with a hot iron. And, 2 Cor. 11:14,15, speaking of deluded seducers of the people, Such are false apostles (saith he) deceitful workers, transforming themselves into the Apostles of Christ. And no marvel, for Satan himself is transformed into an Angel of light. Where among sundry ways of deceiving, he points forth one of Satan's stratagems, to tempt men to make a show of piety and counterfeit appearance of holy zeal, and to pretend the authority of God, to delude the simple. By which delusion, whosoever are ensnared they are ready to put on the same coat; for, being deceived, they deceive others, pretending Scripture, that they may fight against Scripture; and pretending holiness and piety, that they may hinder in others the true exercise of holiness.

As to the causes of ready embracing of errors, 1. there is propension abundant in the natural corruption of the heart to lay hold on any error offered, Jer. 17:9. The heart is deceitful above all things, and desperately wicked, who can know it? Another cause is pointed forth by Christ, Matth. 22:29. You err, not knowing the Scriptures, nor the power of God. A third cause is the want of mortification; for the Apostle doth reckon heresies and schisms among the works of the flesh; and in particular, 1 Tim. 6:10. The love of money is the root of all evil, which while some have coveted after, they have erred from the faith. And concerning the instruments of delusion and division in the Church, the sentence of the holy Spirit doth stand sure: for he knoweth the evils of the heart perfectly, Rom. 16:18. They that are such, serve not our Lord Jesus Christ, but their own belly; and by good words and fair speeches, they deceive the hearts of the simple. Of such men Jude speaketh, ver. 20. These are murmurers, complainers, walking after their own lusts, &c.

As for passive delusion in seduced people, the Apostle prophesieth, 2 Tim. 4:3,4. The time will come when they will not endure sound doctrine, but after their own lusts shall they heap to themselves teachers, having itching ears; and they shall turn away their ears from the truth, and shall be turned unto fables. In which words he holdeth forth the meritorious and adjuvant causes of passive delusion, their lusts, their turning away from sound doctrine, their itching ears, and desire to hear flatterers, who by false doctrine may foster them in their lusts, and making choice of such men to be their Pastors. From this sort of teachers Christ fore-warneth his disciples to keep off, Matth. 17:15. Beware of false prophets which come to you in sheep's clothing, but inwardly they are ravening wolves, ye shall know them by their fruits. Their outward behavior and conversation will not decipher them, for they will seem innocent and harmless lambs, but their doctrine which is the fruits of their teaching and the proper work of the ministry, shall find them out: But the meritorious cause of this giving men over to be deluded, is plainly set down, 2 Thess.

2:10,11. Because they received not the love of the truth, that they might be saved, for this cause God shall send them strong delusion. This judgment, albeit it pursues unto the death only the reprobate, yet whiles in some degree for a time, it may over-take the elect and renewed persons, because some of them, sometime are found to give way to their lusts, and not to take head to the truth which by God's blessing might kill these lusts, therefore God in his justice suffereth them to be infected with a contrary error, and to eat the bitter fruits of their folly, that being corrected they may repent, and forever fall out with their carnal lusts and reject the error whereby they were infected: for God in his wisdom and justice, most holily and powerfully, doth so rule the whole exercise of his elect, that truth shall have no loss, but be the more cleared, and no elect soul perish, as Christ giveth assurance, speaking of the efficacy and power of delusion by the doctrine of false Christ's, Matth. 24:24 There shall arise false Christ's and false prophets, and shall show great signs and wonders, in so much that (if it were possible) they shall deceive the very elect. This is also manifest by what the Apostle saith, 1 Cor. 11:18,19, where he declares, that God hath decreed to permit heresies to arise, that both the truth oppugned by the heresy, and the true converts, may be made the more manifest: for by this means, the lusts and wickedness of some, is brought to light; some are chastised, some perish justly, some have their weakness and folly discovered, by being tainted with error for a time, and in their recovery out of the heresy, the grace and power of God is made more evident, and in these who shall suffer for refusing or resisting heresy, God shall make manifest (for stopping the mouth of Satan and all calumniators) that truth is more precious to his sincere disciples, then goods, or lands, or liberty or life, or whatsoever can befall them in this mortal life for adhering to truth; and of this many martyrs are sufficient proofs in all ages:

The remedy of this fearful condition.

Albeit this delusion draweth the reprobate when they are over-taken with it, unto certain perdition, as the Apostle (2 Thess. 2:10,11) expressly doth teach; and albeit this fearful plague be hardly curable, when it falleth on the elect: partly, by reason of the deep roots of carnal lusts in them, which open the way unto error; partly, by reason of the subtle sophistry of seducers, whereby honest souls are entangled; partly, by reason of new temptations suggested against returning to the truth wherefrom they are slidden; and partly, by reason of the difficulty of coming forth from the bonds of temporal judicial hardness of heart, whereby God hath chastised his child for harboring such lusts in himself as made way for the error: yet the cure of delusion is not desperate, for the Apostle giveth good hope of possible and certain recovery out of it: for, Gal. 5:10. I have confidence in you (saith he to the ensnared Galatians) through the Lord, that you will be no other ways minded, but he that troubleth you shall bear his judgment, whosoever he be.

1. For preveening and curing of this evil, the Apostle commandeth Pastors to hold forth to all sound doctrine, to preach the Word and to be instant upon all occasions, in season and out of season, reprove, rebuke, exhort with all longsuffering and doctrine, 1 Tim. 4:6, and 2 Tim. 4:1,2.

2. Let the deluded person be disputed with, that by arguments drawn from Scripture he may be convinced, as the Apostle dealt with these who denied the resurrection, 1 Cor. 15, and with these who sought to be justified by works among the Galatians.

3. Let the deluded be exhorted to examine accurately his own conscience, how he standeth affected to his own carnal wisdom and earthly lusts; for if he be proud in the conceit of his own wisdom, power or holiness, or any gift he hath received, or be led by the lust of the eye, lust of the flesh or pride of life, and come to God by prayer to solve his doubts, or to teach him the right way, he shall receive such an answer as Balaam received, and such as the Lord threateneth to give, Ezek. 14:2-4. &c, for he hath by his lusts deceived his own conscience, and made it a flatterer of himself when it should have been a grave counselor being well informed.

4. Let the deluded person be exhorted to be humbled for the sins which he granteth to be in himself, and fly to Christ for pardon, pity and help against his own known corruptions, making use of all Christ's offices in the sense and acknowledgment of his standing in need of the benefits thereof daily; for if he do not repent known sins, but go on in them against the light of his conscience, how shall he expect that God shall give him light in his doubts, or errors, who maketh no use, or an ill use, of the light he hath? And if he be in a course of grieving the Spirit of the Lord, and make no use of the grace that is offered in Christ, how is it possible that he who doth not follow Christ, should eschew to walk in darkness?

5. And last of all, let the party deluded consider how from time to time, and most evidently in this time wherein we live, God hath punished the lusts and sinful practices of professed Christians, with giving them over to their own hearts lusts, and letting them not only walk in their own counsels, and in the imaginations of their own ill hearts, but also in his justice, sending to them strong delusions, and false teachers to authorize their errors, and hold them on in the way to perdition. What wonder to see God for the light esteeming of

baptism bestowed on men in their infancy, and the not making use thereof for mortification of lusts and sanctification of life by faith in Jesus Christ, to let loose phanatick Anabaptists, to teach men to renounce their baptism? What wonder to see men's loose-living in the service of their sensual lusts, punished with letting loose antichristian Antinomians, who turning the grace of God in wantonness, do avouch whatsoever they do, it is no sin, and that they are not bound to keep the law, which Christ professeth he came not to dissolve, but by the contrary to establish it? What wonder to see men's carnal confidence in their own wit, worth, strength and ability, works and merits, punished with letting loose lying spirits to harden them in their error? And what wonder to see God punishing the abuse of the Gospel, and refusing to receive the truth in love with giving men over to the spirit of Antichrist and strong delusions, 2 Thess. 2. The patrons and propagators of such errors and delusions are called by the Apostle, ministers of Satan and false brethren, 2 Cor. 11:16, deceivers, 1 Tim. 4:1, and men who were of old ordained to this condemnation. From whose contagion and punishment, let every misled soul pray to God to be delivered.

CHAP. VIII. - Concerning the converts conscience, mistaking vice for virtue, and pleasing himself in this condition.

THIS CASE DIFFERETH FROM the case of delusion, which we have taken for erring in the matter of Religion, whether doctrine or worship, pertaining to the first table of the Law; but this mistaking conscience is in the practice of duties of the second table, when the doctrine of the duty is confessed, but in practice and action, vice is practiced under the notion and pretense of virtue, and the man is pleased with himself in so doing. Whereof it shall suffice to give three instances.

The first instance.

The first instance wherein a convert may be for a time mistaken, is, when a man pleaseth himself in miserly parsimony, and narrow scraping together of money to the hindrance of spiritual duties, under pretense of frugality and diligence in his calling, &c. Whereby he persuadeth himself, that his practice is so far from sin, as it is rather commendable and worthy to be imitate, for he conceiveth that according to God's command he is not slow in the work of the Lord, but fervent in spirit, serving the Lord, Rom. 12:11, that he is working with his hands that which is good, Ephes. 4:18, that he is providing for the necessity of his family, for which if he should not provide, he should be worse than an infidel, 1 Tim. 5:8. If the matter were found so to be after examination, true it is, frugality, diligence in a lawful calling, and provision for a man's family, are commendable; but here is the deceit of the heart found, when anxiety is found instead of moderate carefulness; when hasting to be rich is found, instead of moderate diligence in his calling; when love of money and avarice is found, instead of honest provision for a man's family. We grant also, that this mistake is not easily discerned by beholders, but yet the convert himself, after examination, may discern it, when he looketh upon the effects, signs and concomitant evils, such as are felt impediments, and hindrances of a spiritual disposition: for, this covetousness of things earthly, whereof we are speaking, doth mar the study and endeavor for things spiritual, and diminisheth the fear of sinning in the matter of gain, and taketh up the time due for spiritual exercise. In this case, carnal joy in the getting gain, is a sign and evidence of a deceived heart, and so is also worldly grief for want of success, or for not getting expected and desired gain, a proof of this mistaking.

The causes of this evil, are the too great fear of poverty, an over-high estimation of riches, a diffidence of God's providence, a doubting of God's promises to furnish his own with food and raiment, and things necessary for this temporal life: which diffidence Christ doth expressly discharge, Matth. 6:24,25. But for a remedy of this evil, the person guilty cannot seek after, nor embrace it so long as he is not convinced of his sinful condition; wherefore, for clearing a man's mind in this point, let him examine himself whether in following gain his heart be ofttimes surfeited and overcharged with the cares of this life, and made frequently indisposed for prayer and religious exercises, whether he be too much taken with gladness when he gaineth, and grief when he suffereth loss and worldly damage, whether he useth, for hope of gain or fear of life, to lie and flatter, or dare deal injustly in his bargains, whether he findeth himself slow unto exercises, of religion, but prompt and ready for secular affairs? Whether he spend the time heavily in religious exercises, and is weary of them, but can pass the time pleasantly in the affairs of this life? If he find himself convinced by shrewd signs of this evil, let him humble himself in God's sight, fly unto Christ for fastening his bargain for righteousness and eternal life through Christ; then let him not cast off his diligence in and faithful discharge of his lawful calling, but by a religious disposition of mind, and observance of all religious exercises seasonably, temper and moderate his diligence in secular affairs, and depend upon God more then he hath done for the success of his labors, and take from God loss or advantage as he giveth it, so as he may be found in prosperity and adversity submissive unto God and ready for the discharge of charity and equity, as occasion shall offer.

Another instance.

There is another instance, wherein a convert may be mistaken, to wit, when a man pleaseth himself in in the prosecution of private revenge, that he may pay home to such as have wronged him in the matter of his credit and reputation, or in his goods, or bodily harm done to him or his friends: for, this ungodly disposition he may pretend possibly, a care of following retributive justice, wherein he may seem to himself to come short, except he should watch for a recompense-giving to the person injurious; he may possibly pretend a dutiful respect to public peace and welfare of the commonwealth, of the society wherein he liveth, wherein he may seem to himself to come short if he should suffer the person injurious to him to go away unpunished; he may pretend also his own safety and security for time to come, whereof he may seem to himself careless except he make it evident, that whosoever doth him wrong shall be made sensible of his injury done; he may pretend that the glory of God requireth so much, that sins should be punished, the avenging whereof, if it should be delayed longer then occasion of revenge should offer, or till the Magistrate should take notice of it, no punishment should fall upon the injurious at all; and last of all, he may pretend the good of the party injurer, who by feeling the smart of his wrong done may be led to repentance, and made to learn by his suffering the recompense of his injury done, to carry himself more equitably toward his neighbors in all time coming. All these pretenses may bear weight in the corrupt inclination of a convert, and may harden him in his sinful course of seeking a private revenge on the person who hath injured him. And his corrupt inclination may be observed by himself, 1. by the stirring of his passion and wrath against the injurer, whensoever he doth see the party injurer or call the injury to mind. 2. By dissimulation and hiding from all men the sense he hath of the wrong received, till he find an occasion offered to be avenged on him. 3. By a stop made in his own prayer for remission of sins, by his conscience telling him, he could not subscribe the condition put in the prayer for remission of sin by Christ, which is forgive us our sins, as we also forgive them that sin against us.

The causes of this sinful condition are, 1. corrupt and unmortified carnal self-love, with a too high estimation of himself in pride, which maketh the injury seem so much greater as he hath a higher estimation of himself. 2. A defect in his Christian love, meekness, longsuffering, patience and pity, which should have their exercise specially in cases of provocation of our unmortified affections. 3. The oblivion of the commands of God, and of the manyfold sins daily committed against him, whereof if there were a due estimation had, the fountain and course of carnal revenge, should soon be stopped, that private and carnal revenge should not break forth.

When these evils are found out and acknowledged by the convert in himself, the main remedy thereof is in and by Christ, who hath died for us when we were his enemies, Rom. 5:8, and for whose cause greater sins against God, are daily forgiven to us, then are the injuries done unto us by men. 2. In this case also, the grave admonition of the Apostle should not be forgotten, Ephes. 4:26,27. Let not the Sun go down upon your wrath; neither give place to the devil: Giving us to understand, that if wrath, which draweth with it the desire of revenge, shall lodge all night with a man, the devil will lodge with it also, stirring the man up to pursue a revenge whensoever he findeth opportunity.

A third instance.

A third instance of this possible mistake of a convert, may be found, when he pleaseth himself in his carriage too much for his own carnal satisfaction in meat, drink, apparel and recreations, and here he may be hardened by sundry pretenses which he may have for his excess in the use of things other ways lawful. As, 1. that what he spendeth upon himself is of his own means. 2. That his recreations are lawful and allowed unto him of God. 3, That in all this he hath a care of his health. 4. That he doth not spend more upon himself then his rent and ability may well bear. 5. That God hath said, by the mouth of a wise King, that this course which he doth follow in allowing on himself, is the gift of God, Eccles. 5:19. And last of all, that he might seem justly a miser, if he did not well to himself when he is able so to do; and here are pretenses abundant. But if after examination of a man's own self, he shall find the abundance of earthly things weakening his desire after things spiritual, or shall find the sense of his in-born corruption laid over to sleep in his prosperity, or shall find his flesh wax wanton against the spirit, and to prevail in the conflict: or shall find his compassion toward the poor and afflicted to grow cold, and his delight in things spiritual much diminished, or shall find too great a share and portion of his time bestowed upon his body, and but little time bestowed upon the care of his soul, a wakened conscience may easily convince the convert, that matters are not so right with him as he supposed.

The remedy of this evil, is not for a man to turn unto another extremity, and to a contrary vice, as if there were no place for a wise moderation, or as if at sometimes a more liberal use of the creature were not allowed unto men, or as if a spiritual disposition of a man's spirit, could not consist now and then with any banquet or festivity: for, it is plain from Scripture, that there is a time to feast, and a time to fast, a time to labor and a time to be refreshed, both in body and mind after labor. In which prudence, the Apostle had not a little advanced, when he saith, Phil. 4:12,13. I know both how to be abased, and I know how to abound, everywhere and in all things I am instructed, both to be full and to be hungry, both to abound and suffer need: I can do all things through Christ that strengthens me. But here is the remedy, 1. that distrusting ourselves, and fearing the snares which Satan layeth for us in all things we have our conversation with Christ, and set our affections on things which are above, as the Apostle giveth direction,

1 Col. 3:1,2. Next, that we watch against the lusts of the flesh, least at any time our hearts be surfeited with meat or drink, or anything which is pleasant to the flesh, Luk. 21:34, Rom. 13:14. For we are not debtors to the flesh, to fulfill the lusts thereof, Rom. 8:12, but are bound so to care for our bodies, so as our souls have no loss thereby; for, the lusts of the flesh do fight against our souls, 2 Pet. 2:11. And to this end, let the admonition of the Apostle be well remembered, 1 Cor. 7:29-31. This I say, brethren, the time is short, it remaineth that both they who have wives be as though they have none, and they that weep as though they wept not, and they that rejoice as though they rejoiced not, and they that buy as though they possessed not, and they that use this world as not abusing it: for the fashion of this world passeth away.

Many more instances might be given, but these may suffice our purpose, who mind only to give some taste of cases of conscience in some examples, which may give light unto other like cases as they fall in.

CHAP. IX. - Of the case of conscience, dealing treacherously under pretense of liberty of conscience.

PREVARICATION OR TREACHEROUS DEALING, is strictly taken, when for a bud or bribe the conscience doth betray the cause which it should defend: and it is borrowed from the unfaithful advocate, who for a bribe doth sell the cause which he pretends to defend, and give over the plea of his client, and falleth in to the adverse party. Such is the man whose affection to some lust and worldly advantage, doth blind-fold his conscience and moveth it to speak contrary to its duty, and mean time doth pretend he is only following the light of his conscience, for whose liberty he ought to dispute; the matter may be seen in an example or instance one or two: King Saul receives a command from God to slay all the Amalekites and destroy them and their beasts; when it cometh to execution, Saul conceiveth it shall be for his honor to spare Agag and reserve him for a triumph, and that it should be for his advantage to spare the fattest of the cattle, whereof the people might make use for sacrifice; So advantage and honor do solicit him.

The people's consent who followed him, helpeth on his resolution to spare Agag and the fattest of the cattle: fear to offend the people whom he had drawn on to consent unto his mind, concurreth to the giving forth his decreet, contrary to God's command; and so his conscience being bribed, faileth against the command of God. In which resolution and practice Saul doth please himself.

The like treachery in Saul falleth forth in the matter of the Gibeonites: The Gibeonites preserved from Joshua's time, did grow in number to the detriment of the Israelites as he conceived, the oath of a covenant sworn for sparing their lives standeth up on the one hand to hinder him from slaying of them, the advantage which his kindly subject might have by killing them and possessing their lands and goods, standeth up to entice him to kill them, on the other hand: Saul being taken with the bait of advantage and honor from the people of Israel, for whom he was zealous, inclineth his conscience to mis-regard the oath of the covenant, partly because it was given without God's counsel and consent, yea contrary to his positive command, discharging a covenant with the Canaanites; partly because the Gibeonites deceived Joshua and the elders, and feigned themselves not to be of the number of the Canaanites, but men of a far country; partly because many years had intervened between the day of Joshua's covenant with them and his time, and it seemed unto Saul very unreasonable, that a rash and unadvised oath should be still in force from generation to generation; and partly also because the form of the civil Government was now changed, whereby Saul conceiving himself not to be obliged as successor to the Judges, but as King ordained at God's special direction, as free a Monarch as any in the world, and not bound by the oath of the rash swearing Judges and Elders in Joshua's time, doth treacherously seduce his own conscience, and falleth upon the off-cutting of the Gibeonites by the sword. How many are they who by such enticements, having deceived their own hearts, and for worldly gain or glory, or for eschewing of damage, do embrace errors in religion, and follow that course which most serveth to satisfy their own lusts, or is most applauded unto of them who are in power? From which sort of treacherous dealing nothing can divert, and draw back the man to repentance, except the Lord partly by disputation, and partly by Church-censures and civil punishments, shall discover unto them their treacherous dealing in selling the truth and betraying their conscience for base ends, and so bring them to repentance.

In this case, such as are pretended maintainers of liberty of conscience, but in effect patrons of licentious living after their own lusts, put in their objections.

1. Obj. It is necessary for me, saith one, to do what I do, and to think what I think; I conceive I have reason for me and am persuaded that what I do and profess is lawful, and that that is not lawful whereunto censures and punishments tend to draw me.

Ans. What necessity can be pretended for a deliberate man's actions and profession except a moral necessity of doing duty and of not sinning? Natural necessity he cannot allege for the justifying of deliberate sinful actions: For if he pretend original sin and native corrupt inclination to sin, it is no excuse for sin, but a granting himself a sinner by kind, by natural inclination and custom; or, if he pretend a civil necessity, it is either for hope of gain or fear of worldly loss, and that is but a base reason to move a man to do what is in itself sinful. If conscience be pretended, and that he cannot without sin do what is against his conscience, he must know that a conscience mis-informed cannot warrant a sinful tenet or practice: for except a man renounce the error which he hath embraced, both the error is his sin, and the profession and practice according to the error, doth make his sin double; if he pretend, that except he do as his conscience diteth unto him, he sinneth, because the conscience is the rule of a man's actions, he must know, that the conscience is not the absolute rule of a man's actions, but the Word of God must be the rule of his conscience and of his actions also. Because if he put his conscience in the place of God's Word, and not in subjection and subordination thereto, he must justify the murderers of the Martyrs, of whom Christ giveth warning, that they who kill his servants shall think (to wit in their conscience) that they do unto God good service, John 16:2. If he pretend, that upon this ground, liberty of conscience is altogether destroyed, if men living under civil and ecclesiastic Government, must renounce the light of their conscience and give obedience to men's commandments, he must know, that he is mistaken, and that the true liberty of the conscience standeth in the following God's Word, and doing service unto God. Neither doth sound doctrine tie any man to renounce the liberty of his conscience, but to renounce the error which hath blinded him, and to renounce his lust which hath opened the door unto the error which hath misled him, lest both he perish in his sin, and the society wherein he liveth be infected with the error, and fall under the wrath of God. If he pretend, that neither the will of a man, nor his conscience can be compelled: For, the nature of the conscience and will, is to determine freely what the man shall do; and the Lord's people must be a willing people, Psal. 110:3 He must know, that albeit the will and conscience cannot be compelled, yet the carnal lusts which have seduced the conscience, may be crossed and curbed by ecclesiastic censures and civil punishments, that the conscience and will, being better informed, after the discovery of the deceitfulness of their lusts, which did mislead them, they may freely disclaim the error, and their unhappy venting thereof. If he pretend, that God is the only Lord of the Conscience, and no man may take upon him that power to prescribe unto, and command another man's conscience, let him know that God indeed is the only Lord of the conscience, and because he is Lord, therefore hath he appointed his Ministers to teach men the truth, and to press the disobedient members of the visible Church with censures; and hath put the sword in the Magistrates hand to see his will done, and to punish such as refuse to give obedience to his commands, that so obedience may be procured to God the only Lord of the conscience, In which case albeit the acts commanded by the will and conscience, are curbed and restrained, yet the will and conscience, is not compelled, but is brought to a better determination of its own elicit acts, that having obtained a clearer light about its duty, it may command the outward man to say and do what is right. If he pretend, that religion is not to be propagate and pressed by force, but by the word preached, and heresies are to be rooted out, not by the sword but by the power of truth holden forth to the heretic, let him know, that there is a difference between propagation of religion among Pagans, or people not under the charge of the civil Magistrate, or Church Judicatories, and the preservation or purgation of religion among them that are within the visible Church, and under the power of the civil Magistrate.

For albeit the only way to bring religion in request among heathen nations and strangers to the covenant of promises, be that way which the Apostles did follow, preaching the Gospel to all, and receiving such as embraced the Gospel into Church-fellowship, yet the Magistrate, having civil dominion over heathen Idolaters, may after information of them by the Preachers of the Gospel, break their Idols and

abolish them, and restrain them from doing contempt unto the true
Religion, or abusing of the Sabbath, as the fourth command of the
moral law doth give warrant; yea, and may compel them to use the
means whereby they may be instructed in the true Religion. Again,
let him know there is a difference between dealing with Pagans and
strangers from the commonwealth of Israel, and dealing with these
who have given up their names unto Christ, have entered in covenant
with God, and by baptism have consecrate themselves and their children unto the faith, worship and obedience of God, and do profess
the Christian Religion, and yet go about by their errors and practices
to corrupt and over-turn the true Religion and faith of others among
whom they live: for, such may and should be not only instructed by
Sermon, conference and dispute, but also punished by the civil Magistrate for their deceiving of the people, and troubling the flocks of
Christ, Deut. 13, and Rom. 13. If he pretend, that Church-censures and
civil punishments can serve for nothing but to make men dissemblers
and hypocrites in the matter of religion, which is most odious in the
sight of God and wise men, let him know, that every hypocrite shall
bear his own iniquity: Ecclesiastic censures and civil punishments
concern the words and deeds of the outward man, that they may be
ordered so as Religion and the peace of the Kingdom may not suffer
detriment. If any man say and do that which is right in hypocrisy
and dissimulation, the society wherein he liveth is safe; but for his
hypocrisy let the dissembler answer to God for it. And yet it is not to
be presumed, that all who by censures, and fear of civil punishments
do forsake error and embrace truth, are dissemblers and hypocrites
in so doing, because they are means appointed of God for curbing
and reclaiming erroneous persons, wherewith he giveth his blessing
when it pleaseth him: for by censures and civil punishments, the

allurements which have induced them to error are cut off, such as are applause of men, vain glory, worldly advantage, sensual pleasure, and such like, wherein the erroneous have been taken as in an evil net, which being broken, the ensnared captive may come freely off his error, and embrace the truth, and take in good part the censures and civil punishment which drew him out of the snare into the right way: As we are assured by the prophesy of Zechariah, chap. 13:6. And one shall say (to wit, to the converted sectary) what are these wounds in thine hands? Then he shall answer, those with which I was wounded in the house of my friends. But whether by those means the erroneous be reclaimed heartily or in dissimulation, respect must be had to God's commands and his people's good, by curbing of vice and error, according as God hath given power to the Church and to the civil Magistrate, Rom. 13:3,4, who is appointed the minster of God for the people's good.

If he shall object, that he who chargeth him for his error, is no less subject to error, then he whom he chargeth, yea, that Governor's ecclesiastic and civil are no more exempted from the danger of erring, then private persons, yea, that the determinations of Synods and Councils are not infallible, yea, that he is persuaded the error he is charged of, is no error, but not persuaded of the truth which the reformers of him pretend unto. Let him know that the force of his objection doth assert, that truth and righteousness is settled upon the mis-persuaded sectaries part, and that the Church and Magistrate who findeth fault with him, hath nothing to persuade them of the truth, which they do press upon the sectary, and so cannot condemn or punish him; but he must know, that it is one thing to say one may err in the latitude of a possibility indefinite, another, to say one doth err in such a particular wherein he hath the light of Scripture and reason clear for him. The sectary will not deny he may err, but he will maintain that in such one or other article of his profession he doth not err. Shall he maintain his plea, that he doth not err in such a point of error? And shall not the Magistrate and Church maintain their plea, that they do not err in punishing such an obstinate erroneous person? Christ hath committed the keys of doctrine and discipline to his Church, that private persons may know Christ's will by the ministry of the Church, except he will be holden for a heathen or publican, Matth. 18:17. He hath also committed the power of the sword unto the Magistrate, who doth not bear the sword in vain, Rom. 13. And therefore let the Church and Magistrate do their duty, and let erroneous persons cease to stumble the Lord's people by their error and practice, and suffer themselves to be brought in order by such as have commission and power to move them by censures and civil punishment thereunto.

If still he will insist and allege, that by this means a Christian by censures and civil punishment, is compelled to sin against his conscience, let him know, that a scandalous sectary or licentious libertine, is not compelled at all to sin, but to say and do that which is right and to hearken to the Word of God rather than to his own erring conscience; for the scandalous sectary, schismatic or heretic lieth in a twofold sin, the one is in his spirit, believing and embracing an error, the other in his external words and deeds corrupting the minds and manners of God's people. If after conference and disputation, the sin of his misled mind cannot be taken away, yet the correcting of him by Church-censures and civil punishment may restrain and bind him up from troubling, and infecting others with his leaven and ill example; and so his sinning externally is cut off, and he made in so far to cease from evil: wherein he doth not sin in so far, because sin is not every transgression of the ditement of the conscience simply, but the transgression of the law, and ditement of the conscience speaking according to the law, is a sin. It is true indeed, that whosoever doth judge the ditement of his conscience to be the Law of God, and yet doth the contrary, must by interpretation of his deed be holden guilty of sin, because he who by fear or hope can be moved to do contrary to the ditement of his erring conscience, in effect doth profess he may be moved by hope or fear to do contrary to the ditement of his conscience well informed. Mean time it is expedient, not only for the good of the society of God's people, but also for the good of the erroneous person himself, that he be curbed and hindered, by these that have lawful power, from doing yet more harm, and restrained from following the course of sin and filling up the full measure of sinning, which he was about to do.

CHAP. X. - Of such as do please themselves in a condition not pleasing God, because they conceive they can pray well under any condition.

SUNDRY THERE ARE, WHO think their souls to be in a good case and condition, when they can pray much, and that with freedom of spirit, when possibly they do not watch over their hearts, nor ways as becometh them.

This sickness even converts are subject unto sundry times, but it may be most clearly seen in those, who put a sort of worth and merit in effect, upon their religious exercises, as we may see in many Israelites in Isaiah time, chap, 58. They did reckon themselves among them that did seek God daily, who delighted in his ways and did approach unto him, ver. 2, yet because God did not grant their petitions, they fell on chiding him, ver. 3. Wherefore have we fasted (say they) and thou seest not? Wherefore have we afflicted our souls and thou takest no knowledge? The history also of Korah, Dathan and Abiram is notour, wherein we see what esteem Korah and his accomplices had of their own holiness, and of their access to God in their prayers that they durst hazard and lay their lives in pawn, that God should make them as welcome when they came with their censers to pray before him, as Aaron and Moses, yea and more welcome than they.

Such a sort of deceit is that whereby some fanatics, enthusiasts and heretics do foster themselves in their own folly, and imagine they are no small men in God's account, because they find a sort of eloquence in their prayers, which they conceive God would not give unto them, except he were well pleased with their persons, prayers and ways; and that the true convert also is subject to this sickness, appeareth by this that Moses in charity judged many who countenanced the conspiracy, to be godly persons other ways, and therefore exhorted them to forsake the unhappy society of these wicked men. And sure it is, that sundry of the sons of Korah did repent and fly from the company of the obstinate transgressors, for it is clear that all the sons of Korah did not perish, Numb. 26:11, and frequent mention is made of the posterity of Korah in the Chronicles and Psalms.

But we need not insist much here, seeing experience teacheth, that many go on confidently in maintaining schism and error, persuading themselves of the goodness of their course and condition, because their prayers do flow according to their wish from day today. And many are, who if they find freedom in prayer, for any particular concerning themselves or others, do assure themselves that it shall come to pass which they pray for: And if their spirits be straitened in praying for spiritual and promised graces, they fear they shall not be satisfied in the particular they pray for.

For remedy of this self-deceit, men must know, that it is one thing to pray much, and another thing to be heard and their prayers and persons accepted. The Jews are told by the Prophet Isaiah, chap. 1:15, that albeit they put up many petitions, the Lord will not hear them, because their hands were full of blood. 2. Carnal affection may easily creep in and stir up a fervency of prayer, Jam. 4:3, you ask and obtain not, because you ask amiss, that you may bestow what you pray for upon your lusts. 3. Saints may pray earnestly for that which God is not minded to grant unto them, as Samuel prayed for Saul, that he might be continued King, 1 Sam, 16:1. And David may pray for the life of Bathshebas child and not prevail. 4. On the other hand prayers put up from a straitened heart in a sad condition, may prove no less pleasing unto God then when the supplicant doth find most enlargement of spirit, and freedom of prayer. How oft did the Psalmist cry out of the deeps, when his spirit was overwhelmed within him, when darkness and the cords of death did straiten him, as Psal. 61:1, is holden forth? And the Apostle (Rom. 8) giveth us to understand, that the spirit of the convert may be so straitened by afflictions bodily and spiritual, that they are not able to set their words in order before God, yea, nor have clear notions of their necessities and desires, but instead of an oration, do sigh and groan unto God. Wherefore if a man shall in the sense of his sins and wants, have his daily recourse unto Christ, and be careful to bring forth the fruits of the spirit, praying for what is promised, with submission to God what measure and at what time he pleaseth to give, he may be sure his person and prayers are acceptable, as we are taught, 1 John 5:14,15. This is the confidence that we have in him, that if we ask anything according to his will, he heareth us; and if we know that he heareth us, whatsoever we ask, we know that we have the petitions that we desired of him.

CHAP. XI. - Of the converts esteeming the peace of God to be but a carnal security.

WE HAVE BROUGHT FORTH some examples of the first sort of the conscience erring, by esteeming an evil condition to be a good condition. Now let us look upon some examples of a conscience erring, by esteeming a good condition to be an evil condition. Of the which sort this shall be one.

Sometime some converts do mistake the peace of God granted unto them after hard exercise, and do esteem the quietness of their conscience, to be nothing else but a carnal security and sleepy disposition of the conscience. To which case that we may speak the more clearly, we do not deny that many are, who indeed fall in a carnal security and please themselves therein, conceiving they have the peace of God and a blessed quietness of conscience. Such persons have no doubt nor suspicion but all is well with them, for they do not examine and compare their condition and ways with the Word of God, but sleep sweetly in their carnal security and negligence of spiritual duties, like to these luke-warm Laodiceans, Rev. 3. Of such we do not speak here. 2. Again we do not deny, that true converts are in danger to suffer the peace which God hath granted unto them, to degenerate unto a carnal security. For easily may a convert after consolation divine fall in a sleep, as the Spouse did in the Canticle, 5:2. But we are speaking of the case of a convert, watching unto duties, who after no small vexation in his conflict with the temptations of the devil, with the terror of the law and sense of divine wrath, hath gotten the victory by faith in Christ, and hath obtained peace with God graciously granting his petition; we are speaking here of these converts who after the Lord hath granted peace unto them through faith in Christ, dare not enjoy their peace, but do suspect that their peace is not sound, and at length do count and call it carnal security; and so do breed themselves new troubles of mind. The pretense and seeming reason whereby they do deceive themselves is this. When God, say they, seemed unto us angry with us, when we found no peace and were wrestling under the sense of sin, and in doubt whether such as we should find mercy, then we did pray very earnestly, night and day, then we were diligent in hearing and reading of the Word of God, and were painful in the exercise of all duties of religion and obedience. But now we find ourselves much cooled and slackened in all these duties, whereupon we justly suspect the peace which we now do find, to be nothing else but a carnal security of a sleeping conscience. By this mistake all thanksgiving for the peace granted unto them is well-near suffocate and extinguished. Their former condition under doubts and fears, is judged to be better than their present condition, they wish their former fears may return, rather then they should continue in this condition, wherein their tears are dried up, and their former diligence eaten up. Hence go they on to lay forth their complaints before their intimate acquaintance, concerning God's dispensation and dealing with them, because the spirit of fear and reverence toward God, the spirit of grace and supplication is much diminished and near-by quenched in them. By which complaints they do not only breed trouble to themselves, but also make heavy the hearts of their godly friends, and do tempt them to fall into the like complaints and to grieve the Lord's Spirit.

2, This mistake doth arise, partly from the not considering and esteeming of the gracious gifts of peace, and other graces bestowed upon them, and partly from a wrong comparison of their former and present condition. For, first the afflicted person taketh no notice of the evidences of a new creature in himself, he doth not consider how great a benefit is bestowed upon him, when he feareth to offend God, feareth to be shut out from society with him, and earnestly desireth to be sure of his favor in Christ: he hath not a due estimation of having peace with God and war with sin in himself, joined together; to be freed from the torment of the conscience condemning him according to the law, and withal a desire and delight in the obedience of the Gospel joined together. 2. He doth inconsiderately exact of his conscience, that his soul should be in the same disposition before peace be granted, and after that it is bestowed, or that his affections should be stirred up one and the same way in both these cases: for before peace is given he cannot choose but he must have sorrow, heaviness of heart, unquietness, fear, and such like other sad affections. But after that God granteth peace, these perturbations are quieted, tormenting fear ceaseth, lamentations are restrained, tears are washen away in a good measure, and in their place, do thanksgiving to, and praises of God succeed, and every duty do call for their own place in a pacified mind, so that the man's body be not neglected as before, but care had of keeping health, for enabling to do what is required of him in his calling toward every one with whom he liveth: For, now his condition being changed, why should not his affections, and the effects depending on them be changed also? Who can reasonably exact the same duties of a man in a fight, which he may require of him when he hath gotten the victory? Who can expect the same carriage from a man when he is sick and when he is in health? Doth not the Apostle say, Jam. 5:13. If any man be afflicted let him pray? Is any merry, let him sing Psalms.

3. For remedy of this evil, 1. let the afflicted examine himself whether this peace hath had a conflict of conscience and faith under the sense of sin and fear of the wrath threatened in the Law, going before it or not? 2. Whether this peace hath followed upon flying to Christ by faith, unto whom he did cleave in his sad exercise? 3. Whether this peace hath followed after prayer and supplication made to God for it, that he might without fear of his enemies serve God all the days of his life? 4. And last of all whether his heart still inclineth and endeavoreth to give obedience to the commands of God, and to be grieved for his shortcoming therein? If these things do concur which beseem a convert, let him persuade himself his peace which he hath censured for carnal security, is the solid peace of God mistaken by him. And therefore, 1. let him no more suspect the gift of God, but hold fast the Word of God, which faith of the soul chased to Christ, hath laid hold on, that being now justified by faith, he may have peace with God, Rom. 5:1. For, God doth not give to his supplicant carnal security for peace, a stone for bread, and an adder for fish. But, 2. let him observe the wiles and malice of Satan, who cannot endure that the soul fled from him to Christ should have peace, or in the enjoying of it bless God for his gift of grace. And, 3. let him study to make use of this peace granted to him, going on in the obedience of God's commands cheerfully, and to be ready for new conflicts and

assaults from Satan, and not be afraid of being deprived of the peace of God, while he by faith in Christ is yoked in battle against sin which he seeth in the world and feeleth in himself.

CHAP. XII. - Of the case of a convert, taking some acts of justifying faith to be high presumption in his person.

THIS CASE IS LIKE the former. Some true converts are, who have fled to Christ for remission of sin and delivery from perdition, and have applied the promises made for sanctification and consolation, and full salvation after this life, in such a measure as doth suffice them for encouragement to wrestle with difficulties, wherewith with they may meet in their way to heaven. But when the highest and most excellent privileges of the Gospel are presented to them, and come to be made use of, such as are, sitting together with Christ in heavenly places, Ephes. 2:6, being co-heirs annexed with Jesus Christ, Rom. 8:17. So esteemed of, and loved by Christ, that they who touch his Saints, do touch the apple of his eye, Judging the world and the damned Angels, 1 Cor. 6:3, and such like other privileges, they are at a stand, and dare not apply these privileges for fear of high presumption.

2. Neither must we wonder that a soul should fall in this exercise, and yet adhere to Christ as a convert and true believer: For, when a

sinner for fear of perdition is chased to a Savior, and dare not loose his grips lest he fall in the pit, he may seem to himself to be in good case if he get in to Christ, albeit he do not thrust himself upon such high privileges, and join himself with Abraham, and the Patriarchs and Prophets. Like unto Mephibosheth, who judged himself to have found grace enough at David's hand, that his life was spared, but trembled when he was privileged to come to the Kings table, who, in his own eyes, was like a dead dog for his unworthiness, as he judged of himself. Or like the prodigal in the Gospel, who in his own eyes was not worthy to be counted a child of the family, but content to be as one of the hired servants in his fathers house. And true it is, that the wonderful largeness of the promises of the Gospel maketh the true convert, lately come forth of the slavery of sin and Satan, to stand so astonished, that he dare not take to him so glorious titles, privileges and consolations as the Scripture doth allow him: yea, when he would lift up himself to believe the glory promised, he can no more apprehend the infinite love and grace of God propounded and adjudged unto him, then he can measure the heaven with his span, or comprise in his hand the great Globe, and round of heaven and earth. From such a consideration was it, that Peter did at first utterly refuse to suffer Christ to wash his feet; and that Martha, in the beginning of her conference with Christ, could not think of so great a benefit, as the resurrection of her brother Lazarus before the day of judgment.

2. The convert in this case, doth wrong to himself and to the Word of God, and to the liberality and rich grace of God; for, so long as he suffereth himself to be born down from embracing, as safely he may, the rich allowance of God upon a soul reconciled to him by faith in Christ, he not only cuts himself off from that measure of joy

of the holy Ghost which he may have, but also giveth occasion and advantage to Satan, to brangle and call in question, whether the man hath indeed believed in Christ at all, or whether he hath laid hold on Christ for righteousness and salvation by faith unfained; for, if it be presumption for a self-condemned sinner, flying unto Christ by faith, to lay hold upon the benefits which Christ hath prepared, purchased and offered unto him upon this pretended reason, that these benefits are so hugely great, and the man so small and unworthy in his own eyes, why may not Satan, with as great reason, (if there were any weight in it) call it presumption for such a man to lay claim unto Christ, who is greater than all his benefits, and so beat him off from faith and confidence in Christ the great gift of God, made of God, to poor sinners fled unto him, wisdom and righteousness, sanctification and redemption?

3. Wherefore, to help the convert in this condition, let him consider, he doth well to be feared for presumption, for it is a fearful evil: but, let him remember to put due difference between presumption, and true faith and confidence; for, 1. presumption is proud and puffed up with self-conceit, but we pre-suppose the convert to be humble and laid low in his own eyes, in this condition we are speaking of. 2. Presumption is secure and negligent in the discharge of commanded duties; but the convert we speak of, is about the use of the means, and in some measure diligent in discharging commanded duties in his calling. 3. Presumption layeth hold upon promises not made to the presumptuous, and troubleth not itself with precepts and threatening's; but the convert in this condition we are speaking of, regardeth both precepts and threatening's, and is so far from putting forth his hand, without a warrant, unto promises, that he stands aloof from laying hold on more promises, then he conceiveth necessary to save

his soul from hell. 4. The presumptuous promiseth to himself felicity, albeit he walk in his own ways, and turneth the grace of God into lasciviousness, encouraging himself to sin because God is merciful; but this convert escheweth sin, and followeth the way which may lead him to the possession of all promises. Therefore, 1. let the convert in this condition remember, that Christ and all his benefits are so joined together in the grant of grace, that he may confidently say, with the Apostle, Rom. 8:32, that seeing Christ is given to the believer flying unto him, it cannot be but God with him will give all things also. 2. Let him consider, that it is a dangerous matter, not to give credit unto God's faithful Word holden forth in one promise, as well as in another: For, seeing he is worthy to be believed in the first promise, of receiving into favor a sinner flying to Christ, why shall he not have the glory of truth and grace in the rest of the promises, which belong to the accomplishing of the full glorification of the man reconciled. 3. And last of all, let the convert in this condition consider, how near he draweth to a popish error in this practice; for, Papists do measure the gifts of God unto men, by the man's merit and well-deserving, and not by mere grace only, and upon this ground do reckon it presumption for any ordinary Christians to be assured in this life, that God will guide them with his counsel, and at their departure out of this life, immediately receive them into glory. For, if the convert, being chased by the law to lay hold on Christ (who is the end of the law for righteousness unto everyone that believeth) shall stand aback from laying hold on the highest privileges of Saints, and the greatest promises made to justified souls, because of his own unworthiness, doth he not say in effect, if I were more worthy and like in holiness unto such and such Saints, I could be more confident to lay hold on these high promises: which ground, if it be once holden, it makes the reason of the man's confidence to be his own well-deserving, and not the mere and only grace of God the free promiser thereof, and so the way of salvation by grace should be undermined and over-turned: which is absurd, because the Apostle, Ephes, 2:8, saith, that by grace we are saved through faith, and that not of ourselves, it is the gift of God. Therefore let not the humbled convert think it presumption to lay hold on Christ and the fullness of all promised grace in him, how large soever it be.

CHAP. XIII. - Of the condition of the convert, fearing that the joy of the holy Ghost which he hath felt, be found only to be either the joy of speculation, common to temporal believers, or a mere delusion.

OF THIS SORT ALSO is this case, wherein the convert doth suspect, that the joy of the Spirit which he hath felt at sometimes was either a joy of speculation or contemplation only, such as Philosophers may find in their study of human learning, or else a delusion of Satan also. This case may fall upon the true convert in the time of affliction and felt desertion, when not only the sense of consolation is withdrawn, but also sorrow and heaviness have seized on his spirit, when the sharpness of affliction takes up the whole soul, and sorrow doth fill the heart. At such a time the memory of by-past joy is greatly darkened, and the sense of present grief inflameth the whole man. For as it falleth forth in a man's body, that both sweet and sour liquor, do affect the sense of tasting most, when they are presently felt, but when they are past, the memory of them doth affect the imagination only, and that but lightly in comparison with present sense. As the sense of a fiery coal doth other ways affect us when it touches our flesh, then the memory of the pain we have felt, doth move us when the pain is past; So it is in the passions of the soul, for joys spiritual shine for a while, when they are lately raised up in the soul, but after a time they are darkened, and in some sort worn out, especially when grief doth arise, then they are swallowed up with sorrow, or are well near forgotten, or lightly esteemed and rejected: My soul refused comfort, saith the Psalmist, Psal. 77:2. Such was David's condition, Psal. 116:11, when he said in his haste all men are liars: at which time, whatsoever joy he had felt, in believing the promises made to him by Samuel or other Prophets, he counted all to be but deceiving of him and delusion.

This mistake is strengthened ordinarily by Satan's temptation and wicked suggestion, watching upon all occasions to traduce and slander all God's words and operations. The complaint of Jeremiah savors of this malicious suggestion, which the Prophet layeth out before God to be rid of it, Jer. 20:7. Thou hast deceived me, and I was deceived. Yea, ofttimes it cometh to pass, that our old man and corrupt inclination taketh part with Satan, and when occasion doth offer, scorneth all the spiritual affections of the new man, as Ishmael mocked Isaac's devotion.

2. This evil except it be speedily and solidly cured, not only casteth the convert in a miserable condition, but also calleth in question his state, whether at all he be regenerate, reconciled and in the state of grace: for, if the joy of the holy Spirit granted to the supplicant praying to God in Christ, for confirmation of his faith, granted to the mourner for sin, that he may be comforted, shall be esteemed as the effect of speculation only, then the comfort of the earnest-penny and first fruits of the spirit is lost, the confirmation of faith by that consolation is enervate and weakened; thanksgiving formerly offered for the comfort sometime felt, is recalled, and the testimony of God's Spirit, speaking according to the word in oft-repeated experience, is laid aside. And so the afflicted soul shall seem to himself in worse condition then when he was lying in his sins, because he shall seem to himself to have lost his labor from the time that he renounced his sins. Wherefore it is necessary, that this sickness be speedily cured, lest it prevail.

3. For remedy of this evil, let the afflicted lay aside the dispute for a time whether his joys and spiritual experiences of the Lord's working in him, have been real, as they sometime seemed, and let him turn his eyes upon his present miserable confused condition, let him take a new view of his sins and unworthiness, let him observe Satan's malice, power and wiles to weaken faith, and what need now he standeth in of Christ Mediator, Redeemer Surety and Physician by office, after a new discovery of his sinfulness; and let him look upon the riches of the grace of God offered in the Gospel to every hungry and thirsty soul flying to Christ for refuge, and let him say to God, Lord there was never a time wherein I had more need of Christ for righteousness and salvation, behold I fly unto thee, I welcome and embrace Christ offered in the Gospel, and heartily do consent

unto the covenant of grace through him, and do accept, embrace and rely upon remission of sins through him, and the imputation of his satisfactory righteousness, made over to such as fly unto him, or else I should perish utterly, and do give up myself to thee, that thou mayest write thy law more powerfully on my heart. By this means the confidence of the afflicteds interest in the covenant of Grace shall be more fixed and made sure to him, and Satan disappointed of his design to cast the afflicted by his temptations in mis-belief, and separation from Christ.

4. Thus when he hath renewed the grips of faith in Christ, let him now enter the lists, and dispute the solidity of his former felt experiences, by discussing the objections which did weaken his estimation of the former felt joys of the Spirit. One objection against them was, because they were of short endurance, and therefore seemed not solid. The answer may be this, The short staying of the joy of the Spirit is no proof against it, as not true joy; for, it is sufficient earnest of the promised salvation, if when the Word of God in the Gospel speaketh peace to the man fled to Christ he findeth the Word believed to be confirmed to the believer by peace and joy, albeit the sense of it remain but a short while; After you believed, saith the Apostle, you were sealed with the spirit of promise, Ephes. 1:11. As it is not sufficient to prove, that wholesome water given to a fever-sick person is not a wholesome drink, because the cooling refreshment by it, endureth but a short while; So it is not sufficient to prove, that consolation and joy given to a sorrowful sinner, seeking favor through Christ, is not solid and true joy, because it stayeth but a short while. It is sufficient, that it hath stayed so long as was needful; for, after the word of promise was believed, the joy was sent to ease the afflicted souls present grief, and to give him earnest, that full and lasting joy

should be given in due time unto him. When the messenger hath done his commission, let him return to his master. As the sheet let down in the vision from heaven to Peter, after it had served for Peters instruction, it was taken up to heaven again, Act. 10. The Spouse in the Canticle knew by experience, that her spiritual joys would not last long, and therefore chargeth the daughters of Jerusalem that they waken not her beloved till he pleased.

5. Another objection is this. If my joy had been solid (saith the afflicted) it should have brought forth better fruits then it hath done; but joy spiritual, as I then called it, did degenerate into a carnal security, and I was not the more holy by it. To which objection the answer may be this, the blame of this is not to be laid on spiritual joy, but upon the abuse of this mercy, by ingratitude for this gracious blink of felt favor, negligence in the use of means to entertain this sense, by sleepiness of conscience and other sins, and namely the laying too much weight upon this sense, and not fixing the heart by so much more upon the word of promise when felt consolation may be withdrawn, is a just cause; for, spiritual joy is not given to any to build upon its continuance, but to make the convert hold the confirmed word of promise so much the faster, when for the exercise of faith, comfortable feelings are withdrawn. The spouse in the Canticle after a feast of this kind, falleth a sleep, and giveth slight entertaining to the Bridegroom when called upon by his word, for which she is chastised, by his withdrawing of his comfortable presence, Cant. 5:1-3. &c. But let us put the case, that the felt joy of the spirit were not abused, yet is it not unusual for God to withdraw consolation, and to send trouble and anguish on the soul of his dear child, to try his faith and train him on to hold the word of his grace, in the hardest condition he can be into, as he did exercise Job, and Jeremiah the Prophet, Jer.

20, and the Psalmist, Psal. 77. In which condition, to suspect that the consolation and joy of the spirit, speaking to the heart by his word, is not his gracious operation, or is a delusion, cannot but exceedingly grieve the Lord, and give him cause to chastise this suspicion with desertion.

6. But how may I know, saith the afflicted, that my joy was solid and was indeed the gracious operation of the holy Spirit? For answer, 1. If this joy was given to him when, or after, he was lamenting his sins, and fearing wrath deserved, and flying unto Christ offered in the Gospel, he hath reason to reckon that joy to be such as the Word of the Gospel doth promise and approve. 2. If during the time of his sweet feeling of peace and joy through Christ, he found his faith in God, and love to Christ confirmed and strengthened, if the Word of the Gospel was in more estimation with him, if his heart was enlarged to bless, praise and thank God for manifesting himself in Christ reconciled, if the purpose of following after holiness was renewed in him, he hath no reason to suspect his joy and comfort. 3. If after the removing of this sweet feeling he is going on in the study of holiness, believing in Christ, how heavy in heart soever he may be, by affliction and temptation, he may be assured his sometime felt joy of the Lord's Spirit was solid, and his present suspicion thereof to be an evidence of his infirmity, and of a temptation from Satan. This was the way how the Psalmist wrestled out of his sad condition, Psal. 77.

CHAP. XIV. - Of the converts suspecting, that his zeal for God and against the sins of others hath been fleshly severity and imprudent temerity

IT COMETH TO PASS, that they who love God sincerely, and cannot endure the out-breakings of the wicked, do sometimes transgress the bounds of moderate zeal, and being overtaken in some miscarriage, for which being rebuked by their friends, or by them in power censured or civilly chastised, do instead of moderating their zeal in time coming, grow more slack and remiss in their zeal, suspecting themselves inclined to unreasonable severity and rashness, and ready to be esteemed haters of men's persons by those among whom they live, as in some by-gone experience they have already felt. And upon this occasion the temptation of Satan falleth on, tending to extinguish the fervency of true zeal required in all true converts.

And here there is danger lest true zeal grow cold, and the convert become luke-warm, both in curbing sin in others under his charge, and in pursuing duties in his own person. In which sickness he may be the better pleased with himself, by so much as his friends and others do commend him for his moderation and prudence, as they shall call it.

2. As to the remedy of this evil, there is no doubt, but that may befall true zeal, which is common to other virtues, of which there is none so perfect, but some in-lake or excess may be observed in them. And therefore, as it is without reason to go back from pursuing duty in the exercise of other virtues, because imperfections therein are remarkable from time to time, So is it without reason to grow luke-warm in zeal which may render a man loathsome unto Christ, Rev. 2:3. Wherefore let the convert take heed what the Lord's Word doth require of him in his calling, and labor to discharge his duty towards others, so as he may be found both zealous and prudent, that in the expressions of his zeal against sin, meekness and love to the offender may be manifested. 2. To this intent, let the convert carefully take heed to entertain these three properties of commendable zeal, which are, 1. The fear of God. 2. Humility of heart. 3. The love of his neighbor: for, the fear of God will not suffer the convert to depart from his commandments; Humility of heart will make the man modest in his expressions; and the love of his neighbor will make him mix meekness and compassion toward sinners with his zeal against offenses. This is the right seasoning of zeal, which the Apostle calleth the zeal of God according to knowledge.

CHAP. XV. - Of the converts suspecting his aiming at circumspect walking, shall be found in him scrupulosity.

SOMETIME IT COMETH TO pass, that the convert, being under hard exercise before his consolation, doth put on the whole armor of God, and studieth to walk circumspectly for a while, but after a time he becometh somewhat weary of the yoke, suspecting he hath given too much way unto scrupulosity, whereupon he becometh more remiss and slack in his watchfulness and diligence, laying aside the armor of God, as David laid aside the armor of King Saul, wherewith he was not accustomed.

For satisfying himself in this course, I presuppone he maketh use of three pretended reasons. The first is, because it is impossible for any man to attain to such circumspection in his carriage as becometh him: for, it is no less then to aim at perfect obedience of the law, which the Apostle hath declared to be impossible, because of the weakness of the flesh, Rom. 8:3. The next pretended reason is, because this bending of a man's spirit maketh the conscience unquiet, that a man cannot enjoy the peace of God granted in the Gospel. The third pretended reason is, because it doth restrain Christian liberty in many things lawful, so as a man can neither make use of recreation of body, or mind without scruple; and here we must beware on the one hand lest we give way to any degree of mis-regarding the law, which is the error of the Antinomians; and on the other hand, lest we ensnare the conscience of converts, and hinder them in the lawful use of what God doth allow unto them.

2. For remedy of this evil, let the convert know that there is a necessity of aiming at circumspect walking. This duty is indispensable: for, if a chink be opened here in the vessel for the least entry of water, it may ere long fill and sink the whole ship: for, the command standeth immovable, Heb. 12:14. Follow peace with all men and holiness, without which no man shall see the Lord. And, 1 Pet. 1:15. As he that hath called you is holy, so be ye holy in all manner of conversation. And, Matth. 5:48. Christ hath said, Be ye perfect, as your father in heaven is perfect.

This ground being laid, let us examine these three pretended reasons. As to the first, albeit the attaining unto the perfect obedience of the Law in this life be impossible, because of the infirmity of corrupt nature; yet, the aiming at the perfect obedience of God's Commands is both possible and profitable, and he who aimeth at perfection of obedience in this life, shall attain it fully in the life to come. It is one thing to give perfect obedience unto the Law, for in many things we do sin all of us; another thing to endeavor, according to the measure of grace given, to obey the Law perfectly. For, God, who hath loosed converts, fled to Christ, from the covenant of Works or the covenant of the Law, he hath not loosed his subjects from obedience to the Law-giver, he hath not abolished the ten Commands, he hath not loosed the duties of the redeemed and converted souls, but by receiving them in favor through faith in Christ, he doth augment their obligation to serve the Lord their Redeemer, so much more cheerfully and carefully, as the grace is large in forgiving them their sins, and translating them from the slavery of sin and Satan, into the kingdom of Christ.

Again, albeit it be true, that it is impossible to attain perfect obedience unto the Law, yet there is great advantage to be had by circumspect walking and aiming at perfect obedience: for, this, 1. doth glorify our heavenly Father, when we strive to be conform to his will and to have respect to all his commands. 2. This endeavor adorneth the Gospel and profession of our most holy faith, whereby we lay hold on the grace of free justification, that we may become the servants of righteousness indeed. 3. This endeavor beareth witness of our sincere desire to serve God with all our heart, albeit we attain not to the perfection of obedience in this life. 4. This endeavor giveth unto us daily, new matter of humiliation, when in our aiming at our duty, we come very short of our mark we shoot at. 5. This endeavor and short-coming, for all we can do, maketh us despair of seeking justification by works before God, and to esteem highly, and make use by faith, of Christ's satisfaction for us imputed to us for righteousness, which is a garment able to hide our imperfections and nakedness. 6. This endeavor to walk circumspectly, puts us to the exercise of all Christian graces, and to strive with others and with ourselves, to perfect holiness in the fear of God.

3. As for the second pretended reason, that this endeavor, to walk circumspectly, may make the conscience unquiet, it puts a foul as-

persion on the holy precept of the Apostle, Ephes. 5:15-17, who hath declared this to be a man's wisdom, and so a good mean of making his conscience quiet, and to establish in it the peace of God: For, by this endeavor, to walk circumspectly, believers in Christ are assured, that they are without the reach of condemnation, because they walk not after the flesh, but after the Spirit, Rom. 8:1. Secondly, this endeavor is the evidence of a good conscience, which accompanyeth true faith, and in a manner, doth guard the conscience from just challenges which might trouble the same. Thirdly, by this endeavor, the believer is, by a holy necessity, forced to cleave close unto Christ, to converse with him in heaven, that the pollution of daily sin may be washen away, by new application of Christ's expiatory sacrifice to the believer, and that Christ may let forth more strength to him to walk in the way of commanded duties, and so the convert may stand in the grace of God. Thus the peace of God, offered and covenanted in the Gospel, is preserved in him, so long as this endeavor, to walk circumspectly, is entertained.

4. As for the third pretended reason against circumspect walking, as if by it Christian-liberty shall be crossed and cut short, it is a false pretense; for, the contrary is true, that Christian-liberty is not hurt, but helped and preserved, by circumspect walking: for, this is true Christian-liberty, to have allowance of the use of the benefits which God doth bestow with his blessing, so far as may serve our well-fare; seeing it is not a point of Christian-liberty, licentiously, by intemperance, to abuse God's benefits, and turn them to our own hurt. Wherefore, let our heart be all day in the fear of God, that we may, in lawful manner, make use of lawful things; neither doth the study of holiness make recreations of body and mind unlawful, but restraineth immoderate and untimely use of things lawful. All that

Christian liberty granteth unto us, is, that whether we eat or drink, or what lawful thing else we do, we do all for the glory of God, 1 Cor. 10:31, that is, so as we may be strengthened and set forward, to glorify God in Christ in necessary duties. As for the manner and measure to be keeped in the use of things lawful, prudence must be asked of God, who will direct us in this as in other Christian duties.

CHAP. XVI. - Concerning the converts suspicion, that his softness of heart is nothing but a natural disposition to weep upon any occasion.

WHEN THE LORD HATH taken away from the sinner a heart of stone, and hath given unto him a heart of flesh, so that he dare not anymore harden himself against the threatening's of God's Word, but doth tremble at the hearing thereof, as speaketh Isaiah 66:2, and in his prayer doth pour forth his heart ordinarily with tears, he may (as experience hath taught) fall in a suspicion of this ordinary or frequent melting of heart, as if it were nothing else but a childish or woman-like temper of body and spirit, and no evidence of contrition for spiritual causes, which the Scripture requireth and commendeth in the penitent.

2. In this case there is danger on either hand, if the convert be not wary and circumspect in this condition; for, on the one hand he is in hazard of making light account of the work of God, who hath taken from him the heart of stone, and given him a heart of flesh. On the other hand, he is in hazard of laying too much weight on his tears, if once he be satisfied about the suspicion he hath of his own tears, and made clear, that they were proofs and evidences of his sincerity in his prayers to God.

That there is a danger on either hand, experience hath taught; for, some sincere converts, having entertained the suspicion, that their tears in prayer proceeded from the soft temper of their natural complexion and disposition of spirit, have resisted their inclination to mourn, and striven against letting forth of tears so far, that they have become so dry for a long time, and have prayed more perfunctoriously than before, that when just causes of grief and tears were given unto them, they were not able to bring forth one tear for easing of their grieved heart. On the other hand, experience hath taught, that some, looking upon the expressions of the Saints in Scripture concerning their tears, have laid so much weight upon their tears, as they have numbered, in a manner, all the drops of their eyes, and from the less or more quantity of them, made reckoning of their own better or worse condition, and of God's acceptation of their prayers less or more.

3. This tenderness of heart, and easiness to be moved unto tears, for spiritual motives, is a rare gift. Few they are, who with sense of the body of death and original sin bearing them down, do lament their natural sinfulness in their best condition with Paul, Rom. 7:24. Few shall be found so affectionate, to the glory of God and salvation of people's souls, as to pour out tears both in secret and openly,

for promoving thereof, as the Apostle did, Act. 20:19,21, and 2 Cor.
2:4. Few like Timothy, whose heart was so tender, that the Apostle
could not but observe his tears, and remember them, 2 Tim. 1:4. Yet,
we doubt not, that from age to age sundry be, who by the grace of
God have this constantly melting heart, according to the measure
of God's free donation, some with tears, some without tears. And
therefore, if there be found in such mourners, an honest endeavor to
walk circumspectly, let not the suspicion, that their tenderness is but
natural weakness of spirit or bodily complexion, be entertained. Only
let the giver of the grace of a tender heart be relied upon, and not
their tears, as if they were anymore then witnesses of their honest
affection in spiritual exercises; for, such prayers may prove sincere
and acceptable to God, both when they cannot mourn, and also when
their heart seemeth withered, hard and dry.

CHAP. XVII. - Concerning the converts suspicion, that all his devotion is but lip-labor which is not joined with a tender and melting
heart, and with God's sensible approbation.

As some are suspicious of their condition, because of their ordinary
tenderness and melting of heart; So other some are suspicious of their
condition, because they find not their heart tender and soft in their
devotion. All converts do agree in this, that God must be worshiped
in spirit and truth, and that it is not acceptable worship to God, if
a man draw near him with his lips, when his heart is far from him:
whereupon, every convert, when he is mindful of his duty, goeth
about to worship God with understanding and inward affection of
heart, to confess sin, deprecate wrath, ask of God things necessary,
intercede for others, give thanks to God for his benefits, and praise
him for his works and working, so as his affections may be conform
to his expressions, and the conscience may approve both his words

and his hearty affections, and God may, with his peace and consolation, approve the worshiper. But some converts are, who, albeit in
sincerity they worship God, yet they count all their devotion to be
but lip-labor, except they find their affections wakened up and their
heart tender, and some vigor of spiritual life in their exercises, and
the sense of God's approbation of their worship, by giving sense of his
peace and consolation to them in their worship. Hence ofttimes doth
suspicion arise, without just ground, that they are deserted of God,
that he is displeased with them; and this suspicion being entertained,
doth send forth complaints, and bringeth on coldness in prayer and
discouragement.

2. This unjust suspicion of the grace of prayer, the Lord doth ofttimes chastise by with-drawing peace and comfort, and order in
prayer and of words also, that he who complained that his devotion
was but lip-labor, because he sound not such measure of affection as
he would have had, nor that consolation which he wished to have,
shall find himself in worse taking after his complaining, then he was
in at first, when he began to suspect his condition. It is true, that
confusion of mind, and want of words to express the case wherein he
is, may fall on a convert, by reason of afflictions and manifold temptations, and yet he may be free from this suspicion of God's affection
and acceptation of his person and prayers; as the Apostle doth teach
us, Rom. 8:26. Likeways, the Spirit also helpeth our infirmities; for we
know not what we should pray for as we ought, but the Spirit itself
maketh intercession for us, with groanings which cannot be uttered.
But when this cutting short of the gift of prayer, in any measure,
doth follow after suspicion of God's respect and good will toward the
complaining and discouraged convert, it is a fatherly chastisement
from God, threatening the convert with a greater measure of deser-

tion and heavier temptation, except he repent his folly and return to God, whom by his suspicion and misbelief he hath offended.

3. For remedy of this evil, these five things must be distinguished by the afflicted convert; 1. the labor of the lips, or formality in prayer or devotion; 2. prayer in faith; 3. prayer with felt and observed affection in prayer; 4. prayer approven of God; 5. prayer with the sense and feeling of God's approbation.

As to the first, the labor of the lips, or formality in prayer which the Scripture doth condemn, is when a man prayeth with his mouth for things necessary or lawful and is about the external work of devotion, wherein he pleaseth himself, and doth rest upon the work wrought without affection of heart or faith, as we see, Isa. 58:1-3, and this is not the case of the convert of whom we are speaking; for, because he esteems his devotion to be but a formality, he is displeased with himself and is unquiet.

As to the second, prayer in faith, is when the convert misseth freedom of speech, and answerable affection to his speech in his devotion in prayer, praises, thanksgiving, intercession, &c. yet, because the duty is commanded, he doth offer it up to God with hope of acceptation, and yet is displeased with himself, and humbled in the sense of his coldriff affections, which is the duty of the convert of whom we are speaking, but the not esteeming this his devotion through Christ acceptable, is his fault.

As to the third; prayer or devotion with felt affection in discharging it, is when the convert poureth out his heart unto God with freedom of speech, and yet cannot be quiet, because he doth not feel any sign of God's approbation of him and hearing of his supplication, and this was the case of the Psalmist in sundry Psalms. But this is not the case of the convert we are speaking of; for, he complaineth of the hardness of his heart and want of affection, and doth weaken his own faith, which is his fault.

As to the fourth; prayer approven of God, is when the convert doth offer his devotion to God in sincerity, and prayeth for what is promised, in hope to be heard and answered in due time. And this prayer or devotion is approven by God in Scripture, whether the convert be satisfied with the measure of answerable affection to his words, or not, as the Apostle testifieth. 1 John 5:14,15. And this should be observed by the convert, of whom we are speaking, for rectifying his judgment and quieting of him, albeit he neither find his affection moved as he would, nor find consolation from God as he would.

As to the fifth; prayer or devotion, with the sense and feeling of God's approbation, is when God not only approveth the converts prayer and devotion, by his Word in the Scripture, but also by his Spirit doth sensibly comfort the supplicant, and sends him to his calling with joy. So did he deal ofttimes with the Psalmist David, and so did he comfort Samuel's mother, in, and after her prayer, 1 Sam. 1. This is the thing which the convert we speak of would be at, and which would satisfy him if he could come to it.

4. This condition is the sweetest to the supplicant, and much to be desired, with submission to God's dispensation whatsoever it be, but it is not the only condition acceptable to God, as we see, 1 John 5:14,15. This is the confidence which we have in God, that if we ask anything according to his will he heareth us, and if we know that he heareth us, whatsoever we ask we know we have the petitions that we desired of him. And that the matter is so, may be perceived in David's condition at sundry times; for, Psal. 119, seven or eight times he prayeth, Quicken thou me according to thy word. He findeth in

himself much deadness of spirit, yet he continueth meekly praying to be quickened in the service of God.

5. Wherefore, so oft as the convert is displeased for any defect he findeth in his devotion, let him, 1. humble himself in the sense of his imperfection, and betake himself so much the more to the intercession of Christ, and lay hold more firmly upon the satisfaction made by the Mediator, and draw by faith grace for grace out of his fullness, and let him in faith and sincerity worship God, and live holily in his conversation and not be afraid that his devotion shall be esteemed of God to be but lip-labor. 2. To this end, let him rightly construe God's dispensation, and consider that his gifts are wisely given forth for the good of his people: for, sometime he giveth to will that which is good, without ability for the time to effectuate what the convert willeth; he may give a willing heart to pray affectionately, and not for the time grant ability to pray as his child would, Rom. 7:18. Sometime he may give no more but to sigh and groan, without ability to express the confused desires of his heart, Rom. 8:26,27. Sometime he will suggest words, and make the supplicant in sincerity of faith present the words put in his mouth, Hos. 14:1. 2. Sometime he will grant to the supplicant to bear out much disputation in his prayers, without sensible consolation, Psal. 77. Sometime he will grant the supplicant a loosed heart in prayer and abundance of tears, and yet seem for a time not to regard them, Psal. 6. Sometime he will grant confidence and consolation to the supplicant, as, Psal. 6, and many other Psalms. And certainly, the variety of divine dispensation to his children cannot be told; in all which, he requires of his supplicants meek submission, and perseverance in prayer, with confidence to find a good answer at last: for, if his child do not accept well of the measure which is bestowed on him, he may readily find the measure

he complained of, more scant, and confusion of mind without words to fall upon him, and if yet he shall not wisely submit himself to God's exercising of him, he may fall in harder trouble and questioning of his state in grace, and be tempted to restrain prayer till he cease complaining, and fly for refuge to Christ the Mediator, and come to a better estimation of the measure of presence with him when he began to complain.

CHAP. XVIII. - Concerning the converts looking upon the sight of his faith, as if it were the failing of his faith.

Sincere faith in Christ is the special grace of God, given to the elect only; which grace, the more we do exercise it, the more we please God: for, without faith it is impossible to please him, Heb. 11:6. This saving grace the Lord taketh pleasure to put it unto trial and exercise, that thereby he may train it on, and foster and increase it, and bring it forth to light, both for his own glory and for the commendation of his children, as is told us, 1 Pet. 1:7. In which exercise, the true convert is ofttimes much mistaken, and doth mis-construe his condition. The reasons are, 1. the faith of young converts is very imperfect, knowledge is many ways darkened, and the application of promises is very weak. 2. When Satan by his temptations obscures the truth, which should strengthen faith, the convert finding himself in the mist, may be at a stand, till his sight be cleared up and he freed from the temptation. 3. The sincere convert, in the conscience of his own imperfection, and consideration of the deceitfulness of the heart, is wary and suspicious, that he may be easily deceived, and take historical or temporal faith for true saving faith, and so doth readily lay hold on Satan's suggestions against the sincerity of his faith. 4. In the conflict, which his faith ofttimes hath with mis-belief, strengthened by Satan's temptations, he finds himself now and then foiled by yielding unto the suggestion of Satan; as David's experience teacheth may befall both the elder and younger soldiers, Psal. 116:11. I said in my haste, all men are liars, meaning Samuel and other Prophets, who promised to David in God's name he should be King. 5. In the fight of faith, some infirmity is always manifested, and the convert is forced to acknowledge, that his faith is not so strong as he supposed it to be before the fight, whereupon he is ready to suspect his fight in faith to be a fainting and decaying in faith. 6. Sometime the convert by giving way to sin, doth grieve the holy Spirit, and provoke him to withdraw his comfortable testimony, which he gave in former time to the convert, which bringeth him into suspicion of the sincerity of his faith, which seemed to himself sound and unfeigned before.

2. This case is both troublesome to the convert and dangerous; for, till it be cured, it groweth like a raging fever, and sets upon the vital power of justifying faith, and at least hindereth the exercise thereof not a little.

For remedy whereof, let the afflicted convert put difference between an infirm faith, and felt infirmity in faith fighting: for, albeit the convert, in the conflict of faith against temptations to mis-belief, do feel infirmity, yet is not his faith to be accounted infirm simply, because whatsoever infirmity he feels in his fight, yet his fighting against temptations proveth his faith to be so much the stronger, as he resisteth mis-belief and cleaveth closer to Christ.

2. Let him consider, that the Lord suffereth his child to be exercised with temptations, of set purpose to humble him, and empty him of all confidence in his own wisdom, righteousness and strength, that he may gather strength in his fighting, by Scripture, holden up to God in prayer, and so wax valiant in fight, as believers have been helped before, Heb. 11:34.

3. Let the convert put difference between faith and a settled persuasion: for, settled and full persuasion excludes all dubitation for the time, But saving faith may be where doubting is and unbelief is felt; as the father of the possessed child in his prayer to Christ maketh manifest, Lord, I believe, saith he, help my unbelief.

4. Let him put difference between dubitation suggested, and faith striving to overcome dubitation: for, dubitation bewrayeth infirmity of faith, but striving against dubitation, doth evidence life and vigor in faith to be present, and is acceptable service to God.

5. Let him put difference between the doubting of the truth of the promise and the weak griping of it; for he that doubts of the truth of the promise, is, (Jam. 1:6,7) like a wave of the sea, and can expect nothing, But he that lays hold on the promise, with a trembling hand, and striveth to hold it fast against doubting, may expect to obtain.

6. Let him put difference between his suspicion of the failing of his faith and the right judging of it: for, in the mean time of his fighting and fear of failing, he goeth on in exercise of faith, fearing to succumb, yet resolute not to depart from Christ: In the love and estimation of whose grace, he goeth on and groweth, longing for the victory and for a nearer felt fellowship with him; which if he did observe and consider, his judgment should be rectified.

Last of all, let him put difference between a hasty apprehension of the failing of his faith, and a fixed opinion that his faith is but fancy: for, a strong soldier may be surprised on a sudden (as David, Psal. 31:22, and Psal. 116:11, and Jonah 2:3,4, do furnish instances) who shortly after did gather their courage and entered the lists afresh, and became victorious against their temptations unto misbelief.

Therefore let the wrestler be of good courage; for, nothing can prove the sincerity of his faith more than his wrestling against distrust, and his looking towards Christ through all the clouds which hinder his sight, and his sorrowing for his unbelief, for his weak holding grip of the covenant of grace, and for his inability to glorify the truth of the Gospel, and rich grace of God offered in Christ: Especially when he considereth, that the Spirit of Christ commendeth the exercise of faith, with variety of temptations, for a matter of great joy, Jam. 1:2,3.

CHAP. XIX. - Concerning the converts straitening his charity toward others, more than he did at the first time of his conversion, conceiving his former larger charity, was unwarrantable folly.

ALL CONVERTS MUST AGREE to Christ's saying, John 13:35. By this shall all men know, that ye are my disciples, if ye have love one to another. No man doubteth of this his duty in general; but sundry make question about the exercise and expression of their charity: for, some conceive, that their former charity (in the matter of judging of others, and in the matter of affection to others, and in the matter of actual expression of their charity) hath been ill bestowed toward unworthy and ill-deserving persons. And this they reckon to have been folly; and therefore do resolve to dispose of their judgment, affection and good deeds more prudently then they have done, that their charitable estimation, affection and expression actual, shall be drawn forth toward the worthy and well-deserving disciples of their acquaintance, thus they condemn for folly what was right indeed. The main pretenses of reason for their resolution, are two. The first is, because they perceive many whom they judge wise and godly, to exclude from the number of believers, or disciples of Christ, all in whom the evident signs of regeneration do not appear, and so do think they may draw the circle of their charity in straight and narrow bounds, and may shun to keep Church-fellowship in the pure Ordinances of Christ with any, save approven visible Saints. The other pretense is, because they have found themselves ofttimes deceived by those, of whom sometime they have entertained good thoughts, and no small estimation.

1. As for the first pretense, it belongs to the question of the constitution of visible Churches, whether it be founded upon visible Sanctity or evidences of Regeneration, or upon visible entering in the external covenant of Grace, and profession of subjection to the Doctrine and Discipline of Christ. Of which question, there is enough written by learned and godly men, and and in this place it doth not fall in conveniently to be disputed.

2. Concerning the other pretense, of being ofttimes deceived by sundry, such as were unworthy of respect; we grant, that there are many hypocrites who pretend to be Saints, and worthy to be blamed in that respect: and it is no wonder, that the charity of many wax cold, when so many speak vanity, every man to his neighbor, Psal. 12:2, for this our Lord foretold, Matth. 24:12. Because iniquity shall abound,

the love of many shall wax cold. Yet, it is not justifiable to cut charity short, because of men's ill-deserving; Rivers of tears, saith David, run down my eyes, because they keep not thy Commands. Here is love to God's glory, and pity toward perishing souls; such mourners were spared in the day of God's wrath. Ezek. 9:9.

1. Ob. But some may say, the same Psalmist did hate the wicked and profane. Ans. 1. But he did so with a perfect hatred, not with a carnal and corrupt hatred against their persons, but with a spiritual and sincere hatred, tending to the abolishing of their vice and safety of their persons; for which end, the Psalmist presenteth his affections to be examined of God, and teacheth men, by his example, to purify their hearts in hating sinners. 2. Put case, that God did reveal unto the Prophet the reprobation of some enemies of God, for whose perdition he prayed in sundry Psalms, that the justice of God might be ministered, and the Church preserved from their malice. This his practice is not to be imitate by them who know not of what spirit they are and cannot justify before God the integrity of their hearts in the particular.

2. Ob. But, put case, saith one, that I am a civil Judge, shall my charity hinder justice and cutting off malefactors, man-slayers, or others such-like? Ans. Not; for, charity to the malefactor may stand with the love of Justice and the Common-wealth, when the malefactor is adjudged to death. For, when Joshua was to destroy Achan, he exhorted him to repent and give glory to God, that his soul might be saved, Jos. 7:19. Likeways, the Prophets, when they denounced the destruction of Cities and Nations, had melting hearts in compassion toward them who were condemned by God, Isa. 16:11, Jer. 48:36, and Christ our Lord, charity itself, weeped for the misery of Jerusalem, destinate justly to destruction, Matth. 23:37.

3. Obj. But, (saith he) a special regard must be had toward believers in the exercise of charity, Gal. 6:10. Ans. It is true; but the
Apostles words are, As we have opportunity, let us do good unto all
men, especially unto them that are of the household of faith. Which
household consisteth of all them, who by profession have subjected
themselves to the doctrine and discipline of Christ, and are members
of the visible Church.

4. Ob. But (saith he) as all that are of Israel, are not the Israel of
God, Rom. 9:6. So all that are in the visible Church, are not of the
household of God. Ans. Who hath made thee a Judge either to discern
who are elect, who not? Or to discern what shall become of this man
or that man, whereby thou may abandon charity toward him? God
hath given to us his Spirit, saith the Apostle, that we may know what
saving grace he hath given to ourselves, but not to know what he
hath bestowed on others. 1 Cor. 2:10,11. God, who only searcheth the
secrets of all hearts, hath reserved the judgments of men's hearts to
himself, and he alone can discern who is the hypocrite, and in whose
heart there is no guile.

5. Ob. But (saith he) the judgment of charity is not blind, but
should be according as the truth is; other ways, I shall esteem a man
a true convert, who is not regenerate, and so deceive myself. Ans.
The judgment of charity, concerning other men's inward estate and
condition, is not one always with the judgment according to verity;
for, the rule of the judgment of charity, is equity and commanded
duty, reserving the judgment according to verity to God. For this
distinction the Apostle gives ground, Phil. 1:6,7, in charity judging
all the Philippians to be sincere converts; he saith, his speech and
estimation of them was according as was meet for him to think. Now
equity required, that he should judge the best of them all, albeit he

did not know the hearts of them all, as he saith, 1 Cor. 13:7, charity believeth all things, hopeth all things, endureth all things. But, for the judgment of other men's estate and condition in grace, according to verity, he doth forbid men to judge before the time, 1 Cor. 4:3,5, Rom. 14:4, Jam. 4:12. And, 1 Pet. 5:12, the Apostle, speaking in charity of Sylvanus, saith, he is a faithful brother, as I suppose. 2. If we see it our duty to show charity to our neighbor, whatsoever he be, our charity is not blind, but clear-sighted.

6. Ob. But (saith he) men's profanity, wickedness and atheism, may clearly be seen; for, the Psalmist saith, The transgression of the wicked saith within my heart, that there is no fear of God before his eyes, Psal. 36:1, and Christ, speaking of false Prophets, Matth. 7:16, saith, Ye shall know them by their fruits.

Ans. What the Prophet saith by the Spirit, and what Christ saith, is true; and we grant, that men's ill deeds and corrupt doctrine, do bewray their naughty inward disposition: but what serveth this to justify thy rash judgment of thy brother, that there is no saving work of grace in him, because they cannot perceive the evident signs thereof in him, in whom possibly thou cannot find any reigning vice, or open out-breaking scandals? What doth this serve to hinder expressions and fruits of charity toward open sinners, so long as God waiteth patiently on their repentance? It is one thing to be wary, lest we be infected with the contagion of men's ill manners or corrupt doctrine; another thing to cut them off from being the objects of our charity.

7. Ob. But we are forbidden (saith he) to have fellowship with sinners who may entice us to sin, Pro. 1:11, and to make friendship with an angry man, Pro. 22:24.

Ans. This wariness may consist with charity: for, albeit we cannot be partakers with evil workers, or enter in needless familiarity with those with whom we cannot converse and be free of damage from them, yet we may not exclude them from the object of our charity, or carry ourselves so toward them, as they can take no good from our hand: for, so long as we live in the world, we must follow peace with all men and holiness, Heb. 12:14, 1 Cor. 5:10.

8. Obj. Albeit it be true, that we must in common duties of civility and humanity, prudently behave ourselves, yet we must carry other ways to professed Christians, if their conversation be grossly scandalous; for, with such we are forbidden to eat, 1 Cor. 5:11.

Ans. This place pertains to the exercise of the key of discipline, and execution of the censure of excommunication judicially pronounced by the Church; as, ver. 12, following, doth declare. And this, as it doth not cut off natural duties of parents, or children, or parties married one to another, So it can well consist with charity toward the excommunicate, who, in order to his salvation, should be thus dealt with, that he may be humbled and brought to repentance: And so doth the Apostle give warrant; for when he hath given order to excommunicate such as walk disorderly, 2 Thess. 3:14,15, he subjoins, for keeping charity to the excommunicate person, saying, Count him not as an enemy, but admonish him as a brother.

9. Obj. But I (saith he) have been mistaken and deceived ofttimes when I esteemed charitably of some, loved them dearly, and bestowed not sparingly on those who proved afterward unworthy of such respect and dealing.

Ans. Our Lord's words may satisfy this objection, promising whatsoever is done to a disciple, in name of a disciple, shall not want a reward. Thou therefore needs not count thyself deceived in this respect. But, if thou by rash intruding thyself, to judge better or worse of the man's inward condition, hath deceived thyself, be more wise in time coming. For remedy of this evil, 1. let not the convert, mistaken in the point of charity, be feared to be mistaken and hindered from exercise of his charity, because he knoweth not the sincerity of the man's profession: There are relations enough between him and the party toward whom charity is to be exercised, such as bonds natural, civil, ecclesiastic and spiritual, obliging to the duty. 2. Let him be sparing in judging of his neighbor, even within himself, and far more in expressing his judgment of him to his prejudice. 3. Let him rather judge this, that he lay no stumbling block before his feet, which may hinder him in a good, or harden him in an evil course, Rom. 14:13. Let him not be rigid and censorious in aggreging every sinful infirmity in his neighbor, for this is forbidden, Jam. 3:1,2. In a word, let a convert beware to alienate any man from making use of his charity, whether by injust suspicion of him, or inhumane dealing with him, or imprudent speeches of him, but rather let his whole carriage toward all in every case be such, that a patent door may be for mutual giving and getting good one by another.

CHAP. XX. - Concerning the converts mistaking his condition, because of felt in-lake in his charity and love to God and men.

HITHERTO WE HAVE SPOKEN of two sorts of the converts mistaking of their condition, and have given some instances of their being well pleased with themselves in an evil condition; and some instances of their being displeased with themselves in a good condition. It follows, that we give some instances of a third sort of mistaking in the converts complaining of his condition, as if it were altogether evil, when indeed his condition is partly good and partly evil; and the first shall be of those who do lament their condition, because they cannot be affected with the sense of their sins, nor with the sense of God's benefits and favors bestowed on them, as they should, cannot be affected with the sense of threatened judgments as is required, and cannot be affected with the sense of the miseries and mercies dispensed toward others, and cannot come up to the obedience of the Apostles precept, to rejoice with them that rejoice, and to mourn with them that mourn, which doth so afflict them, as they reckon this their condition altogether evil, and are near unto discouragement, because of their apprehended hardness of heart.

2. For remedy of this evil, 1. let the convert consider, that the hardness of heart whereof he complains, is not that hardness of heart which the Scripture calleth hardness of heart: For, the Scriptures do not charge any man of this sin who lamenteth his sinfulness, but those who do not acknowledge their sins, and go on in them when they hear them reproved, mis-regarding what God saith, commandeth, commendeth or threateneth. Mean time we do not deny, but those in-lakes whereof the convert doth complain, are sinful defects of duty, and inclinations of corrupt nature unto hardness of heart. But we deny, that this defect lamented, is charged in Scripture for hardness of heart. 2. Let the convert consider the difference between the evil whereof he complaineth, and the good gift of God pointing out that evil unto him, and making him to dis-allow it and lament it, and he shall find his condition not altogether evil, but such as he hath cause to be humbled in himself for it, and also to bless God for discovering this defect, and making him lament it. 3. Let him consider, that his lamenting his coldriff affection to God and his small compassion toward men, is good and commendable; for this lamenting the defect, beareth witness of his will and desire toward the duty, and in effect is a part of the exercise of repentance, and of begun renovation of his heart. 4. Let him consider, that there may be made good use of this condition, both for the exercise of humility, because of felt defects of needful graces, and also for the exercise of

faith in Christ, by application of his imputed righteousness, which hideth the nakedness of felt defects, and drawing virtue from Christ to sanctify and renew the heart more and more. 5. And last of all, let the convert under the sense of this defect in his affection, study to bring forth the effects of those affections, that is to say, let him go about to do the work of a lover of God, in having respect to all his commandments, and to do the work of a compassionate affection toward men in misery of soul or body, and so what seems to him inlaking in his heart, shall be found forth-coming in his hand and actions for the greater glory to God and edification of his neighbor.

CHAP. XXI. - Concerning the converts despising of his own exercises of religion, because of his felt vanity of mind therein.

ALL TRUE CONVERTS DO agree in this principle, that God should be worshiped in spirit and truth, and that the more a man strive to be sincere and upright in his worship, the less can be comport with the sin which doth hinder his worship. When therefore a true convert doth perceive in himself so great levity of his thoughts, that in the very time of hearing Sermon, praying to God, or singing of Psalms, his mind runneth out to think of naughty and profane things, impertinent, idle and foolish matters, unworthy of his thoughts at any time, but most untimely and sinful in the time of divine service, he is so displeased with his condition, that he condemns all the service and devotion he is about for the time, and cast it away as altogether polluted; and if he find this sickness from day today cleaving fast unto him, he falleth in discouragement, and in question with himself, whether it be better to break off at least in secret, such ragged worship, or to go on to offer the sacrifice of a fool unto God: for, so he doth esteem of his devotion, thus leavened, with roaming and vanity of his mind.

In this case, the convert doth not only mis-regard what is right in his devotion, or divine service, but also by fretting, discouragement and mis-behavior of his spirit, is ready to augment his sinful condition, and to provoke the Lord to be wroth with him indeed.

2. For remedy of this evil, let the convert judge wisely of his condition, that he charge not himself with guiltiness more then he ought to do, and that he may take a right course to be free of guiltiness, and healed of this sickness where guiltiness is found. And to this end, 1. let him put difference between roaming of mind with interruption of worship, and the natural course of his fantasy and understanding, which may consist with the continued acts of worship; for, as the eyes of a man, running to some place, cannot choose but see every visible thing in his way, and yet runneth on without staying till he come to the place he aimeth at; So the fantasy and understanding, cannot choose but take up, and discern whatsoever is offered unto them in time of prayer from the outward senses, or from the memory, and yet make no interruption of prayer, such is the natural agility of a man's mind; and therefore this natural course of imagination or fantasy, must not be charged as guiltiness upon the worshiper, who followeth on the work of worship notwithstanding. 2. Sundry suggestions may be cast into the converts mind by Satan to mar his worship, which must be charged on Satan chiefly, and the worshiper not always made guilty thereby. 3. When the worship indeed is interrupted, and the mind falleth off from the work of devotion, or divine service, and entereth upon discourses about vain, vile, or impertinent matters, let

the convert not only acknowledge guiltiness here, but also examine, if this his roaming of mind in prayer and divine service, be not also a chastisement from God for his not acknowledging of God in his affairs, and for loosing reins to his mind to rove all the day, which justly meeteth him at night in his devotion, as a rod on his back for his voluntary roaming from God in his former walking.

3. These considerations being premised, and the sins which have drawn on this evil being discovered, and the power of indwelling-sin perceived, and the power of Satan's temptations noticed, and the Lord's chastising rod justified, and his own culpable infirmity acknowledged; 1. Let him humble himself and fly to the rich grace of God offered in Christ, and lay stronger hold on the satisfaction made by Christ, imputed to all believers in him, that guiltiness may be, by free pardon, removed. 2. Let him pray for more assistance of the holy Spirit in all the exercises of religion, and expect a gracious granting thereof, in God's wise dispensation, of the measure of his grace in the use of holy Ordinances. 3. Let his heart be in the fear of the Lord all the day long, making him lift up his eyes from time to time to God in the midst of his lawful affairs, how mean so ever. 4. Let him gather his thoughts before every religious exercise, by way of preparation, lest he take the name of the Lord in vain, by rash and irreverent rushing in upon divine Service. 5. Let him thank the Lord for granting him grace to see his sinful roaming of mind, and to be displeased with it, and to confess it. 6. Let him be comforted in the Lord, who gathereth the ragged and scattered honest desires of supplicants, and taketh away the iniquity of the service of his clients, as our high Priest, bearing, in his appearing for us, as it were, on his fore-head, Holiness unto the Lord.

CHAP. XXII.
- Concerning the converts discouragement for felt want of ability to do the duties commanded, whereunto his renewed will is very bent.

SUNDRY TRUE CONVERTS, FINDING a will to do that which is good, but not finding power how to perform that which is good, do fall in disquietness and discouragement when they should go and seek to make good use of their infirmity, and go to Christ for remedy, as the Apostle did, Rom. 7:18.

The cause of this evil is, the relicts of corrupt natural inclination to seek to be justified by works, and to have in our hand ability to do the good which we would do; for, albeit the convert be forced to seek reconciliation with God by remission of sins in his conversion, yet in his course toward heaven and salvation, he desireth to have a storehouse and treasure of strength in himself, to be made use of as he willeth. For, it seemeth to him, in his carnal wisdom, a poor shift to be, in every good action, put to beg supply from Christ by prayer, and to stand waiting on in a dependence on Christ, till furniture come from heaven unto him. Which furniture of strength, because our Lord doth suspend to give, till his infirm and humble child hold up his heart as an empty vessel to receive influence from him, according to his wise pleasure, the inconsiderate convert doth trouble himself and falleth in a distemper.

2. This case is not altogether evil as the convert doth take it; but this much is right, that he looks upon the Law as holy, spiritual and good, that he desireth earnestly to obey it, and that he loathes himself for his felt unconformity unto it: Yet, this is wrong in him, that he doth not humble himself, but is cast down and discouraged that he doth not make Christ his sanctifications as well as his righteousness, that he doth not consider of the furniture to be brought unto him from heaven by faith in Christ, and that this grace is nearer and more ready to serve his turn, then if it were in his own hand.

3. Therefore let him renounce more and more all confidence in his own righteousness, with the Apostle, Phil. 3:8,9, let him thank God in Christ, in whom an out-gate is to be found in all difficulties, Rom. 7:25, let him trust Christ for supply in all service, in whom if a man abide, he shall bring forth much fruit, and without whom he can do nothing, John 15:5. For, if he depend on Christ in his emptiness and weakness, he shall find by experience, that when he is weakest, then is he strongest.

CHAP. XXIII. - Concerning the converts imprudent censure of himself for felt ingratitude.

SOME CONVERTS SOMETIME, DO pass rash sentence against themselves for ingratitude, namely when after receiving some notable benefit, for which they had made earnest supplication to God, and for which, before the receiving of the benefit, they had obliged themselves by vow to a thankful acknowledgment of the favor prayed for, they find themselves come short of their purposed, promised and hoped-for cheerfulness and alacrity in praising and thanking the Lord; whereupon they not only fall in heaviness, but also in a sort of indignation against themselves, and querulous complaining of their condition, and by this means, are so far from performing their vows, that by their imprudence they do involve themselves in no small guiltiness: and for this distemper of mind and indignation against themselves, they conceive themselves to have just reason; partly, because they find their rejoicing in God, and thanksgiving to him, for the benefit received, nothing answerable to their earnest praying for it; partly, because the benefit received seems to them to have lost much of the estimation it had before they did receive it; partly, because they find even that small measure of joy, at the receiving of the benefit after some few days, to grow cold and likely to evanish. Hence doth suspicion begin to get footing in them, that for their ingratitude the Lord is angry with them, and hath bestowed the benefit on them, not in mercy but in wrath, and so they fall in the guiltiness of ingratitude more and more.

2. For removing of this evil, five practical errors must be removed, which ordinarily concur in this sickness. The first is this, the afflicted, in his promising unto God to be thankful, will be found to have had too much confidence in his own strength; trusting, that in his resolution, his heart could not but melt in the sense of the mercy granted. And this appeareth by his indignation against himself, when he findeth, that in his resolution his heart hath deceived him; as if he had expected the benefit from God, and the thanksgiving from himself; whereas he should have distinguished these two benefits, to wit, the gift prayed for, and the thanksgiving for it, and should have depended upon God for bestowing of both: for, the grace of thankfulness for a benefit asked and received, is greater than the benefit prayed for; which if the afflicted had considered well, he should have humbled himself before God for his not performance of his duty, rather than fallen in a proud quarrelling for his inability to be thankful.

3. The second error is an unequal comparison between the desire he had to obtain the benefit, and the rejoicing in God for the benefit received; for, the desire to obtain the benefit, ofttimes hath in it a great measure of natural and carnal appetite, and seeking of some part of self-perfection; but the rejoicing in God, which the convert purposed to offer for the benefit, is spiritual. And we are much more inclined to seek these things which pertain to the commodity of this life, then to perform spiritual duties; So that it is not to be wondered

at, when our desires, in part natural, are not followed with equal affection spiritual.

4. The third error is, when the convert doth not put difference between the estimation of the benefit, and the joy in God for bestowing of it, but measureth them with the same line, not considering that estimation is the act of the intellect and judgment, and that joy is the act of the affection; and both of them in this case exercised about divers objects: the estimation respecting the benefit itself, the affection of rejoicing in God who did bestow it, respecting the giver of the benefit. Now the estimation of, and delighting in, the benefit, may be less or more, while the estimation of God's goodness, in bestowing of it, remaineth the same. And therefore, the convert should not charge himself for lake of estimation of God and his gifts, albeit he feel much variety in the respective motions of his affections.

5. The fourth error is, when the convert counts all the estimation of, and thanksgiving for, the benefit, temporal or spiritual received, as nothing, because it is not answerable to the worth of what is received, or to the kindness of God who hath granted it: which reason, if it were of weight, there should be no acceptable thanksgiving from any Saint on earth, during this present life; for, it is impossible that any measure of thankfulness from men should be found answerable to the causes of their thankfulness, whether manifested in temporal or spiritual benefits. And therefore, upon this consideration, the Psalmist, Psal. 116:11, crieth out, What shall I render to the Lord, for all his benefits towards me?

6. The fifth error is, when the convert taketh it for an evidence of an unthankful mind, if the fervor of praising God, once kindled after the fresh receipt of the mercy, shall after some time, seem to cool or decay; which if it were true, no room should be left to any holy affection,

except only to the expression of joy for benefits received. But the truth is, that one duty must so be studied, as other duties have their time and place also; for, we are commanded to rejoice and tremble also, to rejoice with them that rejoice, and to mourn with them that mourn. Again we must acknowledge, that some expressions of thankfulness becometh the convert upon the fresh receipt of the benefit, which are not required to be always afterward continued. We read of the impotent cripple restored to his limbs by Peter, Act. 3:8, and that for joy, he leaped and cried out; but no man would require of him that he should always thereafter have danced and cried out, and yet he might be found among the number of thankful receivers of favor from God.

7. These errors then being removed, let the convert, 1. with the Psalmist, Psal. 103, charge his soul to bless God at all times, and to remember all his benefits, and not forget any of them, and to confess his obligation to God, which in the Scripture, and specially in the Psalms, is put for blessing, praising and thanking God; for, the word that signifieth in the Original to confess and praise, or thank, is ofttimes one and the same. 2. Let him beg grace to be thankful for benefits no less earnestly, then he doth beg the promised benefits themselves. 3. Let him put the sacrifices of thanks and praise in Christ's hands, by whom the calves of our lips are made acceptable unto God. 4. Let the convert comfort himself, that in the life to come, he shall be taken up with praise and thanks-giving to God forever and ever.

CHAP. XXIV. - Concerning the converts imprudent censure of himself for his felt impatiency in bearing lesser troubles, after his patient bearing of greater troubles.

SUNDRY CONVERTS, WHEN GREATER troubles do assault them, do humble themselves in the acknowledgement of their inability, and pray unto God for patience and strength to bear their burden. But when lesser troubles surprise them, they are foiled and overcome by their passions. For example, in the smaller pains of body, loss of goods, injuries done to them unexpected, by word or deed; and here they fume and fret, and break forth in some expressions of impatiency. Whereupon, when they reflect, they are so far from humbling themselves and making right use thereof, that their indignation at themselves, and their fretting is increased so much the more, as the cause of their impatiency was so small, as common reason found in heathens hath overcome, and therefore should have been more easily digested by Christians. This mis-carriage useth ofttimes to be past-by, without any fruit further then to acknowledge their infirmity.

2. But the true cure of this evil, is in discovery and removal of the causes thereof, which are three, 1. Carnal confidence of the convert in his own strength, as able to overcome lesser troubles. 2. Neglect of duty toward God in his rencounter with smaller provocations of passion; for, men in great troubles and weighty crosses, use to fly unto God by prayer to help them to bear the same, but when they meet with lesser crosses, they oppose their own strength unto them, and puts not up the matter to God, and so their infirmity is manifested. 3. God's wise correcting his child for neglecting of him in lightest matters.

3. Therefore let the convert afflicted in this case, acknowledge his failing, and be humbled at the sight of his passionate infirmity, and bless God for bearing down by his rod carnal self-confidence. 2. Let him learn of David, Psal. 141:3, not to trust in his own strength in anything, but depend on God for setting a watch before his mouth, and keeping the door of his lips, and mainly for keeping his heart from inclining to any evil thing. 3. Let him make more use both of Christ's open fountain for washing away sin and uncleanness, and of his assistance to mortify the deeds of corrupt nature by his Spirit: for, other ways the convert may look to be oftener foiled in this kind, and oftener to be corrected for not watching over his passions.

CHAP. XXV. - Concerning the converts mistaking his case for want of such a submission unto God's exercising of him, as he would have.

SOME TRUE CONVERTS, SOMETIME esteem themselves guilty of rebellion against God, because they cannot submit themselves in bodily or spiritual chastisements unto God's dispensation, as they would. The pretended reasons of their hard sentence against themselves, are three, 1. because they find in themselves fretting and murmuring against the Lord's dealing with them. 2. They find themselves far from humbling themselves under the mighty hand of God. 3. Because they find in themselves still unquietness after they set themselves to submit; which endeavor to submit, they conceive should have brought forth quietness of mind, if it had been real, and sincere submission indeed. And these thoughts, when they have weight, make way for many suggestions of Satan, and do draw on more and more unquietness and guiltiness withal.

For remedy whereof, 1. let it be considered, that in this exercise a difference must be put between God's part, the flesh, or corrupt nature's part, the new creatures part, and Satan's part.

As for God's part, by his chastisements and exercising of his child, he brings to light the perverseness of corrupt nature in his child, to humble him and drive him to Christ. The part of flesh or corrupt nature, is always to strive against the work of grace and the new creature, and it cannot be submissive unto God, Gal. 5:7, but must be mortified, Rom. 8:7. The part of the new creature, is not to consent to the fretting and murmuring of the flesh, but to oppose it, to yield unto God's dispensation, and to be grieved for the power of corrupt nature, and therefore not the new creature but corrupt nature should be condemned. Satan's part is, still to take advantage of every hard exercise, and to suggest wrong thoughts of God and his work, in the child of God.

Secondly, let a difference be made between the conflict of corrupt nature against the work of grace, and the victory of the corrupt nature; for, corrupt nature may fight, and not prevail, but be keeped from reigning in a man, how much soever it rage.

Thirdly, let a difference be made between the victory of corrupt nature in some conflicts, and its victory in the war; for, corrupt nature may prevail in sundry conflicts, and yet loss its labor in the close of the war, wherein grace is made perfectly victorious through Christ, in hope whereof, the child of God must renew the combat against nature and not faint.

Fourthly, let a difference be put between submission of mind and quietness in mind. Submission may be sincere, when pain of body maketh the convert to cry, when affliction maketh him a man of sorrow and grief; yea, when corrupt nature doth fret and murmur, provided that the convert control and condemn his corrupt nature, and suffer it not to break forth in words of impatiency, but prayeth to God to help him to bear the burden and endure his exercise with patience.

Fifthly, let a difference be put between the sinfulness of corrupt nature and the trouble which doth stir it up, and the sorrow which the convert hath in the observation of both; for, the sin is the work of the flesh and Satan, the trouble and affliction is the work of God, the sorrow for sin felt, is the work of God's Spirit also; and the sorrow for pain, loss, shame, or any sort of trouble, is moderate and sanctified when the convert offereth himself willing to endure it, so long as God shall be pleased to continue it. Last of all, let it be considered, that a wrestled-for submission, pleaseth God no less, then a victorious submission doth please the convert, because in wrestling against corrupt nature, the convert testifieth his will to please God, his glorifying of God's wisdom, justice, power and love, however the Lord deal with him. After which wrestling, the Lord doth give submission victorious, and quietness with it.

CHAP. XXVI. - Concerning the converts mistaking of his condition because of temptations.

GOD'S CHILDREN OFTTIMES ARE not only heavy and grieved because of temptations (which the Apostle, 1 Pet. 1:6, presupposeth to be ordinary, and in some respects needful) but also fall in a mistaking of their condition, as if it were altogether evil and displeasant unto God, because they perceive themselves many ways polluted in their conflict with them. Which pollutions, albeit they cannot be denied to be pollutions, and should not be excused, or extenuate, yet should not darken or obscure the grace of God in a convert striving against temptations, and lamenting his pollutions contracted by occasion of them.

2. These temptations, that they may be the more clearly discovered, we shall divide them in three sorts. 1. some of them are directly from God, in a wise and holy manner, for trial and exercise of faith, hope, charity and other graces, and do not in any way tempt men to sin. 2. Some are from the flesh and the world, alluring or inducing

men to sin; which two we join together, because concupiscence or the flesh, or corrupt nature, joineth itself with the world, and these two help one another, and therefore are joined together by the Apostle, 1 John 2:16. All that is in the world is the lust of the eyes, the lust of the flesh and the pride of life. And when men are tempted by their own lusts, the world doth furnish objects, allurements, and inducements to sin. The third sort are, the temptations from Satan, who beside that he is not idle to take advantage of concupiscence and the worlds inducements, so is he chiefly busy to throw his fiery darts against the convert, and to solicit men to such sins as the convert doth most detest and abhor.

As for the first sort of temptations from God, they are ordinarily by afflictions bodily or spiritual, wherein ofttimes the converts do not observe the Lord's purpose and will revealed in Scripture, or are forgetful of the admonitions and consolations which they have heard from Scripture, which was the case of the afflicted Saints, Heb. 12:5, and so they are more vexed than they should be; and, (Psal. 42:11) dejected and disquieted, and do suspect that God is angry with them and with the way they walk in, Heb. 12:12,13.

Of this sickness, there may be three causes, 1. the bitterness of affliction for the present time wherein it is felt. 2. The sense of by-past sin which the afflicted doth suspect God is pursuing, and making him possess the sins of his youth, Job. 13:26. The third, is the observation of in-born corruption, discovered unto the afflicted much more then in prosperity.

4. For remedy of this evil, let the afflicted convert persuade himself from the Word of God, that in all the afflictions of God's children, the Lord doth intend the trial and exercise and increase of faith, and other grace, bestowed on them. And upon this consideration, the

afflicted should rejoice in this exercise, Jam. 1:2,3. Secondly, let him remember, that with the trial of faith, there is always a discovery of infirmity and corruption of nature in the afflicted: As in the purifying of gold, both the good metal and the dross are discovered, which as he should acknowledge, that he may be keeped from fretting, So must he still remember, that the Lord doth intend the trial of his faith, that he may be constant in believing on Christ, the only help and relief from sin and misery. Thirdly, in whatsoever condition he is in, let him endeavor to go on in patience, experience and hope, which shall never make him ashamed, for this doth the Lord teach us, Rom. 5:3,4, and Jam. 1:4.

As for the second sort of temptations, from the concupiscence of the flesh and from the worlds allurements and terror, let the convert afflicted follow the same course which is prescribed in the remedy of the temptations of the first sort.

As for the third sort of temptations, which are from the devil tempting men to atheism, or blasphemy, or despair, or self-murder, and such like, which even nature doth abhor, whereof something is spoken elsewhere, 1. let the afflicted convert put difference between the devil's sin in tempting to vile sins, and his own seeming feeble resisting, wherein albeit he thinketh himself polluted, yet his not yielding testifieth his dissenting from those fearful sins whereunto Satan doth tempt him. 2. Let him put difference between the consent of his unmortified corrupt nature inclinable to every evil, from the lust of the spirit which fighteth against the lust of the flesh, which hindereth the adversary from getting the victory. 3. Let him put difference between the sufficiency of God's grace upholding him in the conflict, and the full victory against the messenger of Satan buffeting him: for, God useth to suspend the victory for a time, and yet make his grace sufficiently uphold his soldier till the victory be given, as Paul's experience, 2 Cor. 12, teacheth us. And indeed, it is a pleasant spectacle to the Lord to look upon his weak child striving against the flesh, the world and Satan, and standing out by faith in Christ against them all. 4. Let him consider, that by these temptations of Satan unto vile sins, God can, and doth mortify sin, and make his child watchful and strong against both the sinful inclination unto these and all other sins. In the meantime, let him beware of a more sly and subtle temptation, which Satan useth to slide in at the back of these ugly and gross temptations; which is this, when he hath pressed with all violence these fiery darts and vile suggestions upon the convert, he chargeth the afflicted soul with a giving consent unto them, and like a scolding calumniator impudently beareth guiltiness upon him, and all to make him apprehend his condition to be worse than it is, and to suspect, that God, by this exercise, is pursuing him in wrath; and this temptation is not readily observed by the afflicted convert, but yielded unto more then to the gross temptation. Therefore, in the last place, let the convert guard against this temptation which wrangleth his faith, and lay the blame, with the Apostle, on corrupt nature, whatsoever guiltiness is found, Rom. 7:17. Now, then it is no more I that doth it, but sin that dwelleth in me; a speech beseeming a man free of out-breaking and prevailing corruption, and striving against all inward motions of corrupt nature. And for remedy of this and other evils, let him renew the acts of his faith in Christ, laying hold upon the covenant of Grace, that he may more confidently draw near unto God reconciled in Christ, and so no more doubt of God's good will to him, notwithstanding of his hard exercise under temptations: for, thus Satan shall not only fly from the first temptation, being resisted, but also be disappointed of the success he expected in questioning the coverts condition and weakening of his faith.

CHAP. XXVII. - Concerning the converts mistaking his condition when he doth observe some degrees of God's deserting of him.

To speak of the sorts and degrees of God's deserting a soul, requireth a large Treatise, and the case and cure thereof is already publicly set forth by a learned and godly Preacher of the Gospel. It shall suffice, for our purpose, to speak of it only so far as it concerneth the converts mistaking his condition when he apprehendeth himself deserted, whether the desertion be real or apparent only, and falleth into suspicion of God's love to him, or that God is displeased with him, because he findeth not such lively influence of God's Spirit as he hath found, and such assistance of his gracious presence as he did expect in discharge of religious duties, or exercises wherein divine providence hath yoked him. The Scripture and daily experience do furnish instances of sad complaints of the Lord's hiding his face and withdrawing or with-holding of light or peace, or consolation, or strength and ability for spiritual duties, &c.

2. For remedy whereof, 1. let the convert remember, that God doth not leave a believer fled to Christ for relief from sin and misery, always and forever, but for a short time, and that he keepeth love to them constantly, albeit he do hide the tokens of his love sometime, and dispose of the acts of his love, as he seeth sit for the advantage of the work of grace in them. Let him put difference between desertion and the gift of discerning of the desertion: for, albeit desertion be of itself a sad visitation, yet the sight and observation of it, testifieth God's presence with his child, giving eye-salve and light; and thereby doth not only teach that wound to be curable, but also that the Physician is begun the cure of it, by pancing and lancing the wound. 3. Let him not count it a desertion, when God in any service whereunto he puts his child, emptieth him of all conceit of his own ability, that he may open his mouth wyd and be filled: for this emptying of the convert, is the very fitting of him for fresh supply from Christ to go about the service in Christ's strength and furniture, which the Apostle felt by experience, 2 Cor. 12:10. When I am weak, saith he, then I am strong. Poverty of spirit, and hunger and thirst for righteousness, are not to be counted desertions. 4. Let him observe the degrees of God's presence, no less than the degrees of his absence, as the Psalmist did when he recollected himself, Psal. 73:23, after the temptation which troubled him was overcome. Nevertheless, I am continually with thee. Thou holdest me by thy right hand, and ver. 26, my flesh and my heart faileth, but God is the strength of my heart and my portion forever. 5. Let him put a right construction upon God's dispensation, believing always, that God doth what he doth for good to his afflicted subject;

whether he draw forth, by his desertion, the latent-corruption of the heart, as he did to Hezekiah, 2 Chron. 32:31, or whether to prevent out-breaking of corruption, as he did to the Apostle, 2 Cor. 12:7-9, or whether to exercise his faith, love and patience, and to sharpen his prayer, as he did to the Psalmist frequently. And therefore, let him, in the observation of whatsoever degree of desertion, humble himself before God, fly in more closely unto Christ, and patiently wait upon the change of his condition, in the use of the means, and following the duties of his calling as the Lord shall enable him: for, this is the counsel of the Lord, Isa. 50:10. Who is he among you that feareth the Lord, that obeyeth the voice of his servant, that walketh in darkness and hath no light? Let him trust in the name of the Lord, and stay upon his God. And this much sufficeth for instances of the third sort of the converts mistaking his condition.

CHAP. XXVIII. - Concerning cases, wherein the convert is in doubt what to determine about his condition.

IT RESTETH, THAT WE speak of the fourth sort of cases of the conscience of the convert, wherein he is at a stand, and in doubt what to determine of his present condition.

2. In these doubtful cases, the convert is not properly deceived, as in the former ranks of cases it is presupposed of him; because in this sort of cases, the convert doth not positively determine the question wherein he is fallen, but standeth in doubt what to resolve upon.

3. Cases of this sort pertain to the mind and judgment of the convert, and if his judgment be cleared by loosing of the question, incontinent he is satisfied and quiet.

4. It is necessary for the converts clearing, that he form the question rightly; and to this end, 1. let him consider his case and condition in himself, so accurately as he can. 2. Let him ingenuously lay forth the question or doubt he hath, before his Pastor or Christian friend, acquainted with cases of conscience, and ask their judgment what

to think of, or what to do in, such a case. The reason why he must examine narrowly his own condition, before he speak of it to another, is partly because other ways his doubt or question may prove frivolous and unworthy of an answer; partly, because the convert, after examination of his case and prayer unto God, may find satisfaction to his doubt; and partly, because, if his doubt remain, the question may be the more clearly propounded, and so receive the more clear and speedy answer for his satisfaction.

5. Of this sort of questions, we shall propound some examples and give some resolution unto them, whereof use may be made when such like questions shall occur.

The first question shall be, concerning confusion of mind.

It cometh to pass sometime, when a convert is upon examination of his own estate or condition, that such a mist and darkness falleth on his mind, and such a crowd and throng of thoughts within him, that he can discern nothing but mist, multitude of thoughts, and darkness and confusion. The question is, what shall he think or do, for removing of this confusion of thoughts and darkness of mind?

Ans. This case befalleth converts frequently, and therefore had need to be the more carefully cured: Which cure, that it may the better go on, let the afflicted renew the examination of his former behavior, and see if he can find out the meritorious cause thereof in himself; for, this case ofttimes is the castigation of the afflicted, for his former negligence and omission of duties, or slight discharge of religious worship: yea, it may be found possibly, that the afflicted hath been so careless in keeping his heart in the fear of God, that he hath involved himself too far in earthly and thorny affairs, or hath exceeded in the use of things lawful, or by some corrupt communication, hath grieved the Lord's spirit, and so hath drawn on some desertion and with-drawing of illumination from him.

2. This case may also fall out, from some present perturbation of mind and passion, whereby his reason is so taken up for the time, that it cannot discharge its duty: as cometh to pass usually in anger or fear, or grief, or some such like passion as may be seen, when a man is injured by his neighbor, or doth meet with some damage, or is put in fear of some imminent evil coming on him, or findeth sharp pains of body, or some such like cause perplexing him. The question is, what shall he think of this condition?

Ans. If the afflicted shall examine how he is fallen in this case, and shall, in consideration of his weakness, be humbled before God by prayer, he shall not want clearness of mind, and directions from God what to do and how to behave himself, in ordering of his conversation aright, Psal. 50:23, for, the Lord gives wisdom liberally, to all that ask it of him in faith, Jam. 1:5, and this his present condition giveth him an errand to God.

The second question is, concerning the convert, who most part walketh heavily.

There are some true converts, who after examination of themselves, cannot deny, but their heart is toward the ways of God in their calling, and that as they find the imperfections of their service, so they are forced to renounce all confidence in their own righteousness, and to fly to the righteousness of Christ, as the only true garment able to hide their nakedness; yet, they are for the most part heavy in their spirit, seldom they rejoice, but many times they weep; and howsoever they maintain confidence in Christ for the state they stand into, yet, when they consider their ordinary heaviness of heart, they doubt what to think of this their sad condition.

Ans. This condition, if well considered, is very useful, albeit not always comfortable; for, the Lord's dispensation toward such a person thus exercised, is well tempered and wisely mixed: for, he neither suffereth the heavy in heart to cast away his confidence in Christ, nor to be idle and unfruitful in his vocation, nor to glory in his own works, or put confidence in them, but so keepeth him up to the duty of more and more esteeming of Christ's righteousness, and drawing of strength from him by faith, that he goeth on in his course uprightly, albeit not fed as he would be by the consolations of the holy Ghost.

2. For remedy whereof, let him quiet his mind; for, after examination of his own natural inclination, he shall find the reason of the Lord's dispensation toward him, sparingly giving unto him such measure of consolation as he would have, to be this, least he should abuse the same, and lean more to the sensible feeling thereof then to the word of faith: and therefore, however he find heaviness of heart through manyfold temptations, let him hold on his way in the obedience of faith, he shall after a whiles patience and wrestling, meet with as much peace and consolation as may suffice a pilgrim, walking from strength to strength till he appear before God in heaven, where all tears shall be wiped away from his eyes. Meantime, let this ground be holden fast, that God mixeth the cup of his own children as he findeth it fit for their edification.

The third question is, concerning the converts, who for not looking on their original sin and the out breakings thereof, are in doubt what to think of their former condition.

Some converts are, who after a quiet possession of peace enjoyed in a blameless conversation among men, and in the exercises of religion uprightly before God, after examination of their condition more narrowly, do find, that the conscience for a long time hath been silent, and hath not changed for the motions of original sin, but suffered them to go on securely under the guiltiness of the daily sprouting forth thereof. In this case, as they dare not cast away their confidence in Christ, nor their holy purpose of walking uprightly before God; So they cannot justify the silence of their conscience, which hath suffered the motions of sin (although not consented unto) to go away without challenge or reckoning made for them, and here they are in straits, and doubt what to judge of their own condition.

Ans. In this case, the silence of the conscience is not to be excused: And the peace of the convert albeit it may be sound, in order to the converts state in grace, yet the condition wherein he is, is not good, but mixed with much security; for, to make the condition of a convert to be good, it is not only required, that his conscience be keeped free from gross pollutions, but also that he be daily aiming at mortifying of sin, and that to this end, he daily give an account unto God of his wandering and vanity, and of the observed out-sprouting's of the bitter root of original sin, that he may, after his best behavior, perceive a necessity of that prayer, taught us by our Lord for daily remission of sins, and so may daily have the answer of God from the Evangel, saying, Son, be of good cheer, thy sins are forgiven unto thee: For, there is a twofold absolution of the convert, one is in order to his person, which Christ calleth the washing of the whole man, the other is in order to his daily imperfections and blemishes of his conversation, which Christ doth call the washing of the feet. By virtue of the first sort of absolution, the child of God, flying to Christ, is judicially declared free from condemnation; by the other, the believer, making use of the fountain opened up in Christ, is exempted from his acknowledged uncleanness. This is clear from Christ's words, John 13:10. Mean time we confess, that the motions of sin in our mortal bodies are so innumerable, that no man can overtake them, yet must they be counted for a heap at least, as David doth teach us, Psal. 19:12. Who knoweth the errors of his life? Cleanse me from my secret sins. And this same lesson doth the Apostle teach us, Rom. 7:24. Wretched man that I am, saith he, who shall deliver me from the body of this death? I thank God through Jesus Christ. Wherefore, let the convert go on in his former godly and righteous behavior and conversation, not mis-regarding the sprouting's of original sin, but giving account thereof unto Christ, as said is, that he may glorify that righteousness of Christ by faith, and enjoy peace with God, not only in order to his state, but also in order to his condition daily.

The fourth question is, how the convert may know and be certain of his justification.

When the true convert heareth the different opinions of Theologues, concerning the act of justification of a believer, some saying, that it is an act of God immanent, whereby he willeth the absolution of the believer; some saying, that it is an act of God eminent and transient from God upon the spirit of the believer; some saying it is the sentence of the Judge, absolving the believing sinner from the curse of the law. The believer here possibly is at a stand, and knoweth not how to answer the question till his doubt be loosed.

For the satisfaction of the convert, first, we may safely say, that it is not material whether the convert be able to take up the quiddity and formal notion of the act of justification, provided he be a believer in Christ and know that the believer in Christ is justified before God, and that being justified by faith, he hath peace with God, and can apply these truths unto himself, in the exercise of repentance and new obedience. But if possibly, the convert cannot be satisfied till his doubt be answered, let him consider, that he must distinguish between justification actively taken as it proceedeth from God, and justification passively taken as it is terminate on the justified man; as it is taken actively, these four things are to be distinguished, 1. God's eternal will and decree, to absolve from sin and wrath every believer in Christ. 2. God's actual revealing in time this his gracious pleasure in the Gospel. 3. God's judicial application of this general sentence to the believer in the point of his conversion, whether the believer perceive his absolution or not for the time. 4. There is a sensible intimation of this sentence unto the believer, joined with peace and joy, which the Apostle calleth the shedding abroad of the love of God in the heart, Rom. 5:5, and the sealing of the holy Ghost stamping the heart with holiness, Ephes. 1:13. The first three makes the absolution of the believer certain, whether the believer thinks so or not; but the fourth, which is the sensible intimation of this sentence, doth make the believer both sure and joyful.

As justification is taken passively, four things may be distinguished in the believer justified. The first is, his actual receiving of Christ, offered in the Gospel for a perfect remedy of sin and misery. The second is, the Lord's judicial settling of the general sentence of absolution upon the believer, as if he had spoken to him by name, as he did to the Apostles, John 15:3. Now are ye clean through the word I have spoken unto you, that is, you are clean from the guile of sin by my absolving of you. The third is, the believers observing, in a reflect act of his conscience, that he hath fled to Christ for absolution, and therefore justified indeed. The fourth is, the feeling and observing of the testimony of the holy Ghost bearing witness with his spirit, that he is a child of God absolved from sin and wrath. The first two of these, to wit, the act of faith, receiving of Christ and of the right made by Christ to the believer in him of his absolution, may be in, and on the believer without the other two, to wit, his observation of the act of faith, and the felt intimation of this work of grace by the holy Spirit.

2. For solving of the doubt then; as justification is actively taken, as proceeding from the immanent act of God's eternal purpose and decree to justify the believer, it is no more the actual justification in this life, of which we are speaking, then the immanent act of God's eternal purpose to raise the bodies of believers in Christ, and to glorify them in soul and body, can be called the actual resurrection of their bodies, and glorification of both soul and body in this life.

But the transient act of justification in a judicial way, which is the Lord's judicial sentence of absolution of the believer, declared by his Word, set down now in holy Scripture, it is indeed and formally the believer's justification, and is judicially terminate upon every believer in the act of his conversion, whether the believer doth clearly perceive his own conversion, or be in suspicion of his being reconciled and justified.

And this may be made to appear, if we compare the condemnation of the unbeliever with the absolution of the believer fled to Christ, John 3:18. As he that believeth not in Christ is condemned already, because the curse of the law and condemnation, pronounced in the Scripture by God, the sovereign Judge, stands against him so long as he doth not believe in the only begotten Son of God: And this sentence standeth fast, whether the unbeliever take notice of this sentence or not, whether he do apply it to himself or not, do find grief for it or not: So the believer in Christ is relaxed from condemnation and absolved, and hath right unto eternal life and begun possession of it, albeit for the time of his infancy, temptation, trembling and fear, it be not so, albeit he doth not perceive the blessed change of his state, nor doth lay to heart, as he might, the words of Christ judicially pronouncing the sentence, comprehending him as certainly as if his name were expressed, John 3:18. He that believeth on him, is not condemned, and ver. 36. He that believeth on the Son hath everlasting life, and John 6:37-41. Hence we conclude, that the formal act of justification of a man fled to Christ, is to be found in the written sentence of the judge absolving every believer and the man we speak of.

There is another transient act of God, in an actual revelation of justification, wherein the holy Ghost openeth the eyes of the believer to behold and perceive the gift of faith already bestowed on him: Of this speaks the Apostle, 1 Cor. 2:12. And after that the holy Ghost hath pointed out his own grace, bestowed on the believer, he followeth his work, by giving remarkable peace and joy as earnest of life everlasting, whereof the Apostle speaketh, Ephes. 1:13. In whom ye also trusted, after ye heard the word of truth, the Gospel of your salvation: in whom also, after ye had believed, ye were sealed with the spirit of promise, which is the earnest of our inheritance. Therefore, he that desireth to have the intimation of his justification, after flying for refuge unto Christ for relief of felt sin and feared wrath, must read his absolution in the Gospel, as well as he hath read, before that, his condemnation in the law. Unto which sentence of absolution, let him hold fast in his daily endeavor after sanctification.

The fifth question is, how to satisfy the convert who findeth himself pursued for his sins after remission believed, and is brought in question what to judge of his case.

Many converts have fallen in Job's case, and seemed to themselves to possess the sins of their youth, Job 13:26. For, after conversion and felt reconciliation, they find the sins they did repent of, and did believe to be forgiven through Christ, objected to them afresh, pursued with sharp accusations, and signs of wrath joined therewith.

Their reconciliation and righteousness through Christ, they purpose to hold fast; their old guiltiness, and sentence of their conscience writing bitter things against them, they cannot deny: The pinch is here, either the remission they did believe is null, or the challenge is unjust, do they reason with themselves; the nullity of their remission they dare not admit, and the just ground of challenge they cannot deny, and the doubt what to think of this case they cannot shun, not seeing, how these things can consist and stand together.

2. For answer to this doubt, these four things must be distinguished, and how they may all consist one with another, must be timeously considered. The four things to be distinguished are, 1. the reconciliation of a convert with God; 2. the remission of the reconciled man's sins freely gifted unto him by God; 3. a renewed bitter accusation raised by Satan against the reconciled convert; 4. The holy and wise dispensation of God, permitting and ordering these renewed accusations of his child by Satan, for the trial and exercise of his faith and growth of his repentance, and other good ends.

Now for the consistence of these four, we need not doubt, but the accuser of the brethren can cast up to us forgiven sins, and bear upon us that they are not forgiven. Neither need we doubt, but God in wisdom and love to his children, may suffer Satan to renew accusations against them, and so order that matter, as neither Satan shall prevail, nor his child suffer damage by the means: for, there is a great difference between Satan's renewing of accusations for sins forgiven, and God's making null the remission granted, the Lord can suffer the one to be, but the other he will never suffer to be: for, when a true convert groweth negligent, and falleth in such sins after conversion as he lived in before conversion, no wonder Satan be permitted to call his former conversion in question; yea, the Lord may justly cast up to his child his former faults, to humble him and shame him from going on, albeit he doth not disannul the formerly granted remission.

3. When thanksgiving for remission of sin, granted for Christ's cause, beginneth to cool in the heart of a convert, what wonder the Lord not only suffer, but also present the vileness of by-past sins to make the convert sensible of the remission, and to cause him renew the acts of repentance and godly sorrow for his sins by-past, as, Ezek. 16:63, and 36:32. Then shall you remember your own evil ways and your doings which were not good, and shall loath yourselves for your iniquities and abominations.

When the convert groweth remiss in watching over his own heart and ways, and is in danger of falling back into these sins which he had repented of before, what wonder the Lord by remembering him of his natural inclination and former ways, do warn him of his danger to make him preveen his fall?

4. Wherefore, let the convert maintain the solidity of former remission of sins, and make good use of his former sins which went before his conversion, and let him follow the example of Paul, who did not suffer his former sins go out of his mind, but did renew the confession of them upon all occasions for his own daily humiliation, for the edification of others, and for magnifying the glory of the grace of God, and yet for all this, did not suspect the remission of sins received: For, by this means the convert shall preveen accusations, and stop Satan's mouth, and make his accusations have no force. By this means, the convert shall possess firm and stable confidence of God's unchangeable grace and mercy, and of the stability of the remission of sin granted.

The sixth question is, of a convert casten, not only in an uncertainty for the time of his conversion, but also in a doubt whether he be elected or not, and knows not how to do in this case.

Some converts fall in Heman the Ezrahite his exercise, whereof we read, Psal. 88, especially, ver. 14,15. While I suffer thy terrors I am distracted, saith he. Counsel hath been offered by some to the afflicted, to follow the practice and experience of some eminent Theologues, who being brought to such straits with good success, have submitted themselves to God, to save them or destroy them as he pleased; after which submission, they have felt the marvelous sweet embracement's of God's loving kindness, making them sure both of their conversion and election. Whether to follow this example and experience of some notable Saints, is the doubt, wherein the convert is not clear, and knoweth nor how to carry himself toward God in this case.

2. For answer to this question: It is free for God to comfort a soul casten down, when, and how, he pleaseth; it is free for God to pass by the infirmity and error of a terrified soul, coming to him not in the wisest way prescribed to him, and to look to the necessity of the man's consolation, and not to his way of seeking of it. But, howsoever it pleaseth God to comfort some extraordinarily, yet this is not the duty of the afflicted to come with such an unrequired submission unto God: for, it limiteth the Lord, in a manner, either to comfort the man speedily, or suffer him upon apparent refusal for the time, to despair: For, God's order is to bring the sinner under the sense of sin and acknowledgment of deserved wrath for sin, and then to charge him to believe in the name of his Son Jesus Christ, and after believing in Christ, to seal the believer with the stamp of holiness and

the earnest-penny of the inheritance, which is peace with God, and joy in the holy Ghost shed abroad in his heart.

3. Wherefore, as for the conversion of a man straitened in the pains of the new birth and fear of everlasting wrath, and tempted to suspect that he is not elected: It is a more safe way to lay aside all disputation about God's decree (because secret things belong to the Lord) and to look to the Lord's command, and to his own duty of flying unto Christ: So for the recovery of a convert, fallen in Jonah's case, and made to suspect, that he is a reprobate cast off of God, it is a more safe way not to dispute for the time, either his election or conversion, whatsoever suggestions may be cast in by Satan, then to offer unto God an absolute submission to be saved or destroyed as he pleaseth, and then to lie in sorrow till God give an answer of consolation: for, God doth not require such a submission, but calleth for an act of faith and obedience; for, God hath declared in his Word, that he delighteth not in the death of a sinner, but that he should repent and turn to God and be saved. Secondly, in this submission the heart will be found deceitful, which neither will nor can submit to be destroyed. Thirdly, this offer of such a submission as this is, [Lord, I know not whether thou hast chosen me or rejected me in thy decree, but I submit myself to thee absolutely. If thou wilt destroy me, thou shalt be found to be just, and I do confess so much unto thee; but if thou wilt save me, I shall proclaim thy grace] such a submission, I say, is but in effect, a tempting of God speedily to reveal his secret counsel, either by consolation, if the submitter be an elect, or refusal of con-solation, if he be a reprobate. The only safe way in the foresaid case, is to be humbled before God, and fly to Christ by prayer, (as Heman did, Psal. 88, and as Jonah did, who chose to look again to his holy Temple, where the Mediator sat upon the mercy seat between the

cherubim's) and not suffer such a thought as reprobation. Thus did Heman, Psal. 88:13,14. But unto thee have I cried, O Lord, and in the morning shall my prayer prevent thee. Lord, why castest thou off my soul, why hidest thou thy face from me. Let the command of God to every self-condemned sinner, to believe in Christ, prevail against all temptations to the contrary; 1 John 3:23. This is his commandment, that we should believe on the name of his Son Jesus Christ.

The seventh question is, how to satisfy the convert, doubting whether it be better to forbear or go on in the outward exercise of religion, (at least in private) when he finds an indisposition of mind unto it.

Sundry converts, when they perceive the unfitness of their spirits to offer immediate worship to God in prayer, praises or thanksgiving, especially in private, do fall in doubt with themselves, whether it be better to delay the offer of their worship, till they find themselves well disposed for it, or to go on as they may, albeit they apprehend their lips polluted, and their hearts far away from God. Their fear on the one hand is, lest they should pollute the worship and take God's name in vain; on the other hand, they fear lest they fall in the guiltiness of omitting a prescribed duty. The question shall be, what the doubting convert should determine and do?

2. For answer, this case is spoken unto before, 2. Book, Chap. 17, in as far as the convert determineth not, and doth not what is right, but goeth wrong and pleaseth himself in his bad condition. But here we speak to this case, as the convert is in doubt only, and desireth to be keeped from deceiving himself. In which case we say, that as it is the converts doubt, so we must confess, that this case of indisposition and unfitness for spiritual exercises is very frequent, and is ordinarily and ofttimes a chastisement of us, drawn on by ourselves, because

we do not watch unto prayer, we do not study to keep our hearts in
the fear of the Lord all the day long, we do not foster that tenderness
of conscience which might furnish us matter of humiliation, and
of thanksgiving to God upon observation of our faults against God,
and of God's favors daily and hourly remarkably running toward us.
Hence it is, when our ordinary time of secret worship doth come, we
find our roaming minds hardly called home from their wandering,
our conscience challenging us for our loose and uncircumspect walking, our affections dull and dead, and all the powers of our souls taken
as with a palsy, that we cannot bestir ourselves in worship as we
should and would. Therefore, in this case, let the convert be humbled
and confess his fault, and take with this chastisement and fly unto
Christ, who heareth and taketh away the iniquity of our pollution of
holy things; and let him nor defer his worship till another occasion,
but wrestle against all impediments and follow out the work in hand,
blessing God for his pointing out unto him his wants and weakness,
his wandering and vanity of mind, his slipping and sliding in his
ways, and for opening unto him a fountain in Christ, for washing
his pollutions and healing his wounds. And that the convert may
be encouraged to aim at, and follow on, this way, let him consider,
that the converts worship may be pleasant and acceptable to God,
when the convert is much displeased with himself in the discharge
of it: for, there is a worshiping of God in faith, without sense and
feeling of the hearts enlargement; and there is a worshiping of God
with felt enlargement of heart. The worshiping of God in faith is
pleasant unto God, albeit the worshiper in perplexity and wrestling
with temptations and corruptions, be much displeased with himself.
The worshiping of God with enlargement of heart is pleasant, both
unto God and to the worshiper also, as (Psal. 119:32) David gives us to

understand, I will run the way of thy Commandments, saith he, when thou shalt enlarge my heart. But when this enlargement, by sensible assistance of the holy Ghost, is not perceived, the Psalmist is but a dead man in his own estimation; yet, he doth not forbear or delay to worship God as well in bonds as in freedom; Quicken me, saith he, according to thy loving kindness. Therefore, let the convert in this case, 1. follow the example of the Psalmist, who (Psal. 5:3) resolveth to call on God with his voice, that is, to follow the work of prayer externally, pre-suppose his spiritual powers were bound up, and he unable to back his petitions with suitable affections; My voice, saith he, shalt thou hear in the morning, O Lord, in the morning will I direct my prayer unto thee, and will look up. And, Psal. 27:7. Hear me when I cry with my voice, have mercy also upon me and answer me. 2. For his encouragement in this case to go on in his worship, let him confess unto God the truth, as it is presented unto him by his conscience, and say, O Lord my God, these are my sins which I ought to acknowledge before thee with tears, which for the present are dried up, &c. These are thy favors and benefits wherewith I am loadened, which I should acknowledge with joy and sense of thy goodness, &c. but thou Lord delights in truth in the inward parts, Psal. 51:8. This will be found our reasonable service which the Apostle calleth for, Rom. 12:1,2.

The eight question is, how to satisfy the convert, doubting what is the sin which God pursueth by long-lasting affliction.

It falleth forth ofttimes, when a true convert, being a long time pressed under some lasting cross or calamity, doth inquire after the special causes of his affliction; and when he cannot be clear what to determine, doth doubt what to think of his condition: for, he acknowledgeth his sins, common to him and other converts, to be innumerable; but apprehendeth that it is some special sin pursued by God, which is the cause of his affliction, which because he cannot condescend upon, he is at a stand, and doubteth what to think or do.

2. For answer we say, 1. such a case is more troublesome then dangerous; for, so long as he is observing his sins, common to him and other converts, and in the exercise of repentance is daily humbled before God for his known sins, he must not be anxious, albeit he know not the particular sin pursued, as he apprehendeth: for, albeit the Lord afflict no man but such as have sin in them, yet he doth not always, in afflicting of his children, pursue unknown sin in them. For, sometime he afflicteth his child to preveen his sinning, hedging up his way with thorns, lest he should follow after beloved lusts. Sometime he doth afflict him to try his faith, to teach him patience, meekness, temperance and other virtues, such as are dying to the world, seeking after things spiritual, compassion toward others in affliction. 2. When the afflicted hath composed his mind to reverence God's dispensation, whatsoever it is or shall be, then let him yet again look upon his affliction, and it may be he shall read in the rod what is the Lord's quarrel. 3. Whether he shall find the special cause of his affliction or not, let him turn all his indignation, zeal and hatred against the body of death, the bitter root and bulk of actual sins, and watch diligently over the motions of original sin, or concupiscence in himself. 4. And let his whole exercise stir him up to have Christ in greater estimation, to make use of Christ's righteousness imputed to believers, and to invocate his holy name for the right use-making of his affliction.

The ninth question is, how remission of sin may be said to be granted in respect of sins to come.

It is commonly said, that the convert, in his justification, hath the remission of sins by-gone and sins to come: whereupon the question is moved, how this can stand with daily renewed remission of daily sins; on the one hand, daily renewed remission seemeth not necessary, first, because we believe, that remission of all sin, is the privilege of all believers in Christ, and the abridgement of the special articles of faith set down in the Apostles Creed, as it is called, holdeth this forth. 2. Because it is certain, that Christ, in his death, did complete the payment of the price of redemption from all sin, as 1 John 1:7. The blood of Jesus Christ cleanseth us from all sins. 3. We are said to be not under the law, but under grace, and so freed from the curse of the law. 4. Because if daily remission of sin be necessary to be granted, then it presuppones, that both original sin, and every actual sin flowing forth from it daily, must be taken notice of, reckoned for, and repented of daily, which is impossible. On the other hand, the convert seeth, that every transgression of, and disconformity to, the law is sin; and the Apostle, 1 John 1:8, speaking of himself and other converts, saith, If we say we have no sin, we deceive ourselves, and the truth is not in us. And Christ hath taught us, as oft as we pray for our daily bread, to pray also for the remission of sins. The question is, how the doubt of the convert may be cleared?

2. For answer: We must grant to the convert, that original sin remaineth in the believer, and is not only an exceeding sin, as the Apostle calleth it, Rom. 7:13, but also is the fountain of all actual sins which doth pollute the conscience, and sometimes also the outward man. 2. We must grant also, that there cannot be an actual and properly called remission of sins which are not yet committed: for, no man is guilty of that fault wherewith he cannot be charged: for, such a remission were a dispensation and license to sin, such as the Pope granteth to his slaves to gratify them, in allowing their vile lusts for enriching himself with the price of that iniquity. 3. If such an

actual remission of sins were given in justification, the once justified person could never become a daily debtor by his daily transgressions, contrary to the declaration of Christ in one of the articles of the Lord's prayer.

3. For solving the doubt then, we must distinguish the significations and acceptions of remission of sin: For, 1. it is taken for remission purchased by Christ, by virtue of the covenant of Redemption, in favors of the elect, but not applied unto the elect before the man's conversion, Heb. 10:12-14. But this man, after he had offered one sacrifice for sins forever, sat down on the right hand of God: from henceforth expecting till his enemies be made his footstool. For by one offering he hath perfected forever them that are sanctified. 2. It is taken for remission promised by Christ to all that shall believe in him, to be bestowed on them so soon as they shall turn to him, Act. 26:18. Thirdly, it is taken for the sentence of absolution, judicially applied and adjudged to the actual believer, Eph. 1:7. In whom we have redemption through his blood, the forgiveness of sins, according to the riches of his grace. 4. For the actual remission of all sins past before his conversion, Rom. 3:25. Whom God hath set forth to be a propitiation, through faith in his blood to declare his righteousness for the remission of sins that are past, through the forbearance of God. 5. For a constant right to daily remission of sin, and access to the fountain opened up in the house of David, (that is, to all the children of the household of faith in Christ) Zech. 13:1. In that day there shall be a fountain opened to the house of David, and to the inhabitants of Jerusalem, for sin, and for uncleanness.

4. So then, the convert hath, first, the actual remission of all sins preceding his conversion, and withal his state, changed from being a child of Satan, to be a child of God. Secondly, he hath right unto

daily remission of sins, as they fall out after conversion; for, Christ, speaking of the remission had in the time of conversion, calleth it a washing of the whole man, Joh. 13:10 He that is washen needeth not to wash, save his feet, but is wholly clean, to wit, for the state of his person accepted in Christ, and for the application of his right unto daily remission. Christ teacheth all his disciples daily to pray for it, which Christ calleth the washing of the believer's feet, Joh. 13:10.

5. For answer to the objections, made against the necessity of daily renewed remission of sin, let it be remembered, that the article of our Creed is so far from making daily remission of sin not necessary, that of necessity it must be extended, not only to the remission of sins past before conversion, but also to the right made unto us, for daily remission of the sins which run daily from the relicts of corrupt nature not fully mortified; for other ways, the believer could not have quiet consolation in the daily exercise of renewed repentance and faith in Jesus Christ. 2. As to the second objection, concerning the perfect purchase made by Christ of remission by-past and to come; It doth prove indeed, that there is no other sacrifice for sin, nor price of redemption from sin, save that which was completed on the cross; but it doth not prove, that we must only once make application of this purchase; for, Christ keepeth the full purchase in his own hand, and doth let forth the application thereof, as we stand in need, in his own order and by degrees, till he perfect us in sanctification and glorification also.

6. As for the third objection, we must not think, that when we are loosed from the Law as a covenant of Works, we are loosed also from the commands of the Law: for, the covenant of Works prescribed in the Law, is posterior, both in order of nature and time, to the natural writing of the Law in man's heart, Rom. 2:15. And therefore, when

the covenant of the law of Works is taken off, the authority of the Law to direct and command all moral duties doth remain, and can no more be dissolved, then the obligation of the reasonable creature to be obedient to the Creator, can be abolished: and therefore, when the believer falleth in a transgression, he meriteth death and destruction as the wages of sin. But Christ our Advocate, who liveth forever to make intercession for us, holds off the execution of deserved wrath, and giveth to the believer the grace of renewed repentance and faith in him, and so saveth the believer, 1 John 1:9, and 2:1.

7. As for the last objection, taken from the impossibility of knowing, taking notice of, or confessing every sin wherewith we are daily polluted, or from the impossibility of putting repentance and faith in exercise about every particular sin; we answer, first, that the children of God, notwithstanding of this impossibility acknowledged by them, have sought and obtained renewed remission of their innumerable sins, Psal. 40:12, and Psal. 19:12,13.

8. Secondly, such as are justified by faith, upon confession of such sins as they know and do remember, are accepted of God, as if they had confessed all their sins particularly, because he that hath no mind to deny or excuse any sin in himself, but is willing to open up his heart to God in sincerity, and to confess every particular, if he were able, he hath presented a contrite heart before God, which is a sacrifice acceptable to God, Psal. 51:8,9, Psal. 32:5, and this much also Christ doth teach us, speaking of the Publican who made a short and general confession of his sins in sincerity, and went home justified, Luk. 18:13,14.

Thirdly, it is not impossible for a watchful conscience to observe daily, as many particular sprouting's from the root of in-born sin, as may humble him daily, and bear down all confidence in his own righteousness, and furnish to him matter for exercise of repentance and faith in Christ. And this lesson the Lord did teach his people under the Law, by the twice offering sacrifice every day morning and evening, that his people observing daily the running issue of corrupt nature, might daily have their recourse by faith unto the lamb of God, that takes away the sins of his own people, and hitherto we are directed to look, Isa. 45:22, and, 1 Joh. 2:1. Meantime, on the one hand, let us beware to lay any sort of merit upon our daily exercise of faith and sorrow for sin in our repentance, other ways we should be found offerers unto God of satisfaction from us, and not suitors of remission of sins from God; and on the other hand, let us beware to be discouraged, albeit we do not find daily the renewed intimation and sense of remission: but as we apply the Law to ourselves in the exercise of repentance, So let us apply the sentence of absolution pronounced in the Gospel, in favors of every penitent soul that flyeth to Christ for refuge.

The tenth question shall be, concerning spiritual dispositions of mind and qualifications, which may be joined with, or separate from, the special work of true conversion and saving grace.

The Apostle, Heb. 6:4-10, tells us of sundry qualifications which may be found in unconverted men, and also he tells us of better things which do accompany salvation, and are sure evidences of re-generation. Of the first sort, there are, among others, these five. 1. A legal conviction of the vileness of sin and vanity of the world. 2. A renouncing of unlawful pleasures, joined with a refraining even from lawful and allowed worldly delights. 3. A natural desire of salvation and of sanctification, that they may be saved. 4. A purpose to live righteously, holily and soberly in this present world. 5. An outward change of manners and conversation, so far as they may be blameless before men. These and such like qualifications may make a fair show in the flesh, and yet may be found to be not only in true converts, but also in such as are strangers from the life of God: such was the Apostle Paul before conversion; such was Israel, Rom. 9:31. Which followed after the law of righteousness, and did not attain to the law of righteousness. Who being ignorant of God's righteousness, did and going about to establish their own righteousness, did not submit themselves to the righteousness of God, Rom. 10:3. Of this sort are such of the Papists, who go about to be justified by their own works, and do but mock at the imputation of Christ's righteousness, calling it blasphemously, a putatious or conceited righteousness; not considering, that the Pope and his servants do reckon the imputation of the righteousness and merits of men, and of the superfluity of the Saints righteousness, by reason of their works of supererogation, to be worth a great sum of money, as they find their merchants.

Concerning these five qualifications, some converts, especially such as desire to see the evidences of saving grace in those with whom they will join in the society of Church-membership, may make question what to think, whether they be saving graces, or common operations of the Spirit.

2. For answer, we must distinguish between a man's judging of those qualifications in himself, and his judging of another, in whom these qualifications appear to be; for, a man judging of himself, may attain to a clear and certain discerning of saving grace in himself, as the Apostle giveth us to understand, 1 Cor. 2:11,12. In which case of our judging of ourselves, this much may be said; that if a man find in himself, those qualifications joined with faith in Christ for righteousness and eternal life, and is seeking furniture from Christ to bring forth fruits of his faith in new obedience, he may be quiet and

be out of doubt of saving grace in himself: for, unto such a person, the description of a true convert may safely be applied, Phil. 3:3. We are the circumcision, &c. And pre-suppose he hath observed these qualifications in himself, before he hath observed his closing with Christ, or his application of the offer of reconciliation through him, he neither needeth nor should trouble himself or others with questioning, whether such and such qualifications in him, before his fixing on Christ, were the common or special operations of the holy Ghost: for, seeing the kingdom of heaven cometh not with observation always, it is hard to determine of the first beginnings of the working of saving grace by the holy Spirit, because saving faith hath in it the substance of historical, dogmatical and temporary faith. And therefore, when both saving faith, and historical, dogmatical and temporary faith, may produce belief of the law, and convince the man of sin, and wrath due for sin, and produce the belief of the Gospel also, without application of the offer of reconciliation, how shall a man determine whether these effects were produced by virtue of dogmatical and temporary faith, or by virtue of saving faith, until the time that the humbled sinner fly in unto Christ, and seek to draw furniture from him for new obedience of the law of love toward God and man, and so put difference betwixt saving faith, and that faith which may be in an unregenerate and unreconciled man? But, when the man is come up to apply Christ, and cleave unto him for righteousness and life, and furniture to carry him on the way unto salvation, it is not his wisdom to dispute whether these five qualifications were common operations of the spirit or effects of saving faith, not as yet manifested to be such, before the person did close covenant with God in Christ, for not imputing his sins unto him, and making solid reconciliation with him.

3. As for judging of others, when we observe these qualifications, all or some of them, we must not determine positively what sort of operation the holy Ghost hath in hand; but our part is, according to our place and calling, to help on the least preparatory qualifications, which may serve to be inductive and serviceable to beget and foster saving faith in them, even when the sense of sin and unworthiness is like to drive them from Christ, as it did Peter, when he cried out unto Christ, Depart from me, O Lord, for I am a sinful man. For, God hath not made us Judges of the operations of the holy Ghost in this or that person, but to be their helpers unto faith when we perceive any good qualification in them, and helpers of their repentance when we perceive any out-breaking evil in them.

The eleventh question shall be, of the converts doubting what to think of his condition, when he finds more freedom of prayer in the presence and audience of others, then when he prayeth in secret alone.

It is not a case unusual, that some converts do find a great deal of freedom of prayer in the audience of others, more than alone; for, they have experience, that when they pray in the audience of others in their family, or occasionally elsewhere, their prayer is more copious then when they are alone, their style of speech more polished, their words in better order, their expressions more significant, their notions more sublime, more fervent, more zealous, then when they are in secret in their closet; which difference, when they consider, they doubt what the matter doth mean.

2. For answer, first, there is a difference to be put between solitary prayer in secret, and prayer in society with others; for, in secret oft-times the converts worship is carried on in the sense of his sinfulness, unworthiness and indisposition presented to God through Christ,

with sighs and confused groans without words; for he studieth most for affection, and not for words, having no ear to care for but the ear of the searcher of hearts, who knoweth his weakness, fears, temptations and wrestling with doubts. But in company, he studieth most to make use of knowledge, and to express himself so, as he may carry along the company with whom he prayeth with consent, that he may edify himself and them in worship; and in this case, he may find greater freedom possibly then he findeth alone in secret.

Secondly, it is ofttimes found, that God (for his own glory, and the mutual edification of two or three gathered together in his name) doth enlarge the freedom of speech in the speaker.

Upon which considerations, the doubting convert may satisfy himself; only let him beware least vain glory, or studying to have the applause of such as hear him pray, do not blow wind in his sails; and in as far as after examination he findeth himself guilty, let him, when he is in secret alone, be humbled before God for it, and crave pardon through Christ, seeking help and healing of this wicked inclination.

The twelfth question shall be of the doubt which the convert may have in a case contrary to the former.

Some converts do find themselves more enlarged in secret prayer and alone, then in the company of one or more. In company, saith he, I cannot utter my own private condition without a needless and inconvenient discovery of my present case to others, and I can hardly conjecture what may be their necessity with whom I pray, or condescend upon petitions and thanksgiving fit for us in common. I am taken up also with thoughts of what estimation my hearers may have of me. &c. But in secret prayer I am freed of that care, I am not feared that God shall mis-construe my words, or thoughts. I may in secret make a long pause in my petitions, and fall in meditation upon some passage of Scripture, and after a while direct my speech unto the Lord: I may express my affections by voice and gesture, as they fall out, and pour forth my heart to God with tears, without fear of being esteemed a hypocrite, &c. Mean time I doubt what my indisposition to pray in company doth import, when duty calleth for it.

2. For answer, we grant, that God, to some of his dear Saints, whose prayers in secret he will accept and reward openly, hath not given ability to edify others by way of praying in their audience; to others in regard of age of sex, to whom modesty and silence is most suitable, he hath not given confidence to pray in name of others, whether more or fewer, as their mouth. But as for these, to whom God hath given ability and a calling, by reason of a charge in the family, or some occasional exigence, to pray in the audience of others, and yet notwithstanding they do foster their natural averseness from such a duty, they had need to examine themselves, whether they be hindered by fear to loss some of their estimation at the hands of the hearers, if possibly all things should not be found so well digested and expressed in the prayer, as they would.

The thirteenth question, shall be of the converts doubting what to think, when he compareth his disposition to prayer, and God's dispensation toward him in prayer.

Sundry converts, when they compare their own divers dispositions to prayer, with the divers dispensations of God toward them in prayer, they are at a stand what to think. Sometime (saith one) albeit I be very hardly drawn to pray at all, yet when after wrestling, the conscience of the duty doth set me on work, my prayer goeth on as I could wish, light is furnished to me what to confess, what to thank for, what to seek both for myself and others; whereby I gather, for the time, that the Lord is pleased with my person in Christ, and hath accepted my prayer. Sometime it fareth other ways with me: for, when time, place, and leisure for prayer concur, and I am now about to make use of opportunity, and do fall down before the Lord to speak, on a sudden, I have nothing to say; matter, words and light do fail me, darkness and confusion falleth on my mind, and my prayer sundry times is stopped, and closeth with a sigh or groan; which dispositions of my heart and dispensations of the Lord when I compare, I am in doubt what to think.

2. For answer, in the first case, concerning the Lord's blessing of the aiming at duty, the matter is clear and speaks for itself; for, God will have us to aim at a right frame of spirit when we are about the discharge of any part of his worship, but not forbear to do the duty, if we cannot reach that fitness of spirit which we desire; let us strive against all impediments, and God will help us to fight, will give the victory and reward it for our encouragement to set upon our duty.

As for the other case of setting on the duty, and missing, of furniture to discharge it, let us consider, that God in this dispensation is teaching us, that both the discharge of any duty, and the success thereof, do not depend upon him that willeth, or on him that runneth, but upon God that showeth mercy; yea, he teacheth us by experience, that to will and to do are two distinct gifts, the one whereof sometime he will give and not the other, and sometime he will give both, that we may learn not to limit the Lord in any case, but really acknowledge that every good gift it from him, that we may aim at our duty and depend on him for the blessing.

The fourteenth question is, how to solve the doubt of the convert in another like comparison of his disposition and God's dispensation.

Some converts, out of their own experience, may say, I being in a sad condition of heart, have sundry times diligently used all means to be comforted, and have wondered within myself, that my pains have produced no hoped-for effect, but the heart hath lain dead, like the child of the Shunamite, when Gehasi laid the staff of Elisha upon him. At another time I have been surprised unexpectedly with enlargement of heart, with liberty of speech in prayer, with peace and joy in the holy Ghost, to the no small confirmation of my faith, and what to think of this divers dispensation, I cannot tell.

2. For answer, the doubt may be satisfied, by observation of the Lord's grace and wisdom toward his child; in the first case, he giveth grace to use the means, and suspendeth the sensible fruits thereof, to teach us, 1. that he hath indeed tied us to the use of all appointed means, but left himself free to give the fruits thereof, in what time, and in what measure he pleaseth. 2. He teacheth us, that whatsoever benefit he doth bestow upon us in the use of the means, he doth bestow them, not for the using of the means, but by the using of the means. 3. He teacheth us, that there is no inherent virtue, nor effectual power in the means, but that the means are the way wherein we must walk, that we may find the blessing from God in using the means, and not put confidence in them. 4. He teacheth us, whatsoever mean or instrument is made use of, we should, with Paul planting and Apollo watering, give the glory of the increase, fruit and success unto God alone.

3. As to the other case, wherein the Lord doth prevent his child's using of means, and giveth an answer ere he call, thereby he teacheth us the same lesson, to wit, that what blessing God doth give, he doth it freely of grace and not for works. 2. He teacheth us, that what blessing we expect in the use of the means, he will give it, not when we would, nor in what measure we would, but as he sees it fittest for our good and his own glory, that so we should neither be frustrate

of the fruit of the means using, nor yet conceive the fruit thereof as a deserved reward of works, but as a gift of mere grace.

The fifteenth question, shall be about the measure of mortification or sanctification, whether it be growing or decaying.

Ofttimes true converts fall in this doubt, not indeed when they are in a sensible and comfortable condition, for then they seem to themselves to be growing in holiness; neither fall they in this doubt when their condition is sensibly evil, as when the power of in-born sin either breaketh forth in action externally, or defileth their spirit at least; for then they seem to themselves to be decaying. But this doubt ariseth when they are going on in their ordinary way of a blameless conversation, without any observable change of their spiritual condition to the better or to the worse. Then is it, that they seem to themselves in a dubious condition, and cannot say, whether mortification of corrupt nature, or sanctification be on the growing hand, or not.

2. For answer to this doubt about the measure of holiness, 1. it is not safe curiously to inquire, what measure of holiness a man hath attained: for, as it is not good to eat much honey: So for men to search out their own glory, it is not glory, Prov. 25:27.

Secondly, it is hard to determine the question; for, God useth to hide from his children, especially the younger sort, these operations of the holy Spirit, which may in any sort weaken their endeavor in piety, or softer pride in them, but he discovers unto them their sinfulness and the imperfections of their obedience, that he may set forward their repentance and laying hold on Christ righteousness.

Thirdly, there is such an instability of any good condition wherein any convert may be, so great variety of temptations, such a vicissitude of victory of the flesh and of the spirit in their daily conflict, that hardly can any man satisfy himself in the solution of this question:

for, he who thought himself dead to the lusts of the flesh, and to riches and honor, may shortly find himself overtaken in the net, and fall foully in the mire, and be found carnal.

Therefore, let him that stands take heed least he fall, let him watch and pray least he be overcome in temptation, let him study to observe the wickedness of nature, and imperfections of his best works, that the righteousness of Christ may be in greater estimation in our eyes, and we may grow in faith and love toward God, drawing virtue from Christ, and furniture to every good work. This is the way to grow in holiness indeed, and not to be proud for anything in us, or done by us; and this is the way wherein the Apostle did constantly walk, Phil. 3:14-16.

The sixteenth question is, what the convert shall think or do in hard afflictions.

When the convert doth fall in long-some bodily diseases and sad afflictions, by unexpected and long-lasting adversity, when Satan is permitted to vex him with sore temptations, when God doth hide his face for a long time from him, when he exposeth him unto the cruel persecution of worldly men, he cannot choose but fall in many doubts and perplexities: for, when God doth immediately afflict him, he readily suspecteth that God is angry at him; if he louse reins unto Satan to sift him and vex him, if he answer not his supplications, comfort him not readily, what wonder multitude of thoughts arise in his heart? The question is, in this case, what shall the convert think or do?

2. For answer. It is true, the Lord useth ofttimes, in his deep wisdom and unchangeable love to his children, to exercise them, as is said, and Satan will not fail to whisper in their ear, that God doth not love them; in which case, if the convert do not stand fast, in the faith

of the love of God through Christ, in all his temptations, he cannot stand out in the conflict.

Therefore, that he may guard and strengthen his faith, first, let him seek wisdom from God, to expound the Lord's dispensations toward himself, by the word and working of God in his children, set down in the holy Scripture; in exercising of whom by affliction, he hath discovered the corruption of their nature, the bitter fruits of sin, and promoved the work of the mortification of sinful lusts that are in the world, to wit, the lust of the eye, the lust of the flesh and pride of life, and taught them humility, meekness, patience, temperance and compassion toward others in affliction. Secondly, let him set his affections on things spiritual, and on our blessed Redeemer Jesus Christ, who is at the right hand of the Father making intercession for all them that call upon him, that they may be saved, always remembering, that as the Law is a pedagogue to lead us and draw us unto Christ, So affliction is a pedagogue to lead us to the Law, and to Christ the end of the Law for righteousness and life. Thirdly, let him learn, in examination of his own condition, accurately to distinguish the Lord's part exercising him with trouble, for trial, and training him on in the obedience of faith, as for his own glory, so for the good of his afflicted child; and Satan's part, in cruelty, craftiness and malice, tempting and vexing him; and his own part, who hath deserved much more affliction then is come upon him: which considerations may keep him from fretting and murmuring in his trouble, how heavy soever it be. Fourthly, let him put difference between sinning and suffering of trouble, that he may choose to endure affliction, rather than by sinning draw on much more trouble.

3. But if the afflicted convert seem to himself deserted of God, in respect of the special operations of the holy Ghost, let him be of good

courage, he is not altogether deserted who can observe the decaying of saving graces from the measure he hath found before; he is not altogether deserted, who loveth communion with God, and longeth after it, and can go to God and regret his desertion as a sad affliction; for, if our loving Lord Jesus Christ hath withdrawn himself out of the sight of his afflicted child, yet hath he presumed his own foot-steps with the unction of his own Spirit, that he may quicken and kindle his child's love and desire toward him. This regrated desertion is but in part, not altogether, yea, it is not a real but a seeming desertion. The Lord resteth in his love, albeit he hide the effects of his love for a time: He preserveth the habits of saving grace as his own seed in the afflicted heart, albeit he do not always draw them forth unto action: if he withdraw the sight of saving graces, yet he augments the estimation of them, and languor to find the Lord working in him. If the afflicted observe well, he shall see the hand of the Lord in some part of his works, so that in his hardest condition he may say, with the Psalmist, Psal. 73. Nevertheless, I am continually with thee, thou holdest me with thy right hand.

4. If it shall please God, with immediate afflictions from himself, to suffer, not only Satan to fight against the faith and consolation of his child, but also to super-add a fiery trial of his faith, by cruel persecution for righteousness, let him still, for all this, be of good courage, because in all such battles the Lord of hosts shall be with him, who will not suffer his soldiers to be tempted above their strength, but, with the temptation, will give an issue, that they may escape, and will furnish strength to them, that they shall overcome: for, he hath laid up a crown of righteousness for all them that keep the faith, and at last will give it to all that love the coming of our Lord Jesus. Wherefore, let the afflicted convert humble himself under one or all

these exercises, and not doubt of his condition, seeing it is agreeable to the Scripture and lot of the Saints.

5. It is true, that all affliction to the flesh, for the present, is a bitter potion, but yet reached forth to the patient by the hand of our Physician and heavenly Father. It is a fire, but will not consume the burning bush; it is a furnace, but will not destroy any metal but dross only; it is a labor, but shall in due time bring forth the quiet fruits of righteousness; it is a rough file, but the more sharp it be, it shall so much sooner rub away the rust of the vessel of grace, make the soul of the penitent more bright, and, by the blessing of God, render him more humble in his thoughts, more fervent in prayer, mor constant in the faith, more strong to bear whatsoever burden shall be laid on him, more desirous to grow in all virtue, more careful to keep communion with God, more innocent in his conversation, more clean in his conscience, and at last more blessed, Let not then the afflicted convert regard the labor he is put to, but look to the fruit, reckon the worth of healing, and not the bitterness of his potion; let him not look to the pain of the affliction, but to the fatherly love of God chastising him, who expressly hath told us, that he chasteneth all whom he loveth, lest they perish with the world; let him not shift the battle, but set his eye on the crown, and go on in the way of God, how many soever his tribulations shall be: for, as the outward man by trouble doth decay, So the inward man is renewed daily: for, the Apostle, who was most acquaint with such exercise, hath, for encouragement of all who are under the cross, said, Our light affliction, which is but for a moment, worketh for us a far more exceeding and eternal weight of glory, while we look not at the things which are seen, but at the things which are not seen; for the things which are seen, are temporal, but the things which are not seen, are eternal, 2 Cor. 4:17,18.

The seventeenth and last question, shall be about the relicts of sin in the Saints in this life.

The remainder of sin doth often-times drive true converts to many doubts; for, when carnal lusts and sinful passions seem to be sub-dued, and in a good measure mortified, incontinent, upon the least occasion (as dying ashes when sulphureous powder is cast upon them) they kindle and are inflamed: and when their spirit is most willing and ready to do good, corrupt nature standeth up and maketh opposition, so that the convert cannot do the good he would; yea, such is the power thereof, that ofttimes it forceth him to the ill he would not. In which warfare, being oft overcome, he is so weary, that he falleth out, with the Apostle in his lamentation, Rom. 7:24 crying, O miserable man that I am, who shall deliver me from the body of this death? And while he searcheth how it cometh to pass, that such a body of death lodgeth in the children of God, and so powerful relicts of sin remain in the justified man, he cannot satisfy himself, considering, that God doth hate sin, and maketh the new creature hate it also; which God could easily take away in a moment, in the day of the converts reconciliation and justification.

2. For answer to this question; if a reason of God's permission of the relicts of sin, to remain in the Saints all the days of their life, be asked after; a reason superior to the most holy will of God to permit it, can none be given, nor should it be sought after. But to quiet our minds in this case, these following considerations may suffice, 1. it is the will of the Lord our God, our wise and loving Physician, to renew and restore his image in his children piece and piece, till it be brought to per-fection in all the lineaments, parts and degrees thereof, and to heal our sinful sicknesses and infirmities, not in an instant, but by little and little, as he seeth fit; this way of bringing his work to perfection

by degrees, he keeped in the creation of the world, which he did not perfect in a moment, but in six days: So also, the seed that is casten in the ground every year, he doth not bring forth to maturity, for men's use, in less time than some months. He doth not form infants in the womb and bring them up to their appointed stature and strength, in less time than a number of years. And for the relics of sin, how odious and loathsome soever they are in themselves, yet he can, in his deep wisdom, make use thereof in a most holy way for the good of penitent converts: for, as it was fitting, that a difference should be put between the militant Church on earth, and the triumphant in heaven, So it is the Lord's wise will to exercise his militant children, in conflicting against sin and misery in this life, that the next life and triumph over sin, death and hell, may be the sweeter when it cometh, and more desired till it come.

2. Secondly, as the Lord, after subduing of the Canaanites, did not forthwith cast them altogether out of the holy land, but suffered a multitude of them to live, for the exercise of the Israelites with warfare, and for teaching his people by their own experience, that the victory which they had obtained over the Canaanites was not purchased by their sword or bow, but was given unto them from the Lord of hosts, who led forth their armies and prospered them: So doth he not abolish the relics of sin in his Saints in this life, after their conversion, that they may know that the victory which they have received, over the devil, the world and the flesh, in their conversion, is not to be ascribed to the power of their own free-will, but unto God only. For, if the renewed convert cannot over-come the relics of the broken forces of his spiritual adversaries within him, which his renewed will would most earnestly expel, how can he give the glory

of his victory over the devil and the world in his conversion, unto the power of his corrupt and unrenewed free-will?

3. Thirdly, it is required of all that come unto Christ, that they deny themselves, take up their cross daily and follow him; and to make them so do, strong motives are daily furnished from the feeling of the relicts of sin in ourselves: for, how can a renewed convert look upon his own ignorance, errors, folly and vanity of his mind, perverseness of his will, impotency to good and propension unto all sin, and not loath himself, and so be forced to fly to Christ the Redeemer for relief?

4. The remainder of sin being an adversary to all virtues, doth furnish work to all the habits infused by God for the daily exercise thereof, according as inborn sin doth put forth itself to the hindrance of faith, love, hope, patience, temperance, &c. but in special it serves to bear down pride and to foster humility: for, this doth the experience of the Apostle show, 2 Cor. 12:7. Least I should be exalted above measure through the abundance of the revelation, there was given to me a thorn in the flesh.

5. Nothing doth more manifest the infirmity of the strongest soldiers of Christ, then the power of inborn sin, brought forth in the conflict against the new creature; No sharper spur to prayer and imploring of God's help, then the felt power of the remainder of sin: this also doth the experience of the Apostle teach us, 2 Cor. 12:8. For this thing I besought the Lord thrice, that it might depart from me.

6. How much the endurance of this conflict, with the remainder of sin, doth serve to manifest the greatness of the Lord's power, and largeness of his grace towards his weak soldiers, whom he upholdeth and comforteth in this conflict, the answer which the Lord giveth to the Apostles prayer, maketh manifest, 2 Cor. 12:9. And he said unto

me, my grace is sufficient for thee; for my strength is made perfect in weakness.

7. We are slow to believe, dull to apprehend and learn that which the Word of God tells us of the ugliness of the body of sin, the perverse wickedness of corrupt nature, the filthiness of the flesh, the wiles and deceitfulness of the old man, and the enmity of our corrupt nature against God. Therefore, in, and by the frequent and renewed conflicts, now with one lust, then with another, we are forced by experience to learn the lesson more and more solidly, and believe the truth of the Lord's Word speaking of sin that is in us, and to engage ourselves to prosecute the mortification of sin unto the death.

8. The renewed experience of the power of sin in our flesh, should make us so much the more vigilant against it, and daily to put on the whole armor of God: Because we must fight, not only with the flesh, but also with principalities, powers and spiritual wickedness, which take advantage of the sin that naturally dwelleth in us, Ephes. 6:11,12. Put on the whole armor of God, for we wrestle not with flesh and blood, to wit, only.

9. The conscience of the remainder of sin dwelling in us, serveth to move us to pity, and to have compassion on the children of Adam, and meekly to restore our weak brethren, who are overtaken in any offense, as the Apostle doth teach us, Tit. 3:2. Showing all meekness to all men. For we ourselves also were sometime foolish, disobedient, deceived, &c. Gal. 6:1. Brethren, if a man be overtaken in a fault, ye which are spiritual, restore such an one in the spirit of meekness, considering thyself, lest thou also be tempted.

10. Last of all, the permission of the relics or sin, to remain in true converts all the days of their life, doth serve to decide the great controversy between God and men, concerning the way of justification:

For, by nature we cannot admit the righteousness of God, which is by faith in Jesus Christ, flying to his satisfaction of justice for us, and righteousness imputed to us thereby: for, by nature, with mis-believing Israel, we acknowledge no justification, save of, or for works, albeit it be impossible, Rom, 10:3. And as they being ignorant of God's righteousness, and going about to establish their own righteousness, have not submitted themselves unto the righteousness of God. So we, even after conversion, and after embracing of justification by faith, in our conversion, do give ofttimes evidence of our natural inclination to seek after the righteousness of works, for after examination of ourselves, we shall find, that our confidence doth flow and ebb as we are pleased or displeased with our own carriage; and when we have most need to make use of the righteousness by faith in Christ, we forget it or slight it, do not fly to it, do not adhere to it, do not comfort and strengthen our selves in conflicts by it (as hath ofttimes been observed by us) what then would we do, if our going about to establish our own righteousness did prosper? Or if the power of in born sin did not set up itself against us, and force us, by the law, either to despair or fly to Christ? And this our natural inclination, even after conversion, to return and seek after the righteousness of the law, may be seen in the Galatians, who having begun in the spiritual way of justification by faith, sought to be perfected by the fleshly way of justification by works, and did fall in danger of falling from grace, and excluding themselves from the blessing of the promise through Christ.

Wherefore, our infinitely wise Physician Jesus Christ taketh course, as we have said, for his own glory and our good, not to repair at once the image of God in us, not to heal our sinful diseases all at once, but piece and piece, by degrees, that his righteousness, bestowed on those that fly unto him for refuge, may be in higher and higher estimation daily, that the fountain opened up in him, for removing of sin and uncleanness, may daily be made use of, and the benefit of justification may daily be looked upon as a new gift, that virtue may daily be sucked out of him for bearing of good fruits, and out of his fullness we may receive daily grace for grace, and may render thanks unto our God daily, and bless him for his grace given unto us, as did the Prophet, Psal. 103:1,3. Bless the Lord, O my soul, who forgiveth all thine iniquities, who healeth all thy infirmities; And grow in the love of God, for the remission of so many sins as escape us daily, as did the woman, Luk. 7:47, who loved much because many sins were forgiven her; And grow in holiness, without putting confidence in our works, as the Psalmist did, Psal. 71:15,16. My mouth shall show forth thy righteousness—I will go in the strength of the Lord God, and will make mention of thy righteousness, even of thine only. And the Apostle giveth us his example, Phil. 3:8-14.

Wherefore, let the doubting convert make use of these considerations, and long for the coming of Christ, who shall abolish sin and misery altogether. To whom, with the Father and holy Spirit, be glory forever.

Amen.

FINIS.